POWER AND GOLD

POWER AND GOLD

Jewelry from Indonesia, Malaysia,
and the Philippines

from the Collection of the
Barbier-Mueller Museum
Geneva

Text by Susan Rodgers
Photographs by Pierre-Alain Ferrazzini

Prestel-Verlag

First published on the occasion of the exhibition "Power and Gold,"
organized by the Barbier-Mueller Museum, The Asia Society,
and the Smithsonian Institution Traveling Exhibition Service.

Second edition, Prestel-Verlag, 1988, 1990

© 1985 by Barbier-Mueller Museum, Geneva
4, rue de l'Ecole-de-Chimie

Cover illustration: Central Flores
(Cat. No. 81, description p. 326)

Prestel-Verlag
Mandlstrasse 26
D-8000 Munich 40
Federal Republic of Germany

Distribution of the hardcover edition in the USA and Canada by
te Neues Publishing Company, 15 East 76th Street, New York, N.Y. 10021

Distributed in continental Europe and Japan by Prestel-Verlag,
Verlegerdienst München GmbH & Co KG, Gutenbergstrasse 1, D-8031 Gilching,
Federal Republic of Germany

Distributed in the United Kingdom, Ireland, and all other countries by
Thames & Hudson Limited, 30 – 34 Bloomsbury Street, London WC1B 3QP, England

Design: Jean-Louis Sosna, Geneva
Editors: Diana Menkes (Washington)
Fabienne Bouvier and Iolanda Jon (Geneva)
Typesetting: Artcompo, Geneva, using
"Zapf International light" by Berthold AG, Berlin-West
Color separations: Aloha Scan Luthi, Geneva
Printing: Karl Wenschow Franzis-Druck GmbH, Munich
Binding: R. Oldenbourg GmbH, Munich

Printed in the Federal Republic of Germany

ISBN 3-7913-0859-9
(French edition: ISBN 2-88104-010-1)

I am pleased to dedicate this exhibition to Blanchette H. Rockefeller with great respect and affection. Through her I met Allen Wardwell, former director of the Asia Society Galleries, and together they encouraged the preparation of this exhibit, the first ever devoted to jewelry from island Southeast Asia. Without her interest and Allen Wardwell's enthusiasm this book would not have been published and Susan Rodgers would not have done the field research that has led to the preservation of so much valuable information on the roles these ornaments played in the lives of those who made and used them.

Jean Paul Barbier

TABLE OF CONTENTS

WHY THIS COLLECTION,
WHY THIS EXHIBITION?

The precious ornaments of island Southeast Asia, which play such an important role in identifying social rank, in strengthening marriage alliances, and in mediating between the mundane and supernatural worlds, form a little-known chapter in the history of peoples living out of the mainstream of modern civilization. The sculptures and beautiful textiles of these cultures

have been brought to the attention of the public in recent exhibitions; now the artistic dimension of jewelry is being revealed for the first time with examples from our collections.

It is interesting to point out that the Barbier-Müller Museum came across the objects presented here quite by accident. Its collections already included some jewelry acquired between 1920 and 1939 by Josef Müller, who had become the owner of several important sculptures from Borneo, Nias, and the Philippines at the time when he was assembling his collection of "primitive works." This accident happened to be the 1972 purchase in Amsterdam of a wooden effigy brought back to Europe at the beginning of this century. Originating in Nias, this figure represents a person wearing an earring, a necklace, a bracelet, and a crown decorated with a

palm motif (at the left). In order to describe these ornaments, we did some research and discovered a photograph, taken in the last century, of a chief wearing an identical crown. Thus we learned that this ornament was made of fabric stretched on a light frame on which leaves and gold buttons were sewn (right).

We thought that no museum or private collection had a similar crown. But a little later we discovered in a Brussels collection a complete set of Nias jewelry (plate p. 89) including a crown of another type also featuring the Cosmic Tree, so important in the myths that were the basis of the religion of the Nias people until the beginning of this century.

We then learned that on the one hand a rather large amount of jewelry had been brought back as souvenirs by tourists and colonists who had visited island Southeast Asia. On the other hand we found out through researchers that certain noble families in the villages had preserved their family treasures.

By completing our collections with purchases from antique dealers and public auctions (we always avoided acquiring a piece which was still in its place of origin) we have begun to put together all the information relative to the use and the symbolic value of these marvelous ornaments whose forms enchant us.

Thanks to Prof. Susan Rodgers of Ohio University, who agreed to carry out on location an important research project based on a set of photographs of the pieces in our collection, we are now able to publish this catalogue, the first to be devoted to this subject.

We warmly thank Allen Wardwell and Andrew Pekarik, former and present directors of The Asia Society Galleries, for the enthusiasm they showed from the beginning by collaborating with us on the very concept of this exhibition. And we are grateful to Peggy Loar and to Martha Cappelletti of SITES for having joined us in making this accessible to a large number of American museums.

We are certain that the care we have taken in documenting the pieces by the use of archival photographs will permit visitors to the exhibition and readers of this catalogue to better understand the reason for the creation and use of these ornaments, which are sometimes of surprising dimensions. These works of art are proof of the spirit of creativity and aesthetic refinement which go far beyond the activity of a simple artisan.

Jean Paul Barbier, President
The Barbier-Mueller Museum, Geneva

FOREWORD

This exhibition of ritual hereditary jewelry from the island cultures of Southeast Asia is remarkable not only because the objects themselves are unique in their beauty and skilled workmanship but because it provides an occasion to glimpse the strength and vitality of the people who produced them, people whose material cultures are not widely known in the United States. Exhibitions with a theme of beauty are not uncommon and their popularity suggests a high level of interest in all kinds of artistic expression. It is a harder task, however, to look beneath the evident beauty to the meaning which underscores their creation — a meaning which may be somewhat alien to our own way of looking at bodily adornment. Jean Paul Barbier has shown not only great sensitivity in the selection of these pieces but also great wisdom in the decision to look at them from a cultural point of view. The anthropological focus of the text written by Dr. Susan Rodgers points out that these objects are infused with a social and spiritual power that has far-reaching effects in the lives of the people who make and wear them.

The appreciation of non-Western art in the West has historically been linked to the fantasy of a "primitive" world in which people are seen to produce objects as a simple and direct expression of their feelings. While we now know that such an ethnocentric view is inappropriate, alternative perspectives are often difficult to obtain. This exhibit gives us the opportunity to describe the potency of the symbolism which these objects evoke, and to create a better understanding of the cultures that are responsible for them.

We are very grateful to Jean Paul Barbier for his generosity in lending these beautiful objects, for his efficiency in the preparation and production of this catalogue, and for his patient cooperation with every phase of this exhibition's organization. We thank Dr. Rodgers for her ground-breaking work in the field of jewelry symbolism in this part of the world and for her ability to involve us so completely in the real world of their makers.

We are proud to have had the opportunity to work on this project and to share with others the pleasure of seeing these objects and of learning about the people of Indonesia, Malaysia, and the Philippines for whom they are an integral part of life.

Peggy Loar, Director
Smithsonian
Institution Traveling
Exhibition Service, SITES

Andrew Pekarik, Director
The Asia Society Galleries

ACKNOWLEDGMENTS

This museum catalogue is the collaborative effort of many people: citizens of the Southeast Asian countries where the jewelry originated, museum directors, curators, photographers, and anthropologists. My largest measure of thanks goes to Jean Paul Barbier, who sponsored the field research and in fact first thought of the idea of basing the catalogue on ethnographic research. His tireless help in selecting photographs to illustrate the catalogue is also gratefully acknowledged, as is his aid in revising the Nias chapter.

In Indonesia, the Lembaga Ilmu Pengetahuan Indonesia (LIPI) provided research permission to do the short field study in 1983. Thanks are also due to the University of North Sumatra for serving as my institutional sponsor. That university's new program in anthropology generously introduced me to my two superb Batak field assistants, Astina Bangun and Astar Simbolon. Along with the American anthropologist Mary Steedly, they made the North Sumatran portion of the research unusually productive and enjoyable.

Government officials in several local Cultural Affairs offices of the Ministry of Education and Culture are due special thanks, for without their help interviews in villages where I had not previously worked would have proved impossible. Since I was confined to the Indonesian language in all areas but the Batak regions, I also had to rely on the translation services of these men when visiting villages where some people only spoke the local ethnic languages. Thanks are due to Bapak L.T. Tangdilintin of the historical and cultural museum bureau in Ujung Pandang; Bapak M. Masyhuda, head of the excellent new ethnographic and historical museum in Palu, Central Sulawesi; Bapak Dj. R. Tandjimanu, the chief cultural affairs officer in Waingapu, East Sumba; Bapak S.P. Buli, the head of the Education and Culture office for the county of Rindi Umalulu in East Sumba; Bapak H. B. Mude, head of the Cultural Affairs office in Waikabubak, West Sumba; Bapak Donatus Tat and Bapak Silvester Parit of the Cultural Affairs office in Ruteng, West Flores; Bapak Benediktus Toda, head of the Cultural Affairs office for Ngada District, Flores; Bapak Dominikus Pay, of the Education and Culture office in Ngada District, Bajawa; Bapak Jan Djou Gadi Gao, from the Ende Education and Culture office; Bapak Jacobus Ari, of the same office; Bapak H. Mengki Uly, head of the Cultural Affairs office of Kupang District, Timor. Anthropologist Danielle Geirnaert-Martin was also most helpful in a short visit to Lamboya, West Sumba. Roland Beday-Brandicourt deserves much of the credit for documenting the Philippine section.

Thanks are also due, finally, to Ohio University and my department for granting me a research leave for spring quarter, 1983; to my excellent, erudite editor, Diana Menkes of the Smithsonian Institution; and to Andrew Pekarik of The Asia Society and Martha Cappelletti of the Smithsonian Institution for help in revising the text.

Susan Rodgers
Department of Sociology and Anthropology
Ohio University

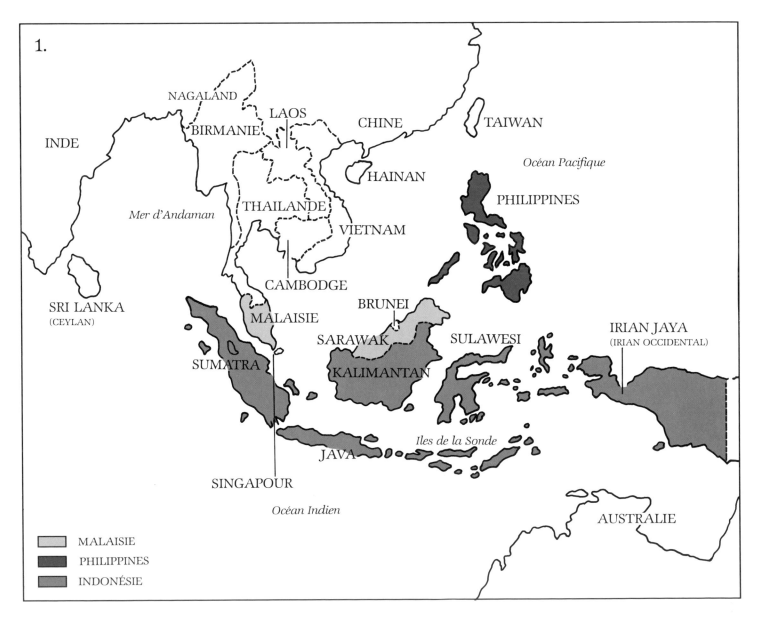

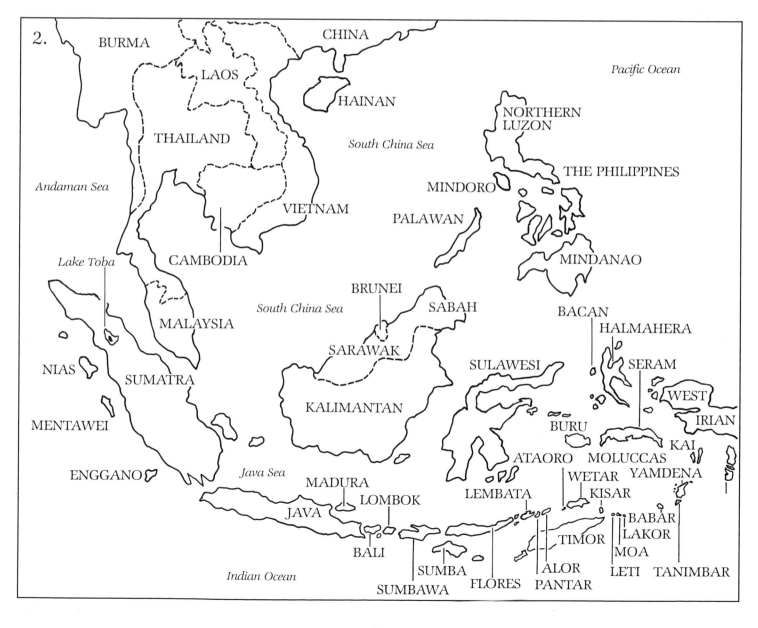

PART I

JEWELRY IN ISLAND SOUTHEAST ASIA

1
ORNAMENTS AND HEIRLOOMS
BEYOND THE OLD COURT SOCIETIES

In the smaller cultures of island Southeast Asia beyond the Indianized court civilizations of Java and Bali, ritual jewelry is somewhat like the region's stunning ceremonial textiles. Both forms of adornment and display are art traditions of obvious beauty but forbidding cultural complexity. In Indonesia, Malaysian Sarawak, and the northern Philippines, jewelry and cloth serve many functions and tap into many layers of social and religious meaning. Jewelry and textiles are often kept as ancestral treasure, and serve as family heirlooms deeply symbolic of their owners' place in the world. Through their shapes, colors, and designs, ornaments and ceremonial cloths are also public representations of important ideas in local systems of traditional politics, kinship, myth, and ritual. Moreover, necklaces, pendants, bracelets, and textiles work as crucial trade objects in elaborate systems of exchange. They circulate among ethnic groups and between coastal peoples and highland societies, drawing culturally distant peoples into common economic leagues. At a more local level, metal and cloth goods are exchanged at weddings and throughout the course of the marriage, symbolizing the larger political alliances formed through such unions. Metal and cloth also represent many of the mythic dimensions of marriage and politics and sometimes symbolize local ideas of masculinity and femininity as well. Frequently, these various systems of meaning are intertwined with each other, and with art. Island Southeast Asian jewelry and textiles are both art in this complicated sense and go beyond the secular decoration of the human body to touch uncommonly deep layers of meaning. Like the intricately dyed and woven traditional cloths of Sumba, Flores, Kalimantan, and Sumatra, old earrings, frontals, pins, and chain belts are small pieces of vast symbolic worlds whose mythic landscapes were well known to their practitioners but are largely opaque to Westerners and, for that matter, to many modern-day Indonesians.

Ceremonial textiles from the region have been described in a number of valuable recent publications, including Mattiebelle Gittinger's *Splendid Symbols: Textiles and Tradition in Indonesia* (1979).[1] The present catalogue, written to accompany the Barbier-Müller Museum's 1985–1987 exhibit, is designed to introduce the museum-going public to the area's rich jewelry traditions, the natural counterpart to the ceremonial textiles. As was the case with *Splendid Symbols*, this catalogue will describe some of the concepts of wealth, power, prestige, sacredness, and exchange that underlie the pieces in the collection. Since ritual jewelry and heirloom objects concentrate so much social and philosophical meaning in their designs and uses, they are excellent entry points for understanding the cultures that created them and traded them among themselves. Like many aspects of island Southeast Asian cultures, jewelry is often part of local "coherence systems" — tightly integrated systems of words, concepts, social organizational patterns, images of time, mythical assertions about the way the universe is ordered, material culture traditions, and performance arts (Becker and Yengoyan 1979). In these cultures the

---

1. See also Gittinger 1980, Adams 1969, Kahlenberg 1977, and Hardi et al. 1976.

1. – Traditional houses and megaliths, West Sumba. Like much jewelry, both reflect local worldviews (Photograph J. Gabriel Barbier-Müller, 1976).

2. – East Sumba man's cloth (*hinggi*), depicting two people working on a traditional house. Like textiles, jewelry often portrays other art forms. Detail (Barbier-Müller Museum, No. 3651-N, not exhibited).

way one domain is structured is often reflected in the way another domain is patterned (Becker 1979). Thus house architectural styles (Fig. 1) represent the local view of the cosmos, kinship is perceived as part of a larger universal order, and textiles replicate (Fig. 2) some of the organizational patterns found in economic and marriage exchange, and so on throughout the culture. Ritual jewelry is integrated into many island Southeast Asian cultures in just this way; as a consequence, studying jewelry obligates the analyst to study virtually the whole culture.

Given the ethnic diversity of Indonesia, Sarawak, and the Philippines, a single museum collection could not be expected to offer an exhaustive display of every type of jewelry from every culture. However, the Barbier-Müller collection does contain representative and often especially fine examples of most of the major types used in the area: bracelets, armlets, anklets, necklaces, headpieces, forehead decorations, combs, chest decorations, belts, rings, pins, and ornaments for religious sculptures and for everyday practical objects such as baby carriers (which themselves sometimes serve protective religious functions to keep infants healthy). What is more important, the pieces in the collection illustrate most of the major functions jewelry served in pre-modern, mostly late colonial island Southeast Asia: jewelry as objects of personal adornment (Fig. 3), as protective amulets, as political badges of rank (Fig. 5), as bridewealth and other ceremonial exchange goods, as family house treasure (Fig. 4), and as sacred altar objects for summoning spirits from supernatural worlds. The jewelry pieces in the exhibit also illustrate most of the major symbolic themes of village social life and cosmology in pre-modern island Southeast Asia: ideas of a common structure in the social order, the house, the village, and the universe; themes of complementarity, opposition, and the creative union of opposites; ideas of life springing from the destruction of life; and concepts of exchange involving ranked giver and taker groups and gifts and countergifts. Lastly, the ornaments in the collection employ most of the major design motifs used by island Southeast Asian metalsmiths and carvers of bone, shell, and wooden miniatures. That is, the pieces are various combinations of crescents, circles, open ovals, ax shapes, and mythically important animals, like cocks (Figs. 6, 7, and 8), hornbills, serpent-dragons, horses, dogs, water buffalos, and crocodiles.

The common themes just noted give some unity to the startling ethnic range of the exhibit. The jewelry pieces from Indonesia — the largest part of the collection — include items from the Karo Batak and Toba Batak of North Sumatra; the Sa'dan Toraja people near Rantepao and the Kaili, Kulawi, Pamona, and Poso Lake groups of Central Sulawesi; the various East and West Sumbanese societies; and the Manggarai, Ngada, Nage, and Lio peoples of Flores. Also included are pieces from the Lamalohot archipelago east of Flores, from Tanimbar in the Moluccas, and from the Atoni and Tetum or Belu peoples of Timor. Over the last one hundred years many of these Eastern Indonesian jewelry pieces were created by itinerant goldsmiths from the small islands of Ndao and Savu near Timor, and so in an important way those cultures are represented in the collection as well. A small number of ornaments from various Dayak peoples in Indonesian Kalimantan and Malaysian Sarawak are also included.

The cultures of Northern Luzon in the Philippines contribute the last range of decorations. Northern Luzon is ethnically fragmented into a great many cultures, and the collection correspondingly has pieces used by the Ilongot, Igorot, Ifugao, Bontoc, Kankanay, and Gaddang (plus a few pieces from Mindanao in the Southern Philippines). The word "used" is employed advisedly here, for in Northern Luzon as in Indonesia many ornaments are made by one ethnic group but used by a variety of their near and distant neighbors, some of whom claim the pieces as part of their own "ancient tradition." As we shall see, in many cases it is laughably inaccurate to assign a definite ethnic provenance to a piece of island Southeast Asian jewelry. These peoples were traders par excellence.

Given the large number of cultures represented in the exhibit, this catalogue, not surprisingly, cannot begin to do justice to any of them, their art traditions, or even their jewelry traditions. In every case that last task would demand a separate anthropological ethnography and social history if the symbolism and ritual and economic uses of local jewelry were to be described adequately. The essays that follow, which were based on very brief fieldwork, aim simply to treat local jewelry traditions in enough ethnographic detail so that their place within area-wide island Southeast Asian patterns of society and art will begin to be evident. This catalogue offers no full anthropological analysis of Indonesian or Philippine

3. — Jewelry as personal adornment, worn by a Northern Luzon woman. Philippine jewelry also marks ethnic identity (Photograph Eduardo Masferré, Bontoc region).

4. — Stone chest carved for a nobleman's feast of merit, in South Nias (Photograph Jean Paul Barbier, 1974).

5. — Mannequin dressed and adorned as a Philippine nobleman from the Ifugao group from Kiangan, in Northern Luzon (exhibited). The central part of the headdress is the red beak of a calao, a hornbill associated with head-hunting. The belt is made of disks cut in a giant clamshell, traded from the coastal area. The man wears a fiber raincoat, a silver necklace (made of assembled earrings). His spear is a ceremonial model; most Ifugaos own at least several of the five different kinds of spears (Photograph P.-A. Ferrazzini).

jewelry; it is an introduction, rather, intended as a spur to further research.

After having carefully examined the Barbier-Müller collection, I went to Indonesia from April 1 to mid-July, 1983, to visit several of the areas where these ornaments were still used and could still be discussed in some detail by village experts and by connoisseurs of village ceremonial life. After trips to the National Museum in Jakarta, I conducted interviews with ritual experts (mostly male *rajas*, or chiefs, and old women familiar with the manufacture and meaning of ceremonial garb) in Lingga in the Karo Batak area and several Samosir towns on the island of Lake Toba in Sumatra; in Kulawi (Fig. 9) and Palu in Central Sulawesi; in Waingapu, Rindi, and Pau in East Sumba; and in Waikabubak, Kampung Tarung, and the Lamboya area in West Sumba. I then went to Flores for interviews with village ritual experts in Kampung Ruteng outside of the big town of Ruteng in the Manggarai region. This was followed by interviews in Bajawa, Kampung Bajawa, Kampung Naru, and the Nage villages of Boawai and Olaewa in Flores. I then interviewed aristocratic families in the Lio coastal village of Walo-topo and the nearby village of Ndona, also in Flores. Next I worked briefly with the museum staffs and officials of the Ministry of Education and Culture in Kupang, Timor, and Tenggarong, East Kalimantan. On leaving Indonesia I visited the national museum in Kuala Lumpur, Malaysia, and the Sarawak Museum in Kuching. Information from village interviews and museums was supplemented by a number of recent Indonesian publications[2] and material in the Southeast Asia collection at Ohio University. Recent anthropology Ph.D. theses were especially useful in investigating the many relatively under-researched societies represented in the collection.[3] The Philippine section, by far the least well-documented, is based on published materials, with no fieldwork.[4]

Although I am a cultural anthropologist, the interviews I conducted while compiling this catalogue

2. The Monografi Daerah series, published by the Department Pendidikan dan Kebudayaan (Ministry of Education and Culture), has a good deal of detailed information about bridewealth exchange involving jewelry, and the local *kabupaten* (subprovincial) offices of the ministry often have mimeographed treatises on *adat* relating to a variety of prestige goods such as textiles and ornaments.

3. See Suggested Readings for citations, under the various ethnic areas.

4. Much information about the individual jewelry pieces from Northern Luzon societies was kindly supplied by Mr. R. Beday-Brandicourt.

probably should not be dignified by the tag "ethnographic fieldwork." True anthropological field research takes long-term residence in an area, not one-day visits, and easy familiarity with the local ethnic language. The most satisfactory rounds of interviews were done in Sumatra: in Karo, where I worked with a Karo Batak field assistant from the University of North Sumatra, and in Toba, where I worked with a Toba Batak field assistant from the same university, and where the Angkola Batak language I speak was close enough to the local language to obviate the need to use Indonesian (the national language, often considered something of an outsider's language in villages). Other relatively rewarding interviews, running to three and four hours, were conducted in Sumba (in Rindi, Pau, and Waingapu in East Sumba and Tarung in West Sumba) and in Ruteng, Bajawa, Boawai, Naru, and Walotopo in Flores. All were tape recorded,[5] and, except for the Toba talks, all interviews were conducted in the Indonesian language. This circumstance immediately artificialized the information obtained, for jewelry in these areas is often part of local *adat*, or village "ways of life" and ceremony, and ethnic *adat* is always indelibly stamped with the structural imprint of the local ethnic language. This makes for awesome translation problems, worth noting here at the onset.

A.L. Becker, a linguist who works with the Burmese and Javanese languages, has reminded students of Southeast Asia in a number of recent publications that the languages of the region cannot be comfortably translated word by word and phrase by phrase into European languages, as if each language was somehow the close equivalent of the other (Becker 1979, 1982). In Becker's view Southeast Asian languages contain and presuppose entire conceptual systems, quite different from those in the West, and adequate translations of oral speech or written passages would have to give Western readers access to some measure of these foreign worlds. Translation thus becomes an effort at "communication across diversity" (Becker 1979) and not some mechanical exercise at finding equivalent words and sentences. "Translation, as every translator learns quickly," Becker writes in the introduction to *The Imagination of Reality: Essays in Southeast Asian Coherence Systems*, "is not just a matter of imi-

5. Fieldwork tapes from this research are available from the Southeast Asia Collection of Alden Library, Ohio University, Athens, Ohio 45701.

6. – The cock seen by three kinds of Sumbanese artists: A man's ceremonial cloth, or *hinggi*, from East Sumba, a prestige exchange good. Detail (Barbier-Müller Museum, No. 3651-AD, not exhibited).

7. – Gold *mamuli* pendant, East Sumba, a royal treasure object. Detail (Cat. No. 131).

8. – East Sumba turtleshell comb, for marriageable women. Detail (Cat. No. 111).

10. – Jewelry as house wealth, displayed on women: young Angkola Batak woman in bridal array, for a verbal duel ritual (*osong-osong*) (Photograph Susan Rodgers, 1983).

tation, of finding our words to imitate their words, but is also the recreation of the context of the foreign text. A culture, to one outside it, is very much like a text, or better, an assemblage of texts, to be translated. No one has seen this so clearly as Clifford Geertz....In his words, 'cultural forms can be treated as texts, as imaginative works built out of social materials...'" (Becker 1979:2 citing Geertz 1972).

What does this mean for the study of jewelry? Take an Angkola Batak example (Fig. 10). In the most extravagant type of *adat* wedding, the *horja mangupa boru* ("ritual for celebrating the bride"), the bride and groom are outfitted as a princely *raja* and his consort, although they may actually be from nonaristocratic families who simply have enough money to stage the *horja*-level ceremony. In a style possibly influenced by Minangkabau culture (Figs. 11 and 12) to the south, the bridegroom is dressed in a metal-threaded sarong and a black and gold hat resembling a bowler. Sumatran wedding costumes often employ military motifs, and the groom here is armed with daggers tucked into his sarong at the waist. Metal armlets and a black, red, and gold cloth (called *ulos*) complete his costume. The bride is turned out in an even more stunning array of daggers, deep-red scarves crossed over her chest, a heavy metallic sarong, armlets, bracelets, and long gold false fingernails. The *pièce de résistance* of her wedding ensemble, however, is her spangled gold headdress. The Angkola bridal headpiece resembles the feminine wedding headgear used in the old court centers of South Sumatra and in many coastal areas throughout the archipelago. Like those ornate head ornaments (more than jewelry, really), the Angkola one is an improbable assembly of gold spikes which support long cascades of thin gold disks. These hang down over the bride's face and shimmer and glint and move about as she walks in the various processionals of her wedding. She must, for instance, wear the gold headpiece when she and her groom take their ceremonial trip to the Tapian Raya Bangunan, the "Bathing Pool of the Rajas and Spirits," a spot thought to be in especially close contact with the spirit world. To a foreign observer this gold head ornament might resemble a crown, and the temptation would be to simply translate it as that. The foreigner, further, might well see the headgear as decorative jewelry to beautify the bride but little beyond that. Angkola see it differently.

First, the gold itself of which the headpiece is made

has much meaning. It is a sign of aristocratic social standing and nobility of character and may not be worn, at least ideally, by commoners or slave descendants. Further, the gold of the bridal headdress recalls the gold given to the bride's family by the groom's family as part of her bridewealth payment. This is an exchange recalled in the ritual speech phrase *omas sigumorsing*, "gold yellow yellowest gold." The bride may well have accused her mother of "loving *omas sigumorsing* more than you love me" when she left her home for the last time and said goodbye in *andung* (mourning wails) to her parents, playmates, her childhood bed, and the doorsill of the house. Furthermore, in the many advice-to-the-newlyweds speeches showered on the new wife, orators often "read meaning" from the different parts of the bride's costume. The old *rajas* tell her, for instance, that the crossed scarves over her chest and the daggers steel her to *tolak bala* (to cast back evil influences from herself, her future children, and the lineage she is marrying into). The gold head-gear is especially full of moral maxims for her new married life. She will be told, for example, that the spangles hanging down over her forehead shielding her eyes on either side teach her to keep her gaze demurely directed to the ground in front of her, not wandering from side to side. In other words, her gold headgear reminds her that a proper bride keeps her attention on her new husband and his family, and not on peripheral people. Beyond these moral lessons the bride well-schooled in the *adat* will also know that the gold headpiece is part of a *raja*'s royal house treasure. This is a set of weapons, ritual textiles, lineage relics, and bridal jewelry that is so full of *sahala* (magical powers) that is must be kept securely boxed in a special treasure cabinet when not used at ceremonies. The treasure can be taken out into the daylight only if a water buffalo ("the livestock of the *rajas*") is sacrificed first.

The Angkola gold headdress — and in fact most of the jewelry objects in the Barbier-Müller collection — are packed with many layers of kinship, political, and mythic meaning of this sort. In other words, they are not just decorative ornaments for personal display — they are full of life and full of very localized conceptual schemes fully understood only by the cultures that created them. This catalogue, because it is largely based on interviews in Indonesian and not the local ethnic languages, can only hint at some of the significance stowed away in these little objects.

11. — A Minangkabau woman outfitted in her family's treasure. These styles from West Sumatra influence other Sumatran groups (Photograph Ulrich Scholz).

12. — Jewelry and personal array from an Islamized coastal society: Minangkabau bride and groom, Guguk village, near Padang. From right to left: the bride, the groom, the witnesses (Photograph Jean Paul Barbier, 1974, West Central Sumatra).

2

THE PEOPLES AND ARTS
OF ISLAND SOUTHEAST ASIA

Before examining some of the common themes running through the jewelry collection, a short description of the several types of cultures found in island Southeast Asia would be helpful, for the Barbier-Müller exhibit draws quite selectively on two ranges of related Indonesian and Philippine societies. These might be called, provisionally, cultures with asymmetric marriage alliance (Fig. 13),[1] and the cognatic,[2] inland cultures (Fig. 14). What anthropologists term marriage alliance cultures build much of their social structures on ideas associated with giving and receiving gifts. Their kinship systems depend on the same motif, and they involve wife-giving lineages and their ritually subordinate wife-receiving lineages. Ideally, at least, a lineage that gives brides to another lineage may not receive women back from that same unit — thus the asymmetrical nature of these marriage systems. Givers and takers are bound to each other through a series of gifts and countergifts of women, textiles, jewelry, livestock, food, and such intangibles as blessings and fertility. The two partners to the exchange complement, or more exactly complete, each other. In this context, metal jewelry is often the countergift to presents of cloth.

In their political organization, these marriage alliance cultures ranged from chiefdoms to small, rather fragile states in late colonial times, when most of the jewelry in the Barbier-Müller collection was produced. In Indonesia, these societies were located at the edges of the sphere of influence of the large, Indianized court societies such as those on Java and Bali, and generally only came under firm Dutch colonial control in the late 1800s and early 1900s. As small, vulnerable minority societies in the shadow of larger, more politically centralized states, these marriage alliance cultures were constantly obligated in late colonial times to negotiate and re-negotiate workable power relationships with their larger neighbors. Gold and silver coins (Fig. 15) were important currencies in this interaction and often flowed from the centralized states to the little marriage alliance cultures, where the coins were then recast into jewelry for the aristocratic class. Several of the cultures included in this broad category are the Batak peoples of Sumatra and a number of societies on Sumba, Flores, and Tanimbar.

The second type of culture represented in the collection — the inland, cognatic societies — also stressed ideas of family giving and obligation. However, although these peoples were certainly fascinated by prestige goods, in general they had no elaborate notions of asymmetrically ranked wife-giver and wife-taker groups. "Cognatic" kinship systems trace family relationship out through both the mother and the father's sides of a person's kin network and tend to focus on loose collections of living relatives rather than on clan ancestors. Included here are the Dayak

---

1. There is a large, contentious anthropology literature on this type of marriage system. Basic works include Lévi-Strauss's *The Elementary Structures of Kinship* (1949), Leach's "The Structural Implications of Matrilateral Cross-Cousin Marriage" (1961), and Needham's *Structure and Sentiment: A Test Case in Social Anthropology* (1962). Rita Smith Kipp's "A Political System of Highland Sumatra, or Rethinking Edmund Leach" (1983) is a valuable comparison of Karo Batak and Kachin marriage systems in the context of the many theoretical debates sparked by this type of kinship system.

2. See Appell 1976 for discussions of this somewhat controversial terminology.

13. — Bawömataluo's *raja* with his family, South Nias. A hierarchical, ranked society, traditional South Nias resembled such marriage alliance cultures as the Batak (Photograph courtesy Koninklijk Instituut voor de Tropen, Amsterdam, before 1930).

14. — A group of Mah Kulit Dayak, in full dress. The Dayaks of Kalimantan and Sarawak have cognatic, inland cultures (Photograph courtesy Koninklijk Instituut voor de Tropen, Amsterdam, before 1930).

societies of Kalimantan and Sarawak and a number of Northern Luzon cultures. None of these societies were organized into indigenous states, and though it is somewhat misleading to characterize them as egalitarian tribes, in general they did not have the firm ideas of rank and class position one finds in the marriage alliance cultures. In these cognatic cultures, prestige for men was often associated with headhunting (Fig. 16) and with war. Their jewelry traditions often glorified these activities and provided a measure of magical protection from mystical attack.

Both of these types of cultures tend to be found in the more isolated regions of their archipelagos, although it is inaccurate to say that these were all highland cultures (some marriage alliance cultures in Eastern Indonesia were located on coastal plains). Located far from Indianized, inner Indonesia (Java and Bali), some of these societies were fairly parochial. State-level peoples tended to consider them rustic barbarians, or "uprivermen" living in wild highland regions.[3] It would be a mistake, however, to pick up too much of this stereotype. It is grossly inaccurate to see these cultures as primitive societies that somehow sailed through Indonesian and Philippine history in splendid isolation. Far from it. They were strongly shaped through contact with the periodically expanding and contracting Indianized court civilizations of South Sumatra, Java, Bali, and Sulawesi. Moreover, seafarers and merchants tied the Indonesian islands together for centuries before Dutch control was established in the outlying regions, and trade during colonial times increased contacts among Indonesian societies of all types still more.

In the Philippines, peace pacts between members of distant ethnic groups allowed for vigorous trade in practical and prestige goods in Northern Luzon before the Spanish arrived in the mid-1500s. In some cases colonial military control and political suppression of these small, geographically peripheral cultures led to further contact between them and to more trade exchanges (and battles) with state societies. The Spanish, for instance, opened a number of trails through the Luzon highlands, the better to pacify, control, and Catholicize the "Igorots" (natives, rustic mountaineers, in the ethnographic stereotype). Spanish contact may well have led to the development of more trade and ethnic contact via the already established Luzon institution of the

3. The Indonesian phrase *orang udik* (a backward, rural person) literally means someone from upriver, or from the interior.

peace pact, which united families from normally hostile groups into regularized trade arrangements.

As we shall see, the leitmotif of the history of all these cultures was change. This included astute adjustment to the frequent incursions of neighboring state-level societies into the ethnic homelands. Another main theme was trade — trade circles of various dimensions that fostered the spread of common ideas, artistic motifs, and, in our case, common jewelry shapes. Many ornaments in the Barbier-Müller collection were in fact a product of such interaction, for through trade small highland ethnic groups or isolated island societies took in highly prestigious, beautiful objects from more politically powerful trading partners, obtained raw materials such as gold, ivory, and shells, and exchanged their feather and shell finery for versions made out of precious metal. This last practice was a common one in colonial times in Indonesia, when Portuguese and then Dutch and British trade ships pumped a steady supply of metal coins into Eastern Indonesia to buy up spices, horses, and fragrant woods. Local chiefs *(rajas)* and their families emerged from such trade encounters strutting about in magnificent ornaments made of gold and silver from coins (Fig. 17). Their house treasures filled up with fine relics and altar objects, testaments to their political acumen. With more wealth pumped into the system, rivalry between aristocratic families increased, until by late colonial times outer Indonesia was the scene of ceremonial activity resembling potlatching (ritualized party-giving by rival chiefs who tried to outdo each other through profligate gift-giving and even outright destruction of prestige goods). It might be said, in fact, that much of the jewelry of island Southeast Asian nobles was a jewelry of political interaction and display.

A time framework into which the jewelry collection can be placed would be helpful at this point. A sketchy picture of area prehistory is emerging, one that concentrates on the importance of trade networks (Solheim 1976, 1981) and the mutual political development of highland cultures, coastal societies, and the large states of India, China, mainland Southeast Asia, and Java, Bali, and South Sumatra (Hutterer 1977). Each of these types of societies influenced the development of the other.

Indonesia and the Philippines have been inhabited for millennia; Java is in fact an important site for *Homo erectus* remains, dating to approximately the Middle Pleistocene. During the Pleistocene the

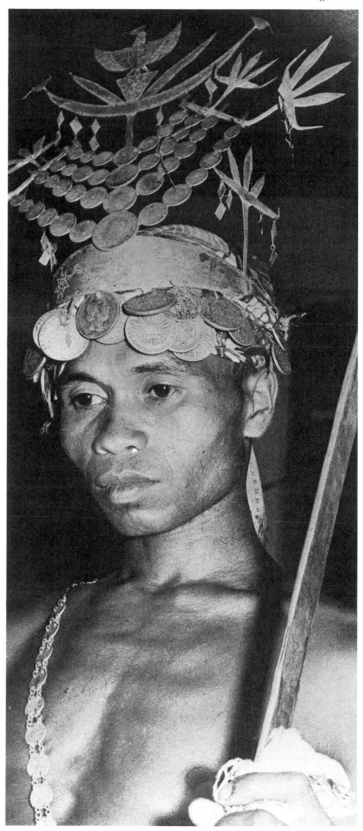

15. – A man from Tetum, in Central Timor. Similar headdresses are used in Atoni in West Timor. European coins, especially from the Netherlands and Portugal, are important in both bridewealth and jewelry. This particular headdress includes a Mexican coin (from Schulte-Nordholt 1971, fig. 10).

ocean level periodically fell around the Indonesian islands, and Sumatra and Java, at some time joined to mainland Southeast Asia, probably served as a causeway for migrations into Australia. In the Philippines the following rough time framework has been proposed: 200,000 or more years ago to 5000 B.C., the Archaic Filipino Period, characterized by a hunting-and-gathering way of life; 5000 to 1000 B.C., the Incipient Filipino Period, a time of small-scale inter-island trade, new tools, pottery manufacture, and fairly egalitarian types of societies; and the Formative Filipino Period, from 1000 B.C. to 500 A.D., a time of increasing agricultural and social complexity and trade contacts with Asian states (Solheim 1981).

Indonesia in historical times has been a focus of trade interest for a number of rival state societies from mainland Southeast Asia, India, China and Europe. This has been largely because of the archipelago's great natural wealth: a collection of 13,667 islands (about a thousand of which are inhabited to a significant extent) with a total land area of 1,906,240 square kilometers, the region covered by the modern nation of Indonesia includes great stores of oil, metals, forest products, and fish. The string of islands extending from the northern tip of Sumatra through Java and out into Eastern Indonesia is generally characterized by mountain chains running down the spines of the islands, covered in heavy forest that is interspersed with cultivated land in rice paddy or slash-and-burn plots. In some parts of Sumatra and Eastern Indonesia there are also stretches of open savannah, and the climate can be quite dry. The more typical situation, however, is a tropical or semi-tropical climate with distinct wet and dry seasons.

As noted, Indonesian history has been marked by the periodic rise and fall of a number of court-centered states which interacted with the great Asian and European civilizations and the small ethnic minorities in Indonesia's highlands and outer islands. Trade contact became established with China sometime after the fifth century A.D.; coastal *entrepôts* began to prosper in such trade, and ancient Borneo benefited from its pivotal location on the routes between Inner Indonesia and South China. The Buddhist kingdom of Srivijaya-Palembang, in South Sumatra, benefited from the same sort of role in international trade. From at least the seventh century to the tenth this kingdom was the main *entrepôt* in island Southeast Asia on the trade route from India to China via the south. Small harbor kingdoms along the Straits of Malacca also came under Srivijaya's control. Since this Sumatran power had close cultural links to the great Buddhist court states of mainland Southeast Asia, it is safe to surmise that interaction with Srivijaya shaped the minority ethnic societies of other parts of Sumatra in important ways.

Srivijaya was eventually eclipsed by kingdoms based in Central Java in the eighth and ninth centuries, whose ruling families had long been linked to the South Sumatra kings. The Javanese states were also legitimated in a language of Indian religious symbolism (that is, the king was thought to rule by divine right and his palace and state were considered to be miniature versions of the cosmos as a whole). Buddhist temples such as Borobudur were constructed as signs of the piety and religious importance of the ruling families. These temples also testify to the agricultural success of these early Javanese kingdoms, for only a prosperous state could support the huge labor force necessary to construct such massive artworks.

After the year 1000 A.D. East Javanese kingdoms gained in strength and extended their influence far into Eastern Indonesia and South Sulawesi. Hindu religious expansions of political power were important in this era. A kingdom centered on Majapahit was established in the early 1300s, with the aid of Gajah Mada. This state exerted considerable influence in Sumatra, Borneo, and Bali. Hayam Wuruk's reign from 1350 to 1389 is recalled as a glorious period of Javanese hegemony.

At the end of the thirteenth century Islam entered Indonesia via Sumatra. Within two centuries a number of small harbor kingdoms had converted to Islam and were led by Muslim princes. These coastal states in turn introduced the religion into the interior kingdoms of Java and into such Sumatran societies as Minangkabau. Indonesia's political center began to shift away from the court societies of interior Java to the fervent, newly converted coastal trade states of the outer islands. In the centuries since the 1400s virtually the entire archipelago has converted to Islam, until today the population is over 90 per cent Muslim. In some areas believers are especially pious, faithful, and knowledgable Muslims, while in other regions the religion is not a central focus of village life.

Islam spread along trade routes and fostered exchange with the Middle East and in turn with Europe. Private Portuguese traders entered this

18. – Forked post, a memorial associated with feasts of merit in Nagaland (India) (from Barbier 1984, fig. 5).

19. – Forked post in the Nage village of Boawai. Note similarity to Naga posts. Sacrificial buffalo were bound to such stakes at community feasts (Photograph Jana Ansermet, 1980).

20. — Megalithic tomb in Tarung village, Waikabukak, West Sumba. A man sits between the horns of a buffalo. The sculpture is said to have been carved prior to firm Dutch control of West Sumba, in the early 1900s (Photograph Susan Rodgers, 1983).

21. — Cross-cultural similarities with mainland Southeast Asian highland peoples: carved door from an Angami village, Nagaland. A man stands between the horns of a *mithan* (buffalo). The human heads were lucky trophies of warriors (from von Fürer-Haimendorf 1946, fig. 7).

competitive economic arena in the 1500s. Malacca in 1511 fell to Portugal, which spent the next one hundred years trying to secure control of trade with the Spice Islands (the Moluccas). English and Dutch traders entered Indonesia in a significant way in the late 1500s. The Dutch East India Company was given its charter in 1602 and formed the basis of the Dutch colony in the Indies. By 1619 the Dutch controlled the region around Batavia (now Jakarta). By encouraging local disputes between rival polities, the Dutch gradually extended their economic and administrative control throughout the archipelago. By 1898 they occupied large portions of South Sumatra, the Moluccas, most of Java, and some parts of Sulawesi and Eastern Indonesia.

Dutch rule was maintained through the manipulation of the plantation system and through control of local elites. Resistance to Dutch occupation of Java and the Outer Islands was frequent and bloody. In 1942, during World War II, Japanese forces quickly occupied the islands. The national revolution of 1945 to 1949 finally succeeded in freeing the archipelago from European control, and the Republic of Indonesia was established under President Sukarno. The years since have been marked by increasing national consolidation, a succession of forms of national government, and rapid economic development. Increasing numbers of people have moved from rural ethnic homelands to the multi-ethnic cities. Today the country includes over three hundred ethnic societies and about the same number of ethnic languages. The Javanese, Sundanese, Madurese, and Balinese make up over half the national population, although the majority of the land area lies in the Outer Islands. In 1983 the population of Indonesia was 160,932,000.

The Philippines today resembles Indonesia in several important ways. Like its southern neighbor the Philippines is an island state, an archipelago consisting of about 7,100 islands covering 300,440 square kilometers. The national population of 53,162,000 (in 1983) is divided into at least seventy-five distinct ethnic groups; there are at least that number of ethnic languages. Like Indonesia the country has a national language — Filipino, or Tagalog. English is widely known as a result of fifty years of United States control after the Spanish American War and before national independence in 1946. The Spanish occupied the Philippines for 333 years (Magellan arrived in 1521, the first permanent settlement in Cebu was established in 1565, and the Spanish remained until 1899, when the United States formally gained control). During the Spanish period European and Roman Catholic influence was especially strong in the lowland areas, while military excursions and missionary efforts in the mountain regions often met with considerable resistance. Today the country is 83 per cent Roman Catholic. Like Indonesia, the Philippines in the national period after World War II has experienced massive social changes as the rural population becomes more urban.

Controversies in the study of art in Southeast Asia

One particularly bitter controversy in the study of island Southeast Asian art has focused on the fact that along with this diversity a number of geographically distant ethnic groups share very similar motifs in their village arts. Some scholars assert a common origin, or homeland, for these elements, which purportedly reached their present location through a process of cultural diffusion. Robert Heine-Geldern is the preeminent champion of this approach (1966, 1982). Anthropologists and many historians, on the other hand, find improbable the idea of large-scale, long-distance migrations of people and look to the social mechanisms of inter-island trade to explain the spread of particular artistic designs. Since there are a number of similar jewelry shapes in the Barbier-Müller collection from geographically distant Indonesian and Philippine cultures, and since a simple diffusionist model might at first seem plausible, some of the drawbacks of Heine-Geldern's approach should be addressed briefly.

Southeast Asian populations vary in terms of their physical anthropological characteristics, religious beliefs, material culture, language, and art forms. The archaeological record also presents observers with considerable cultural diversity in pottery styles, design motifs, settlement schemes, and so on.

Heine-Geldern and others of the diffusionist school assert that the area's cultural complexity is the result of successive waves of migration of culturally distinct peoples who brought definable languages, religions, and art traditions to the Indonesian and Philippine archipelagos from various "homelands" in eastern India and southern China. In this view, contemporary cultures and populations are sort of palimpsests of past societies, each one coming in "on top of the other" and each leaving certain "survival forms" (e.g., art motifs, religious ideas). It should be noted that this way of thinking locates the origins of "all that is worthy" in island Southeast Asian culture outside of Indonesia and the Philippines, which are

22. – Men's house (South Nias), with human skulls hanging from the roof. Headhunting was already recorded in Nias by an Arabic seatrader in 851 A.D. (see Barbier 1977, p. 47) (from Modigliani 1890, plate IX, facing p. 210).

23. – Row of human head trophies in a Dayak house. Note the typical motifs painted on the wall (Tillema n.d., fig. 60).

24. — Ifugao nobleman, Northern Luzon. The headdress is made of horns, feathers, and a hornbill skull in the middle. This was an ornament worn only by Kiangan noblemen (from Worcester 1912: 878).

25. — A Southeast Asian parallel: headhunter in Wakching, northern Nagaland. The headdress is formed of two *mithan* (buffalo) horns with two hornbill skulls and men's hair (from von Fürer-Haimendorf 1946, fig. 85).

thus seen as vessels into which cultural patterns from supposedly more creative and vigorous areas of the world are poured. This idea has become a major focus of criticism of the diffusionists. Illustrative of Heine-Geldern's approach is his 1966 article "Some Tribal Art Styles of Southeast Asia: An Experiment in Art History," which deals with the concept of the Dongson period in Indonesian art, important for the study of jewelry styles.

According to this article, the art of the nonliterate peoples of the mountains of mainland Southeast Asia, Sumatra, Kalimantan, and Eastern Indonesia derives from several basic, distinct traditions, each associated with the migrations or colonial incursions of large groups of people. The oldest tradition is the "monumental style," which can be glimpsed today in some of the village arts of the Naga people of Assam, the hill tribes of Western Burma, and in Nias, Toraja, and, in an "impoverished version," in Northern Luzon (Heine-Geldern 1966: 166-167). The style revolves around megalithic monuments, "all with a predilection for simple, often straightlined forms and contours and even for outright geometrical stylization" (1966: 167). The forked stake (perhaps used at feasts of merit as a sort of sacrificial altar; Figs. 18, 19) is a mainstay of the monumental style; it has survived "later stages" with great resiliency. Also associated with the monumental style are buffalo heads (Figs. 20, 21), a human figure positioned between buffalo horns, female breasts, and a four-spiral design. According to Heine-Geldern, art was dedicated to increasing family prestige; feasts of merit went toward the production of various commemorative artworks (such as stone slabs, carved doors, forked stakes, and stone and wood effigies), all of which glorified dead ancestors while increasing the social lustre of the host. Headhunting was a parallel way of increasing men's prestige (Figs. 22-25).

Heine-Geldern theorizes that this cultural tradition originated somewhere in India and was carried into Southeast Asia in approximately the second millennium B.C. This monumental style purportedly spread far into China and influenced Shang art styles. This path of migration and cultural influence is congruent with Heine-Geldern's usual portrayal of Southeast Asian cultural origins. He has long asserted that Indonesian languages, for instance, were introduced into the archipelago by peoples from far eastern India (1966: 174-175).

The next layer in Heine-Geldern's reconstruction of

the Southeast Asian past is the Dongson style, a term relating to the magnificent cast-bronze "thunder drums" found in mainland Southeast Asia and many parts of Indonesia. These still-mysterious kettle drums, which were possibly used at rituals to produce immense sounds, were decorated with an array of busy human figures sailing funeral boats (Figs. 26, 27, 28), walking in procession, shaking staffs, birds, deer, and frogs. The drums were obviously connected in some way with funerals and a supernatural realm, but beyond saying that these musical instruments were highly successful trade objects, little is clear about the culture that produced them. Heine-Geldern is primarily interested in the drums and associated artifacts as the source of the "ornamental style" in island Southeast Asian art. This style consists of the sort of curliques, inverted triangles (tumpal), "s" designs, and rice-grain motifs that are found on the bamboo carvings, house architecture, and wood sculpture of the Batak and many other Indonesian peoples (1966: 177-190). This style has been blended in some areas such as Kalimantan with Late Chou designs from China (Figs. 29 and 30) (thus, the Dayak's popular *aso*, or stylized, open-mouthed dragon motif). Heine-Geldern completes his breathtaking review of Indonesian art history by noting that "the next great movement that introduced a new art style into Southeast Asia [was] that of Hindu traders, colonists and adventurers, … Brahmans and … Buddhist missionaries … in historic times" (1966: 203). As illustrated, Heine-Geldern advocates the use of art history studies, based largely on the search for visual similarities of form, as a way to reconstruct the social history of Southeast Asia by documenting its supposed migrations.

Heine-Geldern is surely correct in pointing out the influence of the art traditions of neighboring state societies on the smaller minority populations, but he has almost certainly misconstrued the mechanism through which these art traditions travelled around Southeast Asia. A more plausible way than the large-scale migration of peoples for a new style to spread in this region was through trading circles of sailor-merchants. Solheim, in a series of recent publications (1976, 1981), suggests that complexes of religious ideas or artistic styles may have been carried from island to island by traders who had trading partners in these nearby regions. One partner would exchange some conventionalized good, such as sandalwood, for a set type of object, such as shells, and the relationship would become almost ritualized

26. — So-called soul ship or funeral boat on the Dongsonian bronze drum found in Ngoc-lu (end of the first millennium B.C.) (from Goloubev 1929, plate XXVI A).

27. — A Dayak ship of the dead — the mythical soul ship for conveying the souls of the dead to the Otherworld. Note the gongs hanging from the platform on the right. A Tree of Life emerges from the deck, on the left. Spirits and weapons also adorn the ship (from Goloubev 1929, plate XXVIII E).

28. — Another Dayak soul ship (from Goloubev 1929, plate XXVIII B).

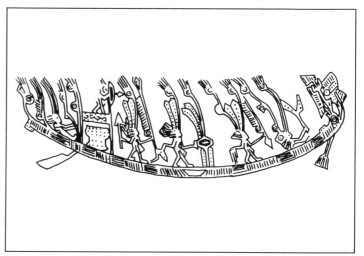

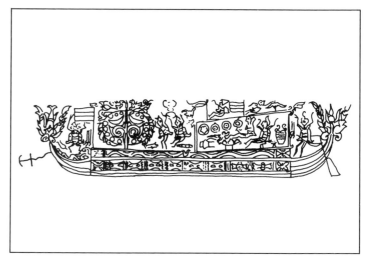

29. – Chariot fitting, late Eastern Chou (third century B.C.). Bronze inlaid with silver (Loehr 1968, fig. 77).

30. – Dayak design on bamboo, with *aso* motif (see Cat. No. 43, nineteenth century) (after Haddon 1905 fig. 8.)

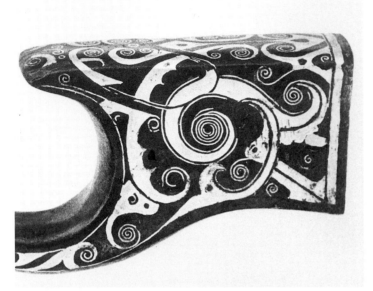

over time. An art style or religious practice could travel from one trading circle to another and eventually spread over huge distances, with most of the local populations seeing only part of the whole system. The region's many common jewelry shapes may very well have developed in this way, up until recent times.

Cultural diversity beyond Java and Bali

In looking at contemporary Indonesian and Philippine ethnic diversity it is important first to remember that minority societies in both countries to some degree all participate in the national, urban-based cultures of those developing nations and are affected by Islam and Christianity. Secondly, it is crucial to differentiate between the densely populated societies of Inner Indonesia (Java and Bali) and the more sparsely peopled regions of Outer Indonesia (all the other islands to the west, north, and east).

Java and Bali have long histories of intensive wet-rice cultivation and centralized, state-level organization. North Sumatra, interior Kalimantan, interior Sulawesi, and Eastern Indonesia, by contrast, have both swidden (slash-and-burn cultivation) and wet rice, and generally supported chiefdoms and small-scale state societies. These include the asymmetric marriage alliance cultures and the inland cognatic cultures represented in the Barbier-Müller exhibition. In the coastal areas of some of these Outer Islands were Islamized mercantile states such as Bugis and Minangkabau. Lastly, there were nomadic hill peoples such as Sumatra's Orang Kubu, groups that are heavily dependent on hunting and gathering forest products. Each of these types of cultures has a definable jewelry tradition.

The Javanese and Balinese states were traditional kingdoms whose leaders promoted the view that the political order was a direct replica of the structure of the cosmos (Anderson 1972). Much as they practiced an intensive and highly productive form of paddy rice agriculture, they had a superheated and truly prodigious artistic output. Figure 31 shows some of the extraordinary jewelry these cultures produced for palace use. The ornaments borrow heavily on Indian court designs, as do the jewelry of other Indianized states in Burma and Thailand. A useful way of seeing these rather overblown artistic traditions is to remember that these highly stratified, socially intricate societies were also great agricultural success stories: they had surplus wealth to convert into ritual systems of comparable intricacy

(Fischer 1961). These states developed a remarkable range of palace arts which included temple and court architecture, jewelry and textiles, *gamelan* orchestras, court dances, shadow puppet plays based on Indian epics, and an extensive religious literature.[4]

The *pasisir* (coastal) states are well represented by the Bugis of south Sulawesi, the Acehnese and Minangkabau of Sumatra, and the Malay sultanates of East Sumatra and Malaysia. Many of these cultures had histories of interaction with ancient Indianized kingdoms in Java and South Sumatra. They generally had capital towns, if not large cities, and somewhat more elaborate class systems than the cultures in the Barbier-Müller collection. The *pasisir* cultures often controlled thriving inter-island trade systems: Sulawesi mercantile states, for instance, extended their influence far into Eastern Indonesia. Some of these merchant societies were islamized as early as the 1400s, whereas the societies represented in the Barbier-Müller collection, by contrast, retained their own religions or came under Christian missionary influence much later (from the mid 1800s to the late 1930s).[5] The "palaces" of the coastal peoples were actually more in the nature of overgrown wooden *adat* houses. Fine Minangkabau noble houses are a good example (Fig. 32): these swoopbacked dwellings set up on wood pilings have long, minutely carved and painted side panels and shuttered windows, lattice-work decorations, ceramic lanterns from Dutch styles, and heavy dark-wood furniture. Personal adornment emphasizes sumptuous brocaded cloth made with metal thread and precious-metal headgear, bracelets, and daggers. Bridal costumes overlap significantly with the royal regalia, and brides and grooms from the noble class in a sense paraded around as kings and queens on their wedding day. This is still true today, when traditional nobles have little secular power. Jewelry styles are very similar from one coastal culture to the next and show the strong influence of Indianized court centers.

In our discussion, as already noted, the societies that dominate the Barbier-Müller collection have been placed in two categories, which, needless to say, are ideal types; some individual societies do not fit

31. – Inner Indonesian court regalia: Balinese girl with ceremonial jewels and dress (from Jasper and Pirngadie 1927, IV, fig. 3).

4. See Anderson's "The Idea of Power in Javanese Culture" (1972) for a discussion of the type of cosmological and social theories used in traditional Java.

5. Among the societies represented in the Barbier-Müller collection, the Toba Batak and various ethnic societies in Sumba and Flores have been converted in significant numbers to Protestant Christianity or Catholicism (particularly prominent on Flores).

32. – Minangkabau *adat* house in the highlands inland from Padang (Photograph Jean Paul Barbier, 1974).

33. – The back board of this "seat of honor" *(pepadon)* of South Sumatra shows a Cosmic Tree, flanked by birds. Noblemen sat on these *pepadon* while giving feasts to rise in social rank. The Tree of Life and feasts of merit are also linked in a number of other island Southeast Asian cultures. Writing of Nias, Steinhart noted that "the purpose [of the feast] is that one… climbs ever higher to the top of the nobility… The Tree (Tola in Nias) is the indicator for feast and feastgiver" (quoted in Suzuki 1959:113), Barbier-Müller Museum, No. 3241-2, not exhibited).

cleanly into either group. The first, termed the asymmetric marriage alliance cultures, are found in the Batak regions near Lake Toba in North Sumatra, and in many parts of Eastern Indonesia in the provinces of Nusa Tenggara Timur and Maluku. Before the profound social changes of the post-World War II national era, the Batak, Lio, Nage, Ngada, and East Sumbanese were hierarchically organized, village-based rice-farming cultures that depended to a high degree on symbols of kin relationship for structuring their social world. Some were advanced chiefdoms, some incipient states, and some should probably be called princedoms. Dutch colonial interference rigidified a number of these cultures into little states. In the process, unwritten *adat* traditions were reconceptualized by the Dutch as "*adat law.*"[6] The very common kinship system of asymmetrical marriage alliance in the Batak areas and parts of Eastern Indonesia involved patrilineal clans and politically motivated marriage alliances between localized lineages of those clans. Marriage ideally involved men and women from different clans, and wife-providing lineages considered themselves the ritual superiors of their indebted, spiritually subordinate wife-receivers.

In these societies wife-givers were often associated with height, the right side, the realm of the spirits, and the centers of *adat* houses and villages, while wife-takers were associated with the complementary opposites: lowness, the left side, the mundane world, and the porches of houses and the rims of villages. The specific symbols vary from culture to culture, but there is a common reliance on ideas of binary opposition and hierarchically ranked giver and taker groups. It is important to note for the study of jewelry that metal, cloth, food, livestock, people, physical protection, farm labor services, ritual labor, and such impalpable goods as blessings and luck were used in structurally similar ways as gifts to bind together wife-givers and wife-takers. A common pattern (although one not borne out in every culture) had wife-givers providing their sisters and daughters as brides to taker groups, along with a series of companion presents such as textiles, spiritual blessings, supernatural protection, fertility, and certain types of cooked and uncooked food. These wife-giver gifts were sometimes associated with femininity, although such an easy English translation obscures the complexities of gender symbolism

6. See Vergouwen 1964 (1933) for a good introductory survey of an Indonesian *adat* system; note that he presents Toba Batak *adat* in a highly systematized form.

in some cultures. It is best to characterize these goods as wife-giver objects, not simply feminine objects. The wife-taking groups would send back countergifts (sometimes but not always described as masculine gifts) consisting of brideprice payments (cash, gold), livestock, metal or ivory jewelry, rifles, spears, physical protection, military services, and labor services in their mother's brother's fields. Metal is thus often characterized as a wife-taker gift to wife-givers, the exact countergift to "feminine" woven textiles.

The mother's brother is especially important in these cultures, because he is the exact provider of a bride to a young man. A generation ago, lineage A, say, sent one of their women as a bride to lineage B. The men of B ideally should look to the same beneficent provider group when it comes time for them to find a wife (these gift-giving alliances ideally persist over many generations). The perfect wife for the young man of B would be a woman from the same household that gave his group his mother a generation before. The mother's brother presumably would have stayed behind in that house, married, and had a large family of children, all members of lineage B. The young man seeks a replacement or repetition of his mother — in other words, he marries his exact mother's brother's daughter. In practice these marriage systems are often extremely flexible, and women outside the ideal lineage can be handily classified as mother's brother's daughters in the kinship terminology. New marriage alliances with previously unrelated women are also quite possible and often are actively encouraged. The Angkola Batak call this practice *pabidang turtur*, or "enlarging the realm of kinship term talk."[7] A man's mother's brother is also vitally important to his own sons and daughters as a source of moral advice and spiritual sustenance, sometimes interceding with the spirit world.

Much of the jewelry in the Barbier-Müller collection was created and used in the context of this particular marriage exchange (Figs. 34 and 35), mainly as countergifts to brides and ritual textiles. However, it should be noted immediately that some types of jewelry go in the opposite direction, and other ornaments are passed down from father to son as holy ancestral heirlooms. In other words, the jewelry plays on a symbolism of clan descent as well

7. Angkola Batak kinship terminology — like much about the kinship system — is classificatory: if a man marries a woman who happens not to be his mother's brother's daughter (the ideal marriage choice), he and his family will forthwith call her "mother's brother's daughter."

34. – Exchange in a Batak funeral feast in Samosir, Lake Toba. A man ritually presents some money to a member of his beneficent wife-giving lineage (Photograph Jean Paul Barbier, 1978).

35. – The same funeral feast: a piece of pork is conferred as a kinship gift (*jambar*, or kin-based division of meat) (Photograph Jean Paul Barbier, 1978).

as marriage alliance. These cultures had two broad types of jewelry and precious objects in general: valuables for *exchange between houses*, used at marriages or other ceremonial, kinship-based occasions; and *house treasure*, which passed down through the family line as heirlooms and ideally was not to be given as gifts to other houses. (Sometimes these valuables did get moved about. The *raja* in Walotopo village in the Lio region of Central Flores, for example, has a house treasure based on several gold chains and old earrings. Early in the treasure's history, its steward gave it to another *raja* in another village, for reasons unknown. This man later repatriated the heirlooms to their original house – or at least so says the family history in 1983).

The asymmetric alliance cultures in the collection also often used quite similar symbols in building their *adat* houses and arranging their villages. The high degree of similarity here and in the kinship realm, in fact, calls for the sort of comparative framework scholars such as Van Wouden (1969) advocate for the study of Eastern Indonesia (Fox 1980b, 1980c; Josselin de Jong 1980). Drawing on the theories of sociologists Marcel Mauss and Emile Durkheim, this perspective sees Eastern Indonesian systems of exchange as total social institutions, or master symbols for constructing social worlds.[8] This enthusiastically cross-cultural approach also asserts that the cultures on Flores, Sumba, Tanimbar, Savu, Roti, and Timor are related to each other on a theme-and-variations pattern. This is especially so in relation to their marriage systems and religious ideas, where certain core symbols such as giving and taking, holiness and mundane life, height and lowness, and so on are employed as a sort of logical language in a great variety of social and economical contexts. Thus an Eastern Indonesian kinship system that calls for a short period of matrilocal residence after marriage (with the new couple living near the wife's original family) and assigns the couple's children to their mother's descent line if the full bridewealth has not been paid can be seen as a particular *variation* of the asymmetric alliance system of the region. This structuralist approach asserts that the many instances of similarity in the symbolic systems of Eastern Indonesian societies are not simply the result of historical contacts and borrowing, but are examples of a fundamental cultural type working itself out in the actual world of diverse island societies in history.

8. See Durkheim and Mauss, *Primitive Classification* (1903) for an early discussion of this idea.

This approach helps make sense of some other common ideas and institutions in these cultures: the prevalence of headhunting in former times; the association of taking life (hunting as well as headhunting) with its complementary opposite, giving life (giving birth to human babies, livestock producing young, gardening); the recurrent idea that the cosmos has an Upperworld, a mundane world, and a Lowerworld, all connected with a Cosmic Tree, or World Tree, which is itself associated with the house, the family line, and the person (Fig. 33; see also Figs. 56-58 below). The structuralist perspective also sheds light on what is perhaps most central to the thought systems of these cultures: the idea that creativity in the universe, whether it be in the form of human pregnancy or wood carving or plant regeneration or recovery after an epidemic, comes from the temporary union of such complementary opposites as male and female spheres or right and left or village and forest or cloth and metal, which are seen as the momentarily separated facets of some aboriginal unity.

The second main category of Indonesian culture, the inland cognatic societies as they are called here, are undoubtedly closely related to the marriage alliance cultures, but for heuristic purposes they will be discussed separately. These cultures include the many Dayak societies of interior Kalimantan and Sarawak, as well as some of the mountain peoples of Sulawesi (the Wana, and perhaps some of the so-called West Toraja groups near Kulawi). The Mentawai people off the west coast of Sumatra should probably also be grouped here.

Calling tribe-like hill societies such as Sulawesi's Wana "egalitarian" is probably a misnomer, for some of these peoples – like their coastal neighbors – employed a hierarchical vocabulary for talking about human society and the universe. They were generally small-scale and relatively isolated village societies practicing slash-and-burn agriculture and, in many cases, pig husbandry. Usually the settlements would move from place to place as they cleared and cultivated new plots of land. Kinship systems generally lacked corporate descent groups with claims to land and property; rather, family relationship was traced bilaterally, out through both the mother's and father's side. This pattern tended to surround an individual or a group of siblings with a personal kindred (a penumbra of living relatives, as Americans have "relatives on both sides"). Personal kindreds multiply until a region schematically might be said to look like a pond covered with overlapping lilypads.

The social horizons of these cultures were often limited. Fear of hostile strangers was endemic; nighttime attack was a common threat. Headhunting dominated politics and male prestige. Taking a head freed a young man from the negative associations of immaturity and gave him his ticket to full, responsible adult status. Powerful men built up stores of prestige by taking many heads. Death also led to life, as headhunting engendered fertility in the human village and the fields. Shamans were socially important persons, but chiefs and their families were generally not distinguished from the rest of society by great differences in house structure or clothing. "Aristocratic" families did own fine house treasures, often composed of trade goods such as old Chinese jars and old beads. Figure 36, of people from the west coast Sumatran island of Siberut, shows some of the sort of jewelry these people had. It was made of forest and seashore products such as feathers, leaves, seeds, stones, wood, and shells. Ornaments were sometimes exchanged at major family gatherings or during healing rituals. Some of these small societies imported metal jewelry, textiles, betel tins, brass food trays, and porcelain from their more politically centralized coastal neighbors.

The nomadic hunting and gathering societies, which have almost disappeared today, apparently had family-based band communities that engaged in silent trade with their various agricultural neighbors. Their jewelry traditions are for the most part unexplored.

Over the course of Indonesian and Philippine history, all of these types of cultures have interacted. Trade goods such as beads, porcelain, metal coins, forest products, and shells were the main currency of this interaction, as expanding states sought to buy the political fealty of the small societies on their perimeters. Let one example illustrate this. East Sumba's house treasures are highly imaginative assemblages of Javanese-made gold ornaments, Chinese porcelain, trade beads, and ancestral heirlooms. Some of these treasures contain beaten gold plates from old Javanese kingdoms, which had been given to local Sumba leaders to secure their political cooperation in Java's expansion into the important trading areas of Eastern Indonesia. House treasures from all over the archipelago have similarly dynamic social histories. If the cultures represented in the Barbier-Müller collection are united in anything, in fact, it is in their ability to take trade goods from beyond their horizons and quickly encompass them within local kinship, religious, and political ideas.

36. – Boy from Siberut, Mentawai Islands (Photograph Tonino Caissutti, courtesy ISME, Editrice Cremona).

3
LOOKING AT JEWELRY

Defining art is always difficult; defining what is artistic about jewelry is even more challenging. Defining art and jewelry across a major cultural divide, such as the one separating the West from Outer Indonesia and Northern Luzon, is more demanding still.

In contemporary Europe and the United States, disputes over the term "art" are likely to center on attempts to label relatively new creative forms, such as photography and video, as art. An important assumption behind disputes like this one is that there is "great art" of enduring value, produced in traditional mediums by "great artists" with more talent and sensitivity than the regular members of society. It happens that questions of this sort are today also becoming important in Indonesia and the Philippines, but the definitional disputes of more immediate concern to the Barbier-Müller exhibition are ones concerning the dividing line between art and ritual, art and religion, and the artist versus the ritual celebrant.

A number of pieces in the collection (Sumba's *mamuli*, the Karo Batak *sertali* bridal ornaments) belong to the "power-full" royal regalia of noble houses. Often these same pieces are also ritual objects used by priests and diviners to get into contact with a supernatural world of spirits or ancestors. Other pieces are amulets for protecting infants and children and people going through dangerous times in rites of passage, when they are unusually open to mystical attacks. Thus these objects are thought of as receptacles for special powers and are located at the borderline between the mundane world and the sacred realm. As religious objects they exist at a considerable cultural distance from secular art objects as defined in the West. An example from the wooden sculpture traditions of Nage culture in Flores illustrates the way in which much jewelry, textiles, sculpture, and house architecture was conceptualized in Indonesian cultures up to the recent past.

Figure 37 shows a *ja heda*, a large Nage equestrian statue from the Boawai region. Before the national revolution of 1945-1949, these horses were apparently sculpted as commemorative effigies to clan ancestors and were placed next to the village *sao heda*, the small ceremonial house commemorating both patrilineal ancestors and masculinity per se. The horns and skulls of water buffalo sacrificed in the various rituals celebrating the lineage were stored in magnificent heaps in these ritual houses. Off on the far periphery of the village was a smaller feminine ceremonial house, accompanied by a small, riderless wooden horse. This smaller statue was identified with femininity. In my 1983 visit to Boawai it quickly became evident that these statues were not locally defined as art in any way resembling the Western sense of aesthetically pleasing objects created by individual artists for public enjoyment, public sale, and private contemplation. Near the masculine ceremonial house lay the insect-eaten remains of the last *ja heda* (Fig. 38). I asked what had happened. One of the village *adat* experts replied that no one in the village was rich enough anymore to provide the many water buffalo necessary to commission a ritual sculptor to go into the forest,

37. — A wooden horse and rider, called *ja heda* (approximately 3 meters long). The *ja heda* stands under the masculine altar house dedicated to clan founders. Nage area, Central Flores (Photograph courtesy Kon. Inst. v/d Tropen, Amsterdam).

38. — Remains of a *ja heda* today in Boawai village, Nage area, Central Flores (Photograph Susan Rodgers, 1983).

select a tree, and bring a new *ja heda* back to the village (that is, carve a new sculpture). Every step of the creation of the statue demanded a buffalo sacrifice, for the sculptor was trafficking with ancestral spirits, so to speak, as he crafted their contemporary "vessel" for contacting their living descendants. With no funds to bring back a new sculpture from the forest, the old *ja heda* — itself an empty vessel without continuous sacrifices — was simply left to molder away. Many ritual jewelry ornaments in Indonesia are part of similar systems of religious belief and practice, at least while the ornaments are still in villages among old people knowledgeable in *adat.*

Jewelry in Europe and America is rarely considered an art form comparable to painting and sculpture, nor are textiles designated full-fledged works of art either; both are generally consigned to the realm of crafts. It is therefore difficult for Westerners to understand the strength and vitality with which Indonesian and Philippine aesthetic expression is channeled into metalworking and weaving. Thus some Westerners may fail to see island Southeast Asian jewelry as anything more than trinkets for personal adornment. Such problems of interpretation are common when Western museum-goers and collectors see objects from foreign cultures that have no readily identifiable counterpart in their own artistic universes. That is, wooden sculptures from Africa and Melanesia are easily accepted as "primitive art" by European peoples with a long indigenous history of wooden sculpture, while beadwork jewelry, decorated textiles, and baskets may be denigrated as handicrafts.[1]

How then to look at ritual jewelry from island Southeast Asia? If abundant information were available about a particular ornament, the piece might be read as a text composed of a number of levels of meaning. Looking at a single ornament could lead the observer outward into studies of local styles, local systems of aesthetics, and such related arts as dance, *adat* ritual, and oratory. The particular shape, manufacture, and place of origin of a piece of jewelry could also open up large sectors of local social history. A careful cultural exegesis of the piece could lead the observer to look at the ornament's place within local social systems of economic, politi-

---

1. Nelson Graburn has an excellent discussion of these points in his introductory essay to *Ethnic and Tourist Arts: Cultural Expressions from the Fourth World* (1979).

cal, and kin relationship. Beyond this, the stylistic features of the piece might suggest ties to art traditions in societies outside the immediate ethnic group, tying the piece to art in Polynesia, for instance, or in mainland Southeast Asia. Anthropologist Clifford Geertz has suggested this sort of interpretive approach for the study of Javanese and Balinese rituals, games, royal processions, and other public events (Geertz 1972, 1973). Interpretation should prove just as possible and just as fruitful for actual objects like earrings and pendants.

Interpretation of this sort is beyond the fieldwork for this catalogue, but the types of inquiries such an analysis would entail can at least be suggested here. Consider a few layers of meaning present in such pieces as the Sumbanese *mamuli*, the Central Sulawesi *taiganja*, or the Karo Batak bridal ornaments (see Cat. Nos. 136, 73, and 11).

One might look first (or rather listen) to the language used to talk about jewelry. Terms vary a good deal among ethnic groups, but the way ornaments are spoken of in the Indonesian national languages gives a primer on some of the important folk concepts associated with jewelry. One common Indonesian word for jewelry is *perhiasan*.[2] This is built on the root word *hias*, an idea associated with notions of adorning, regaling, and bedecking something for public display. Dressing a person or a thing (a sculpture, a house, an assemblage of textiles) in ornaments is also a way of honoring them, literally covering them with "respect." In some Indonesian ethnic languages the full ritual regalia of aristocrats, brides, bridegrooms, warriors, corpses, and ancestor effigies is thought to literally glow with light. This "power shine" demonstrates the concentrated essences of the chieftainship, lineage, house, and so on, according to the political system at hand.

Some words for jewelry also evoke ideas of spell-casting and its correlate, magical protective forces. For instance, a common Indonesian word for earrings is *anting-anting*, which in one sense simply means decorative earrings (the word derives from a

2. In *An Indonesian-English Dictionary* (1963:144), Echols and Shadily define the word *hias* and its related compounds as follows: "decoration, adornment. ber- 1 to dress up. *Ia lagi ~ dlm kamarnja*, She is dressing in her room. 2 dressed up. *Mengapa engkau ~? Apakah akan ada tamu?* Why are you so dressed up? Will there be guests? 3 fancy. ber-kan adorned with. *Ia ~ kalung emas*, She was adorned with a golden necklace. memper-i, meng-i to decorate. *Murid² ~ kelas meréka*, The pupils decorated their classroom. (per)-an 1 decoration. *~ gedung itu sangat indah*, The decorations in the building were very beautiful. 2 adornment, finery. *Ia membeli ~ bagi isterinja*, He bought finery for his wife."

39. – Tattooed legs of a Dayak warrior (from Tillema n.d., fig. 125).

40. – A Philippine parallel: tattooed headhunter in Kalinga, Northern Luzon (Photograph Eduardo Masferré).

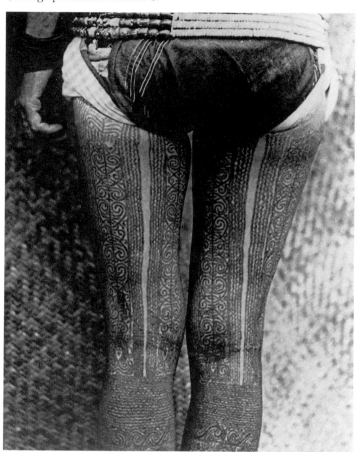

root suggesting the state of hanging down and swaying back and forth); in another of its meanings, however, *anting-anting* means charm — the sort used to protect a small child from mystical harm or to attract healing forces. Words for jewelry have a number of these amulet associations in the various ethnic languages. Sometimes the shape of the ornament suggests a protective mythical animal, and so on. In addition to the individual words for jewelry, one might also investigate the ways ornaments are mentioned in *adat* oratory, as part of praise speeches for brides, eulogies for old *rajas*, blessing speeches for gifts of bridewealth.

Beyond language itself, one might also look at the meaning the piece of jewelry derives from its place in a ritual or in everyday costume. For instance, the Karo Batak *sertali* headdress ornament (see Cat. No. 11) makes full sense to Karo only in relationship to the other ornaments and textiles of the bride's wedding costume. In fact, the *sertali* should be seen against the backdrop of the bridegroom's wedding costume as well. The other rites of passage and village celebrations in Karo *adat* must also be taken as the set of symbols to which the *sertali* jewelry belongs, for it is only within this entire ritual universe that the ornament's repetitive use of the number three, *adat* house designs, bird motifs, and so on makes sense.

A full analysis of jewelry traditions should probably go beyond metal, ivory, and shell ornamentation to consider jewelry's place within other forms of self-decoration common in these cultures. Jewelry, that is, may be part of a set of self-display forms consisting of tattoos (Figs. 39 and 40), clothing, masks, weapons (Figs. 41 and 42), armor, tooth decorations and deformations, and cosmetics (Ebin 1979). Since the decoration of corpses before burial or cremation is important in many island Southeast Asian cultures, funerary traditions should probably be considered at the same time that one looks at the ways living humans are adorned for public view. In pre-national times, teeth filing or facial and upper body tattooing were used in Dayak cultures, the Batak societies, and in some Eastern Indonesian cultures to signal social passage from childhood to marriageable adulthood (tattooing is still practiced in some areas). Haircuts and clothing styles were used for the same purpose. Jewelry was often a part of such complex communicative systems and apparently played an important role in the cultural creation of such social persons as "adult woman" and "adult man" (not to mention "ancestor spirits," for corpses were sometimes sent off to the afterworld decked out in appropriate jewelry).

An individual ornament can also open a window on the local culture as a whole, beyond its ceremonial system. For instance, a gold ornament used as part of the regalia of aristocrats can serve as a text on a local social hierarchy composed of noble families, commoners, and slave descendants. The way a piece of jewelry is handed around from family to family might also be taken as a text on the local village social system, much as Clifford Geertz has used the Balinese cockfight as a text on Balinese status hierarchy in his article "Deep Play: Notes on the Balinese Cockfight" (1972).[3]

Beyond all this, a piece of jewelry can serve as a text on social and stylistic patterns far beyond the awareness of either wearer or creator. For example, patterns of exchange involving prestige goods (jewelry, textiles) may extend beyond the local ethnic group to link several societies into leagues similar to the Kula ring described in "Jewelry and Exchange." The individual societies involved in the trade may not know the full extent of the larger exchange circles. Stylistic similarities and theme-and-variations patterns also draw many of the pieces in the collection into larger symbolic systems of which individual wearers and creators of the jewelry would be unaware. For instance, the open oval shape is repeated in a great number of ethnic jewelry traditions throughout Indonesia and the Philippines (Figs. 43 and 44). This could argue for the possibility of extensive trade contacts or even for a common historical source. The crescent shape, sometimes with an additional piece at the center, is another recurrent design with similar implications (Figs. 45 and 46).

Common designs in jewelry, and in body decoration as a whole, sometimes even extend beyond the broad cultural area itself. In his article "Split Representation in the Art of Asia and America" (1944-1945) Claude Lévi-Strauss examines the undeniable similarities between American Northwest Coast animal designs, Maori body tattoos, and ancient Chinese bronze relief patterns. Such artistic expressions could hardly have come from a single common

---

3. A companion statement on the interpretive approach is available in Clifford Geertz's "Thick Description: Toward an Interpretive Theory of Culture" (1973).

43. – Similar shapes in diverse times and places: four gilded bronze earrings, found in East Java, reportedly from the Majapahit period. Some are very similar in form to the *dinumug*, still used in Northern Luzon (Cat. No. 203). (Barbier-Müller Museum, not exhibited).

44. – The open oval shape in comparative perspective. Compare this basic form in ornaments originating from various cultures. From left to right, top to bottom: Central Flores, Sumba (?), South Moluccas, and the Philippines (Cat. Nos. 84, 122, 178, 204).

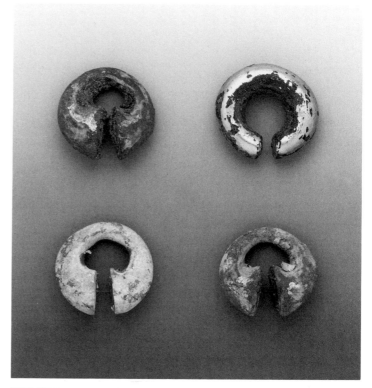

49

45 and 46. – Another widespread shape: the crescent. Crowns or headgear in this form are common throughout Indonesia. A bunch of leaves or feathers are sometimes added to the crescent. Sometimes the whole ornament looks like a pair of buffalo horns, with a palm located in the middle. This resembles the ancestor figure and buffalo horn design of Sumba sculptures (see Fig. 20).
45. Sa'dan Toraja, Sulawesi; 46. Galela (Halmahera).

ancestral culture, but Lévi-Strauss cautions us that in rejecting old-fashioned diffusionist explanations we should not blind ourselves to the fascinating similarities in the art traditions of widely separate cultures. So, island Southeast Asian jewelry might ultimately be studied in a wider context of jewelry traditions of historically distant areas.

In their monograph *Gold and Megalithic Activity in Prehistoric and Recent West Borneo* (1970), Tom Harrisson and Stanley J. O'Connor attempt a rather grand synthesis of this sort, although they do confine themselves largely to Indonesia and Northern Luzon. These authors assert that in prehistoric Borneo (now Kalimantan) the thriving production of gold ornaments was one small part of a larger funerary ritual complex involving the production and dedication of megalithic monuments and wooden sculpture and very probably the staging of elaborate burial ceremonies. Gold ornaments may have been produced in quantity for dispersal at the funerals of important persons and as grave goods. The stone slabs and the carved wooden figures were ostensibly effigy-like objects made in praise of and supplication to dead ancestors (Figs. 47 and 48). At a functional level the erection of many fine megaliths and statues served to increase the prestige of their living sponsor, who was probably engaged in heated competition with his fellow elite. The art system may have been supported by periodic "feasts of merit" in which families strove to outdo each other through the production of artistic works and the widespread dispersal of gifts of food.

This much is standard theorizing about the political basis of art production in pre-state societies, but Harrisson and O'Connor go on to add several insights that illuminate a great deal of the ethnography involved in the Barbier-Müller collection of ornaments. The megaliths may have been replicated in symbolic miniature in the form of pebbles, or micro-megaliths, as Harrisson and O'Connor call them. These small stones connected the big slabs to the earth, or *mediated* that relationship, while wooden sculptures were the symbolic *transformations* of stone monuments, and vice versa. Gold and gold shavings and dust were in a sense "miniature megaliths and micro-megaliths," and gold ornaments, like finished stones, came from the earth originally but emerged into village and cemetery use through human agency. Harrisson and O'Connor also postulate that this sort of ritual complex was not limited to Kalimantan but may have been present, in its transformations, in pre-modern Nias and perhaps other regions of Indonesia and the Northern Philippines.[4] In examining the latter area the authors become particularly eloquent (or over-ambitious) and suggest that the famous flat-topped multilayered rice terraces of the Ifugao may have been part of a similar ritual complex, where the shape of the rice paddies repeated and played upon the shape of masses of flat stone altars. Harrisson and O'Connor's final suggestion, that the stone-wood-gold-ritual complex of ancient Kalimantan and recent Nias may have been present in ancient Bali before conversion to Indian religions, seems more plausible and promising. The reader is referred to Harrisson and O'Connor's book itself and to their earlier *Excavations of the Prehistoric Iron Industry in West Borneo* (1969) for detailed accounts of the metal industries of these areas, their place in Asian trade, and the authors' documentation of their idea that West Kalimantan, not a Malay location, may have been the famed "Gold Island" of Southeast Asia.

Even more ambitious than this approach would be a final analytical use to which Indonesian and Philippine jewelry might be put: like any highly patterned domain of human life such as language or kinship or ritual, or other areas of material culture, jewelry could be used as a text on the human mind. A structuralist like Lévi-Strauss, for instance, might investigate the common assumption in many Indonesian jewelry traditions that the finest pieces combine elements of masculinity and femininity or mundane existence and sacredness. Certain jewelry objects hold these complementary spheres in a tense, temporary alliance thought to contain much creative power and force. This "two-in-one" idea, found in may Southeast Asian cultures, might shed light on basic human thought processes as well as illuminate the philosophical history of the immediate region.

Before going on to the ethnic sections, we will look more closely at the uses of island Southeast Asian jewelry in indicating social position, in gift giving and exchange, in relation to the supernatural, and in processes of modernization.

<hr />

4. The sense of transformation here is that one cultural form (such as wooden funerary statues), somewhat like the sound system of a language, can undergo a series of logical "permutations" quite beyond the knowledge and conscious control of individuals in the society. The basic cultural form can also emerge in different transformations in different societies in a closely related culture area.

47. – Stone seats and slabs fill up Nias' magnificent megalithic villages (Photograph Jean Paul Barbier, 1974).

48. – The megalith and gold complex in Kalimantan and Sarawak: a man on a stone seat, among another megaliths, in the Kelabit highlands (from Harrisson and O'Connor 1970, fig. 48).

4
JEWELRY
AND SOCIAL POSITION

As an unusually condensed form of wealth, easily displayed and carried on the human body, jewelry once served Indonesian and Philippine traditional aristocrats as convenient public advertisements of their high social position. The couple from central Flores shown in Fig. 49, for instance, use their heavy gold garlands to demonstrate their great wealth and power to the common villagers who have no such treasure. This political dimension of jewelry use is an obvious one, but jewelry marked social location in several less obvious ways in pre-national Indonesia and the Philippines.

The noble families of Northern Luzon, the Batak regions, Sulawesi, and Eastern Indonesia often kept the use of precious-metal jewelry to themselves, consigning to the poorer classes shell and bone decorations. Alternatively, the aristocrats claimed exclusive use of certain special designs and shapes in textiles and jewelry. Both the patterns and the types of precious metals were often associated with the very idea of aristocracy and through that, with the idea of a supernatural realm of higher spirits. This is predictable from the way scarce goods are used to mark high social position in other parts of the world, but in East Sumba another, less expected pattern emerges. The *rajas* of such small states as Rindi and Pau owned magnificent royal treasures (crown jewelry, as it were, shown in Fig. 50). The male nobles themselves, however, did not normally wear this regalia. In fact, during my short stay in 1983 in Pau, a member of the village aristocracy laughed at the very notion of the *raja* wearing his gold jewelry; rather, the *rajas* outfitted their personal slaves in the royal jewels, using these men as stand-ins for themselves at major rituals (today there are no actual slaves, just people from certain families who act as a ritually subservient class). A clue to how this symbolic reversal worked comes from Sumbanese *adat* funerals. As the *raja's* body was prepared for final burial, slaves were dressed up "as *rajas*" in the full regalia of ritual textiles and gold chains and pendants. The slaves-cum-*rajas* went into trances and, in a core event of the funeral, served as intermediaries for communicating messages between the living members of the community and the world of ancestor spirits, toward which the newly deceased *raja* was slowly making his way.

Considerable symbolic ambiguity often attaches to mediator figures like these in the myths and rituals of other cultures around the world. For instance, heroic savior figures such as Jesus Christ combine elements of humanity with a supernatural, spiritual status. It could be that the "decorated slave," transformed through his ornamentation into a *raja*, was a mediator figure in several senses. During the *raja's* lifetime the slave outfitted in the royal finery could serve as the *raja's* mediator to the general public, and after his death the slave could offer the *raja* and his ancestors a small road back into the community of humans. In the section on Sumba, below, we will see how this mediator role and its peculiar symbolic ambiguities also characterized one of Sumba's famous jewelry types, the gold *mamuli*.

Jewelry marked social position in other ways. Island Southeast Asian societies dramatized a person's progression through a series of life stages by means of

49. – Husband and wife in a Lio village, Central Flores. The woman's necklace is seven generations old, according to the family (Photograph Susan Rodgers, 1983).

50. – Family splendor: the sacred treasure of a Sumba *raja*, including gold ornaments, ivory bracelets, and beadwork (Photograph Susan Rodgers, 1983).

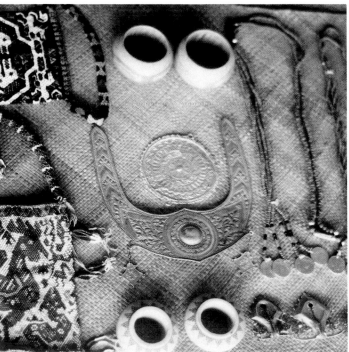

elaborate rites of passage. These ceremonies were used to mark pregnancy, birth, the first haircut, the presentation of a name to a child, the passage from childhood into nubile adolescence, and from adolescence into marriage. The birth of the first child and the first grandchild was sometimes also marked. In line with this, many societies used tekonyms, or names for parents derived from the names of their children, such as Father-of-Parulian. Death, which was sometimes presented as an ascension into ancestor status, was also ceremonialized with great care and at considerable expense (Fig. 51). Often, many water buffalos or pigs were sacrificed and distributed to villagers and visitors. In a way, all of these rites of passage were attempts to create new social persons. A pre-adolescent Batak girl, for instance, would be transformed into a woman through a ceremony in which her teeth were blackened and filed down to an even row. To Batak of the past she would not be a woman without this alteration, no matter what her chronological age.

Such practices can be seen as the cultural control of the maturation and aging process, a process that would make no sense to societies without the addition of a specific ideology and technology of personhood. The local Batak or Lio or Kaili culture defined each stage of personhood through its own standards of beauty and through its own decorative techniques. Pygmalion-like, these cultures called women and men into being. Tattoos, face makeup, manicures, clothing, and weaponry were enlisted for this task of creating a series of socially recognizable persons, and transferring them safely from one stage of life to the next. Sumbanese girls announced that they were marriageable through their hairstyle (short bangs, Fig. 52); when they married they would proclaim that fact by coiling their hair in a long loop on top of their head. Adornment with specific types of jewelry was an integral part of this well-controlled ritualization of the human life cycle.

Heirloom treasures kept in the family *adat* house were a vitally important means of establishing group social status. This is true in many areas even today. These house treasures are quite similar throughout Outer Indonesia and Northern Luzon. They generally consist of some combination of old metal weapons; gold, silver, copper, brass, or bronze ornaments, sometimes made of old European coins; old textiles; and Chinese jars, bowls and old glass, carnelian, and agate beads. These are loved as family relics and sometimes have special names and long mythlike histories about how they entered the house treasure. Some societies think that their treasures literally glow with powers[1] and should never be sold to outsiders or exchanged at marriage. (Actually, pieces do enter the treasures through bridewealth exchange; in societies where this occurs, there are often several categories of house treasure, some movable and some inalienable.)

The great amount of oratory, thought, and worry focused on these relics in Indonesia and the Philippines suggests that Lévi-Strauss's concept of "house societies" (or *sociétés à maisons*; 1983) would be a highly productive framework for understanding these cultures and their heirlooms. "House societies" refers to a structural type of culture found in the Northwest Coast of America and out through Polynesia into island Southeast Asia. Lévi-Strauss uses "house" as an alternative to the more usual anthropological categories of clan, lineage, tribe, and village. In house societies, a corporate body owns an estate, which consists of land, tools, and livestock, and also such intangibles as family stories, names, titles, "powers," and character. House relics are crucial in this type of culture, for they condense a great deal of feeling about the family's ancestry, social position, and future prospects into an observable and subjectively quite beautiful form. The various ethnic sections in the catalogue detail the care Indonesian and Philippine peoples often take in storing, hiding, praising, and ritually manipulating their splendid house treasures.

1. See Anderson 1972 for discussion of related power concepts in traditional Java. In that culture, the *keris* (daggers) of the aristocrats also glowed with power, which had to be kept under tight ritual control lest they "discharge," to put the matter somewhat anachronistically.

51. – Buffalos (as well as horses) were sacrificed at funerals in East Sumba (Photograph Lionel Morley early 1970s).

52. – Defining the person: the hairstyle of this East Sumba girl from Rindi indicates that she is not yet married (Photograph Susan Rodgers, 1983).

5
JEWELRY
AND EXCHANGE

As small, portable, precious, lovely objects jewelry has often been used by traditional societies without monetized economies for a variety of socially important exchanges. Jewelry offers a handy means for displaying the social rank of jewelry-givers and jewelry-receivers. Ornaments transferred from one family to another can also be used to symbolize the importance of the social relationship itself that holds between giver and taker. Engagement rings with precious stones are familiar examples of this type of exchange in Western societies. The French sociologist Marcel Mauss (1959) has characterized the exchange situation well by noting that pre-money cultures were held together through obligatory networks of gift-giving and gift-receiving; gifts, Mauss implied, were the social cement of small-scale societies.

In island Southeast Asia through the colonial period, many ethnic cultures were bound together internally and to one another in this way, through gifts and countergifts of precious goods, labor services, food, livestock, and even people (brides, slaves, war captives). Precious ornaments such as those in the Barbier-Müller collection were crucial items in these systems of exchange. Further, the shapes and designs of the jewelry pieces involved sometimes symbolized the social worth of the givers and the takers and their relationship as a whole. In this, jewelry served these cultures as indispensable mediating objects uniting a variety of opposed social categories and, as we shall see, opposed gender categories and opposed cosmological categories.

Traditional exchange in the region was of two main types: the circulation of wealth within the ethnic group and between ethnic groups. Internal exchanges consisted of such transfers of wealth as the payments and counterpayments traded between families, or houses, during a wedding, or the gifts a high chief bestowed on his politically beholden lesser chiefs, to gain and hold their fealty. It is possible that institutions of redistribution resembling the potlatch (discussed later in the chapter) were present in late colonial Indonesia in some of the outer islands, although this has not been fully documented. Exchanges that linked together several ethnic groups involved, for example, the circulation of trade objects and raw materials between coastal peoples and highlanders (for instance, salt and shells for hornbill beaks) (Fig. 53). Some Indonesian peoples may once have been involved in ritualized trade circuits similar to the Kula of the Trobriand region in Melanesia, discussed later in this section. The Kula trade circle worked to unite ethnically distinct and distant peoples into a common economic league in the absence of firm political centralization.

Another sort of trade between societies involved large states and the small polities at their borders or in their interior highlands. The kings of the Indianized court states bestowed gifts on local *rajas* in small islands, such as Sumba and Flores at the edge of their domains, to command their loyalty. European colonial powers entered into this last type of political exchange with a vengeance. In fact, much of the gold in Eastern Indonesian jewelry came from gold coins transferred to local *rajas* by the Dutch in their efforts to enlist aid in pacifying and administer-

53. — This Kalinga girl from Northern Luzon wears butterfly shaped earrings (*bawisak*), made of mother of pearl obtained through trade from coastal peoples (from Worcester 1912: 867).

ing the various islands of the Dutch East Indies. One of the major processes by which local societies acquired their sacred heirloom jewels and other house treasures was by accepting the munificent gifts of expanding state societies and then incorporating these precious metals into their mythological, ritual, kinship, and political systems.

Jewelry was a mainstay in all these forms of exchange. In some types of trade it even seems to have been the element that kept the whole system working smoothly, by promoting a passion for lovely, exotic objects, which were then accompanied by the transfer of more practical goods such as food and raw materials. Most ornaments represented in the Barbier-Müller collection provide abundant examples of these types of exchange. We can take just two societies here, the Batak and the East Sumbanese, to illustrate the general patterns found in the small societies of the entire region.

The six Batak societies (Toba, Karo, Dairi-Pakpak, Simelungun, Angkola, and Mandailing) are divided by dialect differences and small variations in material culture, but they are united in their wholehearted fascination with the notion of giving and receiving gifts. These are farming cultures, using a mixture of dry field and paddy rice agriculture. None of the six societies attained a full state level of political organization in colonial times, although the southern homelands of Angkola and Mandailing had fairly centralized chiefdoms with aristocratic, commoner, and slave classes (Castles 1975). The exchange of practical objects, prestige goods, and such intangibles as blessings and fertility provided the underlying structure for pre-modern Batak village life.

The Batak kinship system is based on asymmetrical marriage alliance with patrilineal clans, localized lineages, and hierarchically ranked giver and taker groups. Women are "the greatest gift," to use the Angkola phrase (*silua na godang*). A focal lineage would have wife-giving groups on one side and wife-takers on the other; each of these groups themselves would have wife-givers and wife-takers. In Toba and the southern homelands this three-part structure, much eulogized in Batak ritual oratory, is called the *dalihan na tolu,* a phrase which literally means the three stones on the hearth for balancing a cookpot. In that domestic saying, if one stone is out of place the cookpot will tip over into the fire. Batak kinship, similarly, is thought locally to be dependent on the close interdependence of the three lineage partners.

These units demonstrate their reliance on each other by exchanging gifts. Bride-givers provide their bride-takers with fertile women, fertility itself, good luck, "blessing-laden" ritual *ulos* textiles, and cooked and uncooked foods.[1] Bride-takers for their part give their marriage alliance partners bride-wealth payments of livestock and gold (today, cash), physical protection, and such metal goods as knives and weapons (all of which are termed *piso*, "knife gifts," in Toba, although knives may not actually be part of the gift).

Thus feminine cloth is counterbalanced with masculine metal, and mystical blessings are counterbalanced with physical protection. Bride-givers portray themselves as the spiritual and ritual superiors of their financially and spiritually indebted wife-receivers. A constant flow of the designated gifts and countergifts throughout the course of a marriage, and indeed over many generations, is thought to be necessary if the wife-receiving group is to continue to produce children and tend fertile fields (agricultural and human fertility are explicitly linked in the *adat* oratory and then associated too with the plumpness and fertility of the livestock). Earrings for the bride and certain headdress ornaments are involved in this series of exchanges between marriage alliance partner.

The Batak jewelry exchange was not simply between bride-givers and bride-takers, however. In northern Samosir wife-giving lineages in the past sometimes bestowed special earrings on their daughters as they left home to live in their new husband's village. The Batak cultures were also involved in complex trade relationships with their Gayo-Alas and Acehnese neighbors to the north (Fig. 54), with Minangkabau to the south, and with the Malay sultanates along the Deli coastline in East Sumatra. A number of jewelry styles were surely imported from these outside societies, no matter how thoroughly the individual Batak cultures were able to incorporate the pieces into their *dalihan na tolu* kinship system. This openness to exchange with neighboring groups is typical of many small societies of island Southeast Asia. Sumba provides a fine illustration of these more complex levels of

1. See Vergouwen 1964 (1933) and Gittinger 1979 for information on such exchanges in Toba.

54. – Inter-ethnic trade: the chief's treasure in the Toba village of Simanindo (northern Samosir) includes many pieces of Karo origin (Photograph Susan Rodgers, 1983).

55. – The *rato* (priest-diviner) of a village in East Sumba showing a splendid textile, part of the late *raja*'s treasure (Photograph Susan Rodgers, 1983).

exchange, some of them reaching out to Java and even to Europe.

Sumba is a small, partially arid, economically hard-pressed island a bit over halfway between Bali and Timor. Its culture is situated squarely in the Eastern Indonesian complex, with tightly integrated mythic and social worlds, much ritual oratory, and strong metaphors of clan descent and marriage alliance used to structure village social life. It also has a general philosophical reliance on binary opposition and mediation: that is, on contrastive but interdependent pairs such as wife-givers and wife-takers, sky and earth, right and left, inside and outside, male and female, village and forest, and human and supernatural. In terms of its social organization West Sumba is divided into about a dozen small ethnic areas (Needham 1980) while East Sumba has more cultural uniformity (Adams 1969). All Sumbanese cultures, however, share many features. In each area there is an aristocratic class claiming special ritual status and special favors from the *marapu*, or ancestral spirits. A class of priests serves the *rajas* as public spokesmen and intermediaries with the divine realm.

Houses in East Sumbanese *raja*ships are linked to each other through ties of common descent in a clan or through the sort of ranked wife-giver, wife-taker relationships just described for the Batak. Textiles, livestock, jewelry, labor services, and intangibles such as blessings flow between houses in a constant ritual economy of gifts and countergifts (Adams 1969). Beyond this, the *raja*ships along the east coast apparently traded such littoral goods as salt and fish for the forest products controlled by their upland neighbors in the center of the island. In former times aristocratic women living in villages near the coast produced patterned textiles that were highly prized by noble families living in the interior highlands (Fig. 55). Gold jewelry may also have been used as a trade good between coastal aristocrats and their highland counterparts, although this exchange was mediated through marriage and ritual. Especially wealthy aristocrats apparently commissioned large numbers of new gold ornaments for large ceremonies and gave them to their political followers. Heaps of fine textiles and gold ornaments were also buried with prominent *rajas*. This sort of periodic ritual destruction of wealth acted as a spur to the production of new ceremonial goods.

This pattern suggests something like the classic potlatch first described by ethnographers of Native American societies in the Northwest Coast. Rival chiefs from different villages would invite each other to lavish gatherings where the host and his guests would try to outdo each other in giving away valuable objects. The chief who still had some property in reserve when his competitors had exhausted theirs would emerge as the victor, sometimes raising his political ranking as a consequence. Potlatching also involved the public destruction of valuable goods (e.g., copper disks, which were broken before the assembly to show the owner's wealth and daring) and the exchange of blankets and gifts of food. Cultural ecologists have pointed out that this pattern of competitive gift-giving and destruction of prestige goods was probably only one side of the potlatch (Piddocke 1965). Foodstuffs as well as ritual goods were exchanged at potlatch gatherings, and chiefs who were offered large gifts of food were obligated to accept them. This of course has a political dimension (in accepting the gifts the chief is lowering himself *vis-à-vis* his benefactor), but the exchange also had the practical effect of redistributing food from areas of surplus to areas of relative need. Despite the stereotype of the Northwest Coast as a region of great food surplus, especially in salmon, in some historical periods there may have been regions which suffered near-famines. In the absence of enough central political control to assure the regular redistribution of food to these needy areas, the ritual system accomplished much the same thing through the obligatory rivalry and gift-exchange of chiefs from all over the region. Further historical and ethnographic research in Outer Indonesia in ecologically variable places like Sumba and Nias might uncover similar patterns.

Another type of exchange that may have existed in Indonesia is called Kula trade after the Melanesian system, first described by Bronislaw Malinowski in his book *Argonauts of the Western Pacific* (1922). The Kula, it happens, focused on the exchange of jewelry. Although the Melanesian societies in the group of islands east of New Guinea near the Trobriands spoke different languages and had no central political unity, they were united through jewelry exchange. Men would cultivate trading partnerships with other men on other islands, meeting periodically to exchange one type of jewelry for another.

Shell armbands and necklaces, often too big to actually wear on the body, were the main currency of the Kula trade. Armbands circulated from man to man and from island to island in a counterclockwise direction, while necklaces circulated in the other direction. Each trading partner, who probably was not aware of the full extent of the Kula circuits, felt ritually obligated to play his role in the trade, and the emotional intensity of the whole system was heightened by the possibility of trading and momentarily possessing one of the more famous Kula necklaces or armbands. These special pieces had names and elaborate mythical histories about their origins and trade background. Like the potlatch, the ritual aspects of the Kula trade seem to have covered up another type of exchange involving trade in food and raw materials. Women's trade activities in the Kula system seem also to have been important.

To return to Sumba, in addition to the various sorts of inland and coastal exchanges the island was also involved in trade with other societies. Precious metal came into the island from other Eastern Indonesian cultures, and Sumba apparently exported some of its ornaments to Flores, either directly or via goldsmiths (a few *mamuli* pendants are part of the house treasures of Central Flores aristocrats). Goldsmiths from the small islands off the west coast of Timor provided their services to noble families throughout Eastern Indonesia between Flores and Timor. Today, Indonesian-Chinese art dealers are buying gold ornaments from noble families and selling them to Western and Japanese dealers, who in turn sell them to museums and private collectors. Jewelry exchange in this way stretches from bride-wealth transactions to the international art trade.

6
JEWELRY
AND THE SUPERNATURAL

Some jewelry from island Southeast Asia is used primarily for simple ornamentation, but many pieces are essentially miniature religious objects. Understanding them demands a knowledge of the myths and rituals of the region, as well as the religious systems of the individual ethnic cultures that surround each type of sacred jewelry object. The myths and rituals of the islands from Sumatra to Northern Luzon have some common themes, despite the great ethnic diversity of Indonesia, Sarawak, and the Philippines. Moreover, the religious uses of ornaments throughout the area are of several common types. In a number of cultures jewelry is used as amulets for protecting the well-being of children. In a similar way, warriors are protected from the mystical and physical attacks of enemies by being adorned with charm ornaments. Jewelry is thus used often as an indispensable part of magic war costumes. In fact, jewelry in this sense may better be termed military regalia, for it works as a combination amulet and row of battle ribbons and medals. Sorcerers and diviners use pieces of jewelry to strengthen their control over the supernatural, and some ornaments, such as Sumba's *mamuli*, are themselves used to make contact with the spirit world. This last type of religious jewelry is probably the richest in symbolism, for here the object mediates between the world of humans and the world of the ancestors, incorporating representations of both domains in its shape and design.

Some of these religiously charged objects (the *mamuli*, the Karo Batak *sertali*, and Central Sulawesi's *taiganja*; see Cat. Nos. 124, 11, and 73) are also used as bridewealth exchange goods, which adds an extra layer of gender symbolism to the supernatural-human complex. That is, jewelry objects are employed as metal, masculine bridewealth goods that the groom's family gives to the bride's family, but at the same time their shapes and decorative motifs portray femininity and they are often worn by women as well. This use of jewelry reflects one of the major religious tenets of island Southeast Asia before widespread conversion to Islam and Christianity: the idea that creativity and power come from the temporary, dangerous union of complementary opposites. Note how this idea also draws on a symbolism of the sacred center. In this one can see a thread uniting the folk conceptualization of jewelry, house architecture, village layout, and cosmic order.

The mythological systems of these ethnically diverse cultures have many similarities. The religions of Kalimantan, interior Sulawesi, and Northern Luzon form one rough subgroup and the religions of Eastern Indonesia and the Moluccas form another. Some cultures, such as the Bataks and the Nias peoples, have ties to both groups. Among the most obvious resemblances in these mythic systems are similar characters and storylines. Batak and Dayak myths both celebrate the hornbill, for instance, and associate creation and social order with a Cosmic Tree, often identified with the banyan tree (Figs. 56, 57, and 58). Many Eastern Indonesian myths use similar animal symbolism (the crocodile, the horse, the water buffalo, the chicken) while the *naga* serpent-dragon is found throughout the myths of

56. – In front of a Toba Batak *adat* house a sacrificial post takes the form of the Cosmic Tree. The head of the mythical *singa* animal which appears on the upper part of the picture, is adorned with foliated horns that also recall the Tree (Photograph Jean Paul Barbier, 1980).

57. – Another representation of the Cosmic Tree, on the side wall of a Toba house. Here it is accompanied by stylized birds and a spirit figure, at left (Photograph Jean Paul Barbier, 1980).

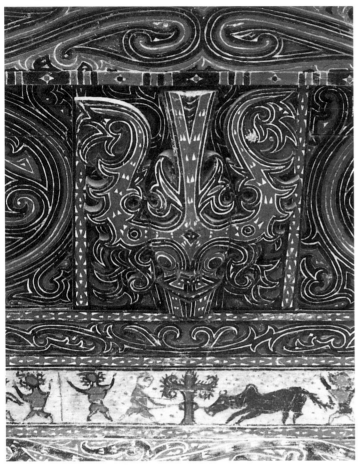

the entire Indonesian region. Opposite-sex twins, dangerous feminine ogres living in the forest or just beyond the edge of the village, tiny clever mouse-deer who slay or outwit big lummoxes, and many other stereotyped characters and situations recur in myths throughout the region. Many have a cosmology made up of a Skyworld, a mundane world, and an Underworld. Sometimes two additional realms, such as an Upstream region and a Downstream region, are added.

At a less superficial level, these myths from widely separate societies also share more fundamental concepts. Life is often thought to come from the destruction of life, an idea probably once important in making headhunting intelligible and socially prestigious in Nias, Kalimantan, Eastern Indonesia, and Northern Luzon. Much as death and the regeneration of life are linked, the forest, outsider peoples, secrecy, and danger are all juxtaposed to life in the village (in culture, in the human sphere), and family, *adat*, safety, and control. Ritual life was designed in an important part to unite such distinct spheres for very short periods of time, under tight control, so that the powers thus released could be employed for the commonweal.

The most immediate and enjoyable way to get a feel for these myths is to listen to one; failing that, to read one. This is a version of the Ngaju Dayak myth of creation, retold by Vredenbregt in his book on Dayak religious sculpture:

In the beginning everything lay in the jaws of the coiled watersnake. There existed only a small pool in which the moon, the female Jata, bathed and in which the princesses of Mahatala refreshed themselves. Then there welled up the Gold Mountain together with the Jewel Mountain. On the Gold Mountain was elevated its master, the hornbill, Ranying Mahatala Langit. The Jewel Mountain moved back and forth and on it moved its Lord, Raja Tempon Hawan, master of the sky. The Gold Mountain and Jewel Mountain touched in their movements, clashing several times, and in succession were created: the clouds, the sky, the mountains of the earth, the sun, the fish lla-llai Langit, the creature Didis Mahandera (with eyes of Jewels and Saliva of the water of life) and a golden head-dress moving to and fro in the sky and beautifully ornamented with a high-reaching jewel.

Then Ranying Mahatala Langit raised his gold-decorated fingers and lightning flashed out of the Gold Mountain, and sent light from the Jewel Mountain which changed into moon-shaped ear-ornaments. These moved to and fro in the ears of the sister of Ranying Mahatala Langit, Putir Selong Langit. Ranying Mahatala Langit stretched out his ten fingers and overshadowed the sea with them, and water ran from his fingers and caused the female Jata to emerge. The earrings of the moon, the female Jata, swung back and forth, stirred by the benevolent wind. The female Jata cast on high the jewels which her earrings were fastened to and they changed into the earth. Ranying Mahatala Langit raised his gold-ornamented fingers and rivers and mountains were created. Ranying Mahatala Langit raised his voice and showed his glittering golden ornaments and his shining jewelled teeth, and he called the female Jata. Jata emerged and came to Ranying Mahatala Langit. Together, the water-snake and its sanger (a term used reciprocally between those whose children have married) created the ancestors of mankind on the banks of the river of the world. Ranying Mahatala Langit conferred with the sanger, Jata Balawang Bulau and the Ranying Mahatala Langit raised on high his golden head-dress. The golden head-dress changed into the Tree of Life. The Tree of Life put forth leaves of gold and fruit shining like white ivory. Putir Belong Langit gathered the ivory fruit and looked for the buds. She mixed them with the Water of Life, the creator of life, and the fruits changed and assumed the form of the tree Andong Nyaho (the tree in the Upperworld from which rice originated). From this time onward Putir Selong Langit was called Putir Selong Tamanang i.e. the creator of life. (Vredenbregt 1981; from a version given by Schärer 1963.)

A number of other myths in the region also stress splendid jewels.[1]

Many island Southeast Asian cultures have origin myths for agriculture, weaving, house construction, and so on. The creation of metal and metalworking is also sometimes given mythic attention. Variations of the name for "Master Iron-Forger" (e.g., Pande Besi, Puang Matua) are found in cultures as distant as the Batak in Sumatra and the Sa'dan Toraja in Sulawesi. Notably, forging and crafting metal are often specifically contrasted to spinning thread and weaving cloth. Much additional meaning is attached to this basic binary opposition. Weaving, for instance, is often characterized as a feminine activity, while metalworking is considered masculine. But this scheme, as noted, is too simple to capture the actual situation in many cultures, for women weave garments for their menfolk and men make jewelry and metal household implements for women to use, and sometimes it is inaccurate to label cloth bride-wealth gifts as feminine and metal countergifts as masculine (see, e.g., Barnes 1974: 282-283).

The Sa'dan Toraja draw mythic connections between present-day iron-forging activities (Fig. 59),

---

1. See Harrisson and O'Connor 1970 for a consideration of possible mythological meanings of jewelry in prehistoric times among Dayak peoples.

58. — The Tree of Life is also the central figure of Dayak drawings used by priests. Such drawings depict mythological landscapes of the Underworld and the Upperworld (from *Kalimantan, Mythe en Kunst*, 1973).

59. — Toraja woman in deep trance. The man behind her is pulling a *la'bo to dolo* (sword of the ancestors) against her abdomen (Photograph Charles Zerner, 1977-78).

the origin of metalworking, and the creation of humankind. In his excellent article "Signs of the Spirit, Signature of the Smith: Iron Forging in Tana Toraja," Charles Zerner examines some of the associations between creativity and iron working:

In ritual verse, Pong Sirintik from Seko, the mythical master smith, "sees the mother of iron." For the Toraja, iron not only has a progenitor or "mother," but iron forging itself is generative, the paradigm formative process. The characteristics of forging as a process, its site, its tools, and its products as well as the technical properties of iron itself, suggested an idiom in which the creation of 'the contents of the world', including mankind, could be described. (Zerner 1981: 94.)

In Toraja creation myths the creator god, Puang Mata:

Forged the heavens
Forged the earth
Forged the ancestor of the earth
Called Patal Bunga
Forged the ancestor of cool water
Called Patala Merang
Forged the ancestor of fire
Called Patala Lamma
Forged the ancestor of mankind
Called datu Laukku
(verses recited by Tandi Datu, Mount Sesean; Zerner 1981: 94.)

Gold as well as iron has considerable mythic significance in Tana Toraja. Citing a myth collected by Van der Veen, Zerner notes that the ancestor of rice was "forged" from gold nuggets thrown into a pair of gold bellows "like unhusked rice." In this version of the myth, Puang Matua "desires children, and is told by his wife to pan for gold at a well. There he fills his betel nut pouch with nuggets which are heated and fused in a cooking pot. This mass of gold is thrown into a pair of bellows and eight children are forged, including Datu Laukku', the ancestor of mankind" (Zerner 1981: 94).

In Tana Toraja gold is associated with aristocratic status as well as creativity. Deepening the metaphor, the aristocracy, and gold as metal and as color, are all associated with the Upperworld (Nooy-Palm 1979: 175). Prior to 1906, when slavery was officially abolished, slave families were not allowed to use jewelry made of brass or precious metals, and female slaves were also forbidden to wear shell armlets (Nooy-Palm 1979: 64). Through the colonial period only noble families could own large stores of gold jewelry. These ornaments were an important part of the heirloom wealth stored in imposing carved wooden houses constructed by the highborn families. This house treasure held powers; it was dangerous to treat it in a cavalier fashion.

A number of Toraja myths mention the golden jewelry of the noble class. A famous myth about a girl named Pano Bulaan (*bulaan* = gold) links such seemingly diverse concepts as gold, iron, snakes, skin diseases, and house treasure. Like many Toraja myths, this one concerns a series of binary oppositions (female and male babies, snakes and humans, death and life). Because it gives a feeling for the complex narratives evoked by gold and golden jewelry in Tana Toraja the myth is worth retelling. This version was first recorded by Adriani and A.A. van de Loosdrecht and is cited again by Nooy-Palm in *The Sa'dan Toraja*. Note here how the masculine figure provides gold objects for his wife. But that is only a tiny part of this wonderful myth:

Pano Bulaan (the Golden Skin Disease; *pano* is a skin disease causing the skin to flake off, a kind of fungus) was pregnant and went into the forest to find some sour fruits to eat. She tripped over a snake (a python) who, when she touched his head, wanted to swallow her. Pano Bulaan said that the snake might marry her (if he gave up the idea of eating her). The snake consented, whereupon Pano Bulaan said that she would put him into a hollow tree. This happened; the snake thereafter provided Pano Bulaan with food, and with golden krisses and golden jewelry (*rara'* = jewelry worn by upper class women).

When the moment that Pano Bulaan's child would be born drew near, the snake said that he would let the child live if it was a girl and that he would devour the baby if it proved to be a boy. Pano Bulaan gave birth to a son, Panggalo'-galo' (The Bold One), whom she concealed. The boy grew up and ordered shipbuilders to make ready an iron vessel for him. When the snake was off again scouring for food, the ship set out for the open sea with Pano Bulaan and her son on board. They had taken along the goods and jewelry. The ship was well-protected, for it was covered with swords and sharp iron.

The snake saw their departure and swam out into the sea. He pounced upon the ship but was cut into three pieces. The snake's head fell onto the iron proa [ship]; Panggalo'-galo' picked it up and the head turned to gold (what happened with the remaining sections of the snake's body is not reported).

The son then asked his mother what course to follow. She answered him:

"Look for the coconut palms standing in a row,
The areca trees stretching in a line,
Point your proa in their direction..."

Panggalo'-galo' struck out as his mother had directed. Then she told him to climb a coconut palm (which belonged to Pano Bulaan's plantation). When he had reached the top he heard a woman's voice: "Who is that? Who comes climbing the coconut palm of Pano Bulaan as if he were some god, seeing that the owner has disappeared and the dishes have been shattered for her and the rice-pounders broken into pieces?" Panggalo'-galo' turned back and told his mother that he had been spoken to "from above". This repeated when he climbed up an areca palm.

Pano Bulaan then revealed to her mother — for, it was her mother who had reprimanded the youth — who she was and she introduced Panggalo'-galo' to his grandmother. Since Pano Bulaan's husband had remarried, mother and son took up residence with the grandmother. First they celebrated the merok-feast and then the mangata'.

As a result of her skin disease which causes the skin to peel away, Pano Bulaan has some snake-like features. The forest, however, is not her true habitat; she comes from a village. She is of high status: she has a golden colour and receives jewelry... from the snake which is appropriate to women from the upper class. (Nooy-Palm 1979: 175-177.)

The association of gold jewelry and other metal treasures with aristocracy and a sort of cagey cleverness is apparently a common one in Toraja religion. In a similar myth, about a girl named Rangga Bulaan, the snake husband and his human wife set up housekeeping in a nest. The snake ventures out periodically to collect food and gold and silver riches, which he brings back to the nest as family treasure (Nooy-Palm 1979: 175-177). Note the image evoked here of a character who gathers in treasure for himself, his family, and his house.

Island Southeast Asian cultures abound with stories like this, many of them considerably more complex than these Toraja snake myths. Jewels, and the metals they are made from, evoke myth after myth of this sort. In trying to understand Indonesian ritual textiles Western observers have to learn that these are not silent pieces of cloth but mnemonic devices packed with layers of stories and myths; gold jewelry is similarly eloquent.

7
JEWELRY
IN CONTEMPORARY ISLAND SOUTHEAST ASIA

Many of the social institutions and beliefs described in this catalogue have fallen from practice over the last one hundred years or so, a time of political consolidation under colonial administrations and then national governments after World War II, and a time of increasing Christian and Muslim missionary efforts in the Indonesian Outer Islands and in Northern Luzon in the Philippines. I have not taken care to write "in former times" every time I describe a practice such as teethfiling or earlobe enlargement, but the reader should be particularly careful not to see the cultures represented in the exhibit in terms of exotic, anachronistic images. Literacy, the electronic mass media, paved roads, and national knowledge and allegiance are spreading to most of the remotest regions of the Indonesian and Philippine archipelagos today. Jewelry use has also changed a great deal over the last century: indeed, many of the genres of ornaments in the Barbier-Müller collection have negotiated the transition from ethnic ritual object to inter-ethnic and even international art object in this period. This transformation of ceremonial goods into art seems to have been particularly characteristic of the 1970s and 1980s, when the international primitive art market "discovered" Indonesian and Philippine jewelry.

The field research for this catalogue did not address such topics of social change in any systematic way, but a few general trends that seem characteristic of Indonesian ritual and art can be mentioned here. Consider first four aspects of Indonesian life in 1983, when the fieldwork for this catalogue was done.

Foreign tourists and well-heeled Indonesian visitors to Jakarta are encouraged to "see Indonesia" by spending a morning at Taman Mini Indonesia Indah (Beautiful Mini-Indonesia Park), a few kilometers outside of town. This is a theme park celebrating the many ethnic cultures of the country. Here small artificial islands in a large man-made lake replicate the geography of Sumatra, Java, Kalimantan, and other islands of the archipelago, while outsize *adat* houses in Minangkabau, Batak, and Bugis styles decorate the park's winding roads, separated by soft drink concessions. Each pseudo-*adat* house is a museum of sorts, with displays of bridal bowers, mannequins in traditional wedding costumes, and ritual textiles. Ethnic jewelry figures prominently in the exhibits of the islands of Eastern Indonesia, Sulawesi, and Sumatra, and is dominated by fancy filigree work associated with such Islamized coastal societies as Minangkabau. In the display-case captions, jewelry is lauded as part of the "authentic cultural heritage" of the various societies. A larger museum on the park grounds also presents the different Indonesian ethnic cultures to its audience of tourists, largely through mannequins dressed in ceremonial garb and jewelry.

From Jakarta one can turn to North Sumatra and the overgrown farming and fishing village of Tomok, on Samosir Island in Lake Toba. Tomok and the mainland lakeside town of Prapat are Batak tourist traps par excellence. In addition to the usual profusion of cheap *losmen* (small hotels), Indonesian-Chinese eateries, bus stations, and spectacular mountain

60. – Souvenir shop in Tomok, Samosir Island, facing the famous little tourist town of Prapat (Photograph Jean Paul Barbier, 1978).
61. – It is not only in Batak regions that fakes are offered to visitors: so-called fetishes and amulets are displayed in South Nias in a picture taken in the early 1970s. Old fragments of stone sculpture and authentic shields and swords were offered at the same time. Here, one can see modern statuettes, with artificial patinas. In the left corner is a beautiful piece of iron armor, probably dating from the last century (Photograph Jean Paul Barbier, 1974).

scenery, both Tomok and Prapat (Fig. 60) have extraordinary tourist strips full of souvenir shops. These are tiny stalls packed with Karo and Toba *ulos* textiles woven specially for the tourist trade, postcards, Japanese film, and miniature versions of old Toba wooden sculpture (Fig. 61) and sorcerer's wands. Jumbled in among the fake Batak primitive art are lengths of factory-produced Javanese batik, tourist versions of Javanese shadow puppets, and Balinese wood carvings like those sold in Kuta Beach. Amidst this conglomeration the tourist can also find a number of jewelry pieces — mostly fakes, some Batak, some Javanese, some Minangkabau, and some of more imaginative ethnic origin.

Next, consider Flores in Eastern Indonesia. Figure 62 shows an old man from the Nage high village of Boawai looking at a Dutch archival picture taken in the 1920s of a group of Boawai noblemen in full ceremonial dress and jewelry. On my 1983 visit to Flores, I took the old photograph (Fig. 63) along to ask *adat* experts about the meaning and names of the various gold pieces the men were wearing. To my surprise the man standing at the far right in the 1920s picture was still alive. The people I was interviewing called him over to talk to me and see his photograph. The conversation that ensued dealt with the Nage gold regalia as art, and as part of the Nage ethnic cultural heritage.

In Sumba a few weeks before, a Savunese goldsmith told me that chiefs' families sometimes send a family member by plane to Bali to have an old *mamuli* pendant repaired or copied into a new version. In addition to this, younger members of East Sumba noble families who inherit the family house treasures after their older relatives die are now apparently selling off their heirlooms at a fast clip to Indonesian-Chinese art dealers based in Bali. In fact, the heavy gold *kanatar* chains and big *mamuli* (even the most sacred "holy of holies" *mamuli* kept in special attic storage places for contacting *marapu* spirits) are virtually streaming out of East Sumba to Kuta art shops in Bali and from there, to Western and Japanese primitive art collections, museums, and the art auction houses of Paris, London, and Amsterdam.

The list of such contemporary social scenes in which "traditional" jewelry plays a part could be extended by many more examples, but let these suffice. As noted, much of the jewelry in the Barbier-Müller collection was generated through the interaction of different ethnic groups having different levels of political centralization. So it is surely mistaken to speak of "archaic" jewelry pieces coming from unchanging primitive cultures. Beyond this, though, relatively new social forces (Figs. 64, 65) do seem to be at work in national times in reshaping Indonesian ideas about ethnicity, history, and art. In fact, it is not going too far to say that the existence of the multi-ethnic state of Indonesia has created, for many local populations, the very idea of salable art.

There are several social processes affecting jewelry like that represented by the Barbier-Müller collection. Anthropologist Nelson Graburn's introduction to *Ethnic and Tourist Arts: Cultural Expressions from the Fourth World* (1979) provides a useful framework here, and demonstrates that many of these patterns are found in other parts of the Fourth World (the small tribal, chiefdom, and traditional state societies located within developing new nations in Africa, Latin America, Asia, and the Pacific).

First, for Indonesia's mass media and public school system, and certainly in the eyes of most foreign tourists and casual observers, Indonesia's small ethnic societies in Sumatra, Sulawesi, Kalimantan, and Eastern Indonesia exist in the shadow of Javanese and Balinese court-based "high civilizations." Java and Bali have *gamelan* orchestras, court dances, written literatures, mystic traditions, temple festivals, and extraordinarily ornate court costumes of batik cloth, metal headgear, and fancywork metal jewelry. These courtly cultures have been appropriated as national Indonesian symbols, to the detriment of the cultures of the outer islands, which continue to suffer the stigma of primitiveness. In reaction to this, these ethnic societies seem to be rescuing and refurbishing certain portions of their own village-based material culture, oral literature, and ritual heritage and transforming these into ethnic identity symbols worthy of public approval and comparable in form and value to Javanese and Balinese traditions. In a sense, too, these smaller outer-island societies are competing with each other in multi-ethnic cities and are enlisting parts of their village-based cultures as weapons in this inter-ethnic competition. In other words, "village traditions," and *adat*, are being created today for very contemporary political purposes.

62. – An old man from Boawai (Nage region, Central Flores) looks at the photograph of himself as a young man, taken in the 1920s (Photograph Susan Rodgers, 1983).

63. – The original archival photograph from the 1920s, showing the same Nage nobleman as a young man, wearing a fine gold crown (Cat. No. 81). (courtesy Kon. Inst. v/d Tropen, Amsterdam).

64. — Old carved house boards deposited on a junk pile, next to a Honda. Bajawa village, Ngada area, West Central Flores (Photograph Susan Rodgers, 1983).

65. — Batak men carving guitars for the tourist trade. The village where this picture was taken is far from tourist areas, but obviously touched by that trade (Photograph Jean Paul Barbier, 1980).

Secondly, only some parts of village culture can be rescued and revised in this way. Much of the exquisite oral poetry of the outer islands is virtually untranslatable for foreign audiences in other parts of Indonesia, since it is so tightly bound to the local languages and to local ideas of kinship and non-monotheistic religion. However, textiles, sculpture, *adat* houses, and jewelry are eminently usable as ethnic symbols for communicating with outside groups (witness Taman Mini Indonesia). These objects have long proven their marketability as exchange items for communicating important ethnic messages to other Indonesian societies, to participants in the national culture, and sometimes to foreign tourists and art lovers. Jewelry made of precious metals is an especially astute choice in these inter-ethnic negotiations, for gold and silver have high prestige value in the West and jewelry is small and portable. Graburn notes that traditional village arts sometimes undergo a process of miniaturization as they become tourist arts and primitive arts attractive to foreign collectors. Jewelry, though, is already a diminutive art form, and Indonesian jewelry of course has long been a prime trade object. Moreover, to foreign eyes ornaments from Eastern Indonesia and Kalimantan have a definite exotic air, a quality that much increases their social and market value in an era when primitive art from other regions of the world is becoming passé.

Different audiences obviously see these ethnic arts differently. Graburn points out that village material culture, redefined in an inter-ethnic context as primitive art, can act like "obvious visual cross-cultural code(s), rather like pidgin languages are when used in trade. At this level, we might say that their content consists of signs rather than symbols" (Graburn 1979: 17), since the audience looking at the objects understands very little of their deeper meaning.

In becoming transformed into primitive art for consumption by outside ethnic groups, Indonesian village sculpture, ancestor effigies, altar-piece jewels, and sorcerers' ornaments lose a measure of their powers. In this process, which is just one part of a larger secularization affecting much of Indonesian culture, the objects shrink in symbolic scope to become badges of ethnic identity, or even mere things of aesthetic interest to outsiders. To contrast a storage room of a prosperous foreign primitive art museum with a nineteenth-century Toba Batak diviner-sorcerer's supply of magic wands, conjurer rings, and ancestor relics: the modern storage room holds a collection of silent, impotent wooden, metal, and stone *things*, while the Toba *datu*'s treasure was full of animate holy riches touching the supernatural.

Finally, there is the financial aspect to all of this. Sumba aristocrats are selling off their gold treasures to Indonesian-Chinese dealers (Fig. 66), and the exchange does sometimes give them enough cash to send a child to school or launch a relative into a job outside the island. The price of Sumba gold jewelry rises again, when the pieces — clothed in a new aura of primitive art — are sold to Western and Japanese dealers or collectors.[1]

66. — The Chinese owner of this shop in Waingapu, East Sumba, sells old ivory bracelets, bronze bells, and necklaces. Gold jewelry is sold directly to Balinese dealers (Photograph Susan Rodgers, 1983).

67. — A government official in Kupang, Timor, dressed in Savunese noble regalia — for purposes of this research (Photograph Susan Rodgers, 1983).

---

1. Of course there are Indonesian collectors as well; among them former Vice-President Adam Malik is well known for his collection of textiles and traditional jewelry.

PART II
ETHNIC GROUPS

NIAS

In pre-national times, Nias had an intense, almost superheated culture characterized by warfare, family rivalry, social class tensions, and perfervid artistic activity. The social order of this small island off the west coast of North Sumatra was divided into an aristocratic class, free commoners, and slaves. Noble families claimed special ties with the supernatural world of deities, who like the nobles were associated with height, magnificence, and the central spaces of villages. Aristocrats vied with each other for power by staging extravagant *adat* feasts to commemorate their dead ancestors. An important part of such feasts was the erection of commemorative megaliths in the stone-paved high villages. Building such monuments was one step along the way toward constructing an *omo sebua,* or large *adat* house (Fig. 68). This structure too was dedicated to the memory of the ancestors and was in a sense as much shrine as home. Another aspect of rivalry and another step in the process of building the great houses was the production and distribution of gold ornaments. These were also conceived as commemorations of family values, high social status, and ancestors. As Nias's richer villages filled up over time with stone monuments, they also built up large stocks of gold jewelry. Pre-modern Nias had just the sort of ritual complex involving the energetic, coordinated production of gold ornaments, megaliths, "micro-megaliths" (smaller stone

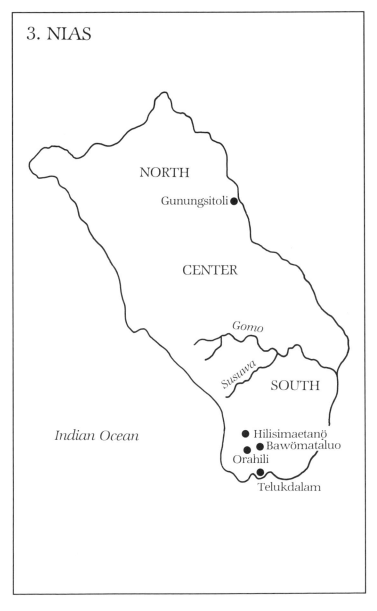

3. NIAS

NORTH

Gunungsitoli ●

CENTER

Gomo

Susuwa

SOUTH

Indian Ocean

● Hilisimaetanö
● ● Bawömataluo
Orahili ●
●
Telukdalam

---

1. See the brief discussion of this work in the "Looking at Jewelry" chapter; see also Marschall 1958 and 1976 for much more detailed research on the theme.

◄ Man's ceremonial jacket. Patchwork made with imported fabrics. Local embroideries. Silk, cotton. South Nias, Indonesia. Detail. (Barbier-Müller Museum, No. 3292-1, not exhibited).

68. – Large house of the chief's family in Bawömataluo, South Nias (Photograph Jean Paul Barbier, 1974).

69. – Chief's house in Orahili Gomo, East Central Nias. Four years after this picture was taken, the stone sculptures in front of the house had been heavily damaged, and lost much of their value for villagers (Photograph Lionel Morley, 1972).

objects), and wooden sculpture described in Harrisson and O'Connor's *Gold and Megalithic Activity in Prehistoric and Recent West Borneo* (1970).[1]

This sort of highly politicized artistic activity reached its peak in the nineteenth century. Today the island is somewhat less prepossessing. Nias is now a stopping-off point for Dutch cruise ships. Passengers disembark at a preserved, reconstructed village to see the famous stone-jumping contests held in the paved plaza between the imposing *adat* houses. As is the case with the Batak cultures on the mainland, Nias people today have given up many parts of their older village culture under the influence of Christian missionaries and the national Indonesian government.

Nias has attracted a relatively large amount of scholarly attention (Barbier 1978; Feldman 1977, 1979; Holt 1971; Kleiweg de Zwaan 1913; Marschall 1976; Modigliani 1890; Schröder 1917; Suzuki 1959; Wirz 1929). This is partially due to the island's reputation as an unusually "complete" and vigorous megalithic, ranked society, and to its intriguing cultural similarities to the Dayak societies of Kalimantan. Indeed, although the theme of Nias's traditionalism has occasionally been overplayed, up until very recently the society and its stunning art forms almost inevitably gave the outside observer the sense of witnessing an ancient type of megalithic Southeast Asian culture.

In most other parts of Indonesia such cultures have been more heavily syncretized with other traditions than they are in some parts of Nias, although of course this island too was shaped by ethnic interaction (Suzuki 1959: iii-iv). Through the colonial period to 1942 Nias existed in relative isolation from Sumatra's other cultures. Choppy seas separate the small island from Sibolga, about 75 miles away on the coast (see Map 4). Nias is ecologically diverse, with both heavy forests and dry regions. Conversion to eating rice came only in late colonial times; tuber crops and coconuts are still important to the rather fragile island economy. Art historian Jerome Feldman provides a concise ethnographic and artistic survey in his article "The House as World in Bawömatulua, South Nias" (1979). He writes that there were three distinct cultural regions: South Nias, where high-walled villages, almost completely paved with fitted-stone plazas and walkways, testified to the considerable power and wealth of an aristocratic class of intensely competitive families;

Central Nias, a heavily populated area with much megalithic activity but less grand *adat* houses (Fig. 69) than in the south; and North Nias, an area where villages had little stone paving, and megalithic activity was comparatively modest (1979: 127-128). South Nias seems to have had the greatest profusion of art, to Western eyes: its great houses, architectural wonders in themselves, were filled with finely detailed wooden sculptures of deities and animals; village plazas were crowded with megaliths (Fig. 70); jewelry work was varied and abundant; dance, which often took the form of mock battles in full armor, was surely among the most impressive in Indonesia (Holt 1971). Feldman implies that South Nias culture was something of an intensification of themes found elsewhere on the island in simpler forms. The megaliths were larger here, the sculpture was more finely worked, and the more prominent villages were especially well stocked with *batu wa'ulu* (vertical stones which increased the status of the living) and *daro-daro* (seats) and *owo-owo* (stones shaped like ships), which commemorated the dead (Feldman 1979: 127-128).

Art and Aristocracy in Nias

Why did Nias, and especially South Nias, develop into such an artistically intense part of Outer Island Indonesia? No full anthropological or art history study has yet answered this, but part of the solution probably lies in the particular political status occupied by Nias chiefs. More than village headmen but less than full-fledged kings of state societies, Nias chiefs were locked in perpetual battle with each other for position. Their main weapon for increasing power was artwork — stone monuments, wood sculpture, and gold jewelry, all of which demonstrated the chief's piety toward his ancestors and his munificence toward lesser humans.

A class-stratified society, pre-twentieth-century South Nias was dominated by noble families. These were called *siulu*, although that term has recently come to mean chief. These aristocrats were thought to have a special character and special "noble features" (beauty spots, finely formed cuticles). Their importance in the universal scheme of things was revealed in their names in the ritual oratory: *si alawa* (that which is high); *ulu* (upstream, river's source); *sofutö dzihöno* (the oracle of the people); and *ola-bua dzato* (the man to whom one turns [for aid and advice]). Gold was the noble metal, or put another

70. — Stone monuments in the paved square of a South Nias village (Photograph Stéphane Barbier-Müller, 1976).

71. — In the abandoned village of Adelasiki (East Central Nias) stone monuments recall the lavish feasts of merit of the last century. The column on the right side with a hook was used as a place to hang the gold ornaments and yellow clothes made for the feast-giver. The round mushroomlike stones were called *niogaji* (Photograph Lionel Morley, 1972).

79

72. – Nobleman (*siulu*) in festive attire. The picture was taken before 1914 in Bawömataluo, where the megalith on the left side can still be seen (courtesy Kon Inst. v/d Tropen, Amsterdam).

way, equally Niassian, nobles were goldlike. Their shining gold ornaments, further intensified by blazing-yellow silk clothes (likened to flashes of lightning) announced their high status and separation from less splendidly outfitted mortals. Highborn people wore their special clothes and gold jewelry at funerals and village feasts (Fig. 13). Aristocratic men in effect also wore the *kalabubu*, or necklace of honor, as a badge of their high status (Fig. 72, 73 and 76), although theoretically any freeborn man could wear one once he had proven his prowess in headhunting. Heirloom porcelain kept in attics also symbolized family magnificence. There were other ways to demonstrate class structure: noblewomen, for instance, were carried about in ceremonial litters when they went on formal visits, and had their own special baths in their own homes, distinct from the communal public baths. (Suzuki 1959: 34-35.)

Commoners were marked by a range of symbols opposite to the images of height, yellowness, light, strength, and Upperworld existence (Suzuki 1959: 39-40). Their emblematic clothing was red cotton flannel, they had modest funerals (where the term for the mortuary rite meant "to throw away"), and they erected no commemorative megaliths or stone statues. They lived in small houses, without heirloom dishes or gold ornaments. It is interesting that Suzuki notes: "What gold they do have is usually called 'red gold' or 'false gold' for much of it is a copper alloy, but more important because it is possessed by the 'red people'" (1959: 39-40). They served the aristocrats as farm laborers, warriors, night guards, and house builders. The nobles indulged their commoner followers with periodic small feasts involving the allocation of food. These feasts were obligatory parts of larger feasting cycles the highborn engaged in to praise their departed ancestors.

In sum, the common people complement the nobles according to the following scheme (adapted from Suzuki 1959: 43):

nobles	commoners
height	lowness
gold	"false gold"
yellow	red
silk	cotton flannel
wisdom	ignorance
strength and decisiveness	indecision
beneficence	receptivity
spiritual blessing	physical protection

As we shall see in a moment, the two sides "complete" each other, and their cooperation keeps the Upperworld and the Lowerworld in a creative union that empowers the cosmos.

South Nias slaves were nonpersons, without any charter in Nias creation myths (Suzuki 1959: 45-48). They were the ultimate outsiders: "They have no past nor future, living as they do, on the whims and mercy of their masters. They live on the fringes of the cosmos and are viewed as being almost on par with animals" (Suzuki 1959: 45). They were "immature," savage, not fully human, and so logically enough they had no claim to live in standard houses — they lived in field huts. Domestic servants or farm laborers, they were chattel in the exact sense of the word. Unlike everyone else who came from the aboriginal World Tree, Nias slaves had no rights, and of course, no splendid house wealth in porcelain or metal.

South Nias culture legitimated this whole social system with reference to a sacred universe made up of an Upperworld (associated with nobles and the god Lowalangi) and its corresponding Lowerworld (associated with commoners, mundane life, and the god Lature Danö). Birds were associated with the Upperworld and serpents with the Lowerworld. Creation myths and even the terms for deities vary from region to region (Suzuki 1959: 7), but there is a consensus that the two main gods were twin brothers, two separated halves of some aboriginal good-and-evil, all-things-at-once unity. After the creation, the universe and all its contents strove to regain the primordial unity. Thus aristocrats and commoners "must" work together at their complementary tasks of spiritual protection and agricultural and military labor, for they naturally complete each other's destiny and keep the universe working smoothly in the process. Women and men come together in sexual union, not as true opposites but as temporarily separated complementary parts of the same original unity. Such unions produce children — products of the same sacred union that unites sky and earth to produce crops.

Not surprisingly, Nias thought is greatly concerned with mediator figures.[2] One of the main ones is

2. The concept of mediator figures and symbols has been explored by a number of anthropologists. For basic works that can serve as an introduction to this literature, see Lévi-Strauss' "The Structural Study of Myth" (1955) and Leach's *Culture and Communication* (1976). Lessa and Vogt's anthology *Reader in Comparative Religion* (1979) has articles on symbolic mediation in the sections on "The Interpretation of Symbolism," "The Analysis of Myth," and "The Symbolic Analysis of Ritual."

73. – Villager of Bawömataluo in festive dress, in 1974. The shield, the sword and the necklace (*kalabubu*) are part of the man's heirlooms. Today, ten years later, it is reported that a great number of these old pieces have been sold. However, some villagers have kept their dress and weapons in order to perform war dances for tourists (Photograph Jean Paul Barbier, 1974).

74. — This stone seat comes from Central Nias. It has feet like those of the crocodile, an animal belonging to the realm of Lature Danö, god of the Underworld. However, the head and tail are those of a bird, a symbol of the Upperworld. Furthermore, the beak of the bird (a hornbill) has fangs, like the serpent and the crocodile. This sculpture illustrates the way Nias people conceived the totality of the cosmos and its divinities (Barbier-Müller Museum, No. 3253-D, not exhibited).

75. — Houses belonging to Nias commoners, in the central street of Bawömataluo. The chief's house is visible in the background on the right (Photograph Jean Paul Barbier, 1974).

Silewe Nazarata (Suzuki 1959: 11-12; Feldman 1979: 130-131), sometimes thought to be the sister of Lowalangi and Lature Danö. Silewe Nazarata is the primordial Nias priestess, the intercessor with the gods who live near them but also close to humans. She is the intermediary between humans and Lowalangi, but she is also the one who serves as the mediator between Lowalangi and his brother Lature Dano. She is perhaps the most protean character in Nias myth: in some narratives, for instance, she is presented as her brother Lowalangi's wife, and the pair occupy opposite ends of rivers, downstream and upstream. Silewe Nazarata's followers (her priestesses and priests) live on the various layers of the Nias cosmos, which consists of nine heavens. She first took on her duties after being approached by a human mother who was anxious about the existence of sickness in the world. Silewe Nazarata told her how to make wooden images (*adu*) to help prevent illness. Beyond this, Silewe Nazarata is also tied to agriculture. In some myths one of her messengers first brought rice grains to the earth; in another, she helps humans know when they should plant their fields (Suzuki 1959: 11).

South Nias art emerged from this imagery of a balanced, interlocking cosmos. Works of art, in a word, unite worlds. As a consequence, Nias art very often combines the attributes of two spheres in a single piece, as for example in the most powerful *adu horö*. These famous wood sculptures represent Silewe Nazarata with penis and female breasts, or female genitals and a bearded male face (Suzuki 1959: frontispiece). Other, simpler statues combine Upperworld and Lowerworld characteristics (Fig. 74). The strong dualism of South Nias art can be explored by looking at the *adat* houses, in addition to wood sculpture and its "transformation" — stone mortuary monuments — and finally gold ornaments. All are excellent texts on multiple aspects of Nias thought, since in the local worldview there is no sharp distinction between persons, social space, political structure, and ideas about cosmological order. Since jewelry was a part of this tightly integrated coherence system, to understand the island's gold ornaments one must first understand its traditional religion and politics.

Cosmic Houses and Monuments

The *adat* house is the apotheosis of these ideas, and so it is the appropriate place to start. Feldman's 1979 article "The House as World in Bawömatalua,

South Nias" is the main source here. Note in the discussion below how one cannot describe house building or stone-monument construction without discussing their ancillary arts.

A nobleman in Bawömatuluo sought to defeat his rivals by constructing a grand *omo sebua* house full of ornaments and wooden sculpture. In constructing this house he was in a sense recreating the universe itself, and a number of ritual regulations governed his architectural activities. In order to erect his house he would have to pass through five levels of communal feasts (Feldman 1979: 148-149; other authors dispute this number). He would first have to sacrifice and distribute at least twenty-four pigs and dedicate a *batu ma'ulu* (a vertical stone monument). This first step was called *fa'ulu* (upwards). In a second ritual, called *simboto*, he distributed twelve pigs at a village meal. The next level of ritual involved goldsmithing: in this *mambu ana's* level the man would stage a number of feasts to produce and distribute gold ornaments to the other members of the village. (Feldman 1979: 149, writes that "The gold must meet certain weight requirements. Ornaments of fifty, one hundred and two hundred (standard weights) are commissioned.") At the fourth level the stakes were raised still higher, for this one involved taking a human head. In this *mobinu* level, a head from the Central Nias Aramö district must be brought back to help "empower" the house-building activities. The actual construction of the house was the fifth and final level, and this involved installing more human heads in the structure.

Houses have many attics — these are the "heavens", as the space underneath the floorboards is the Underworld. The house is conceptualized in a symbolic vocabulary of binary oppositions, with noble status associated with the first list of concepts in the following scheme (from Feldman 1979: 148):

society	wilderness
Upperworld	Lowerworld
human	world
male	female
nobleman	commoner
lord of the village	interpreter of wisdom of ancestors
up	down
center	periphery
front	back
private	communal
"that which overlooks"	peripheral areas of the village

76. — Women's status was linked to that of their husbands, but some had priestly roles. Women's gold jewels were signs of their rank. Here a South Nias priestess with heavy bracelets, necklaces (one is a masculine *kalabubu*) and head ornaments (from Möller 1932, plate XXXII).

77. – This tall androgynous statue (2.55 m. high) is a typical *adu horö*, carved in hard wood. It includes breasts, masculine sexual organs, and a forked ornament on the head. The *adu horö* never had arms. There were more than 100 sorts of *adu*, for each kind of magic purpose. Moreover, priests (*ere*) continually invented new forms of *adu* for specific ritual cures (from Möller 1913, plate 11, fig. 12).

As noted, slaves, like livestock, were seen as falling entirely outside of human society.

The houses of the common people were smaller and less ornate than the *omo sebua*; they were also located away from the village center. Figure 75 shows a row of such houses. Nobles live at the village center, which is bordered by a *bale* (men's ceremonial house) and the chief's *omo sebua*. This central area is the highest part of the village, and the village itself is up on a hill, away from the wilderness (the abode of animals). As a sign of sacredness and high social status, the village streets get wider as one comes nearer the center, until all four paths open up onto a sort of plaza – the village center, which was at the same time the center of the universe and thus full of powers. The *bale*, which also had all the structural features of the South Nias cosmos, served as the council meetinghouse where men decided *adat* matters. Implements for distributing gold were also stored there. Feldman writes that "on the right side there is a flat stone which serves as a surface for dividing fragments of gold which are then weighed and distributed. In the rafters overhead there are hooks on both sides of the *bale* which are used to suspend bamboo containers for gold dust" (Feldman 1979: 136, after Schröder 1917: 154). Heads were also stored in the *bale*, some apparently dedicated to Lowalangi, the god of the Upperworld, associated with the front of the *bale*, and some dedicated to Lature Danö, the god of the Underworld, linked to the back or base of the building (Feldman 1979: 137).

The *omo sebua* included a front room and a private room to the rear. A miniature house called a *malige* was set into the main room and was a replica of the front portion of the house. Noblewomen used the *malige* as a sort of bower from which to watch the village feasts (Feldman 1979: 139). The house was full of sculptures of animals, "tamed" through the human agency of sculpting. That is, animals were brought out of the forest and into the house as sculpture; real animals were antithetical to good house and human order.

Wooden sculptures and their counterpart, stone monuments, served several overt functions in the culture (commemorations of dead ancestors, altars through which spirits could communicate with humans and vice versa) and several hidden ones (master symbols of cosmic order, prestige objects whose production increased the standing of a nobleman, emblems of chieftainship). Ancestor effigies, called *adu zatua*, were thought to be inhabited by the souls of the dead (Modigliani 1890: 650–656; Feldman 1977: 67). *Adu siraha salawa* protected village chiefs and celebrated their dead ancestor's standing (statues often wore the high headdress of noblemen and one earring, plus a warrior necklace or aristocrat's breastplate), his virility, and that of his family line (the sexual organs of these statues were oversize and prominent). The dual-sexual *adu horö* statues (Fig. 77) mentioned previously served a protective function for the house, and extraordinary rows of little human figures (*adu bihara*), attached to a stick, may have represented a lineage.

If Nias noble houses abound with "tamed" wooden animals and ancestor effigies, the village plazas are heaped full of stone slabs, carved seats, mushroom-like collections of stone disks on pedestals, and vertical megaliths (Fig. 78). These work much like the wood sculptures — as altars, testaments to past merit-making feasts (*owasa*), and commemorative monuments to family forebears.

Nias Ornaments: Prestige and Power

Jewelry in Nias was varied, plentiful, and included gold and coconut shell necklaces, gold earrings (Fig. 79) and crowns, shell bracelets, and extraordinary war jewelry for men. Goldsmithing was similar to stone and wood carving, for like those ritual endeavors the creation of fine metal ornaments was a means of storing up merit, power, and splendor for the family. Gold, a main emblem of the aristocracy, was tinged with ambiguity: it was both loved and feared (the great dangers of the sacred gold ornaments could only be "counteracted" through the sacrifice of a slave, whose head was to be buried at the base of the stake upon which the ornaments were hung during the ceremony). Red was the color of death, while gold was a life hue; the darker colors were associated with serpents and the Lowerworld, while the light colors were linked to birds and life forces. Suzuki summarizes the literature on the golden headdresses, which only makes sense against this backdrop of color symbolism (1959: 25–26):

The Golden Crown of [North] and [Central] Nias is called nandrulo, tuwu or saembu ana'a. This head gear is usually in the form of a palm leaf; this piece juts forward at an angle resting upon a basis of woven rattan. The "leaf" is covered with gold plating upon which is often carved a human face.

78. – Stone seats (*sobaqi mboho*) whose shape recalled the wooden chair (*osa-osa*) in which the feast-giver was carried in the village. The monuments with one head were carved for the man, and those with three heads for his wife. This picture was taken in an abandoned village in East Central Nias, in the region of the Susuwa river (Photograph Thierry Barbier-Müller, 1978).

79. – Man wearing the same kind of earring included in this exhibition (Cat. No. 2) (from *Peoples of all Nations*, V: 3724).

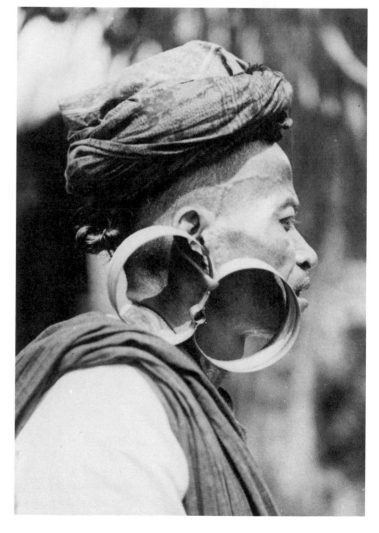

80. – Wooden panel from a chief's house (*omo sebua*) in South Nias. In the middle supported by two human arms is a treasure chest. Underneath, the crescent-like ornament called *saita* may represent the gold ornament on the chief's helmet. The two palms in the upper part are the gold elements of the headdress. The necklace and the single earring indicate that it is a masculine monument (Barbier-Müller Museum, No. 3270, shown in the exhibition, Photograph Otto E. Nelson, 1984).

81. – This picture, taken before 1914, shows the right wall of the chief's house in Bawömataluo. One can easily see the two *laso sohagu* carved on the wooden panels. Swords and precious Chinese wares, protected by wicker boxes, hang in the house (from Schröder 1917, fig. 114).

The rattan is woven into a band. Aside from the "leaf" protuberance, on the back are also two smaller protuberances. The base band is mostly made of white cotton with a strip of red cotton in the middle, a piece of blue on one side and the edges sewn with red cotton. Along the band are four holes wherein are fitted four pieces of wood provided with red flannel flags on top.

In [South] Nias this crown is called takula ana'a. It too is a golden crown with flags; on top are golden "branches" (lagene), sometimes substituted by leaves from the eho tree and furthermore provided with golden leaves, feathers or flags. Sometimes for the golden feather real chicken feathers are substituted and the main protuberance is said to take the shape of a fern while at other times, a hornbill motif is placed on the very top; the flags are red and are placed on both the right and left side.

The shape of the crown and its foliage may have represented the Cosmic Tree. Another head ornament, a crown called *rai bowo zicho*, worn by women, could have been associated with the moon. The warrior's *kalabubu* necklace, although often made of coconut-shell disks, is somewhat similar to these more lavish crowns in that it is associated with gold and aristocratic standing. Suzuki describes this headhunter's ornament in detail (1959: 27).

In [North and Central] Nias, the necklace is called nieto as well as a more common term, kalabubu. Fischer [1909] calls the necklace a "sign of honor" worn by the chieftains and noblemen as a mark of prestige and rank which was formerly awarded for taking heads. The necklace is more or less circular and is composed of thin discs either cut from shells, wood or metal alloys; the center of the necklace is the thickest and tapers off towards the two ends. Very often such necklaces are gold-plated while not infrequently one finds an alligator as decoration on it. In [South] Nias this necklace has no other name than kalabubu and is similar in size, shape and structure to those of the other regions. Only in [South] Nias, the brass alloy as material for it predominates; here too it is a sign of bravery being awarded for heroic deeds. Schröder [1917] posits a [South] Nias origin of this necklace. By Steinhart [1934] we are informed that they were originally made from coconut shells; only those who had taken a head were permitted to wear them while all others were said to become deaf if they did. That this necklace represents the serpent is obvious from reference to it in Nias texts as a "Brustschlange" and "snake of gold" to say nothing of some of them being decorated with alligators.

Nias costumes for warriors and aristocrats were also miniature mythological statements about how the world was structured. In this, clothing resembled jewelry. Gold crowns depicted both the Upperworld and the Lowerworld, the gold branches on the the crown representing the heavens and the various colors on the base portraying the Lowerworld. Sometimes a hornbill (associated with the Upperworld) would be used as a decoration for the top of the crown, and this would signify that the higher realm dominated that particular crown. The Nias robes for men and the jackets for women evoked much the same theme of dualism through the use of the cosmological colors (black, gold, red). In fact, virtually everything a well-dressed Nias aristocrat wore had mythological implications: the *kalabubu* necklace had the shape of the world-snake, and the same mythological reptile was also represented by the shape of war shields. The amulet-basket worn by warriors also suggested the two-part structure of the universe, for this openwork container was outfitted with little wooden images carved with hornbills and crocodiles, animals associated with the Upperworld and the Lowerworld. (Suzuki 1959: 31–32.)

As religiously important signs of high noble and spiritual status, some of the major pieces of headgear were not only worn but were carved in relief sculpture on wooden panels inside the *adat* houses (Fig. 80). The association of jewelry with houses was not an accidental one, for in several important senses the house could wear jewelry. Feldman points out the deep symbolic redundancies in Nias thought between houses and persons (Fig. 81) and houses and villages — and between all of those and the structure of the universe itself (1970: 150–151):

Since the tuha (the secular and sacrifical village leader) is likened to the cosmos, which is also his house, it follows that the house is modelled after the tuha, that is, a human. The ehomo (major house posts) are compared to his legs, the main structure contains his body, and the superstructure corresponds to his head and head ornaments. Indeed the fully dressed ruler has many corresponding iconographic details to the house. His jacket bears many of the same motifs which are painted on the facade of the omo sebua. These included the cotton sepals (sabawo gafasi) and the sides of the facades, ta'io sebu (literally arm-braces) correspond to arms, while the central curved brace, fuso danedane (naval brace) represents the navel. The royal sword telogu has a lasara handle.... On top of the lasara there is a monkey which watches the sculpture found in the omo sebua.... The head-dress is composed of wild plant motifs, including the coiled fern (ni'o woliwoli) — sometimes birds are also included in the headdress. The coiled fern also appears at the ridgepole of the house.

The great house had carved panels depicting the full set of gold ornaments in detailed relief. These panels, called *laso sohagu,* came in male and female pairs (Feldman 1979: 168–169, 142; Barbier 1978: 24, 65–67). It is interesting that some of these panels combine male elements (single earrings) and female elements (double fern or palm-frond decorations). This could mean that these panels are representations of powerful male and female cosmic combinations, but this is an uncertain interpretation.

In sum, in a number of ways much of Nias religious life was concerned with mediating the gulf between such binary opposites as humans and gods, society and wilderness, and male and female. The monkey sculptures in the *adat* houses mediated the forest and village, *ere* priestesses mediated society and the sacred, the house mediated the high villages and the supernatural world, and gold ornaments mediated high chiefs and other villagers (as the *rajas* distributed ornaments to their followers) and served as a bridge between humans and supernaturals (in the use of gold jewelry as part of priestly garb).

NIAS
Crown, earrings & necklace, gold. Cat. Nos. 1, 2 & 5. Descriptions p. 319.

SOUTH NIAS
Necklace, gold. Cat. No. 7. Description p. 319.

NORTH SUMATRA:
TOBA AND KARO BATAK

Some Indonesian ethnic groups have unusually controversial and contradictory reputations. The Batak societies of Sumatra are one of these. By Indonesians and outsiders alike, they have been characterized as fierce, rough-mannered *(kasar)*, abrasive, and hot-tempered. At the same time both detractors and admirers often admit that Batak are generous, loyal to their families, and astonishingly successful in establishing themselves in well-paying jobs and powerful political positions in the *rantau* (the area beyond the ethnic homelands). Such stereotypes are probably best seen as weapons in Sumatra's long history of inter-ethnic competition among the various Batak peoples, the Acehnese, the Minangkabau, and the Javanese and Malay living along the East Coast of the island.

In more dispassionately descriptive terms, the six Batak societies (Map 4) are village-based, rice-farming cultures with similarities to those of Eastern Indonesia. Batak communities, like many in Sumba and Flores, are based on marriage ties between wife-givers and wife-takers. That is, they have an asymmetric marriage alliance system in which giver groups may not receive brides from their taker groups, and givers are deemed the spiritual and ritual superiors of their indebted, subordinate takers. A group that has received women as brides from another group in turn passes on its sisters and daughters to a third group. A similar system was described in the Kachin highlands of Burma by E.R. Leach in his book *Political Systems of Highland*

◀ Toba Batak ritual cloth (*ulos ragidup*). Supplementary weft and warp ikat. Cotton. North Sumatra, Indonesia. Detail. (Barbier-Müller Museum, No. 3175-6, not exhibited).

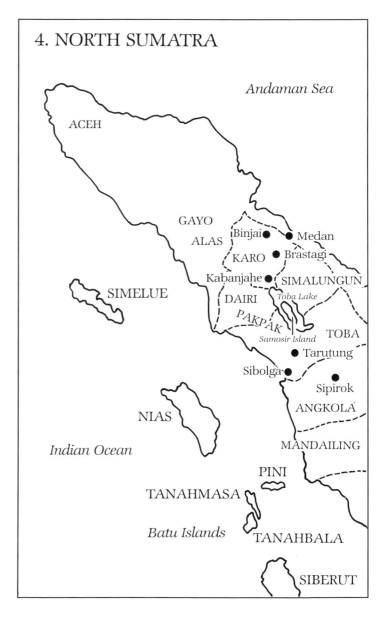

4. NORTH SUMATRA

Andaman Sea

ACEH

GAYO
ALAS

Binjai ● ● Medan

KARO ● Brastagi

Kabanjahe ● SIMALUNGUN

SIMELUE

DAIRI *Toba Lake*

PAKPAK

Samosir Island TOBA

● Tarutung

Sibolga ●

Sipirok ●

ANGKOLA

NIAS

MANDAILING

Indian Ocean

PINI

TANAHMASA

Batu Islands TANAHBALA

SIBERUT

82. – *Adat* houses in a Toba village (Photograph Jean Paul Barbier, 1980).

83. – Toba architecture: detail of a traditional house. The creature called *singa* is often seen on bracelets and rings (see Cat. Nos. 29 and 30). (Photograph Jean Paul Barbier, 1978).

Burma (1954).[1] Considerable amounts of prestige goods, livestock, food, and such intangibles as blessings and spiritual protection are exchanged along with brides between the marriage alliance partners. Chiefs' families from different villages are linked through the same idiom of wife-giving and wife-receiving. Patrilineal clan ancestry is stressed, and, with marriage alliance, forms a focus for village ceremonial life. The Batak arts, like those in Eastern Indonesia, flow from the ritualized obligations of "ancestor worship" (an inaccurate term since Batak are more cajolers and complainers than worshippers) and gift-giving between marriage alliance partners.

Much of the Western literature (for a bibliography see Siagian 1966) asserts that there are six major Batak cultures: Toba, Karo, Dairi-Pakpak, Simalungun, Angkola, and Mandailing. This division into ethnic units is somewhat misleading, however, since villagers often have little use for such general words as "Angkola" and identify themselves in much more local terms as members of a ceremonial league or a group of village clusters. Ethnic identity is also situationally defined (R. Kipp 1983). The sixfold ethnic division may reflect relatively new ethnic designations created in contemporary Indonesian cities as members of different homeland groups come into contact and competition with each other (Bruner 1973). In addition, the Batak populations share many items of material culture across very permeable ethnic boundaries (Karo depend on Toba, for instance, to weave some of their *uis* ritual cloths). Whatever the case, the six large Batak units do have a few identifiable cultural variations that are useful to note as background to a more detailed discussion of Karo and Toba (Figs. 82–85).

The Mandailing are predominantly Muslim, while Toba, Dairi-Pakpak, and Simalungun are largely Protestant Christian. Karo include large numbers of traditionalists still practicing an indigenous Batak religion based on ancestor spirits and animistic forces, although in the last twenty years Karo have been converting in increasing numbers to Christianity and Islam. This is in part because membership in a monotheistic religion is an important badge of national Indonesian loyalty. Angkola, in the south, is

1. See also Leach's *Rethinking Anthropology* (1961), a collection of his articles that put the Kachin ethnography into a wider theoretical perspective. In addition, see the references suggested in note 1 in the "Peoples and Arts of Island Southeast Asia" chapter above.

also a mixed Christian and Muslim region, but here after more than one hundred years of monotheism most traces of an older Angkola religion have been thoroughly syncretized into line with the teachings of the church and the mosque. Another point of difference among the six societies is language: each group speaks a separate dialect of Batak, and the more geographically distant of these, such as Mandailing and Karo, are mutually unintelligible. The influence of neighboring Sumatran cultures has also caused divergence among the Batak groups. The *adat* of the southern Muslim Batak, for instance, has borrowed many myths, ritual practices, and clothing styles from the Minangkabau, while the Acehnese trading states have strongly influenced the village *adat* chiefs' families and the art of the Karo.

Despite such variation, all the Batak societies share a single core culture based on certain organizational and symbolic principles. In this sense, each Batak culture is related to the others on a theme-and-variations pattern.[2] The fundamental theme of Batak thought concentrates on kinship, or, in the Toba and Angkola phrase, on the *dalihan na tolu*.

In its literal meaning, *dalihan na tolu* refers to a familiar image: the arrangement of three equidistant stones set on the hearth for balancing a cookpot. In Batak ritual speech, the image has much deeper meaning. One stone is said to be a man's own patrilineage mates, a small group of clansmen linked to an ancestral village founded by their fathers' forebears. A second stone is said to be this group's wife-givers – another small localized lineage, of a different clan, that has given their sisters and daughters as brides to the first group over a number of generations. This giver group (*hula-hula* in Toba, *mora* in the south, *kalimbubu* in Karo) is seen as the holy, high, superior partner in the marriage exchange. The wife-givers have special links to the supernatural world of beneficent forces, and if their supplicant wife-takers flatter and serve them properly, they will provide a continuous flow of blessings and good luck to their daughters and wife-receiving men. Chief among these blessings is agricultural and human fertility. The third stone in the *dalihan na tolu* is said to be the focal group's own wife-takers (*boru* in Toba, *anakboru* in Angkola, *anakberu* in Karo). They belong to a different clan from those of the two other partners. The focal, first group is

2. For a discussion of this approach, based on Van Wouden 1968, see Fox 1980b: 1–20 and 1980c, and Josselin de Jong 1980.

84. – *Adat* houses in a Karo village (Photograph Jean Paul Barbier, 1974).

85. – Detail of the roof of a Karo nobleman's house. Note the use of carved buffalo heads (Photograph Jean Paul Barbier, 1978).

86. – Stone sarcophagus in Tomok, Samosir Island, Lake Toba (Photograph Jean Paul Barbier, 1980).

87. – Stone sarcophagus in the village of Huta Raja, northwest Samosir (Photograph Jean Paul Barbier, 1978).

responsible for giving brides, luck, and blessings to this third group, just as their own wife-givers provide for them. If one of the partners of marriage pact fails to act his part, Batak social order (according to *adat*) will break down. Before monotheism, such a breach of kinship *adat* would also have cosmological implications, and the very order of the universe would be threatened.

This type of marriage arrangement encourages the circulation of women in one direction, from giver to taker. In other words, if lineage A has given brides to lineage B, women from B should not be "sent back" as brides to A. This is what makes the system asymmetrical. Ideally, lineage B will bestow their women on a third group, C. The exchange of tangible and intangible goods is also highly patterned and asymmetrical. Wife-givers and wife-takers trade a number of set gifts and countergifts. The situation can be presented in the very simplified form of a diagram which glosses over a number of important local variations.

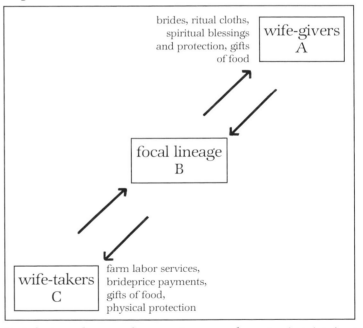

brides, ritual cloths, spiritual blessings and protection, gifts of food

wife-givers
A

focal lineage
B

wife-takers
C

farm labor services, brideprice payments, gifts of food, physical protection

Batak jewelry exchange is complex. In intriguing contrast to some of the patterns of cloth and metal exchange found in Eastern Indonesia, metal jewelry often serves Batak cultures as an important gift for conveying blessings and good health from wife-givers to wife-takers. On the island of Sumba, on the other hand, elaborately worked earrings and pendants are presented by the wife-takers to the wife-givers as major bridewealth objects and serve as "masculine" countergifts to the "feminine" ritual cloths, sent to the marriage along with the bride.

Batak ritual life — and the arts that emerge from it — is essentially an extended paean to the twin *dalihan na tolu* themes of patrilineal clan descent and asymmetrical marriage alliance. Angkola Batak *tortor* ritual dances, for instance, involve *anakboru* (wife-takers) dancing in a protective circle around the *mora* (wife-givers). The *anakboru* keep their heads lower than those of *mora* and wear their *ulos* on their left shouldres, whereas the *mora* drape theirs on their right side (the holy side).

Although the practice is changing under Muslim influence, Mandailing wife-givers once sponsored trance-producing *gondang* (gong and drum) performances for their wife-takers' benefit.[3] And, in perhaps the most spectacular example of Batak village art, in the Karo and Toba homelands huge saddlebacked or peak-roofed *adat* houses were constructed to provide a common home for a family and its complete complement of marriage alliance partners. These *adat* houses were Batak societies in miniature. The floor plan of a traditional Karo house, for instance, surrounded the homeowners with protective wife-givers, loyal clanmates, and supportive wife-takers.

Other Batak material arts also celebrated descent and alliance. The role of village chief, or *raja*, was attained through genealogical position in locally dominant clans and through astutely contracted marriages. The finery of the *rajas* was often a combination of locally produced textiles; Dutch, Minangkabau, or Acehnese weapons; and "power-filled" ornaments from neighboring Batak groups. In Toba, clan ancestors were commemorated through carved stone sarcophagi (Figs. 86 and 87) and stone *tugu* (funeral obelisks), often constructed today from cast concrete. On Samosir Island in Lake Toba the sarcophagi sometimes took the form of boats, playing on the mythic motif of a sea journey to the Afterworld and recalling the boatlike shape of *adat* houses and coffins. The Toba house, in fact, was in a sense a boat carrying the lineage through time, allowing its living members occasional access to the wise counsel of their dead forebears. Another art form — puppets — was used at funerals to represent the deceased. (For a discussion of *si-gale-gale* puppets see Vergouwen 1964 : 274-275). A second range of art work (*ulos* textiles, some metal jewelry,

88. — Toba *datu* or priest-diviner at the beginning of this century. He has a magic book *(pustaha)* containing recipes and holds a carved wand, topped with horse hair *(tunggal panaluan)*. A horn *(naga morsarang)* containing magic ingredients is hanging from his left arm (courtesy Kon. Inst. v/d Tropen, Amsterdam).

---

3. Ethnomusicologist Margaret Kartomi has a valuable discussion of the Mandailing *gondang*, stressing its symbolism of binary oppositions, in her article "Lovely When Heard from Afar," in Kartomi, ed., 1981.

specially arranged mounds of food) consisted of marriage alliance goods that were transferred between wife-givers and wife-takers, as companion gifts for brides, or as countergifts to bridewealth.

One category of Batak art goes a bit beyond the conceptual framework of local kinship into the realm of divination, magical protection, and sorcery. This was the domain of the *datu* (the Toba and Angkola word; Fig. 88) or the *guru* (the Karo term). This person was the master spirit conjurer and spell-caster of Batak village life (and contemporary city life, for that matter, since *datu* sorcery has proven to be one of the most resilient and adaptive areas of Batak culture in this last century of rapid modernization and integration into national life).[4] Toba *datu* and Karo *guru* outfitted themselves with a panoply of magic wands, amulets, conjurer's rings, and potion pouches. All these objects were designed to take evil influences from the sorcerer, his patient, and his village and cast them back to their source.

These common themes of kinship and folk religion take somewhat different forms in Karo and Toba and result in somewhat different jewelry traditions.

Karo Batak

The Karo homeland is in the rugged mountains north of Lake Toba, centered on the market towns of Brastagi and Kabanjahe. Karo culture as a whole, with its vibrant performing and material arts, bears witness to the importance of ethnic interaction in this corner of the Indonesian and Malay world. Far from being an isolated aboriginal hill tribe, the Karo have historically operated at the crossroads of Acehnese and Malay trade history and Dutch and Indonesian interaction. Rather impressive local Karo "kingships" developed under Acehnese and Dutch influence, and many purportedly Karo metal jewelry styles entered the village chiefs' treasures from the more centralized surrounding states. Design motifs seen by villagers as quintessentially Karo, for instance, show unmistakable Acehnese and Malay influence. Other "Karo" pieces are used by Simalungun and northern Toba Batak as well, who claim the designs as part of their own ancestral culture. In fact, Karo metal jewelry traditions thwart any rigid attempt to divide the map of Indonesia into clear-cut ethnic homelands with definite artifacts. Karo culture, in other words, is a document

of Sumatra's history of shifting political systems and exuberant cultural borrowings.

The Karo village is an eloquent text on Karo culture. These settlements, or *kuta,* which today are often a mixture of *adat* houses and modern Malay-style homes (modern structures divided into rooms, with verandas), range in size from about ten families to nearly 800; about 95 percent consist of fewer than a hundred families (Singarimbun 1975: 13-14). The *kuta* is a land-owning unit, and access to rice paddies is determined according to *adat* family inheritance law (Slaats and Portier 1981, 1983). In pre-national times and sometimes even today in this fairly conservative homeland, villages include several rice barns *(jambor).* In addition to food storage they are used as sleeping quarters for young men and male travellers and in the colonial era served as minor courts, or *bale'* (Singarimbun 1975: 19-20). Villages have separate bathing places for men and women, a graveyard outside the village rim, and a *sembahen,* or village shrine. In the *Perbe'gu,* or traditional religion, the guardian spirits of the village were said to live in the *sembahen.* The village aristocrats were the only ones who could communicate directly with the village's spiritual protectors, and as a consequence they controlled a large share of village ritual life. A myth associated with the shrine gives some of the flavor of the *Perbe'gu* and indicates in its imagery of incest between opposite-sex twins the Karo's many cultural ties to other Indonesian peoples with similar twin stories:

The chief spirits of every village shrine are Pa Megoh and Nande Megoh who, according to a myth, are husband and wife but also brother and sister. They were twins and because they were born on an inauspicious day their parents deserted then under a pandanus tree downstream from the bathing place. A civet cat took them away to the forest where they grew up as spirits and got married. One day a traveller passed the forest in which they lived and through him they sent a message to their parents telling them about their dwelling place. The parents were astonished to hear this news and went to the forest to visit their children. A voice came from a tree saying that they, the twins, were now husband and wife, the husband called Pa Megoh and the wife Nande Megoh. They would become guardian spirits, they said, and would guard the village on the condition that a special ceremony were held and offerings made upstream from the bathing place. The villagers performed the ceremony as directed and the shrine was created upstream from the bathing place. (Singarimbun 1975:21.)

Karo art emerged from this system of kin relation-

4. See Gloria Davis, ed., *What Is Modern Indonesian Culture?* (1979) for articles on social change in Indonesian ethnic groups.

ship and religion and from the Karo's cultural inter-action with the Malay sultanates, Minangkabau, Aceh, and the other Batak cultures. It is necessary to point out first that "art" has apparently only recently developed as a meaningful idea for the Karo them-selves. Many of the Karo masks, textiles, and orna-ments in Western and national Indonesian museums were seen by their original Karo creators and users as religious ritual objects, or more accu-rately as part of Karo *adat*. Secondly, the Karo mate-rial arts such as jewelry, *uis* textiles, funeral masks, and *adat* houses can only be fully understood as parts of a larger set of symbolic activities including ritual dances, gift exchanges, oratory, folklore, and proverbs.

The Karo jewelry in the Barbier-Müller collection is first of all the regalia of an aristocratic class. The *padung curu-curu* earrings (Cat. Nos. 17 and 18), for instance, were worn by women of chiefs' families to symbolize both their high social rank and their wealth (1983 fieldnotes). According to a Karo *guru* from Tanjung, the conical shape of this earring represents the nest of a certain type of bird that spends much of its time accumulating twigs, berries, thread, and other little objects to stuff into its fat nest. The *guru* said that the behavior of the bird illustrates the wealth-accumulating behavior of the highborn Karo women of the past, who also would bring all manner of prestige objects into their *adat* houses. The man's ornate bracelet (Cat. No. 26), worn by bridegrooms at their weddings and by the sons of deceased chiefs at funerals, is another example of aristocratic display. Today, families that own such treasures lend or rent them to commoner families when the latter put on *adat* weddings or funerals (Fig. 89).

A second aspect of Karo jewelry is that it is part of the larger array of ritual objects, including *uis* textiles and *adat* houses, tied to local kinship patterns. Sev-eral of the pieces in the collection are magic objects used for fostering the marriage most encouraged in the *adat* — the union of a young man and his mother's brother's daughter. In cultures with patri-lineal clans, matrilateral cross-cousin marriage means that in seeking this wife a young man has gone back to the same household where his father found a wife a generation ago. The relatively simple necklace, or *rante* (a Batak spelling of the Indonesian *rantai*, Cat. No. 23), is one such magic ornament that works to firm up a promise of marriage made when

89. – A pseudo-funeral with sham corpses made of wood. Note the *gelang sarung* bracelet in the lower part of the picture (similar to Cat. No. 26) (cour-tesy Kon. Inst. v/d Tropen, Amsterdam).

90. – Karo woman in bride dress: she wears a *sertali* headdress ornament (Cat. No. 11), a *bura-bura* ornament (Cat. No. 21) and *karabu kudung-kudung* earrings (Cat. No. 15). (Photograph Anthony Pardede, Nov. 1984).

91. – Karo woman wearing *padung* earrings. Note that the heavy silver ornament (Cat. Nos. 13 and 14), inserted into the ear, is attached to the head cloth (Photograph Tassilo Adam, before 1920).

the prospective couple are still young children. The *rante* works this way: when a family has a baby girl, the infant's father's sister comes on a visit bringing the girl the necklace as a "sign of unity" symbolizing the woman's hope that her own infant son and her new niece will get married when they grow up. The double clasp on the necklace represents the two spouses, the father's sister's son-mother's brother's daughter pair. It should be noted, though, that the double clasp can be opened, and the marriage may never actually take place. This droll observation, made by an old *adat* chief from Tanjung, aptly illustrates the Karo's fine sense for the flexibility of their *adat* (see R.S. Kipp 1982 for a sensitive discussion of this point).

Other pieces, such as the gilded silver jacket clasp shown in Cat. No. 25, are worn by unmarried girls to give them luck in finding mates. The stars inside the disks were said by one informant to give the girls luck in locating their *jodoh* (ideal mate, destined by fate). Other ornaments, such as the famous and distinctly Karo *padung* earrings or headdress ornaments (Fig. 91 – Cat. Nos. 13 and 14), teach lessons about marriages which have already been contracted. A standard way to wear the *padung* is to affix one to the textile headdress (Fig. 91), pointing up and back, and let another swing free from the ear on the opposite side of the head. Several informants in 1983 asserted that the "one up and one down" pattern represented a husband and wife over the course of their marriage: sometimes one partner is up and dominant in some dispute but later will be on the losing end in a disagreement.

Larger kinship patterns are also evident in the ways that fine Karo jewelry is transferred from person to person, or, more accurately, from household to household. Three patterns of transmission are common. First, a mother and father may outfit their marriageable daughters with expensive earrings and jacket pins to advertise their social standing and nubile status. Second, a household may bedeck its son and his wife with objects of their house treasure, which they display to the public at important *adat* rituals involving the lineage. Also, the *kalimbubu* wife-givers may bestow luck-bringing rings on their subservient *anakberu* wife-receivers when the *anakberu* have suffered a run of bad luck or ill health.

The heavy *karabu kudung-kudung* ear pendants (Cat. Nos. 15 and 16) are prime examples of jewelry used by a household to advertise its wealth and social standing. The ornaments can be worn by a woman as part of the full bridal costume, with the *sertali* headdress ornament, or later at the funerals of her husband's parents. The bride's structural position in the household is important here: until she has produced sons she remains something of an outsider, a symbol of the wife-giving group's generosity. After this, she is adorned with the fancy earrings at the funeral of her husband's father or mother (persons considered her father's sister's husband and father's sister).

Karo rings are particularly important vehicles for conveying the luck of the wife-giving *kalimbubu* to down-on-their-luck wife-receivers. In 1983 a Karo art shop dealer in Brastagi described a possible situation this way. Say a man invests in a series of business ventures at the vegetable marketplace in Brastagi but fails to realize any return; or perhaps one of his children falls ill and fails to recover. Such an unfortunate householder would be a likely candidate for emergency jewelry aid by his *kalimbubu*: the wife-givers will commission or purchase a *kerunggun* ring (Cat. No. 34) and affix two smaller, plain rings onto the large one. The group of rings represents the *sengkap sitelu*, the threefold partnership of *kalimbubu*, *anakberu*, and *sanina*. The wife-giver *kalimbubu* present the rings to their *anakberu* while saying luck-bringing words. Conveying the ring and the powerful words together is thought to have the magical effect of bestowing some of *kalimbubu*'s store of good luck on *anakberu*.

Such ornaments as the *kerunggun* ring contain a sort of *upah tendi* power, the ability to "protect and firm up the soul" of the wearer. In fact, this is a major characteristic of Karo jewelry. A related concept is the notion that certain combinations of jewelry pieces can be used by *guru* (sorcerer-shamans) to *panggil roh* — to call back souls or spirits to their proper abode. Like other Batak peoples the Karo assume that certain ailments and mental anxieties are caused by loss of the soul. If startled, an individual's soul (*tendi*) can fragment and escape from his body to wander in the fields, where it becomes subject to attack by spirits. *Guru* are hired by concerned family members to call back the wandering soul and replace it in the patient's body. Calling back souls demands a particularly powerful shaman, armed with particularly powerful amulets. It is of interest that these tend to be assemblages of jewelry that combine diametrically opposed categories such as male and female. The wedding ornaments and necklaces of the newlyweds are sometimes used in just this way, for a shaman's seance. For instance, a *guru* takes the bridegroom's *bura layang-layang* necklace (symbolizing, in the buffalo-horn shape of the three major pendant pieces, maleness and nobility) and combines its pieces into a new necklace with the elements of the feminine *sertali*, the bride's headdress ornament. The *guru* then stands and swings the new ornament downward through the air while maintaining his hold on it. This motion serves to call back the patient's lost soul.

As noted, many Indonesian cultures base much of their philosophical systems on this idea of a creative, powerful center uniting, for several tense moments, opposing categories. Batak thought is filled with this pattern. The bride herself is a powerful go-between uniting her father's lineage and that of her husband, and Batak concepts of femininity play on the ambivalent, Janus-faced structural identity of women in the marriage alliance system. Some Batak art systems make even more explicit use of a two-in-one theme. In Mandailing music, for instance, masculine and feminine elements are apparently combined in the *gondang* gong and drum ensemble (Kartomi 1981). In Toba house architecture male snake figures are united with relief sculpture representing female breasts to convey luck and fertility to the inhabitants of the home. It is to these Toba artistic ideas that we turn next.

Toba Batak

In some versions of Batak history, the Toba region is the cradle of the other Batak societies, an ancestral land associated with Si Raja Batak, the first human. He fathered ancestors of the various clan founders, who migrated from Toba into outlying areas to the north and south to establish the other Batak homelands.[5] With typical panache many Toba say that their culture is the *asli* (genuine, original) Batak one from which all others have descended — and degenerated. Cultural objectivity is not a Toba strong suit.

Toba kinship, politics, and art are similar to those aspects of Karo culture centering on ideas of patrilineal clan descent, marriage alliance, and veneration of spirits. *Hula-hula* (wife-givers) provide women

5. Vergouwen 1933 includes long accounts of Toba Batak origin myths.

92. — Upper part of a *datu*'s magic wand or *tunggal panaluan*. (Barbier-Müller Museum, No. 3102-H, on loan to the Dallas Museum of Art. See Barbier 1983, plate 14).

and *ulos* gifts to their subordinate *anakboru*, who give back *piso* (literally "knife") gifts to their wife-providers (Vergouwen 1964:58-63). *Ulos* gifts, which literally refer to *ulos* textiles, convey *sahala* (magical protective power) to the *anakboru*. This idea is dramatized through the action of placing an *ulos* cloth around the shoulders of a daughter and her new husband in the *adat* wedding (Gittinger 1979:79; Myers 1983). In addition to cloth, *ulos* gifts include parcels of land a father bestows on his daughter early in her marriage. Such property is called *ulos na so ra buruk*, the *ulos* that never wears out, and is normally given in perpetuity. Vergouwen notes that cattle, money, rice, houses, and trees can also be used as *ulos* gifts, and "formerly male and female slaves were so used as a sign of the prominence of the donor" (1964:60). Sometimes a young woman would present her firstborn child to her father, grumbling "your grandchild has to eat." In response to this the father would perhaps turn over some of his riceland to the woman and her husband, causing her brothers to complain that their sister had gotten some of their own land through unfair wheedling. This sort of dissension and distrust is typical of Batak village life.

The countergifts to the *ulos* are called "knife or sword gifts," *piso* gifts. Normally these are not actual metal implements but consist of money, cattle, rice, and similar practical commodities. All of these can be called *piso hajojahan*, or a "knife with which to support oneself" (Vergouwen 1964:61). Wealthy *boru* were also expected to support their wife-providers through occasional financial assistance outside of marriage.

Ulos and *piso* gifts thus both cover a fairly diverse range of objects. Toba do not conform to any neat schematization linking metal objects irrevocably to wife-taker gifts which are then inevitably balanced by ritual textile gifts. Rather, metal objects of various sorts (weapons, special ancestral relics) can be passed down the patrilineage, or given by a lineage to its daughters or *boru* men (the bride is outfitted in jewelry for her wedding, a pattern perhaps borrowed from the southern Batak homelands; bracelets such as shown in Cat. Nos. 28 and 29 can be given to a young man by his mother's brother). Beyond these uses, metal jewelry can indeed be given by wife-takers to their wife-givers, or more exactly to the bride herself. For instance, in the Tarutung area, the *simanjomak* earrings (Cat. Nos. 19

and 20) are sometimes given to prospective brides by their wife-takers (father's sister's husband, or husband's father). If the union is an exact matrilateral cross-cousin match, the young woman will expect such a gift as an incentive to actually go through with the marriage. It happens, though, that fathers can also give this same type of earring to their daughters. Note the slight contrast with Karo here. In that homeland, wife-givers present luck-bringing rings to their wife-receiving *anakberu*, while rich lineages give some of their house treasure to their son's wife for her to wear at large *adat* rituals. This woman also gets *padung-padung* earrings and jacket clasps from her parents, to attract young men and later to carry to her new marriage. In Toba, wife-givers give bracelets to their *bere* (sister's son), and father's sister's husbands give rings and earrings to the young women they hope will marry their sons.

Jewelry and a larger range of amulets and spirit-summoning objects were also important to *datu*, the Toba sorcerer-diviner-priests. These men acted as the chief's intermediaries with the spirit world. Before Christianity, Toba apparently had a rather generalized concept of God (Debata), which was seen as a pervasive supreme force in the universe. There were five deities (Batara Guru, Soripada, Mangalabulan, Muladjadinabolon, and Debata-asiasi), three of which had clear Hindu antecedents (Vergouwen 1964:68). The five did not appear to have distinct characters, locations, or functions — there was probably in general a great deal of local variation in the religion. In addition to the gods there were several personified natural forces (e.g., Boraspati ni tano, a lizard god associated with the earth, its fertility, and the protection of houses). *Begu*, or

spirits, also abounded. Since these spirits controlled health and illness, the *datu* healers figure importantly here. To ward off the harmful *begu* there were "antidotes, *pagar*, such as carved images, *gana-ganaan*, and amulets, *porsimboraan*, of which the magical ingredients are prescribed by the *datu* and strengthened by his ritual" (Vergouwen 1964: 69). *Datu* were also important religious personnel in ancestor veneration rituals. The *sombaon*, "he-who-is-revered," were distantly remembered clan ancestors so far from human society as to almost approach the status of deities (Vergouwen 1964:71). Their descendants would sometimes commemorate the *sombaon* with a large sacrificial feast, which the *datu* led. This sort of ritual indicated another role for the Toba *datu*, his activities as the priest for the ruling class.

Datu adorned themselves with a veritable armamentarium of potent amulets and jewelry used for calling back *(mangalap tondi)* the lost souls of sick people or casting back evil influences such as enemy attacks or epidemics. The village *pangulubalang*, a squat anthropomorphic stone statue set at the rim of the village, should probably be included in this set of protective objects. Primary among the *datu*'s magical implements was his *tunggal panaluan* (Fig. 92), magic staff or wand. A number of humanlike figures and mythic characters, each with an open mouth, were carved into the wand. To invest the staff with power the *datu* would "feed" each little mouth with a concoction of magic material made in part from mashed human viscera from a sacrificed victim. According to a Toba art dealer in the Lake Samosir coastal town of Prapat, a cock ring (Cat. No. 38) was part of a *datu*'s armory of magic objects used in such a ritual.

NORTH SUMATRA
Earring, silver. Cat. No. 14. Description p. 320.

NORTH SUMATRA
Necklace, gilded silver. Cat. No. 22. Description pp. 321–322.

NORTH SUMATRA
Bracelet, gold & gilded silver. Cat. No. 26. Description p. 322.

NORTH SUMATRA
Bracelet, silver. Cat. No. 29. Description p. 322.

111

NORTH SUMATRA
Ring, brass. Cat. No. 38. Description p. 323.

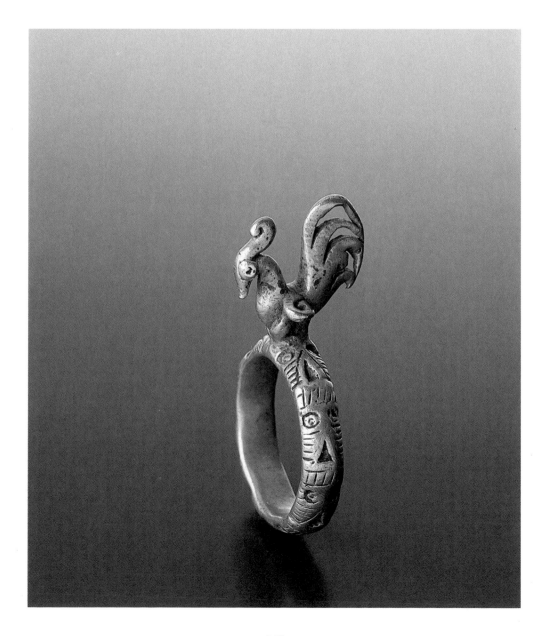

KALIMANTAN AND SARAWAK:
DAYAK

Kalimantan is a heavily forested island of great natural wealth covering roughly 750,000 square kilometers. It is positioned like the center of a wheel between the Indonesian and Philippine island chains and mainland Southeast Asia (Map 5). China lies directly to the north beyond the South China Sea. Today Kalimantan (called Borneo before national independence) is divided among three nations: Indonesia, Malaysia, to which Sarawak and Sabah belong, and the newly independent state of Brunei. With its location on important ancient trade routes, Kalimantan's history is a variegated mix of Chinese, Javanese, Sulawesi, Malay, Dutch, and English influences. The island's coastal cultures interacted most vigorously with outside states, and they resemble Malay sultanates with pronounced English and Dutch overtones. Inland along Kalimantan's great rivers live the many Dayak cultures. These are hill-farming societies with relatively egalitarian social ethics, at least in the sense that rigid hierarchical chiefdoms are absent.

There are many Dayak cultures (including the Apo-Kayan, Kenyah, Bahau, Ngaju, Melawi, Murut, Punan, and several others). In pre-national times, inter-village conflict was frequent, and warfare was a perennial theme of village artwork. Dayak cultures (which for our purposes here will be defined as including Sarawak's Iban) had close social structural and artistic ties to the cultures of Mindanao, Northern Luzon, interior Sulawesi, and the islands off the west coast of Sumatra. The Dayak religions

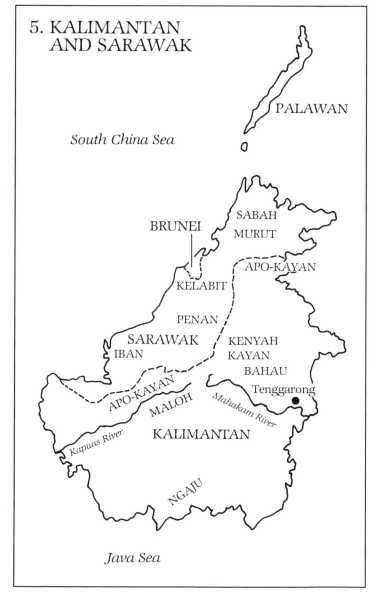

5. KALIMANTAN AND SARAWAK

PALAWAN

South China Sea

BRUNEI

SABAH

MURUT

APO-KAYAN

KELABIT

PENAN

SARAWAK

IBAN

KENYAH

KAYAN

BAHAU

Tenggarong

APO-KAYAN

MALOH

Mahakam River

Kapuas River

KALIMANTAN

NGAJU

Java Sea

◄ Ceremonial cloth (*pua*). Warp ikat. Cotton. Iban. Sarawak, Malaysia. Detail. (Barbier-Müller Museum, No. 3462-9, not exhibited).

93. – Dayak people (probably Iban) in festive dress. The wooden human figures are *hampatong*, protective sculptures to ward off evil spirits. Note that the two men sitting in the first row wear necklaces similar to Cat. No. 55 (color plate p. 127) (courtesy Kon. Inst. v/d Tropen, Amsterdam).

made explicit connections between death (in the form of headtaking, as in pre-modern Nias) and the regeneration of life. Much ritual life, house architectural styles, village wood statuary, and textile art were dedicated to this idea and to the closely associated concept of protecting the village and the person from evil influences. Sickness was religiously charged, and amulets and wood sculptures called *hampatong* were central religious, and medical, devices. The creation myth of the Ngaju Dayak cited in the chapter on "Jewelry and the Supernatural" shows another important theme in Dayak worldviews: the association of fine jewelry with high social status[1] and mythical ancestors.

Dayak Cultures

The Dayak have suffered from unusually harsh stereotypes in the popular Western literature on Indonesian and Malaysian peoples. Living in their longhouses far upriver, dressed in feather headdresses, covered with tattoos, wearing extraordinary metal earrings that weighed down their earlobes into loops four or five inches long, the Dayak seemed the very image of primitive pagan man to many early European visitors. The titles of adventure books and early monographs show this: *Men of the Inner Jungle* (Alder 1923), *Life in the Forests of the Far East* (St. John 1863), *Black Borneo* (Miller 1942), *The Head-Hunters of Borneo* (Bock 1882), and even *Natural Man* (Hose 1926). Such ethnocentric stereotypes have persisted until very recently. Writing in 1956, for instance, Malcolm MacDonald employed remarkably florid captions for photographs in his book *Borneo People*. He described one group of Dayak men in a picture as "Fierce, Husky Savages" and noted for another photograph that "On Gala Occasions Their Costume Assumes Barbaric Splendour" (1956:99,16) (Fig. 93).

Part of the incentive for such images of primitiveness may well have been the Dayak's practice of inserting increasingly larger and heavier earrings in children's earlobes, causing them to hang down in what to Western eyes are grotesque loops. For Dayak, such practices are not cruel deformations of the body but signs of beauty and a way to allow individuals to wear a major part of the family wealth all at once.

1. Harrisson and O'Connor offer an exhilarating discussion of prehistorical Borneo goldsmithing in relationship to status rivalry and funerary art in their monograph "Gold and Megalithic Activity in Prehistoric and Recent West Borneo" (1970).

The Dayak have a fondness for costuming the body in a surfeit of rich textiles, silver disks, bracelets, hair ornaments, and anklets. Big earrings on elongated earlobes were often used as signs of maturity or marriageable status for women. For men (Fig. 94), enlarging the earlobe allowed them to wear the earrings that signified that they had taken a head. As Victoria Ebin notes in *The Body Decorated* (1979), her valuable monograph on body "deformations" of this sort, a number of cultures have used the manipulation of human flesh to convey crucial social messages whose import can only be grasped once Westerners move beyond their initial distaste for elongated earlobes, stretched necks, and so on.

Ethnocentric stereotypes aside, actually the Dayak were not as isolated and pristinely traditional as the early books implied. As riverine peoples they kept in contact with the coastal settlements. Their material culture abounds with imported items, ranging from colored beads and old Chinese porcelain to Malay cannons, suitable, according to W.R. Geddes (1957:27), for welcoming visitors to villages. Dayak art forms, and particularly their jewelry, show this sort of openness to outside influences as well as allegiance to Dayak patterns of thought. A better way of phrasing the situation is to say that those Dayak patterns of thought are themselves the product of Kalimantan's long history of ethnic interaction.

The glass, porcelain, iron, and clay beads Dayak use so imaginatively in their clothing arts are good examples of this sort of ethnic interaction (Dunsmore 1978). Patterned beadwork is used to decorate caps, rattan hats, vests, tunics, baby carriers, and various ritual objects (Fig. 95). Sarawak's Iban peoples have used beads for centuries and may have obtained some of their most prized varieties via ancient trade routes linking the Middle East, India, and island Southeast Asia (Dunsmore 1978:3-6). This cosmopolitan history was also characteristic of other forms of Dayak jewelry (Harrisson and O'Connor 1970) which, like beadwork, is best seen against the backdrop of the other ritual arts and their intellectual framework of myth.

Dayak Village Arts

Dayak settlements are contentious places without well-institutionalized political hierarchies. Dayak kinship can be described as cognatic, although this is a controversial designation (Appell 1976). As

94. – Penan Dayak man in full regalia. He wears very heavy brass earrings similar to Nos. 46 to 50 in this catalogue. His body is tattooed with *aso* motifs (Photograph Lucas Chin, courtesy The Sarawak Museum).

95. – Dayak woman in festive dress. She wears a beaded cap and waistcoat. The blue beads forming one of her necklaces are the most precious variety. Note the elongated earlobes and the heavy earrings, similar to Cat. No. 52 (Photograph Lucas Chin, courtesy The Sarawak Museum).

117

96. – Dayak woman with several brass earrings. She totes her child on her back in a baby-carrier. Her large hat (in her right hand) is decorated with beads and appliqué-work of fabrics (courtesy Rijksmuseum voor Volkenkunde – National Museum of Ethnology, Leiden, Archief Tillema).

discussed in Chapter 2 in the introduction, for heuristic purposes most of the cultures represented in the Barbier-Müller collection are roughly divided into cognatic types and asymmetric marriage alliance cultures. In cognatic societies, individuals trace kin relationship through both their mother's side of the family and their father's. This mode of conceptualizing the family envelops the individual in a circle of living kinfolk rather than focusing on clan genealogies going back through time to dead ancestors, which is a main feature in such asymmetric alliance cultures as the Batak of Sumatra.

As in Nias, the Batak regions, and Eastern Indonesia, the Dayak house is the best entry point to Dayak culture. Homes in the inland villages are usually built along streams or riverbanks. They are literally longhouses, often accommodating fifteen or more households. Each "hearth" group has its compartment, which opens out onto a common central space. The longhouse has a porch running the length of the structure which is used for greeting visitors and doing household tasks. Children run about, babies hang in cloth slings from the ceiling rafters, families cook their meals. The longhouse is set up on stilts for protection from enemy attack. It is usually entered by a single door, a portal which has considerable religious importance as a gateway through which spirits can pass. Fierce protective faces, some employing *aso* (dog) motifs, are carved on the door to keep evil spirits at bay. Some Dayak groups also protect their homes through curvilinear roof decorations which also make heavy use of the *aso* motif. Although the word *aso* literally means dog, *aso* figures in Dayak art are serpentlike creatures with wide-open jaws. In a detailed discussion of the importance of the design in Dayak art, Heine-Geldern asserts that the motif was probably borrowed from Late Chou styles in China (1966: 126-205).[2] The *aso* in various highly stylized forms is used on everything from baby-carrier beadwork (Figs. 96, 97, and 98) to funeral sculpture.

Protection from spirit attack is a constant theme in many spheres of Dayak art and ritual (which were not distinguished in any significant way until the recent past). Wooden statuary in the village center, war costumes, weaponry, and textiles all played on the idea of using amulet objects to cast back evil

2. Heine-Geldern 1966 puts the use of *aso* motifs into useful historical perspective; see also Chin 1980 for many illustrations of the basic *aso* shape in various Dayak wood, metal, and bead arts.

influences. Jewelry was connected with all of these arts.

The Ngaju Dayak word *hampatong* is often used by Western art historians as a general term for statue or figure (Ave 1982:97-98; Vredenbregt 1981). Carved of wood or bone, *hampatong* can take the form of humanlike spirit beings, animals, or threatening mythical creatures (Cat. Nos. 64-66). *Hampatong* come in a variety of sizes: from 2- or 3-inch-high amulets to 4- or 5-foot-high statues placed at the entryway to houses to fend off dangerous spirits. Other *hampatong* called *tajahan* (in Ngaju) are placed atop poles or pedestals and represent ancestors (see Schärer 1963). They convey messages back and forth between human and spirit realms. All *hampatong* are protective objects in one way or another. The tiny figures are sometimes suspended in groups across the back of wooden baby-carriers to help maintain the good health of the infant. These small *hampatong* are probably best seen as part of a larger set of similar amulet objects including tree roots, oddly shaped stones, magical beads, and the teeth of bears, crocodiles, and pigs (Vredenbregt 1981:32). Small *hampatong* are also attached to the special beaded tunic used by the *balian* (shaman) in exorcizing evil spirits (Vredenbregt 1981:33). The little figures not only strengthen the *balian*'s magic but represent major ideas of Dayak mythology, such as the complementarity of the Lowerworld and the Upperworld (Vredenbregt 1981:33-35). Some of the larger statues, carved to represent recognizable human figures, provide temporary homes for dead souls, or simply commemorate deceased loved ones (Ave 1982:98). War costumes bristling with the skins and fangs of fierce animals also offer protection to humans in dangerous circumstances.

Woven textiles serve similar functions and are again closely linked to jewelry. Decorated cloths of the Iban of Sarawak are famous for their busy arrangements of mythical beings. Fine *pua kumbu* textiles (Vogelsanger 1979) sometimes include whole societies of anthropomorphic supernatural figures woven into the designs. Each cloth conforms to the highly individualistic inspiration of the women who weave them. Vogelsanger reports that Iban women think that design patterns come to them directly from feminine supernatural helpers contacted in dreams. She writes:

The most frequently mentioned celestial helper is Kumang, a mythical ancestor of the Iban, wife of the cultural hero Kling

97. – Wooden baby-carrier, with beadwork decoration and different kinds of pendants, including imported Chinese bronze bells (and domestic cast models), silver coins, animal teeth, etc. The upper part of the beadwork shows two *aso* (Barbier-Müller Museum, No. 3480-A, not exhibited).

98. – Detail (drawing) of one of the two *aso* in the beadwork decoration of the baby-carrier of the previous illustration.

119

99. — Barkcloth jacket (Mahakam River area, Kalimantan) with *aso* motifs (Barbier-Müller Museum, No. 3414, not exhibited).

100. — Beadwork jacket with human figures and geometric motifs, Sarawak (Barbier-Müller Museum, No. 3462-26-A, not exhibited).

who resides in the heavenly longhouse Panggau Libau… [Kumang] is the protectoress of women and sometimes also of valiant warriors. To her domain belong, among other things, love and beauty as well as all kinds of feminine arts and skills — in short, feminine intelligence. (Vogelsanger 1979:115-116.)

The messages conveyed by dreams are concretely expressed in the *pua* textiles. A young girl just learning to weave will use one of her mother's or grandmother's old *pua* as a model or — better put — as a pattern for sparking inspiration from spirit familiars. The first several cloths the girl weaves will not be very "pótent," and if a spirit is incorporated in the design (that is, if a mythical being is represented in the weaving) an older woman will ritually help the girl control the situation by tying the dangerous part of the textile (Vogelsanger 1979:117). Women who are in unusually close contact with the female ancestral spirits are able to produce their own distinctive designs with little reliance on others' work. Jewelry and its ritual counterpart, medicines, enter at this point: "Some women protect themselves by charms (pengaroh), medicines (obat), and other magical precautions; others maintain that they do not need charms being strong 'from the heart'" (Vogelsanger 1980:118). Much Dayak jewelry should probably be seen as charms in this sense.

Once completed, the *pua* cloths serve a variety of protective functions. They are suspended from the longhouse ceiling as slings for newborns; they are placed underneath offerings and over temporary shrines; they cover a child for his first meeting with his grandmother; they wave away eclipses and cover children during name-giving and adoption ceremonies (Vogelsanger 1979:119). They are also combined with jewelry of various sorts to make up the complete ritual costume of the different ethnic societies.

Pua are also linked to death. Not only do cloths envelop the corpse for its journey to the grave, *pua* were also once used to wrap human heads taken in raids. The women would stand ready to place the newly severed heads in *pua* cloths when the longhouse men returned from a raid (Vogelsanger 1980:119). Taking life meant giving new life in many Iban religions — a theme also found in cultures of interior Kalimantan. Human fertility, agricultural wealth, and the general prosperity of the village all depended on periodic "life-giving" infusions of human heads, which would be carefully stored in ceremonial houses.

The idea that death was linked to the creation of life was joined to local gender concepts and through those back to metal and cloth. Weaving cloth was sometimes referred to as "the warpath of women" (Gittinger 1979:32, 218-219), much as newborn babies were contrasted to their symbolic opposites and symbolic equivalents, severed heads. The latter were the product of men's energies. Longhouse communities observed ritual taboos similar to those in force for childbearing when the yarns were being prepared before they were dyed (Gittinger 1979:218-219). If cloths are babies for women and heads are babies for men, then joining such separate spheres becomes a dangerous but eminently potent ritual activity. Indeed, uniting complementary opposites is a central preoccupation of Dayak religion. Gittinger (citing Schärer) reports a stunning example of this involving metal, the mythic counterpart to cloth. Metal and cloth are joined in Dayak representations of the Tree of Life, a major symbol of creation:

This symbol of totality, the cosmic whole, or the unity of upper and lower worlds, is seen in many groups, among them the Ngaju of Borneo and the Serawai and Abung of southern Sumatra. Cloths joined to a pole or spear become the sacred tree. Renewal is dependent on the ritual destruction of the tree, just as the transition represented in life-crises is a form of death and rebirth. Concerning the Ngaju, Schärer writes [1963:26], "The emblems of the supreme deities are the spear (Mahatala) and cloth (Jata). They are usually represented in their totality as the tree of life. The fruit and roots of the tree of life are the goods of the total godhead which have been bestowed upon mankind. Most of these fruits possess religious meanings and are used at every religious ceremony. These fruits are: cloth, agate beads, gold ornaments, brass ornaments, sacred jars, gongs, and weapons." In the most solemn ceremonies, the Ngaju ritually destroy the "fruits" of the tree and the tree itself so that the community can go on to a new stage of existence. (Schärer 1963:139-141; Gittinger 1979:33-35.)

This suggests that the Dayak practice of constructing elaborate ritual costumes from metal jewelry and woven textiles was not simply predicated on ideas of secular beauty but may have drawn on religious ideas of combining powerful opposites. Gittinger also notes that barkcloth and beadwork (Figs. 99 and 100) were associated with men and masculinity in some areas of Kalimantan. This would make beadwork-decorated Dayak textiles combination masculine and feminine objects, endowed with an extra measure of protective power because of it (Gittinger 1979:222; J. Maxwell 1980).

Metalworking was also associated with masculinity, but in a rather convoluted way. In Ngaju thought, Mahatala was the god of the Upperworld, a masculine domain, and Jata was the goddess of the Lowerworld, which was feminine. Their sexual union created the world and all its contents. Schärer is quoted above as noting that the emblems of Mahatala and Jata were the spear and the cloth, but Mahatala is also associated with a golden dagger, another clear phallic symbol, while feminine mythical characters are often associated with golden cages (Vredenbregt 1981:26). The two spheres and their two gods are also portrayed as hornbills and water snakes, and in addition the Upperworld was associated with the sun, skulls, and flagpoles, while the moon, flags, and other reptiles such as crocodiles were associated with the female Lowerworld.

KALIMANTAN or SARAWAK
Earrings, brass. Cat. No. 49. Description p. 324.

KALIMANTAN or SARAWAK
Earrings, brass. Cat. No. 51. Description p. 324.

125

KALIMANTAN or SARAWAK
Necklace, wickerwork, etc. Cat. No. 55. Description p. 324.

CENTRAL SULAWESI

Jagged, four-armed Sulawesi (formerly Celebes) is located at the center of a circle of Indonesian and Philippine islands, a geographical fact that helps explain its cultural ties to these neighboring regions. To Sulawesi's north is Mindanao, the ethnically complex southernmost Philippine island. To the west is Kalimantan with its Dayak peoples and coastal trade states, and to the south lie the Lesser Sunda islands of Lombok, Sumbawa, Flores, Lembata, Alor, Savu, Timor, and Roti. To Sulawesi's east lies the crowded Moluccan island group, a center of early Muslim and Christian missionary activity. The Mollucas also have ties to Melanesia.

Sulawesi itself (Map 6) is made up of a number of ethnic groups which all have been shaped to a greater or lesser degree by contact with the surrounding societies, by the Dutch colonial state before 1945,[1] and by the Indonesian national government. There are the Muslim Bugis and Makassarese state societies near Ujung Pandang; these were great mercantile centers whose influence extended far into Eastern Indonesia and up the east coast of Kalimantan. Today Bugis remain successful traders and entrepreneurs in Sulawesi, Kalimantan, and East Java. Sulawesi also includes the Sa'dan Toraja and related societies near Rante Pao in the interior mountains north of Ujung Pandang. In colonial times before 1945 these were highland chiefdom societies

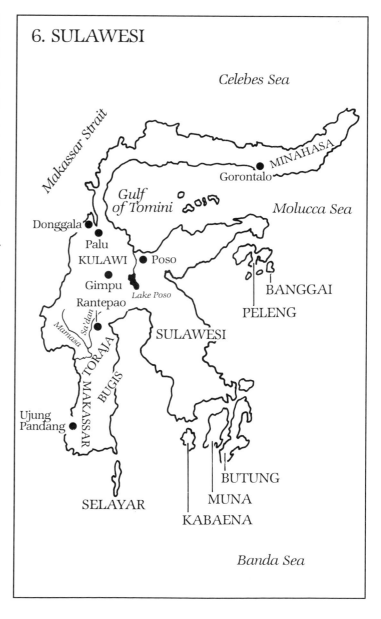

6. SULAWESI

Celebes Sea

Makassar Strait

MINAHASA

Gorontalo

Gulf of Tomini

Molucca Sea

Donggala

Palu

KULAWI

Poso

Gimpu

Lake Poso

BANGGAI

PELENG

Rantepao

Mamasa

Sadan

SULAWESI

TORAJA

BUGIS

Ujung Pandang

MAKASSAR

BUTUNG

MUNA

KABAENA

SELAYAR

Banda Sea

---

1. Barbara Harvey (1974) provides historical detail for the post-Revolution period.

◄ Piece of ceremonial cloth. Painted barkcloth (vegetal colors). Lake Poso region (?). Central Sulawesi, Indonesia. Detail. (Barbier-Müller Museum, No. 3620-10, not exhibited).

101. — The great *adat* houses (*tongkonan*) of the Sa'dan Toraja are carefully repaired or when too damaged, reconstructed. Here, a detail of the construction: showing a buffalo head fixed on the main facade (Photograph Jean-Luc André, 1979).

102. — Two women in Gintu Village. Their beautiful jackets adopt the form of the old *tapa* cloths of the same region; see Grubauer 1913, fig. 300 (Photograph Evelyne Robin, 1984).

somewhat similar to Sumatra's Batak. The Sa'dan Toraja have been discovered of late by the international tourist market and the European art world, and their impressive carved wood *adat* houses (Fig. 101) and village rituals are taking on new life as tourist attractions (Volkmann 1982) and "primitive art."

Farther to the north near the Gulf of Palu and the Gulf of Tomini are the so-called West Toraja societies. This particular ethnic designation, favored by some Western scholars such as Kruyt and Adriani, is probably inappropriate. These societies, many of them fairly centralized small states (sort of miniature Bugis societies), are more properly considered cultures in their own right and not derivative, outlying Toraja societies (Pakan 1977; Masyhuda 1971). Beyond these cultures Sulawesi also includes the Gorontalo and Minahassa peoples on the island's long northern arm stretching toward the Philippines. Minahassa was strongly influenced by Christian missions in the colonial period and remains one of Sulawesi's more outwardly directed societies today (Fig. 102).

Finally, there are a number of small, tribelike, relatively isolated, and somewhat egalitarian societies scattered through the mountains in the center of the island. These societies, which include such groups as the Wana, Lo'on, Sea-Sea, Kahumanoan, Lavje, and Daya, are designated as *suku terasing*, or isolated ethnic groups, by the Indonesian government. They are Sulawesi's last unconverted groups — unconverted in large part to Islam, Christianity, or to Indonesian nationalism. Even these relative xenophobes, however, have seen their cultures shaped and reshaped through interaction with nearby Sulawesi societies and faraway foreigner groups such as the Indonesian state and Christian missionary groups. Cultural interaction, in fact, is a keynote of Sulawesi's social and artistic history.

The jewelry in the Barbier-Müller collection is drawn from the chiefdoms and petty states that clustered around the coastal towns of Palu and Poso near the center of the island and extended back into the interior mountains in the Kulawi region (a few Sa'dan Toraja pieces are also included). In this ethnically and politically diverse region, similar ornaments were often used by quite different cultures and were given different names and uses. The *taiganja* pendants, the snake-shaped copper *sanggori* head ornaments, and the small brass *tau-tau* figurines in the collection were also often mixed among jewelry traditions that used bead ornaments, decorated barkcloth costumes, holy "scrolls," and chiefly regalia resembling that of coastal states like Bugis. Figure 9, for instance, shows a young Kulawi woman dressed up in the village festive costume, a style that has obvious ties to the coastal court centers of the island. The shape of her many-tiered skirt, however, and the use of *taiganja* pendants in the village link Kulawi to societies in the interior highlands. A brief ethnography of Sulawesi's main types of cultures will show why simple labels such as West Toraja cannot accurately pinpoint the social origins of the jewelry in the exhibit.

Ethnic Groups in Sulawesi

The coastal court states such as Bugis were highly successful mercantile powers whose trade boats sailed far into Eastern Indonesia, as well as Java, Bali, and Kalimantan. Ruling families legitimated their power position by claiming their blood was purer and whiter than that of commoners (Errington 1983). Court centers maintained arts of ornate wood carving (incorporating Islamic styles) and brass-work (rice trays, betel boxes, various ceremonial utensils and weapons). Textiles tended to be brocades and silks rather than the rougher woven cloths of the highland societies.

A second type of Sulawesi culture might be termed the inland chiefdoms. This group is well represented by the Sa'dan Toraja (Nooy-Palm 1979; Volkmann 1982; Zerner 1981; Crystal 1974; Crystal and Yamashita 1982). Toraja today is one of Indonesia's ethnic minority societies created in interaction with larger state societies. Through the Dutch period, though, and indeed partly as a result of the colonial presence, the Toraja heartland was an area of sturdy, fiercely competitive village leagues. Society was divided into three main classes: the nobility, the free commoners, and the slaves. The aristocrats, called *anak patalo* (Nooy-Palm 1979:44), claimed ancestral ownership of the paddy rice fields, the villages, the great wooden houses, and the *adat* of the region. Their title to all this was validated by myth. A symbolism of metalworking, it happens, was a crucial element of these origin myths. As noted in the chapter on "Jewelry and the Supernatural," precious metals were important signs of sacredness and high social rank in Tana Toraja

(Zerner 1981). Nooy-Palm relates a representative version of an origin myth setting out the aboriginal separation of free men from slaves in her book *The Sa'dan Toraja*. This myth, called the Passomba Tedong, is taken from a chant recited at a buffalo sacrifice at a mortuary feast:

Pande Nunu (the skillful observer) married Kandaibubun of Illin. This woman, also called Tumba Bollan, wore a bracelet made of clay, and an anklet fashioned of an alloy, probably not including gold, silver or brass; these ornaments betray that she was a slave. Female slaves were not permitted to wear ornaments of such precious metals. Pande Nunu consumed the left-overs from his brothers' meal, an act further associated with the class of the unfree. Two children were born to this pair, two sons, Datu Bakka' and Pong Malaleong (though datu means "lord", the little datu is not associated with nobility). When the "House of Iron" in the upperworld has been completed... and the buffalo for the primeval merok-celebration was about to be sacrificed, fire-wood had to be chopped, and branches which would cast dense shadows needed to be inserted in the earth. These tasks were assigned to Datu Bakka' and his brother, but they refused. What is more, they wanted to marry with women from the group which they considered as their equals; because, they replied to their brothers: weren't they all one big family, Datu Bakka' and Pong Malaleong and the rest who took part in the feast? Hadn't all their fathers originated from the cinders of Puang Matua's forge? The others conceded this point, but confronted the pair with the fact that their father had taken a wife from Illin who wore a bracelet of clay (in traditional Toraja society the children of the marriage between a free man and a slave, usually belonged to the class of their mother).

The two objectors did not want to be treated like buffalos that had to work on the sawah [rice paddies]. Then, from the center of the firmament, it was solemnly declared that they should give in; nevertheless, they remained headstrong, even after divine judgement was delivered through means of a cock-fight. Only after they were beaten in a fight did they yield. There were no women, however, who were willing to become their wives. Puang Matua then sculpted a doll from clay, calling it potto Kalembang. The Prince of the Wind blew life into the image, however, only after he had been trapped in a net and persuaded by Puang Matua. Since then Datu Bakka' and Pong Malaleong laboured in the sawah just like a buffalo; they bent under the yoke, even as animals. And in this way the division into classes became established almost immediately after the creation. (Nooy-Palm 1979:43-44.)

Aristocracy was associated with art in another way. As in Nias, Sumba, Flores, and the Batak areas, rivalry among chiefs and among families was played out through the construction of great *adat* houses, the accumulation of prestige items, and the erection of funeral monuments to ancestors. In the case of Sa'dan Toraja, naturalistic wooden sculp-

103. – Wooden ancestor sculptures *(tau-tau)* placed in galleries carved in high cliffs (Photograph Evelyne Robin, 1984).

104. – Other ancestor sculptures in the Toraja region (Photograph Jean-Luc André, 1979).

tures dressed in clothes representing deceased people (Figs. 103 and 104) were placed in little galleries in the cliffs, behind lattice porches where they could look out at their living descendants.[2] Nobles also engaged in extraordinary competitive feasts, which involved the slaughter of dozens and sometimes even hundreds of water buffalo and the distribution of the meat to all the participants (Nooy-Palm 1979). These rituals sometimes had an almost potlatch intensity to them.

The Sa'dan Toraja arts focused on similar themes of warlike competition, nobility versus commoners, and life versus death. The last theme was particularly important, for the Toraja world was divided into the two realms of life and death, with a separate group of priests handling the ritual activities of each sphere. Many specific artistic motifs evoked ideas of highborn status and war. Buffalo horns, omnipresent in Toraja village art, represent a blend of ideas – prosperity, success, luck, nobility, wealth. Entire stacks of buffalo horns adorned the *tongkonan,* the Toraja *adat* houses.[3] This was a sign that many feasts had been held there by wealthy owners. Buffalo horns were also important components of Sa'dan "war suits" *(baju pa'barani)*. At one level these costumes provided soldiers with actual armor (the vest is reinforced with shell disks). At another, the ensemble afforded the warrior a number of magical amulets for repelling the mystical threats of enemy soldiers and spellcasters: the hat is topped with buffalo horns (Fig. 105), symbolizing luck and success; the boar-tusk necklace plays on themes of fierceness; the shells on the jacket have magical protective qualities.

A third type of Sulawesi culture is represented by the *suku terasing* (isolated societies), the politically uncentralized and vulnerable ethnic groups in the interior mountain forests. As slash-and-burn farmers dependent as well on hunting and gathering forest game and plants, these societies have neither the economic surplus nor the political organization to support elaborate art systems like those found among the prosperous Sa'dan Toraja. The Wana have recently been described by anthropologist Jane M. Atkinson (1983); the culture is also the subject of a long section in the *Monografi Daerah Sulawesi*

2. See the discussion and photographs of these statues in *Art of the Archaic Indonesians*, pp. 78–92.

3. Nooy-Palm 1979 includes a great deal of information about the construction and symbolism of these houses.

Tengah published by the national government (Masyhuda 1977). This booklet, it should be noted, is mainly concerned with describing the interior hill societies so that they might be swiftly brought into the Indonesian national pattern of settled village life, school attendance, rice cultivation, and eventual monotheism. Drawing on these sources, one can take the Wana as an example of the upland cultures.

There are only about five thousand Wana today (Atkinson 1983:686), living in small, mobile villages. Wana communities are composed of households, called *rapu* (hearth) or *tina* (woman); these generally consist of a conjugal couple and their young and old dependents. A new couple is married by the village leaders, who preside over what seems to be a fairly balanced exchange of marriage gifts (brass trays, china plates, and cloth). These items indicate the Wana's ties to lowland, more centralized Sulawesi societies. Atkinson notes in fact that this interaction is "creating culture" for the Wana today, especially as they discover their fragile status as a small ethnic minority in the Indonesian nation. Atkinson asserts that the Wana are culling through their spiritual beliefs and shamanistic rituals for cultural materials from which to construct a religion (an *agama,* in Indonesian) that "looks enough like a religion" to satisfy the national government. Indonesian officials tend to identify civilization, national loyalties, and forward-thinking ways with belief in a monotheistic religion.

Ornaments and Heirlooms in Sulawesi

Few things in Sulawesi are culturally simple, and the provenance of the metal ornaments in the Barbier-Müller collection certainly bears this out. Their origin lies somewhere between the three types of Sulawesi cultures just described. The *taiganja* pendants (Fig. 106), the small (brass) human figurines, and the serpent-shaped *sanggori* (Figs. 107 and 108) came from cultures in Central Sulawesi that combined elements of the inland chiefdoms and the coastal Islamic states. As noted, this range of jewelry is identified in some accounts as West Torajan. Bodrogi notes that the region around Palu and Kulawi was a regional center for metalworking. Coppersmithing was especially important, and artisans provided bells, pendants, *sanggori* coils, and human and animal figurines to neighboring societies. Bodrogi writes that little human figures in male and female pairs were sometimes given to newlywed couples, along with copper figurines of

105. – Mamasa Toraja men with war suits and weapons. Sacred textiles are displayed on the helmet, adorned with metal horns (courtesy Kon. Inst. v/d Tropen, Amsterdam, photograph taken in 1937).

106. — *Taiganja* pendants were worn in different ways, here on the cap of a nobleman (courtesy Kon. Inst. v/d Tropen, Amsterdam).

107. — *Sanggori* were apparently also used as ornaments for funeral puppets (from Grubauer 1913, fig. 235).

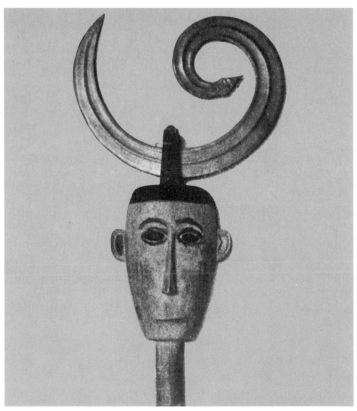

water buffalo. The married pair would carry these charms into their new house with them, as aids to fertility and prosperity. Bodrogi also notes that the *taiganja* ornaments were worn around the neck as pendants, or suspended in front of the genitals, as protective amulets for children (Bodrogi 1972:56).

Apparently Bodrogi tapped into only one of several cultural areas using these ornaments. The *taiganja*, for instance, are important parts of the ceremonial house treasures of the aristocratic class of Palu. In that coastal town, the center of an Islamized trading region, the ornaments have several other uses beyond the ones noted by Bodrogi. It is more accurate to see the *taiganja*, the figurines, and the *sanggori* coils as artifacts used in both coastal and inland regions. The ways these three pieces are used in the culturally heterogeneous region stretching from Palu back into the mountains near Kulawi illustrate their complex origins and local interpretations.

Before national independence Palu exemplified the type of backwater court culture found in coastal trading posts in many islands in the Indonesian archipelago. The Donggala-Palu area was introduced to Islam in stages, starting possibly as early as the seventeenth century (Masyhuda 1977:11). Contact with Ternate, Islamized since the late 1400s, and Makassar, introduced to the religion in 1603, predated large-scale conversions in the Palu region. According to Kruyt and some local historians (Masyhuda 1977:10-13), a charismatic religious teacher from Minangkabau named Datok Karama brought Islam to Palu. By about 1900 the Dutch had succeeded in eliminating Portuguese influence in Central Sulawesi, and they set about supporting local *rajas* and sending military units into the uplands to pacify the villages there (Masyhuda 1977). On the eve of the Japanese occupation of Indonesia in World War II the Palu *rajas* had considerable wealth and power and often lived in spacious Malay-style porched houses filled with heirlooms. Such house treasures, constituting a large part of Palu art, were the usual assembly of brass serving platters, filigreed betel tins, bridal regalia, and inherited trade cloths found in many of the minor Islamized Indonesian *entrepôts*. An important sign of royalty was the *mbesa* cloths, which were dark cotton textiles imported from Bali and possibly elsewhere in Indonesia. Coming from faraway courts, these cloths carried an aura of importance and regal authority (Masyhuda 1982-3:69-71).

Jewelry added some distinctive Sulawesi elements to the generally predictable pattern of Islamic coastal art. The ornately curvilinear *taiganja* pendants, which appear in a multitude of stylistic variants (see Cat. Nos. 73-77), link Palu societies to cultures in the interior mountains. At the same time the *taiganja* form bonds between this local region and island Southeast Asian art as a whole, for the pendant's open oval shape, with a decorated channel up the middle, is one of the basic jewelry shapes of the entire culture area (see Fig. 44 in "Looking at Jewelry").

Taiganja apparently had multiple uses in Palu, or at least multiple interpretations. Some sources indicate that these pendants were status objects used by the nobility, whereas other sources associated them with the free commoners. The excellent new provincial museum in Palu, part of the national system of local ethnographic museums, includes a large selection of copper *taiganja* and specifies several functions for these pieces. Bodrogi's suggestions in the quotation above, that these ornaments were used as amulets suspended in front of children's genitals, is not mentioned. Rather, the museum describes the *taiganja* as ritual objects used in the early stages of marriage arrangements to *membuka kata* — to open negotiations for the various gift-giving activities which accompany the union. In other words, *taiganja* were conciliatory gifts exchanged to pave the way to a successful marriage and a successful alliance between families. The museum further specifies that it was the commoner class, called the *ada sasio* (*sio*=nine), that used the *taiganja* in this way, while the aristocratic families used the human figurines for the same prenuptial purposes. A second ritual use for *taiganja* in Palu involved rites of passage for adolescent girls: during their *mokesa* ceremony, which ushered them from childhood into adulthood, the girls would wear three *taiganja* suspended from a headband. One pendant would be worn on the left side, one on the right, and one would be positioned at the back (Masyhuda 1982-3:39-49).

Another use and another social location for the ornaments were offered during a 1983 interview with a *raja*'s family in a village within the confines of the city of Palu. A motley collection of the last *raja*'s descendants lives in the house, presided over by the *raja*'s widow. The family has no jural authority today under the national government and appar-ently suffered from the taint of feudalism in early national times. That is, they were branded "feodal" (feudal in Indonesian usage) by their former follow-ers in the early days of independence. Possibly as a result of this and their much-reduced political circumstances, today they keep a low profile in Palu and only call the very occasional *adat* ritual. At those rare ceremonies, though, the family arrays itself in its extraordinary heirloom jewelry. The house treas-ure, which is kept in a wooden box in an inner room, includes a number of brass *taiganja* like those in the Barbier-Müller collection. In addition, there are at least six splendid solid gold *taiganja*, once part of the widow's bridewealth payments. Women in wealthy families sometimes get *taiganja* like these from their mothers to wear at rituals. The women of this family either wear the pendants singly on a plain gold chain or wear all six pendants hooked onto a sumptuous gold necklace made of a thick chain and big gold Dutch coins. This arrangement is called *nagalo-ngalu suka-suka*. Sometimes the *taiganja* are worn on gold filigree necklaces.

The old widow and her relatives said that women and little girls wear these *taiganja* necklaces at *adat* rituals; the ornaments are never worn by men. The group also asserted that the jewelry pieces are no longer made, although up to about a hundred years ago Palu goldsmiths produced them. The old woman noted with some consternation that a few years ago she wanted a miniature *taiganja* made from some old gold she was willing to have reshaped. She tried commissioning a Chinese-Indo-nesian goldsmith in town to make the ornament for her, but he refused, saying that he could not get all the curled designs right. So, she said, these pieces are now just "stored things" (*simpanan*, in Indonesian).

In this village within Palu, the *taiganja* and other house treasures have only recently started to come out of their storage boxes into public view. The widow and her relatives feel that the ornaments have special powers to bring disasters if they are mishandled, sold outside the family, or used without the proper *adat* rituals. Another *raja*'s widow in the area is reported to have a solid-gold figurine of a cat which she refuses to bring into the sunlight (much less sell) for fear that some natural disaster such as a great thunderstorm would befall her village.

The *taiganja* have yet another interpretation in the

108. – Man dressed for a funeral ceremony wears a *sanggori* on head (from Kaudern 1929, fig. 118).

upland village of Kulawi, several hours away from Palu by bus. Before national times Kulawi society had five social classes: the aristocrats, religious specialists, officials working for the *raja*, the general populace, and war captives and slaves (Soelarto and Albiladiyah n.d.:10-11). The aristocracy was strongly influenced by coastal styles of house architecture and ceremonial dress, as shown above in Fig. 102. Shamanism, sometimes involving men dressed as women, was the centerpiece of Kulawi religion, although today the Salvation Army has made a significant number of converts. That missionary group is critical of Kulawi's practice of gift exchanges at weddings and of communal feasts at funerals, but some aspects of Kulawi *adat* ritual have survived. Several days before my short stay in Kulawi there was a large *adat* feast celebrating a wedding, where *taiganja* were reportedly worn by some of the women in attendance. The ornaments, which are worn suspended individually from simple necklaces, are supposed to be used only by the noble class. A woman inherits these pendants from her parents, and, according to my sources (a Christian school teacher, her adolescent children, and her sister) *taiganja* are not part of Kulawi bridewealth payments. Those normally include cash, a large copper tray called a *dulang*, water buffalo, and *mbesa* cloths. Note that in Kulawi cloth gifts are given as exchange goods by the man's family to the bride's family. This is in contrast to the Batak and Sumba practice of using textiles as gifts from the bride's family to the groom's family (countergifts to metal objects).

My informants in the Palu village and Kulawi did not hazard any interpretations of the various designs on the *taiganja*. The Palu museum staff was more ambitious. In the catalogue notes for a typical specimen the authors attach considerable metaphorical meaning to the oval shape of the ornaments and to its designs:

Taiganja, no. 43. Bronze. Palu. 4.2 x 4.3 cm.
The middle section is rounded, the front and back sides are identical, the left side and the right side are divided in two by a narrow channel running between them, which widens out at the top, forming the shape of the female genitals. On the edges of the narrow channel are decorations like beads in four rows, while the wider part of the channel opening at the top is decorated on its edge by rice grain designs. The decoration on the side has a water buffalo horn motif, with three of them, while on the upper middle section there is a gallows, and one the lower part the motif takes the shape of the aerial roots of a tree. The decorative motifs found on this taiganja symbolize:

fertility, permanence, and resolute determination in upholding adat rules. (Masyhuda 1982-3:41, my translation.)

None of my informants offered or confirmed the sexual-imagery interpretation.

The pairs of male and female figurines (sometimes called *tau-tau*) are variously identified as marriage negotiation gifts, lucky amulets for warding off misfortune, and fertility objects that newlywed couples carry into their marriage, as noted before. In brief interviews in Kulawi, the *tau-tau* were not recognized. The Palu Museum's catalogue stresses the figurines' role in marriage negotiations among the upper class, but no mention is made of the use of these objects as "fertility-enhancers" brought into newlyweds' homes. The catalogue identifies a typical male and female pair as follows:

Bronze Statue, no. 18. Bronze, From Marawola County, Donggala. 8.2 cm high.
This statue of a human is made from bronze that has been worked by a smith. [The figure] is standing upright, its head is oval-shaped and pointed at the top, its ears are wide and placed a bit low even with the chin. At the temples are found a pair of horns. The arms dangle straight down, and there are only four fingers and four toes.

This statue was found in Marawola County, in the Subdistrict of Donggala. The residents call this statue "sunia" because it is a male. It is used as a gift object of great value during the time when the bridewealth is brought to the bride's family, when [the male statue] is given in a pair with a statue of a woman (*jamboko*). Besides this it is also considered a magic, lucky thing that can cast back evil influences.

This statue represents a prehistoric relic that shows that there was ancestor worship, and also symbolizes the idea of casting off evil.

The female partner:

This statue of a naked human is made of bronze that has been worked by a smith. Its left ear is wider than the right ear. The hands and feet face outward with five fingers and toes, and the upper part of the arm is a bit raised.

This statue was found in Marawola County, in Donggala Subdistrict. Residents name it "*Ntoedi*" because it is of the female sex, and it represents the pair partner of the sunia statue. It is a very valuable gift object used when presenting the bridewealth payments, and besides this it is considered a magic lucky object that casts back evil influences… (Masyhuda 1982-3:17-18, my translation.)

The *sanggori* or coiled head ornament seems to have been used in a fairly large area of central and northern Sulawesi. Bodrogi reports finding the piece far up on the northern peninsula: "A peculiar copper ornament is the sanggori, which can be found practically everywhere in Central Celebes [Sulawesi], and which occurs also with the Loinang group and the Minahassas" (1972:56). He identifies the ornament as a sort of magical armor against harmful mystical forces, signifying heroism in war. The ornament has the shape of a snake (sometimes with well-defined eyes), but the meaning of this is unclear. Bodrogi writes that the piece had several functions: for magical healing, amulet protection in battles, and exorcism of demons. It was also sometimes attached to the top of the *pemia*, a funeral mask that had the shape of a human face. When used this way and by people in ritual festivities, the *sanggori* was worn pointing upward to the right (1972:56-57). It may also have been worn by warriors to cast back the harmful forces of their enemies through its powerful shine: the coil was polished until it glinted brightly in the sun, and this gleam would repel the magical forces of enemies or simply blind the rival soldiers. Sometimes the *sanggori* was worn tilted backward at an angle.

In 1983 interviews in Kulawi, the piece was readily identified as a head ornament for both men and women. The ornament's local name was, however, not *sanggori* but *balalungki*. It was reserved for high aristocrats and worn during ritual dances. The Palu catalogue identifies a similar ornament from Kulawi somewhat differently, using the term *sanggori*. This source notes the ornament's powerful shine.

No. 81. Sanggori. Bronze, Kulawi, Donggala Subdistrict. 23 x 17.5 cm.

This sanggori is made of bronze in the shape of a tail that coils around, resembling a spiral, with no decoration. On the inside bend are found three small holes, places for inserting a string to hold it with at the inside point, at its two pointed ends.

The technique for making it is to stamp it out. It is used as a shield (a headdress), and beyond that is can be used as… something that blinds the enemies' looks in bright daylight because it is always used in a shiny state. It is placed on the head when going to war, or in ceremonies to welcome visitors. (Masyhuda 1982-3:75, my translation.)

In other Central Sulawesi regions, the *taiganja*, the little human *tau-tau*, and the *sanggori* almost certainly have other interpretations and other uses that were not uncovered in the field research for this catalogue.

CENTRAL SULAWESI
Head ornament, brass. Cat. No. 70. Description p. 325.

CENTRAL SULAWESI
Pendant, brass. Cat. No. 74. Description pp. 325–326.

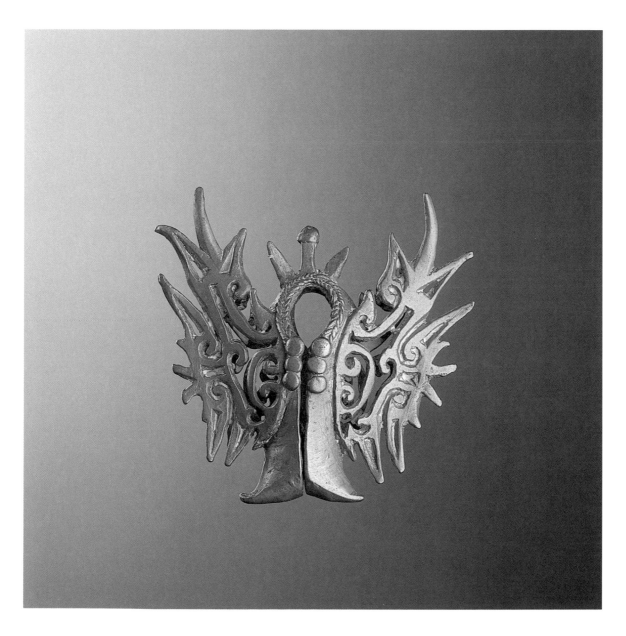

CENTRAL SULAWESI
Figurines, brass. Cat. No. 80. Description p. 326.

FLORES

Flores jewelry, like Sumbanese self-decoration, has a good deal of ebullience and extravagance to it. The ornaments worn by the old Lio noblewoman in Fig. 109 illustrate this well. She is wearing a spectacular if rather whimsical gold necklace festooned with three-dimensional water buffalo and chicken figurines. As if this were not enough, the heavy front part of the necklace is balanced by a sizable gold chain suspended down her back. Flores aristocrats

also outfitted themselves with masses of gold conch shells and gold feathers, perhaps indicative of a relatively prosperous late colonial era that allowed them to indulge in gold versions of older shell and feather finery. Even today Flores noble families have unusually well-stocked house treasures, although the descendants of the old *rajas* often live in reduced circumstances. These treasures include large numbers of gold earrings, chains, and figurine pendants augmented by etched ivory bracelets and stacks of the island's distinctive somber-colored textiles.

In their use, religious significance, and artistic ties to

◄ Woman's ceremonial sarong (*lawo butu*). Warp ikat, decorated with beads and shells. Cotton. Ngada. Central Flores, Indonesia. Detail. (Barbier-Mueller Museum, No. 3535-21-E, not exhibited).

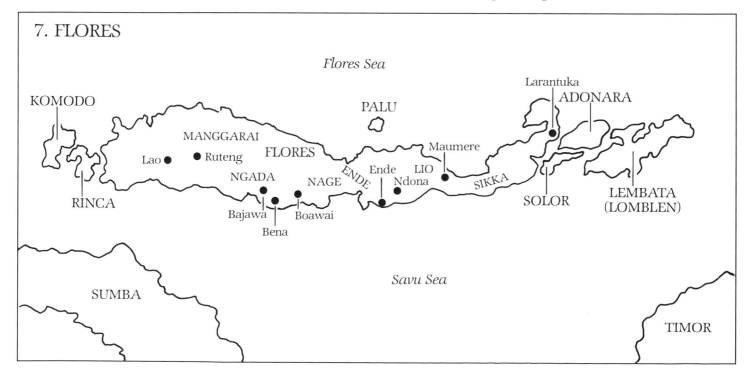

7. FLORES

Flores Sea

KOMODO

MANGGARAI

Lao ● ● Ruteng FLORES

NGADA NAGE

Bajawa Boawai

Bena

RINCA

PALU

Larantuka
ADONARA

Maumere

Ende LIO
Ndona

ENDE

SIKKA

SOLOR

LEMBATA
(LOMBLEN)

SUMBA

Savu Sea

TIMOR

109. — Lio noblewoman in a village near Ndona, Central Flores. See also Fig. 49 of this woman with her husband — (Photograph Susan Rodgers, 1983).

other cultures in the region, these heirlooms recall the aristocratic arts of Sumba, Timor, Roti, and Savu. There is, moreover, a direct historical link between Flores jewelry smithing and the cultures of Roti and Savu, for itinerant goldsmiths from those two impoverished and arid islands migrated to South and Central Flores to practice their trade and supplement the meager economic opportunities at home. As we shall see in the chapters on Sumba and Timor jewelry, these Rotinese and Savunese goldsmiths introduced and promoted a number of common jewelry shapes in various islands in Eastern Indonesia.

Flores art has many local styles. In fact, villagers in one ethnic homeland will not at times recognize the textiles or jewelry of a neighboring society not more than 50 kilometers distant.[1] In my 1983 interviews in the Nage region of Central Flores, for instance, jewelry used in nearby Lio was unfamiliar to Nage villagers. Along with this pattern, however, one finds the common island Southeast Asian practice of trade in prestige goods among ethnic cultures and between coastal mercantile peoples and highland chiefdoms. This makes it almost impossible to pinpoint the ethnic area of a particular piece of jewelry, for many ornaments are known over a wide region. And, as is often the case in Eastern Indonesia, Flores' ethnic societies are linked in a complex web of trade relationships involving jewelry, textiles, ivory, raw materials, foodstuffs, livestock, and marriage alliance. These networks sometimes extend beyond Flores proper to the small islands to the east in the Lamalohot Archipelago.

Flores is a long, narrow island with exceptionally rough mountain terrain and few passable roads. Its geography helps explain its ethnic fragmentation (Map 7). From west to east the island and the Lamalohot Archipelago that extends beyond it include some twelve ethnic societies: Manggarai, Ngada, Nage, Keo, Ende, Lio, Sikka, and the Solor, Adonara, Lembata (Lomblen), Pantar, and Alor islanders (Maxwell 1981). Even today, communication among these ethnic groups is hampered by geographic barriers and by such social factors as distrust and fear of witchcraft.

Flores exhibits a rich social diversity reminiscent of the ethnic situation on the much larger island of

---

1. Needham 1980 discusses a similar situation of ethnic fragmentation in West Sumba. Flores is apparently open to the same sort of analysis.

Sumatra. There, the Batak cultures with their patrilineal clans, asymmetrical marriage alliance, and ceremonial leagues border the matrilineal Minangkabau with their much more centralized polities. In Flores, the forms of social organization also run the gamut. We can look briefly at several Flores cultures as background to discussions of their jewelry traditions, again moving from west to east. Several common themes characterize Flores cultures and their styles of body adornment. Aristocratic status is put on public display through spectacular decorations for the upper part of the body. Beyond this, much jewelry is part of war costumes, which started to change into mere war *dance* costumes under the Dutch pacification efforts early in the twentieth century. Some ornaments, thought to be invested with cosmic powers, serve as signs that the *rajas* are similarly empowered. When used as part of entire ritual costumes, Flores jewelry is sometimes employed in trance ceremonies to make contact with ancestor spirits. And, to no one's surprise, precious ornaments made of gold and ivory are important exchange goods in marriage alliance transactions.

Society and Exchange

Manggarai culture (Fig. 110), which extends over roughly a third of the island, traditionally recognized three main social classes. There were the *kraeng,* or members of dominant lineages; the *ata leke,* or commoners (peasant farmers, artisans, laborers); and the slaves, who were generally war captives, debtors, or persons expelled from their home villages. In this area and the rest of Flores, slavery was abolished under Dutch colonial rule, which was not firm in this region until the first decade of this century (Gordon 1980:49). Manggarai's three-part social order is of course a common one in Indonesian cultures outside Java and Bali, and patrilineal clanship and the practice of asymmetrical cross-cousin marriage among certain noble lineages (Lebar 1972:82) also link Manggarai to a mainstream outer-island type of culture. However, Manggarai's political history distinguishes it from other Flores societies to some extent. In a 1983 interview in Kampung Ruteng outside Manggarai's administrative town of the same name, a group of old men and women insisted repeatedly that their art forms all came "from outside," "from Bima and Goa." Historical and anthropological accounts bear this out (Lebar 1972; Gordon 1980). In his summary

110. – The ethnic societies of Flores are linked via strong megalithic traditions. Here, four ancestor statues on a pile of stones. In the middle, the sacred tree as a forked post. West Flores, Manggarai, Lao village. (courtesy Kon. Inst. v/d Tropen, Amsterdam; photograph taken in 1939).

111. – Megalithic monuments (some erected recently) in the village of Bena, Ngada, Central Flores (Photograph Jana Ansermet, 1980).

112. – The two structure with central pillars are altars for the masculine ancestors. Village of Bena, Ngada (Photograph Jana Ansermet, 1980).

113. – The two rectangular miniature houses behind the small megalithic complex (a tomb) are altars for feminine ancestors, same village (Photograph Jana Ansermet, 1980).

of Manggarai history, Indonesian anthropologist Koentjaraningrat notes the impact of Sumbawa's expanding kingdoms on the little polities of traditional Flores.

The Manggarai seem to have developed a political organization beyond the village level prior to the early seventeenth century, when the Bimanese kingdom of East Sumbawa dominated various coastal areas in the northern and southern parts of West Flores. The early indigenous Manggarai principality had its center in today's Cibal, at the center of West Flores. The major explosion of the Tambora volcano on East Sumbawa in 1815 greatly weakened Bima, and the Manggarai revolted. Supported initially by the Dutch, the Bimanese regained control over Manggarai in 1851; however, in 1907 the Dutch established their colonial administration in West Flores, and the Bimanese finally gave up control over Manggarai in 1929.... In 1917, Catholic missionaries began to survey the area, and missionary activity subsequently itensified. (Koentjaraningrat 1972 : 81.)

Manggarai today is administered as a *kabupaten* (subprovince) of the Indonesian nation.

Ngada culture near Bajawa has a similar social class system, with nobles, commoners, and slave descendants (Fig. 111). However, Ngada kinship sets the culture apart from the Manggarai. Descent in Ngada is cognatic, and relationship is recognized through both the mother's and father's sides of the family. In the Bajawa region there are two types of marriage, called *pasa* and *dii sao* (1983 fieldnotes). In the first sort of marriage the husband's family succeeds in paying the entire brideprice, which generally consists of cash, buffalo, horses, and jewelry (it once included slaves). After the wealth is transferred, any children of the marriage are claimed by the husband's clan. The bride moves in with her husband near his parental home and is urged to sever all ties to her own family. In *dii sao* marriage, by contrast, the man's family finds that it takes them years to pay the negotiated bridewealth. The new family lives near the bride's original home, and her clan claims their children. As we shall see shortly, this complex mode of figuring descent reverberates through Ngada art, cosmological belief, and the layout of villages (Figs. 112 and 113).

Nage culture of the east of Ngada has a similar political structure but a different kinship system, one that resembles the Manggarai pattern. The ideal Nage marriage unites matrilateral cross-cousins, but the Roman Catholic church is reportedly waging a strong campaign to forbid marriages involving descendants of a brother-sister pair any closer than five generations in the past (1983 fieldnotes). The village of Boawai, celebrated in art history circles (Barbier 1983; De Hoog 1982), illustrates Nage's main cultural patterns (the village is discussed briefly in the introductory chapter "Looking at Jewelry"). With an active volcano as a backdrop, this high village near the modern small town also called Boawai is arranged in a circular pattern of houses all facing a *peo*, or forked stake. This was part of an ancestor shrine, and water buffalo were tethered there before being sacrificed in rituals. On the periphery of the village is a male ceremonial house, for storing buffalo horns after sacrifices commemorating ancestors. Near this structure is a *ja heda*, a wooden sculpture of a stylized horse and male rider (Fig. 37). Beyond this, still farther from the village center, is a smaller ceremonial house identified with femininity and marked by a riderless equestrian statue, smaller than the masculine one. As in Ngada, Nage art frequently plays on the themes of the opposing but complementary masculine and feminine spheres. This theme in fact draws the various Nage arts into a coherent conceptual whole.

The next ethnic complex centers on the port town of Ende, a gateway to Sumba a short distance to the southwest and to Roti, Savu, and Timor to the southeast. Ende's culture is somewhat different from that of Lio, an ethnic group centered in the highlands with a few additional coastal villages such as Walotopo. Ende is a Muslim trading town with a *pasisir* (coastal) culture similar to that of Palu, Padang, Ujung Pandang, and any number of other seacoast towns throughout Indonesia. Writing in 1955 Kennedy noted that Ende people are fairly parochial and preoccupied with local *adat* despite the presence of a modern bureaucracy and school system (cited in Lebar 1972:86). In my short trip to Ende in 1983, my impression was just the opposite. Ende has good roads, hospitals, a bustling market stocking Western goods, a small airport, and many Muslim schools. In social organization Ende has patrilineal clans, noble lineages, and marriage alliance (Lebar 1972:87).[2] Society was divided into aristocrats (*mosa laki*), commoners, and slaves captured in wartime; today Ende is a modernizing port town. Some Ende are Christian (half the population in 1955, Kennedy estimated). The two mono-

theistic religions have both cut wide swathes into the conceptual terrain occupied by indigenous Ende religion, which included a concept of a high god, Ngga'eh Dewa. There were male and female priests, curers, and clan rituals involving livestock sacrifices.

Lio culture has some residue of material culture of a megalithic society, despite widespread conversion to Catholicism. Lio has patrilineal clans, and children observe ritual taboos symbolic of their mother's clans. There are aristocrats (*mosa laki*), commoners (*tai walu ana kalo*), immigrants to established villages (*ata mai*), and slave descendants (*ata koo*) (1983 fieldnotes). Children take the class status of their mothers, and women are discouraged from marrying men of lower social status.

Sikka exhibits the familiar Flores pattern of domination by foreign states. Fox writes that Sikka's territorial area has been variously defined as the region around Maumere, the highland domains of Nita and Kangae, and the area once dominated by the Raja of Sikka (1972:88-89). According to Fox's review of the ethnographic literature, a Sikka child is considered a member of his father's descent group after the payment of bridewealth. However, there seems to be considerable regional variation: "In eastern Sika, descent is flexibly ambilineal; bridewealth is unimportant, and children apparently become associated with the descent group with whom the parents choose to reside" (Lebar 1972:89).

The cultures of the small islands east of Sikka have attracted relatively little anthropological or art history research (among the few studies available on this important area are DuBois' 1944 monograph on Alor, Barnes' excellent 1974 ethnography of Lembata society in his book *Kedang*, and Maxwell 1980, 1981). Barnes writes that Adonara, Solor, Lembata, and especially Pantar and Alor are as much out islands in the Timor orbit as they are cultural neighbors of East Flores (1974:1-27). A subsistence pattern based on dry-field rice and maize augmented in some places by trade and fishing is found throughout the region, and considerable linguistic homogeneity overlies significant cultural diversity. Villages are generally organized around patrilineal clan descent, and symmetrical marriage alliance is found in some regions (Barnes 1980:71-73). There is a still-thriving exchange system involving ritual textiles and ivory tusks (Maxwell 1981).

As this last point illustrates, Solor archipelago

---

2. Ende seems to have the sort of coastal (*pasisir*) culture found in Sumatra's Sibolga to Padang region, or the Palu area in Central Sulawesi.

114. — Man in festive dress, with traditional jewelry, in Ruteng, Manggarai (Photograph Susan Rodgers, 1983).

115. — Woman in Walotopo (Lio region) wearing a necklace made of some twenty earrings (mostly like the Cat. No. 93 type but also like Cat. No. 88) (Photograph Susan Rodgers, 1983).

cultures are united on at least one point: their fascination with ceremonial gift-giving. This structures their kinship systems and their political life, which overlap in most of these cultures. Bridewealth on Flores and in the Lamalohot islands deals in a few common currencies. Manggarai's large bridewealth consists largely of water buffalo and horses (Koentjaraningrat 1972:82); Ngada's is a combination of money, buffalo, horses, and jewelry, and once included slaves (Lebar 1972:85). Ende's marriage payments draw on a symbolism of maleness and femaleness. "Traditional marriage was a clan affair," according to Kennedy: "An exchange of gifts was necessary, conceptualized as 'male things' from the groom's clan (ivory tusks, gold, animals) and 'female things' from the bride's clan (cloth, mats, rice). Nowadays a brideprice is paid, chiefly in money and buffalo" (Lebar 1972:87). In Kedang on Lembata, bridewealth historically consisted of jewelry for the bride: bracelets, anklets, earrings, and silver clips for the edge of the ear. Barnes writes that wife-takers today often give bronze gongs or elephant tusks, which are interchangeable, and the less valuable silver earrings and ivory bracelets. The countergifts from the bride's father's clan are textiles (Barnes 1974:283 ff.; Maxwell 1981), although the metal and ivory goods are apparently not categorized locally as masculine nor are the textiles classified purely as feminine (Barnes 1974:282-283). Traditional Alor probably had the most impressive bridewealth gifts: metal drums, called *moko*, which were each apportioned a set value in cash and pigs. The drums were "the coin of the realm," according to DuBois (1944:22), and circulated in quantities at weddings and funerals.

It is probably valid to say that Flores has few arts separate from ideas of giving and receiving gifts as set out in the *adat*. Local woven cloths illustrate this well and also demonstrate the ways in which ethnic identity is dramatized through an art form. Textiles, moreover, are logically part of the exchange systems involving metal and ivory jewelry. In some regions, ritual textiles have more to do with social class than with marriage exchange. In Ngada aristocratic women once announced their high social status by wearing black *lawo butu* textiles decorated with fancy bead designs (see p. 144). These cloths, whose animal designs evoke local myths, are emblematic of Ngada ethnic identity as well. The brown and black textiles of the Ende and Lio regions demonstrate the importance of trade with foreign ethnic groups. These cloths make frequent use of designs borrowed from the *patola* trade cloths of Indian origin, although weaver women today sometimes see these designs as "ancient *adat*" of purely local origin (Maxwell 1979).

Textiles and elephant tusks are crucial exchange objects in Lamalohot marriage transactions, as Maxwell has explored at length. Dark woven cloths, sometimes in association with black embroidered blouses, are important items of family wealth. These textiles are given as wife-giver counterpayments to *belis*, or bridewealth, at weddings. In this area *belis* consists of magnificent ivory tusks, which are also a central part of a family's house treasure. Maxwell writes that ivory gifts from wife-receivers are associated with masculinity, and cloth gifts, woven by women by secret processes, are linked to femininity (1981:48-49). Exchanges of ivory and cloth also take place at funerals and other major ritual occasions where wife-givers and wife-takers meet. These two currencies of exchange are even employed in areas of East Flores and the Lamalohot islands where no weaving is done. Local families import their cloths from other parts of Flores, just as the whole area once imported its tusks. This pattern of course links the region to other ethnic homelands. Not surprisingly, aristocratic families participate in the gift exchange to the largest extent.

Jewelry in Flores Cultures

Examples from other Flores cultures provide illustrations of equally important principles underlying the manufacture and use of jewelry on the island. Flores' complex political history is evident in Manggarai's syncretistic jewelry forms. Lio examples show the reliance of jewelry on local kinship systems. Ngada jewelry and jewelry from the Lio village of Walotopo and the Nage village of Boawai also illustrate the fact that social class standing as well as art must be seen against the backdrop of local cosmological myths.

Students of Manggarai culture invariably point out that this West Flores society has historically been a subject people (Gordon 1980:49). As noted earlier, the small Manggarai village polities have alternately been controlled by the Bimanese of Sumbawa, the Makassarese of Sulawesi, and the Dutch starting in 1907. Manggarai's position as a vassal society on the edges of imperial state societies has left it with art traditions borrowed from Sumbawa and South Sulawesi. At the same time, Manggarai has indigenous art traditions linked to other small societies in Eastern Indonesia and the Philippines. In other words, local arts, syncretistic in themselves, have blended with the imported arts from Manggarai's colonial past. The small village of Ruteng has noble house treasures and dance costumes that illustrate Manggarai's position as a society at the confluence of many cultures.

Ruteng is arranged in a circle, centered on a circular raised burial altar where the bones of patrilineal clan ancestors are interred. These clans are called *wai*. In its kinship organization, village layout, and house design Ruteng resembles other high villages in Eastern Indonesia. It makes all the familiar associations between aristocratic status and height and central position, and links cosmic order to the layout of the village and the house. According to residents interviewed in 1983, this village was a successful military center some eighty years ago when intervillage warfare was still common. The village is set up on a hill, approached by a long flight of stone steps. After a successful war raid, the *raja* and his soldiers would march up the stairs to be greeted by the women of the aristocratic class. One type of jewelry and costume is associated with warfare (Fig. 114). Another range of jewelry, however, is made up of imported items from Sumbawa or possibly from South Sulawesi. The decorated disk (Cat. No. 101), the cone-shaped ring (Cat. No. 108), and the curved gold pendant with applied filigree work (Cat. No. 100) in the Barbier-Müller collection are all examples of jewelry brought from the Islamized Indonesian trade states to West Flores and put to local uses. The pendant and the disk were used in Ruteng up until the last several years as cheek ornaments, suspended from a headband.

If Flores jewelry is a document on the island's political history, it is also a testament to the importance of local kinship systems and the exchange traditions associated with marriage. Lio culture provides a range of typical illustrations of this. In 1983, interviews in the coastal village of Walotopo quickly uncovered some of the kinship underpinnings of Lio jewelry use. Walotopo is a well-preserved megalithic village stunning in its sheer numbers of stone altars and stone terraces. A huge Catholic church dominates the village, though, forestalling any attempt to classify the place as a traditional village

116. – Nage men in the 1920s, wearing gold necklaces imitating shells, and crowns of the type shown in Cat. No. 81 (courtesy Rautenstrauch, Joest Museum, Cologne).

117. – In the Ngada area, carved boards on interior house walls are decorated with mythical animals (horses, dragon-like animals) framed with curvilinear designs looking very much like the motifs of Maori art in New Zealand. Inserted in the spirals are representations of jewels: pendants (see Cat. No. 105) and earrings (see Cat. Nos. 83 and 84) (Photograph Susan Rodgers, 1983).

pure and simple. It happens that Walotopo is a migrant village founded about three hundred years ago (the local view) by Lio from the highlands north of Ende. Since the village is not connected by roads to any other settlement, many residents today make the hour-long hike to Ende for marketing, school, and salaried work.

Walotopo has the familiar hierarchical social structure of the region. The village is divided into *mosa laki* (nobles), *tai walu ana kalo* (free commoners), *ata mai* (recent immigrants, families not descended from the village founders), and *ata koo* (descendants of slaves). People belong to their father's *embu*, or patrilineal clan. At the same time they trace a sort of ritual affiliation on their mother's side by observing *kunu*, which is a ritual prohibition on eating certain food, a taboo that one shares with one's mother's clanmates. *Kunu* also refers to the social category of people with whom one shares the prohibition. In *adat* rituals a household will both commemorate its patrilineal clan ancestors and ask its *kunu* mates for blessings. Marriages can involve people from the same or different villages, and young women are encouraged to marry their fathers' sisters' sons (in other words, the culture has asymmetrical marriage alliance). Inheritance *adat* decrees that sons inherit land and gold house treasures from their fathers. These *pusaka* are impressive collections of gold chains, necklaces made of masses of earrings, and various pendants (Fig. 115). They are passed from family to family and from generation to generation according to local rules of descent and marriage alliance. The treasure in the photograph is said to be six generations old, according to my informant. Da Seko, the *embu* founder, started the treasure rather modestly with seven gold *wuli* (shell-shaped pendants) and two gold earrings (called *wea*). At one point Da Seko gave the treasure to a friend in the village of Ngalupolo, but in a later generation it was returned to Walotopo, where it has remained ever since. Da Seko's descendants added a cosmopolitan collection of other ornaments in later generations, until now the whole assemblage is a good illustration of the syncretism of Flores aristocratic art.

The gold treasure was also used as a set of ritual objects for contacting clan ancestors. In the *maru* ceremony, women representing each *embu* in the village would be called together for a trance ritual when the roof was being put onto a new *adat* house. The women would gather in the space between the ground and the floorboards of the new house and stay absolutely immobile, saying nothing, while praying continually to the clan ancestors. They would be outfitted in the full gold regalia from their *embu*'s house treasure. A single male dancer would perform during the entire *maru* period.

Lio jewelry use was also shaped by marriage alliance. For instance, the bride had a prescribed set of gold jewels that she would use as her personal jewelry when she went into her marriage. This *teo kinga* set ideally consisted of a gold bracelet and two types of *wea* earrings, called *ome mbulu ina* and *ome mbulu*. Part of the bridewealth was used to buy ornaments for her, the actual number of each style depending on the amount of her bridewealth.

Any Flores culture would provide ample documentation of the next themes, the linkage between the jewelry arts and the local aristocratic classes. Examples from the Ngada and Nage regions show the same thing as the Lio material did — that jewelry made of precious metal was a badge of rank for the wealthy upper class. In late colonial times the aristocrats of Kampung Bajawa in Ngada bedecked themselves with gold chains; in a 1983 interview one man wore one of his family's old *loda*, or gold chains of office. The piece is quite similar to the one used in Sumba and Roti. Ngada ritual dancers outfitted as warriors also wear an abundance of jewelry around their necks and chests. In the 1920s Ngada warriors dressed in full regalia wore conch-shell necklaces called *wuli* and chain-link chest ornaments called *wonga uwi*. In some exceptionally prosperous regions such shell ornaments were made of gold. This is the case in Boawai. In Fig. 116, also taken in the 1920s, a group of Boawai noblemen are turned out in a variety of gold crowns, chain-link ropes, and necklaces.

Flores jewelry, finally, is part of larger systems of art objects (house architecture, wood sculpture, stone monuments) and ritual activities (trance dances, war dances, house dedications, sculpture-carving rituals). These traditions are themselves part of even larger philosophical and mythic systems concerning the nature of human life and the way the universe is structured. The full dimensions of these systems are quite beyond the scope of this catalogue, but a few points can be mentioned, using the village of Boawai as an illustration.

The gold crown, called a *lado* (Cat. No. 81), is at one level simply a prestigious symbol of chieftainship. At another level, it is also worn by members of a group of seven noblemen from Boawai who go into the forest to select a special tree to be carved into a new village *peo*, or forked stake erected as an ancestral shrine. The forked stake itself is part of a set of ritual objects including the male and female ceremonial houses at the village edge and the equestrian statues associated with those shrines. After the men choose a tree, they transport it back to the village, trunk end first, with one man sitting at the front and a second man, also in full regalia, sitting on a plank balancing the two branches. Ritual music accompanies this procession. The *peo* is further linked to another ritual triad, made up of the forked stake, inherited farm land, and *ate sage* earrings (Cat. Nos. 93 and 94). These are all considered to be the sacred, inalienable property of the patrilineal clan, or *ili woe*.

Most of the major types of Nage jewelry probably have these complex associations with Nage village life. Further research, in fact, would very likely uncover symbolic linkages of this sort for the jewelry of almost all Flores cultures.

CENTRAL FLORES
Frontal, gold. Cat. No. 81. Description p. 326.

CENTRAL FLORES
Earrings, gold. Cat. No. 85. Description p. 327.

CENTRAL FLORES
Earrings, gold. Cat. No. 86. Description p. 327.

CENTRAL FLORES
Earrings, gold. Cat. Nos. 93, 94 & 95. Descriptions p. 328.

CENTRAL FLORES
Pendant, gold. Cat. No. 106. Description p. 329.

SUMBA

Jewelry in Sumba's several closely related ethnic cultures illustrates every major theme of decorative body adornment and family treasure in island Southeast Asia. The island's abundant gold, ivory, tortoise shell, and bead jewelry is at once a material representation of local myths, a series of marriage exchange objects, a treasure for demonstrating the wealth and mystical power of noble lineages, and a collection of holy altar pieces used to contact the *marapu* (ancestor spirits) through trance prayers. In

pre-national times Sumba's jewelry participated in a large range of exchange transactions, which included bridewealth transfers between aristocratic lineages, exchanges between local *rajas*, and trade between ethnic groups in this ecologically diverse island.

As noted in the "Jewelry and Exchange" chapter of the introduction, in late colonial times East Sumba may have had something similar to the classic potlatch rituals of the American Indian societies of the Northwest Coast near British Columbia. In potlatches, rival chiefs competed for political

◄ Man's ceremonial cloth (*hinggi*). Warp ikat. Cotton. East Sumba, Indonesia. Detail. (Barbier-Müller Museum, No. 3651-H, not exhibited).

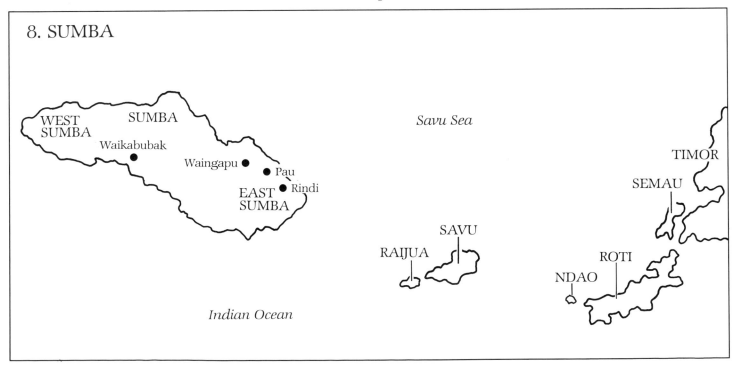

118. — The late Raja of Pau, T.U. Windi Tanangunju, with a *lamba* (frontal) and a *tabilu* (gold disk). (Photograph courtesy Perry Kesner, taken in the mid 1970s).

119. — Rambu J., "Queen" of Rindi. She still owns an important family treasure (Photograph Susan Rodgers, 1983).

supremacy over an area by calling great festivals where each attempted to prove himself the wealthiest and most generous participant. House treasure was used as a central weapon in their efforts to best their rivals: the chief who could give away or destroy the largest amount of prestige goods won the contest and established himself as the paramount leader of the region. Profligate gift-giving and the burial or even outright destruction of such ritual goods as precious-metal objects and fine textiles sometimes masked another important series of economic exchanges in which competing chiefs bestowed great amounts of food on their rivals, who were obligated to accept such largesse. This type of exchange served to equalize food supplies in a region where some small polities may have had food surpluses while other groups suffered periodic famines (Piddocke 1965).

Beyond these local, intra-island systems of exchange, Sumba's jewelry was used in a historically complex series of interactions between Sumbanese societies, the Dutch colonial administration, and other cultures of Eastern Indonesia and the Javanese and Balinese sphere. In fact, Sumba's more luxuriant jewelry traditions were largely created in this international arena. Gold came into the island as Dutch payments in coinage to secure the cooperation of local *rajas*, who could provide the colonial administration with herds of Sumba's famous sturdy little horses. The already heated rivalry between noble families increased in intensity with this new influx of wealth, until by the end of the colonial era Sumbanese house treasures had filled up with gold ornaments (Figs. 118-120) much as Nias village plazas had filled up with stone monuments commemorating ancestors. In both cases ritual artworks were ostensibly dedicated to supernatural beings but actually went toward the greater glorification of competing *rajas* (Fig. 121).

The political implications of jewelry did not disappear with national independence in 1945 and central government control from Jakarta. Today the magnificent gold treasures of East Sumba noble families are becoming part of another type of exchange, this time with Chinese-Indonesian art dealers and, through them, with European and American primitive art museums. East Sumba is an arid place virtually without exploitable natural resources, beyond the grassy rolling hills used to graze horses and imported cattle. A number of local aristocratic

166

families have recently fallen on unusually hard times and are selling their inherited house treasures piece by piece to art dealers, who transport the jewelry to shops in Bali and Jakarta. From there, the ornaments make their way into Western and Japanese collections, with the prices rising every step of the way. This situation makes Sumbanese jewelry an excellent if poignant example of another theme in island Southeast Asian jewelry traditions: the transitional nature of material culture as it moves from ritual to art — as sacred family treasures become marketable *objets d'art* appreciated for their aesthetic qualities by an international audience of connoisseurs.

This chapter will introduce these various themes through ethnographic sketches of the way jewelry is conceptualized and used in three aristocratic villages I visited briefly in 1983. Rindi and Pau in East Sumba and Tarung in West Sumba are villages whose histories and house treasures amply illustrate the almost Byzantine complexities of Sumbanese jewelry. In all these areas jewelry is a small part of larger systems of myth, ritual, kinship, politics, and economic exchange. A few general ethnographic features of the island's societies can be set out first before looking at the individual villages. This short account draws on the generally excellent anthropological literature on Sumba (Kuipers 1982; Hoskins 1983; Needham 1980; Onvlee 1980; Adams 1969, 1970, 1973, 1979, 1980).

Kinship, Royalty, and Art in Sumbanese Societies

Lying somewhat out of line to the south of the chain of islands stretching eastward from Bali to Timor, Sumba is a hilly, partially dry island made up of two subprovinces *(kabupaten)* covering a total land area of 11,911 square kilometers. Mountainous West Sumba has heavy forests and sufficient rainfall for farming, while East Sumba, with an area of 7,711 square kilometers, is a dry, economically fragile region of savannah, rolling hills, and widely separated settlements. Large numbers of Savunese immigrants are found in villages along the north and east coasts near Waingapu. This ethnic group once dominated goldsmithing in Sumba, although a Waingapu smith interviewed in 1983 said that many Sumbanese have now gone into the same business. (Some wealthy East Sumbanese families patronize Balinese or Chinese-Indonesian goldsmiths in Bali when they want a new piece made or an old one repaired.) In the late 1800s East Sumba approached a tradi-

120. – This photograph was taken at T.U. Windi Tanangunju's funeral, in 1981 (courtesy Garuda Airways).

121. – The tomb of T.U. Windi Tanangunju in Pau (Photograph Susan Rodgers, 1983).

167

122. — Mummified body of a dead member of the family of a *raja* in East Sumba, waiting until enough wealth has been accumulated to hold a proper funeral feast. The textiles wrapping the deceased are buried with them (Photograph Lionel Morley, 1977).

123. — In Sumba, like Nias and Flores, village plazas were full of stone monuments, dedicated to revered ancestors. Funeral feasts entailed the slaughter of an enormous number of buffaloes. This picture, taken in West Sumba near Anakalang, shows the horns of the killed animals, which will be affixed on the houses (Photograph J. Gabriel Barbier-Müller, 1976).

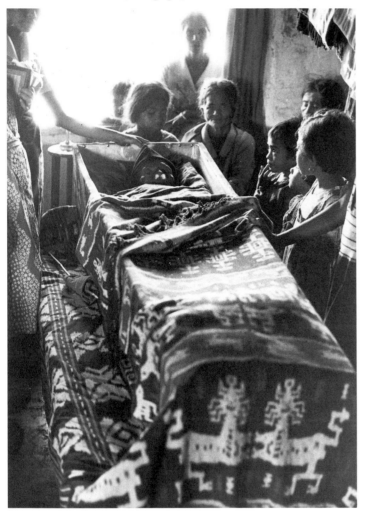

tional state form of government, with several distinct social classes. These included *maramba*, or noble families; *kabihu*, or free commoners (*kabihu* also refers to lineages); and *ata*, or slaves. Helping the nobles as their priests and public spokesman were the *rato*. There were also many residents with mixed class background, all carefully categorized in East Sumba's painstaking folk class taxonomies (Adams 1969). East Sumbanese spoke a single language, Kambera, and made up a single ethnic group. West Sumba, by contrast, was fragmented into a large number of ethnic groups (Map 8), and its societies varied considerably in dialect, *adat*, and kinship system within the general bounds of a core Sumbanese cultural type (Needham 1980).

In most parts of the island through the late 1800s warfare and headtaking raids were fairly common, although the Dutch had established an administrative post in 1866 and undertook pacification efforts which continued through the first decade of this century. Sumbanese were stubborn resistance fighters, at the same time that some of the noble families were capitulating to the Dutch and reaping their rewards for such cooperation in gold coins. This particular exchange fits into a larger range of trade relationships, and is in fact a good entrée to Sumbanese culture as a whole.

To understand the island's various systems of exchange one must first investigate local social structure. In the east this revolved around an asymmetrical marriage system involving ritually superior wife-giving groups and subordinate wife-takers. Old-style East Sumbanese villages consisted of imposing, steep-roofed *adat* houses *(uma)* arrayed around a central plaza (Figs. 123 and 125 show West Sumbanese examples). This central area was sometimes filled with stone tombs and carved stone posts dedicated to the ancestors of the patrilineal lineage. Descent, inheritance, and political leadership within an *uma* followed the male line, and household units were seen as the living representatives of the larger *kabihu*, or lineages. The *adat* house of a village founder was home, shrine, and political center (Adams 1969:8-11). These houses of aristocrats were built around four large posts, which served as foci for consulting the ancestral spirits, or *marapu*, beings associated with the upper reaches of the house, where the family stored its food supply and heirlooms. The core of this family treasure was the sacred *tanggu marapu*, "possessions of the *marapu*"

(Adams 1969; Oe. K. Kapita 1976a; Forth 1981). This included fine old textiles (Figs. 122 and 124), heirloom weapons important in lineage history, porcelain, looms, and gold ornaments such as *mamuli*, chains, *tabilu* disks, and *lamba* forehead crescents. These pieces were sometimes taken down from their attic storage chests by the *rato*, or priest, and employed as a sort of altar for making contact with the *marapu*, who were thought to be vitally concerned with the doings of the living descendants.

Balancing this stress on patrilineal descent was a reliance on asymmetrical marriage alliance, involving wife-giving lineages called *yera* and wife-receiving ones call *laiya*. These were ideally of different clans, and each wife-taking unit would itself play the role of wife-giver to a third lineage. This marriage system resembled that of the Batak in North Sumatra. In East Sumba *adat*, brides given to a receiver group should not be "paid back" in kind, through corresponding gifts of women. Rather, the wife-givers provide their taker groups with women, textiles, and beadwork, while the *laiya* respond with countergifts of brideprice objects and livestock. *Mamuli* pendants are crucial brideprice goods in this marriage system, and in fact some scholars term the jewelry and other metal gifts "masculine" goods, counterbalanced by "feminine" textiles (Adams 1969, 1980). Adams summarized the East Sumbanese marriage exchange system in the following way (1969:47):

Masculine goods (banda muni)	Feminine goods (banda kawini)
Goods	
pendants	textiles
gold chains	beadwork
spears, swords	ivory bracelets
heavy brass bracelets	porcelain
Live creatures	
slaves	personal attendants
horses	pigs

Much as the exchange of practical and prestige goods acted to cement social relationships within and among *uma* households, gift-giving and -receiving were also important in maintaining relationships between social classes (Adams 1969:18-24; Oe. K. Kapita 1976a). The aristocrats controlled access to land, livestock, and such ritual goods as fine textiles,

124. – This East Sumbanese noblewoman is displaying the precious textiles belonging to her family (Photograph J. Gabriel Barbier-Müller, 1976).

125. – West Sumbanese village with stone tombs (Photograph J. Gabriel Barbier-Müller, 1976).

while the lower classes would generally only receive such things through the gift-giving largesse of *maramba*. Commoners gave aristocrats agricultural and military labor, and the *raja's* slaves acted as their masters' servants and ritual representatives in return for their physical upkeep.

Beyond this, East Sumba was involved in another type of exchange: trade between the coastal regions near Waingapu and the more populated central highlands, and trade between the north and east coastal regions and outside islands (Bali, Java, South Sulawesi, Flores, Timor). In the intra-island trade, Adams notes, "Sumbanese accord preeminent status to such foreign goods... as decorated textiles, colored thread, metal goods (knife blades, gongs, coins, jewelry of gold, silver, copper, and brass), ivory, beads, and porcelain. The only local products that rival the foreign articles in value are buffalo, horses, and the decorated textiles made in the coastal districts" (1969:4-5). These ritual cloths, ornamented in the *ikat* technique with a profusion of mythic animals, are woven only by the noble women living along the north and east coasts. When the East Sumbanese *raja*ships still exercised political authority, only aristocrats could wear these textiles, and inland Sumbanese nobles had to obtain them through trade with families near the coast. These coastal nobles, in fact, largely controlled the inter-island trade, which involved such highland goods as rice, horses, and forest products (lumber, fruits, dyewoods) and such littoral goods as textiles, cotton, dried fish, lime, salt, and coconuts (Adams 1959:5). Jewelry was part of both sorts of trade: Savunese goldsmiths living in the coastal areas produced ornaments for Sumbanese noble families, who traded the ornaments among themselves, and the metal flowed into the island from the Dutch colonial state. East coast *rajas* sought to extend their control of ever-larger areas through the increased production and distribution of gold ornaments.

The prodigious artistic output that resulted made sense against the backdrop of Sumbanese myths, recounted through the island's vast oral literature (Oe. K. Kapita 1977; U. H. Kapita 1979; Kuipers 1982; Adams 1979; Forth 1981). A striking characteristic of Sumbanese ritual speech in many ethnic areas is its reliance on poetic parallel phrases, such as *kuru nduu bokulu, kuru nduu kudu* (great sea, small sea), *ina pakawurungu, ama pakawurungu* (which Forth translates "mother and father clustered toge-

ther"), and *taruhuku la baba, manggomalu la lima* ("slipping from the lap and arm," which according to Forth (1981:201) refers to the protection the ancestors provide for their living descendants). In Rindi in East Sumba creation myths combine references to a rather distant deity (sometimes called Ina pakawurungu ama pakawurungu) with detailed accounts of the lives of clan founders, which in this area are the *marapu* (more recent deceased relatives are not classified). *Marapu* are associated closely with houses, while the spaces outside the house and outside the village are identified with somewhat ambiguous, part-beneficent, part-malevolent powers of the earth and forest (Forth 1981:104-132). Binary oppositions of this sort (inside/outside, village/forest) are extremely common and quite explicit in Sumbanese myths (Adams 1979; Forth 1981).

In Rindi's *marapu* religion (a local way of distinguishing the indigenous ritual and belief system from Christianity and Islam), humans cannot communicate directly with the divinity. A host of intermediaries provide bridges between the two spheres: *marapu* themselves stand between humans and deities; the *raja's* priest, the *rato*, intercedes for the nobleman with the *marapu*; and the priest himself makes use of special sacred heirloom objects to make contact with the *marapu*. Forth stresses the strong association the Rindi make between divinity and metal (1981:94-95; 104-132). Gold ornaments from the *tanggu marapu*, as the possessions of the *marapu*, can serve as relics through which their original owners can be contacted. Rindi religion, and indeed many local Sumbanese *marapu* religions, have numerous altars of various sorts for contacting the closer denizens of the supernatural realm. *Tanggu marapu*, jewelry, houses, stone carvings, "skull trees" once used for displaying captured heads, as well as trances and sacrificed animals might all be considered altars in this sense.

The Rindi claim that the sky and earth were once so close that only a man's height separated them. This state itself followed an earlier age when Father Sky and Mother Earth copulated and produced the original group of beings (four males and four females in some versions, eight of each in others). These ancestors' descendants separated, moving to two opposite ends of the cosmos, the Base of the Sky and the Head of the Earth. The two sides then intermarried, giving rise eventually to the clan founders and, after that, to contemporary Rindi society. Interwoven with such narratives is an idea that the Rindi ancestors came from outside Sumba (Forth 1981: 89-90). It should also be noted that Sumba myths of this sort exist today in wary coexistence with missionary Christianity (Hoskins 1982).

To understand Rindi myths further and through them to grasp Sumbanese religious life in general it is necessary to look in more detail at one of their main material representations, the *tanggu marapu*. For this we can turn to my visit to the village in 1983 and supplement this material with Forth's exhaustive ethnographic study. The village of Pau offers a good contrast to the jewelry traditions in Rindi.

Jewelry in Rindi and Pau

Figure 126 shows what is apparently only a small portion of Rindi's treasury. The ornaments photographed in 1983 were those that Rambu J., the presiding monarch (if such a term can be used in a realm with only ceremonial power) allowed to be taken down from their usual storage place in a dark recess of her late father's *adat* house. As the eldest daughter of a family with no sons, she is the guardian of the *tanggu marapu* for the house and village, ensuring that this treasure is safely enclosed in wooden boxes nestled in three layers of palm fiber baskets. The baskets are themselves contained in an absolutely dark room whose wall cracks are shuttered with thick buffalo hide. Rambu J. presides with considerable aplomb, with the help of several sisters, over her nearly deserted village. All of the daughters are unmarried, for no one has ever been able to amass the necessary brideprice payments (according to a Waingapu government official). On brief acquaintance, Rambu J. is a no-nonsense, obdurate lady with an air of having seen it all. In terms of East Sumba's jewelry traditions, she probably has.

Her *ratu*, or priest-spokesman, explained the various ornaments in the treasure while Rambu J. sat silently off to the side of the house porch where the conversation was taking place. The priest was her intermediary with the public, it seemed, much as he served as her specialist for contacting the *marapu*. The village is largely unconverted to Christianity, and large stone slabs commemorating buried ancestors fill up the central plaza.

126. – Part of the sacred treasure of a noble family in East Sumba. Such heirlooms maintained links to ancestors. The long ropes of orange beads ending with gold coins (*anchida langgelu*) are especially prized (Photograph Susan Rodgers, 1983).

127. – Slave (?) wearing a gold forehead ornament (*lamba*) on a woman's textile (*lau*). Detail (Barbier-Müller Museum, No. 3651-AB, not exhibited).

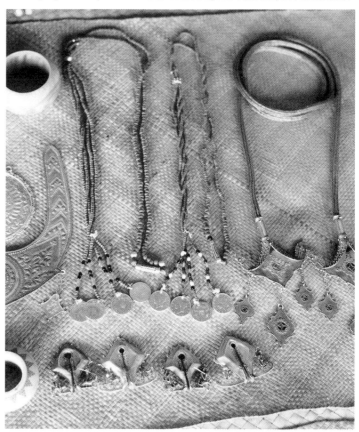

128. – Villagers in Rindi never agreed to pose with gold chains *(kenatar)* outside the proper ritual context. Two government officials accepted this task. Note the length and the enormous "heads" of the chains (Photograph Susan Rodgers, 1983).

In the interview, a government official explained that a "man who could work marvels" from Savu brought *mamuli* pendants to Rindi; he went on to say that the goldsmithing technique was later learned by Sumbanese craftsmen. Savunese also reportedly introduced the *lamba* forehead ornaments to Rindi. The *raja*'s house keeps a "full set" of jewelry for major *adat* rituals. For women these ornaments include ritual textiles woven in the village, tortoise shell combs for adolescent girls, ivory bracelets and long ropes of orange *mutisala* beads made into necklaces called *anchida langgelu.* These last ornaments are magnificent affairs hanging down below the knees, ending with a fistfull of old gold coins. For men the full regalia is even more impressive, but it is not part of the costume of actual *rajas*. Rather, it consists of ornaments for the *raja*'s slaves (Fig. 127) (or their ritual equivalent after slavery was abolished under colonialism). When fully turned out, the slave would be attired in a *tabilu* gold disk around his neck, a crescent-shaped *lamba* ornament for his forehead, a long *anchida langgelu* bead necklace, a huge gold *kanatar* chain looped around his neck, and thick ivory armlets. Two or sometimes three *mamuli* would be suspended from the forehead ornament. Details about the Rindi interpretations of these various ornaments are included in the plate notes.

Why this magnificence for slaves? The institution was a somewhat paradoxical one in East Sumba. Powerful *rajas* cultivated powerful slaves, who ate with their masters, advised them closely, and in a sense became the *rajas* at certain *adat* rituals. Bedecked in the house treasure's full complement of gold ornaments the slave served as the *raja*'s double for the general public. At the *raja*'s death, four or eight slaves (the numbers are symbolic equivalents) would be adorned in the full set of jewelry and go into trances induced by continuous dancing. This allowed them to contact the *marapu* and convey messages back and forth between this world and the next during funerals, which were in a sense windows between the two spheres. The Sumbanese social historian Oe. K. Kapita explained this institution of trance dancing in full costume in his book *Masyarakat Sumba dan Adat Istiadatnya* (1976a: 64-65, my translation):

When [the *raja*] dies it is said of him: "meti papamananyaka – Rara Raumananujaka" [died like the dead midrib of the palm leaf, the leaves all red], like a tree whose leaf ribs and fruit are old and have to fall off; a death like this is not mourned but is celebrated by: singing, beating the gong, dancing and "kamangu" [horse races]. The custom is now rare, for it is rare that people die at such an age.

We demonstrated above that this dead one was a mysterious occult being, and because of this he was a holy being, [and] he could not be contacted in the ordinary way but only via holy ways. So, only persons who have been made holy, who have been purified can contact him and the ancestor beings who come to meet him. For this purpose the maramba nobles and Kabihu bokulu high commoners prepare a person or several persons from the slave class to carry out this duty, drawing lots to see who among the slaves is the favorite. Whoever is selected by lot is then purified with a ritual service, and after this is outfitted with clothing and jewelry that is the best and most expensive in the family. These ones here are the medid [or intermediaries] between people who are living and people who are dead, at the time they are entered by the spirit of the dead one. They go into a trance, and it is at this time that the dead one or other deceased persons put forward their wishes and by the same token it is also at this moment that living people from the family put forward their wishes to the dead one and the other deceased. When he or they [the slaves] are in a trance state, they cannot stand or walk by themselves, to the point that they must be "papah'ed" [helped to walk], and that is the origin of calling them "pahaga nggangu" or "papapanggangu" [those-who-are-papah'ed]. The number of pahapanggangu for nobles is generally four persons, but there are sometimes as many as eight persons among some rajas, each one with his own set duties. These duties do not need to be detailed, but it is enough to simply say that all these duties have a spiritual purpose, which symbolize the essence of the life of a person who possessed the qualities of greatness, glory, and bravery throughout his life, but now in confronting the spirit world must be purified. This is what we see in the clothing, jewelry, and bearing of the pahapanggangu as they wear rich material and sarongs, mamuli, kanataru gold chains, and "anahida" [*mutisala* beads] along with carrying betel holders for males and females, chickens, veils, spears, and so on. This pahapanggangu duty is only carried out once a life-time, and after he has done it he is free of it. While they are carrying out the duty they are highly respected and feared; this is especially true of the one who rides the horse – he is honored as the deceased one himself. This pahapanggangu is always taken from the "ata raja" slaves or the "ata bokulu" slaves [slaves of high nobles and high commoners]. At the time of his death he is treated like a nobleman himself.

No resident of Rindi interviewed during 1983 would agree to pose in the full *papangga* funeral jewelry, for fear of spirit retribution for using the regalia outside of its very specific proper ritual context (their exact fear was that wearing the jewelry would cause an early death). In their stead, two apparently more secular government officials posed with the gold chains of office (Fig. 128).

The Rindi people interviewed also had much to say about their exemplary collection of *mamuli*. Very

129. – A *mamuli* is hanging from the ear of this old man of East Sumba (courtesy Kon. Inst. v/d Tropen, Amsterdam, photograph taken in the 1920s).

173

simple versions, joined in masculine and feminine pairs, are used as gifts that wife-taking groups present to their prospective wife-givers at various stages of marriage negotiations. The gift-giving can start as early as the infancy of the future bride. Large, more elaborate *mamuli* like those shown in Cat. Nos. 131 and 132 are used by slaves in the *papangga* funeral procession, described above. This same type can be used as part of the *tanggu marapu*, the ornaments of the house ancestors, which are stored in the attic. Very occasionally they are taken down, placed in a rattan tray called a *tangawahil*, and used by the *raja*'s priest for summoning *marapu*. A chicken must be sacrificed for such a prayer session, and its innards are inspected as auguries of the *marapu*'s messages. We will return to the *tanggu marapu* jewels shortly.

A third, quite different type of *mamuli* (represented in the Barbier-Müller exhibit by Cat. Nos. 134–136) is much larger than the others and is decorated with naturalistic, movable little figures of horsemen, warriors, or monkeys. These special *mamuli* are part of the *banda uma*, the *adat*-house heirloom wealth. These are almost never taken out of the dark, for fear that their huge powers would kill onlookers and bring natural disasters. From 1983 Rindi discussions, it appears that these jewels are the very essence of the lineage and its political and religious powers. Ideally they must not be exchanged between houses as marriage gifts, much less sold to outsiders. The ones in the museum collection are from Pau, which as we shall see is a more secularized village.

Forth provides more detailed information about Rindi's *tanggu marapu*. He writes that there are three classes, a scheme which seems to encompass what my 1983 informants called *banda uma*:

The first are the original or oldest clan relicas, sometimes distinguished as the pingi marapu, "trunk of the marapu", which are stored in a sealed wooden chest kept in the loft inside the peak of the clan's ancestral house (uma marapu). These reputedly comprise golden and silver pendants, chains and other ornaments, and sometimes metal images of the ancestral couple, boats, called "the portion, possessions of his (the ancestor's) soul, the staff on which he rides" (tanggu hamanguna, toku kalitina). They are thus the means by which the presence of the ancestral spirit is secured and signified within the house, and they serve as a medium in rites addressed to the marapu, performed before the principal house post (kambaniru uratungu). This provides us with an important instance of the association of metal with divinity…

The second type of tanggu marapu consists of metal ornaments or pieces of beaten metal (kawadaku) that are added to the oldest relics on major ceremonial occasions. These too are kept in the peak of the house, but they are placed in a separate container – a small basket or other compartment inside a larger chest that also holds the oldest relics. The third category is rather more general, as it includes several varieties of clan heirlooms: old and valuable pendants, chains, and other ornaments used as ceremonial decoration and alliance prestations…; old spears and shields; and cooking and eating vessels, gongs, and drums used in rites that concern the ancestor. In this sense, tanggu marapu would also include the marapu horse (njara marapu), an especially fine stallion brought to the clan's ancestral house on important ceremonial occasions. In contrast to the two sorts of relics kept in the house peak, these items are stored in the lower section of the building. The two categories are thus distinguished as the tanggu la hindi, "possessions in the loft," and tanggu la kaheli, "possessions in the house floor".

The three classes of marapu possessions are further contrasted with regard to the extent to which they are the object of prohibitions. It is strictly forbidden to view or touch the oldest relics and were anyone to do so they would become ill and most likely die. The Rindi thus describe them as extremely hot. The more recently consecrated relics are also normally out of bounds. But when first placed in the loft they may of course be viewed and handled, albeit only by the older men; so these objects are considered somewhat less hot. The heirlooms, by contrast, may when necessary be openly viewed and handled by women as well as men. That they are not entirely cool, however, is shown by the practice of placing inside each container of old metal heirlooms one or more cheap, recently made metal pendants in order "to cool (i.e., render safe) the valuable" (pamaringu wangu banda). Were this not done anyone who touched them should fall ill. (Forth 1981:94-95.)

This degree of conservatism regarding the tanggu marapu objects was exactly my impression after the short 1983 interview. The impression was jolted several days afterward, however, when a number of fine, big mamuli with movable figures were offered for sale, apparently as the result of my visit to the village – this, despite my clear statement that I had no interest in buying jewelry. A Chinese-Indonesian dealer living in Waingapu played the middleman.

The village of Pau a short distance away also demonstrates the fragility of such notions of sacredness and inalienable family treasure. Where Rindi jewelry is apparently just beginning to break away from its ritual moorings, the Pau treasure actually exists more in the Western primitive art market than it does in the home village. The last raja of Pau (Fig. 130) died several years ago, and his younger brother is now selling off the family treasure to dealers. In fact, this man is virtually emptying out the uma's attic. He is not only selling the smaller tanggu marapu jewels but is digging deep into the most sacred banda uma treasury, Forth's first category described above (see the large mamuli, Cat. Nos. 127, 129, 136).

West Sumba

Much as the western part of the island has more ethnic variety than East Sumba, its uses of such jewelry pieces as mamuli, gold chains, and forehead ornaments are more diversified than in the eastern rajaships such as Pau and Rindi. In West Sumba women and unmarried girls wear mamuli, for instance, whereas only special categories of men wear them in the east. These ornaments serve as earrings in the Lamboya, Anakalang, and Lauli cultures. In addition, girls often wear mamuli as necklace pendants and gold kanatar chains as part of their adat dance costumes. West Sumba societies also have a chest ornament called a marangga (or sometimes maragga) that is not used in the east according to all I interviewed in 1983. This thin, flat beaten-gold piece of jewelry is so large that it is almost a breastplate. Marangga designs figure prominently on West Sumba stone mortuary sculpture much as mamuli shapes are woven into the textiles of the Kodi region.

Although the house treasures of many West Sumba aristrocrats are perhaps somewhat less prepossessing than those in larger rajaships in East Sumba, jewelry is just as integral a part of village politics, kinship, and religion in the west. It is also somewhat overblown. Adolescent girls in adat dances in the Anakalang region, for instance, nearly drip with fussy gold decorations. Tabelu crescents decorate their foreheads, mamuli hang from their ears, big mamuli decorate their neck on gold chains, even larger marangga serve as additional chest ornaments, and suspended under all this by yet another heavy gold chain are solid gold turtles of the size of live box turtles. Not to be outdone, some dancers top off their marangga with another plump mamuli. Such an ensemble was worn several years ago by the daughter of a bupati (chief administrator) for the Anakalang district. The bupati is a representative of the national Indonesian government. Sumbanese metal finery may have found a new stage for political display.

There is a growing anthropological literature on

132. — The stone monuments are filled with representation of the sorts of ornaments that symbolized the high status of nobles. Here, one can distinctly see two *mamuli*, West Sumba (courtesy Kon. Inst. v/d Tropen, Amsterdam).

West Sumba cultures, most of it concentrating on ritual speech, kinship, and gender symbols (Kuipers 1982; Hoskins 1982; Needham 1980). Few jewelry pieces in the Barbier-Müller collection actually came from West Sumba, but the general categories of ornaments such as *mamuli* and gold chains were readily recognized and discussed in my series of 1983 interviews in Kampung Tarung near Waika-bubak, in the Lamboya area, and in an additional series done for this research by H.M. Mude in the Kodi region. It was quickly obvious that there is far too much variation from culture to culture in jewelry use and interpretation to capture in a few days of study. Let Kampung Tarung serve as our only example from the region, remembering that it probably cannot be taken as typical of this diverse area.

The village is situated atop a steep hill, with another small settlement called Weitabar located nearby on slightly lower ground. The highest *adat* houses belong to the founder clans. Height is also associated with ritual importance, for the higher village of Tarung serves as an important ceremonial center for a larger area of Lauli. Every November closely associated clans or *kabisu* gather there for an agricultural increase ritual called Wula Poda. Many of the village's stone plazas, stone slabs (Fig. 132), monuments, and human-shaped statues are associated with this ceremony. The *rato*, or priests, make offerings to the *marapu* during Wula Poda and superintend the other village communal rituals. According to the head *rato* there, part of his duties is to periodically remove the *tanggu marapu* (the *kabisu*'s stock of holy jewelry and wooden plates) and use them to contact the *marapu*. In this area, *marapu* seem to be defined a bit more broadly than in East Sumba, and they may include the spirits of more recent dead. In Tarung, *tanggu marapu* jewelry is all made of gold and consists of very special *mamuli* never used for dancing, as well as *tabelu* (crescent-shaped forehead ornaments, called *lamba* in East Sumba), and *marangga*.

The Wula Poda is one example of a ritual that demands use of the *tanggu marapu* jewels; another is the special rainmaking ceremony also held in Tarung, near an "ancestral tree." In either of these rituals the *rato* takes the jewels from their dark attic storage place atop one of the main houseposts and washes them carefully in coconut milk. Blood from a sacrificed animal (usually a chicken) is sprinkled over the gold surfaces and the priest then contacts the jewels' owners *(marapu)*, who in a sense animate the objects.

The priest went on to say that all three types of jewels — *mamuli, tabelu,* and *lamba* — come in a form that is less sacred and much less dangerous than that used as *tanggu marapu.* The less portentous ornaments are used for body decoration in *adat* dances and other village rituals. This second type of jewelry is also sometimes used by children and young people as part of their festive parade costumes on August 17, Indonesian Independence Day.

Beyond concerns of farming and fertility, much Lauli ritual life at one time apparently centered on warfare, although the area is pacified now. In the village there are several stone altars once used for suspending skulls. A special house called a *rumah andung* (probably simply an Indonesian rendering of a Lauli phrase) is a sort of shrine where soldiers would gather before setting off on a war party. Much Lauli jewelry may once have had some connection to inter-village warfare and the philosophy linking death, headtaking, and the regeneration of life that animated it. In the 1983 interviews, however, these associations between jewelry, gold, and warfare were not made.

In Lauli there was no practice of outfitting slaves in the royal regalia as one finds in East Sumba. *Rajas* themselves reportedly did not wear gold jewelry to any great extent but would dress their sons and daughters in the metal finery of the lineage on public ceremonial occasions. The *marangga* and *tabelu* were especially important in such displays, and the triad of *marangga, tabelu,* and *mamuli* do indeed form a set. *Marangga* were worn by both girls and boys, as well as by the priests in their rituals.

Mamuli are also used as marriage exchange objects. Wife-takers give rifles, horses, pigs, and *mamuli* to their wife-givers, who respond with brides and ritual cloths. After the marriage negotiations have been opened the future wife-givers demand an initial gift of twenty to forty pigs and a certain number of *mamuli.* This daunting order can be paid in several small steps, with ten or so pigs accompanied by a few *mamuli* opening the way for later payments. Wife-givers play their hand rather cagily here. They examine each *mamuli* with great care, pointing out its defects and noting the low quality of gold used in its manufacture. They look up from their inspection of what are probably uniformly excellent *mamuli* and announce that they must have a whole bowlful of new *mamuli* for the negotiations to continue. "*Good* mamuli, this time," they say (all of this is according to the *rato* in Tarung, who was playing both speaking parts with enthusiasm). The negotiation session ends with a handshake — a "filled handshake," for the wife-takers slip their wife-givers a fine *mamuli* in their palm. After the marriage transactions are finally completed, the *mamuli* can be worn by the bride and later by her daughters, or used in further gift exchanges among families. *Mamuli* can be worn on the right ear, or as pendants on a necklace, but they are reportedly not used as decorations for *tabelu* forehead crescents.

Further details on Lauli jewelry uses are included in the plate notes. Documenting other West Sumba jewelry traditions[1] awaits further research by Sumba specialists.

---

1. See H. B. Mude's excellent survey of jewelry in Kodi 1983.

EAST or WEST SUMBA
Frontal, gold alloy. Cat. No. 114. Description p. 330.

SUMBA

Chin ornament, gold & beads. Cat. No. 117. Description p. 330.

EAST SUMBA
Earrings or pendants (*mamuli*), gold. Cat. Nos. 121, 129 & 132. Descriptions pp. 330–331.

EAST SUMBA
Mamuli, gold. Cat. No. 136. Description p. 331.

WEST SUMBA
Earring or pendant, gold. Cat. No. 123. Description p. 330.

WEST SUMBA
Pectoral, gold. Cat. No. 139. Description pp. 331–332.

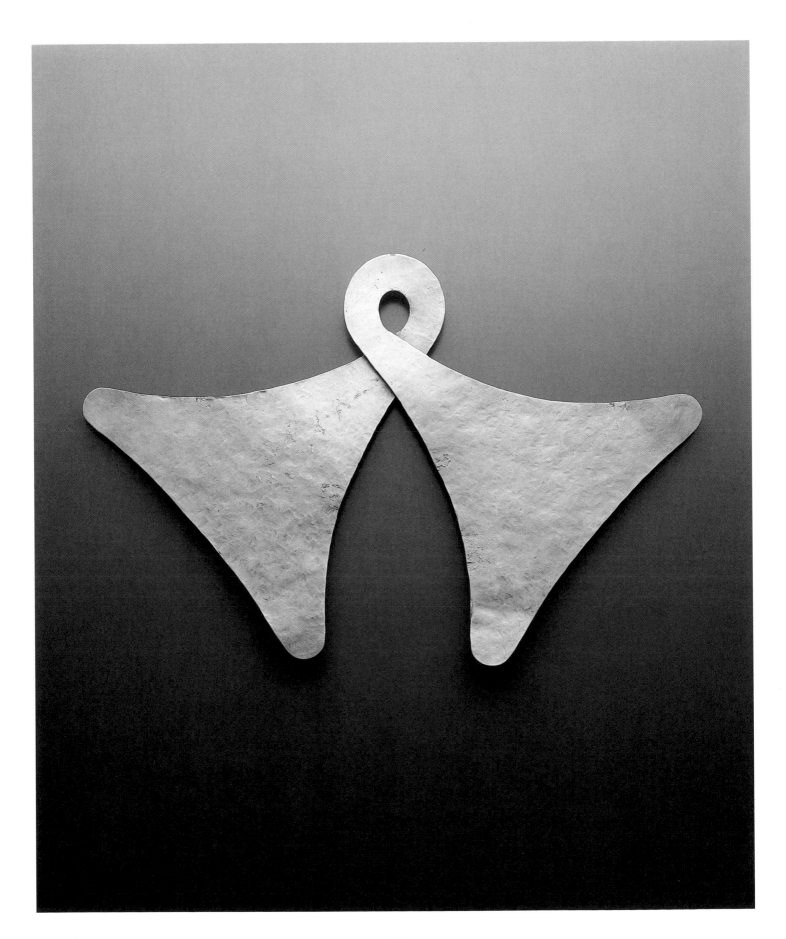

EAST SUMBA
Disk, gold. Cat. No. 141. Description p. 332.

EAST SUMBA
Chain, gold. Cat. No. 143. Description p. 332.

EAST SUMBA
Chain, gold. Cat. No. 144. Description p. 332.

niously carries him out of the sacred, feminine interior of the house into the secular, masculine yard outside (Hicks 1976:29-37). Given all this, it can be readily seen that such activities as farming are deeply religious (uniting rain from Father Sky and soil from Mother Earth). Other Timor societies also attach many layers of meaning to seeds, rain, the sky, and the earth (Friedberg 1980; Traube 1980).

In Tetum, marriage alliance gifts at new weddings include considerable amounts of metal goods, dominated by old European coins (Hicks 1976:83-84). Both symbolic gifts and practical gifts are involved. The first sort of is made up of the *na'an* ("the meat") and the *modok* ("the green vegetables"). Hicks writes that the *na'an* consists of "a buffalo, a horse, a pig, and fifty patacas [a Mexican coin brought to Timor by the Portuguese].... Patacas are included among the sacred artifacts of the clan. In the bridewealth, the fifty patacas are known as the pataca lima nulu. The modok is made up of five patacas and a sacred cloth..." (1976:83).

Many other Timor peoples use old coins (Fig. 135, 137 and 139) in this way and also make head ornaments or costume decorations from them. Figure 137 shows a South Belu man wearing an assemblage of Mexican and Dutch coins in a headdress which is also typical of the Atoni region (Schulte Nordholt 1971:illus. 10, after p. 48). Like horses, fine textiles, and certain weapons, such ornaments are used to indicate high class status. Aristocratic standing is also associated with elder brother status, with certain colors, and with the interior of houses (recall the opposite meaning of interior spaces in Tetum; these symbol systems, like language, are subject to transformations of this sort).

Figure 133 shows an Atoni *meo*, or warrior-headhunter, in full armor. In pre-modern Atoni, heads replenished village fertility and prosperity. Beyond that, headhunting (Fig. 138) was associated with secular political activity, a masculine domain, as opposed to ritual activity, associated with femininity. But that oversimplifies matters. Schulte Nordholt (1980) discussing the situation in an essay on Atoni symbolic classification, notes that the Atoni had two leaders, a sacral lord responsible for ritual and for maintaining cosmic order, and a secular lord, charged with organizing headhunting raids (Fig. 140) and ordering everyday political affairs. The sacral lord was associated with femininity, interior spaces, and immobility, while the secular lord

138. – Carved doors in Central Timor are ornamented with angular designs and geometric spirals as well as human figures carved in high relief. Here, a human's head with the hornlike headgear worn by headhunters (Barbier-Müller Museum, height: 132 cm, No. 3724, not exhibited).

139. – Man and woman riding in Central Timor. They wear full festive regalia, with numerous coins: on the man's chest, a silver disk worn only by successfull headhunters (from Schulte-Nordholt 1971, fig. 25).

140. — Headhunting was a basic feature of Timor political life in pre-modern times (from Vroklage, pl. XLIII, fig. 201).

141. — Central Timor: woman wearing accoutrements of a headhunter, at the end of the seclusion period following a childbirth (courtesy Kon. Inst. v/d Tropen, Amsterdam).

was masculine, active, and associated with areas outside the house.

In *The Political System of the Atoni of Timor* (1971: 340-342) Schulte Nordholt explains some of the meaning behind the *meo*'s intricate war costume. He also asserts that headtaking and war raids should not be classified in any simple way as secular pursuits. After noting that *meo* in a literal sense means cat (which is sometimes linked in Atoni oratory with dog, its symbolic opposite), he reports that war and headhunting were rituals initiating a *meo* into the *atoni au-besi ma nakfatu* status (literally, a man with a body of iron and a head of stone; i.e., an invulnerable man). He then recounts the various meanings associated with the textiles, ornaments, and weapons of the headhunting costume, drawing on a description by Heijmering (1846):

The meo naek's attire was the expression of the leader's courage and glory... [The] meo naek of Amfoan... wore a red and white checked kerchief embroidered by his wife with gold-thread and adorned with small gold and silver disks which flashed in the sun with every movement of his head. They were probably suspended from the silver comb on the right side of his head.... The top of this comb consists of a silver crescent (noin funan) or a silver horn (noin sunan). These names denote growth, as symbolized by the waxing moon, and power and courage, as symbolized by the horns of the buffalo. Kruyt's observation that the latter is probably the original symbolism of the ornament is associated with the moon as well. This crescent or horn frequently has three prongs, the meaning of which is not (or no longer) known. The three-pronged moon or horn also features on the hilt of the sword. According to Heijmering the latter had seven prongs, the longest one in the centre... the middle prong is replaced by a bird which is obviously stylized, like the Indonesian garuda.

The meo further wore a scarlet jacket with gilt buttons and with flowers embroidered in gold at the hem. His white belt was covered with gold and silver disks and fastened with a clasp at the back. In photograph 25 [Fig. 139] the silver discs on the cartridge pouches attached to the belt are clearly visible. He had seven of his upper and seven of his lower teeth covered with gold. Around his neck he wore twenty to thirty strings of coral beads interspersed with silver and gold beads... these coral beads constitute the most important part of the bridewealth by means of which a woman, who is a smanaf (=soul, life), may be obtained for the nono (circle, fertility, fertility power) of the group. Perhaps the meo's wearing strings of coral beads is symbolic of the fact that he also introduces a human being into the nono of the community. This supposition seems to enable in the light of the story according to which refugees from Amfoan saved their lives by handing over their strings of coral beads. His muzzle-loader had silver strips mounted on it and similarly his sword was covered with many such strips. His horse was covered with a red cloth which came halfway between its ears, it wore a silver, three-pronged crescent mounted with small red and white tufts. The rest of the horse's adornments consisted of brass bells, Chinese red horse-hair on its bridle and reins, and four silver shin-guards which were open at the back and tied with cords to its body and legs. Clearly such adornment made escape impossible for "the princely horseman." But according to Heijmering "an Amfoan prince never retreats." Clearly the chief usif, the second most important man of the realm of Amfoan, here is the war leader. (Schulte Nordholt 1971:340-341.)

Recall from the discussion of East Sumba jewelry styles how the full panoply of a *raja's* ornaments were worn not by the nobleman but by his slaves. Timor cultures employ another symbolic reversal: women sometimes dress up in the war costume and ornaments of male headtakers (Gittinger 1979:33; Francillon 1980). Francillon shows a woman attired in male costume receiving a container of war medicine in a ceremony in Wehali, a small princedom in Belu in central Timor. Wehali men leave their villages periodically to venture into other areas seeking war medicine, which Francillon (1980:250) suggests may be a symbolic substitute for heads. Upon their return the men hand over the potions to women dressed as men, who help "cool" the hunters and the objects they have carried back into the villages. This helps control the excessive "heat" associated with headhunting.

Wehali is a matrilineal enclave in predominantly patrilineal Timor (Francillon 1980:26). Wehali lords, playing "feminine roles" (in the ritual sense) controlled a number of outlying patrilineal states. The exact symbolic implications of women dressing in men's ornaments are unclear from Francillon's work, but Gittinger clarifies the situation a bit for another Belu ritual, involving new mothers (1979:32-33). Women were once confined to their houses for the first two months after they had given birth. Their re-entry into village society was controlled through a ritual in which the new mother would dress up in the costume of a male headhunter (Fig. 141). A number of symbolic equations were put forth in this ceremony. For example, men endure dangers to go into enemy territory and take heads in raids; women endure dangers in going through the "journey" of their pregnancies and surviving the rigors of childbirth. Men come back from a raid with severed human heads; woman come back from pregnancy and their two-month isolation with human babies.[1]

As these short notes indicate, the Timor symbolization of jewelry is unusually rich and could certainly bear close ethnographic attention. This is especially so at a time when war raids of the old-fashioned sort are things of the past, and war costumes and ornaments are being converted into dance costumes, much as Timor princedoms are being fit into the developing Indonesian nation.

---

1. Hicks discusses the symbolism of gender, and the association between femininity and sacredness, in his monograph *A Maternal Religion* (1984).

WEST TIMOR
Head cloth with silver elements. Cat. No. 150. Description p. 333.

CENTRAL TIMOR
Earrings, silver. Cat. No. 156. Description p. 333.

WEST or CENTRAL TIMOR
Anklet. Cat. No. 166. Description p. 334.

MOLUCCAS: TANIMBAR

In their rituals, social organization, and magnificent if little understood wooden sculptural arts, the Moluccas are a crucial transitional area linking Timor and Eastern Indonesia to New Guinea and Melanesia. Village ritual activity illustrates this. The Moluccas include societies where gift exchange between wife-givers and wife-takers occupies center stage in life crisis and village renewal celebrations (a pattern reminiscent of Eastern Indonesian cultures). On the other hand, there are cultures here which have men's secret societies – institutions associated with New Guinea. This culturally complex area on the edge of the Indonesian world has unfortunately received little recent scholarly attention, and its art forms remain largely undocumented in an era when many pieces of sculpture and metalwork have been summarily taken off to European museums without ethnographic description (not to mention local blessings).

Village ritual life is also changing rapidly, and older carving and metalworking traditions are either disappearing or undergoing energetic reconceptualization under the influence of the Christian churches, coastal Islam, and the national development efforts of the Indonesian government. Fortunately for the study of south Moluccan jewelry, an excellent, exhaustively detailed ethnography of Tanimbar marriage and political structure has recently been completed. Anthropologist Susan McKinnon's "Hierarchy, Alliance, and Exchange in the Tanimbar Islands" (1983) examines the central role of the

◄ Woman's sarong (*tais*). Warp ikat. Cotton. Tanimbar. South Moluccas, Indonesia. Detail. (Barbier-Mueller Museum, No. 3572-5, not exhibited).

10. MOLUCCAS

Pacific Ocean

TALAUD

Halmahera Sea

MOROTAI
TERNATE
● Galela
HALMAHERA
TIDORE
WAIGEO
BIAK
WEST IRIAN
OBI
MISOOL
BURU
AMBON SERAM
KAI
SERUA
NILA
TEUN
ARU
ROMANG
YAMDENA
DAMAR
Tanimbar
Islands
MOA
BABAR
LETI LAKOR
KISAR
SELARU

142. – Old woman from Tanimbar, wearing gold earrings of the type shown in Cat. No. 180 (from Drabbe 1940, fig. 47).

143. – Tanimbar men ritually cutting an elephant tusk (from Drabbe 1940, fig. 43).

house, and house wealth, in Tanimbar's village and inter-village political arenas. McKinnon shows how noble families and commoner households are bound together through thickets of "exchange pathways" based on ideas of wife-giving and wife-taking, elder brother to younger brother relationships, and "life-blood" – the vital force coursing through women that wife-givers bestow on their wife-takers. Gold pendants and silver earrings like those in the Barbier-Müller collection are important exchange objects in these systems of house wealth and marriage alliance, and McKinnon's estimable fieldwork allows us to place these pieces in their local social contexts. In Tanimbar, as in many other cultures represented in the Barbier-Müller catalogue, jewelry serves as objects through which to play out the major themes of social order.

Ethnic Groups in the Moluccas

The entire island group from Morotai and Halmahera in the north to Tanimbar, Kai, and Aru in the south (Map 10) is administered by the Indonesian government as a single province, called Maluku. Its capital is Ambon and its 1980 population was 1,411,006 persons, making Maluku the most sparsely populated province in the country (Biro Pusat Statistik 1982:46). Maluku in fact lies on the literal and sociological fringes of the Republic of Indonesia (tellingly, the Moluccas have historically been used as a place to which political prisoners have been exiled). This sprawling province is divided culturally into roughly three areas: Halmahera and its penumbra of islands equidistant between New Guinea and the long northern arm of Sulawesi; the Central Moluccas, consisting of Ambon, Seram, and Buru; and the southern Moluccas, which are composed of the Southwestern Islands stretching eastward from Timor (Roma, Damar, Nila, Teun, Serua, Wetar, Kisar, Luang-Sermata, and Babar) and Tanimbar, Kai, and Aru.

Halmahera is an ethnically diverse archipelago divided into about thirty distinct societies, some of which speak non-Austronesian languages (Lebar 1972:119). Halmahera's coastal areas are polyglot regions with long histories of trade and missionary contact with Europeans and Islamic proselytizers from Java. The Central Moluccas, the focus of great Dutch trade interest because of their spice crops, had developed a virtually *mestizo*, partially Europeanized culture by the time the colonial period ended with the Japanese invasion in World War II. Kai, Aru, Tanimbar, and the Southwestern Islands were relatively removed from these busy trade currents and retained rather parochial village societies until this century. Inter-village warfare and headhunting raids gave the region a particularly fierce reputation.

The theme of relative isolation should not be overstressed. This is especially true in the study of south Moluccan jewelry. Just as the Tanimbarese mythical founding ancestor, Atuf, came from outside the archipelago, much of the gold, silver, and ivory used in Tanimbarese jewelry and house treasure was imported from other parts of Eastern Indonesia (Figs. 142–144) and ultimately from the colonial European sphere. McKinnon reports that there were probably three main channels of trade supplying Tanimbar with its precious goods for jewelry-making (1983:87-88). Tanimbar sailors engaged, first, in trade with other south Moluccan islands (going to Aru for bird of paradise plumes, to Kai for boats, and to the Southwestern Islands for gold pendants and earrings, bead necklaces, and sarongs). Makassarese and Buginese traders from south Sulawesi maintained the second range of long-distance exchange relationships: they regularly sailed east to the southern Moluccas to buy copra, shells, and tortoise shell, using elephant tusks as payment. Citing Riedel (1886:288-289) McKinnon notes that these merchants "may well also have traded with gold pendants, earrings, swords, and bead necklaces" (1983:87). The Dutch and English ships coming into the Spice Islands furnished the third avenue by which precious metals entered the region (Figs. 142 and 144).

A brief sketch of Moluccan history might be useful for locating Tanimbar jewelry traditions within Indonesia. A key theme here is syncretism, with a stress on the interplay between the island trade empires and the monotheistic religions introduced by the trading peoples.

The Central Moluccas and Ternate and Tidore in Halmahera were *entrepôts* as well as missionary centers for spreading Christianity and Islam through the Moluccas and in fact through part of Sulawesi. Ambon is known as a bastion of Protestant Christian culture, while Ternate and Tidore grew into rich sultanates and Islamic centers whose secular and missionary influence extended over a huge swath of Indonesia from East Kalimantan to their home

144. – Young man from Tanimbar. He wears earrings similar to Cat. No. 183 as well as two breast plaques, perhaps imported (compare this plaque with Cat. No. 186) (From Drabbe 1940, fig. 102).

213

145. — Women from Luang, in the Babar Islands, wearing gold crowns and dishes that they display on their breasts as ornaments. First quarter of this century (courtesy Kon. Inst. v/d Tropen, Amsterdam).

islands. The Protestant villages of Ambon have a representative religious history that demonstrates the influence of great trading centers on the small village societies of the region.

Cooley reports that in 1966 a few Ambonese villages were Alifuru (adherents of the indigenous religion); all others were either Muslim or Protestant. These communities had been under the sway of outside rulers since the late 1400s. Cooley lists the following succession of foreigners controlling the Ambonese villages:

… the kingdoms of Ternate and Tidore in the North Moluccas, the Portuguese from 1520 until the end of the 16th century, the Dutch East India Company from 1605 til the end of the 18th century, the British for the first two decades of the 19th century, the Netherlands' Crown until 1941, the Japanese during the Second World War, and finally the Dutch again from 1945-49. Indonesian jurisdiction over this part of the Republic of Indonesia in January, 1950. (Cooley 1966:137.)

Some Central Moluccans remained loyal to the Dutch after the Revolution in 1945-1949 and emigrated to Holland.

Far from being isolated, then, the Moluccas have been a veritable grand concourse of competing ethnic, international, and religious interests (Figs. 145 and 146). The following account of Tanimbar art and jewelry focuses on artworks in their local political, mythic, and kinship meanings, but, as McKinnon suggests, further research might eventually set Tanimbar traditions within their regional framework.

Tanimbar Jewelry:
Alliance Gifts and House Treasures

Tanimbar is actually an archipelago of sixty to seventy limestone and coral islands, located in the Arafura Sea about 300 miles north of Australia and 300 miles southeast of Ambon. The 1979 population was 62,704 dispersed in eighty-two villages on twelve islands (Kantor Sensus dan Statistik Propinsi Maluku 1980:7-10, cited in McKinnon 1983:15). Four distinct Austronesian languages are spoken (Yamdenan, Fordatan, Selaruan, and Seluwasan). The east coast of Yamdena is the most heavily populated area (McKinnon did her main research in Fordata, which has a total population of only 3,675). Most villages (Fig. 147) today are down on the beaches, although formerly they were generally built on cliffs, partly for defensive purposes. Villages center on stone altars formed in the shape of boats, sometimes outfitted with beautifully carved wooden prowboards. (See McKinnon 1983:136-147 for a superb description of Tanimbar wood carving.) Ritual offerings were once presented to the supreme deity at these boat altars before and after inter-village raids and when alliances were renewed. Four or more rows of houses face the boat altar. Villages are divided into hamlets, which are themselves composed of house complexes. These are made up of aristocratic houses with names (these houses are likened to elder brothers) and unnamed houses for commoners (houses that are the "younger brothers" to the homes of nobles). Villages in pre-modern times were linked to each other through long cycles of revenge and counter-revenge, as well as through "elder brother-younger brother" protective alliances. Raids are no longer undertaken, but the village alliances are still strong and much celebrated through ritual dances and gift exchanges.

Tanimbarese aristocrats resembled their counterparts on Nias, Sumba, and Flores in that they competed with each other through ostentatious displays of gold ornaments, but Tanimbar's nobles historically went about the business of regal one-up-manship with particular verve. In McKinnon's phrase, they "flashed" their gold at each other (1983:28-29). She explains the situation this way. Villages are allied into enduring partnerships in which two settlements are said to be like elder brother-younger brother pairs. As brothers, they share food (a major symbol of their family relationship), and in pre-modern times they also enjoyed a sort of mutual defense pact in which they came to each other's aid when attacked. (Any important village would have from five to fifteen brother villages of this sort.) The village-to-village relationship was a basically egalitarian one involving two powerful groups that nurtured each other — an important contrast to the fundamentally hierarchical and unequal relationship that held between wife-giving and wife-receiving houses, where one partner provided blessings to an eternally indebted associate. Allied villages would renew their ties once every ten years or so through lavish ceremonial visits. These rituals had a double focus: tight camaraderie between brothers and an undercurrent of hostility. Gold enters at this point to symbolize both relationships:

Despite the obligations that bind two villages as brothers, it is on the very occasion of the renewal of their alliance that an

146. – Inhabitants of Kisar with different kinds of pendants. These disks or crescents are related to ornaments in Sumba and Flores although Kisar is part of the South Moluccas (courtesy Kon. Inst. v/d Tropen, Amsterdam).

147. – Monumental stone staircase with a stone human figure, in a village in Yamdena Island, in the Tanimbar Islands. This kind of megalithic work is very similar to that in Nias (from Drabbe 1940, fig. 110).

148. – Old man from the island of Yamdena (Tanimbar) with a shell necklace, gold earrings and a pendant (from Drabbe 1940, fig. 8).

underlying competition and hostility are manifest. On such occasions, the visiting villagers sail to the host village in a great fleet, disembark and march into the center of the village chanting incantations for the destruction of their host village. They then dance for four to five days a measured, but spirited, dance (which is in the formation of a boat) until the host villagers (also in boat formation) aggressively "crash into" or break up the circle of dancers. The nobles of the two villages then stand each other off and – dressed in greatcoats under which all the important gold of their respective villages is pinned – flash this gold at each other in an ultimate test of rank and power. (McKinnon 1983:28-29.)

Once they have stood each other off – or perhaps one should say shined each other off – "the two groups of villagers sit down in two straight lines opposite one another and negotiate for several days what valuables the host village will give their visitors" (McKinnon 1983:29). Several years later the villages change places, and the members of the first host village pay a visit to the second community, where the dance and the gift-giving ceremony are replayed.

In another pattern that recalls the aristocratic arts of Nias, Sumba, Flores, and Sulawesi, Tanimbarese associate metal and metalworking with the supernatural world as well as high social status. Tanimbarese ideas of "life forces" which are kept coursing through human society via marriage exchange are particularly important here.

The supreme deity of the indigenous, pre-Christian religion is a male-and-female-in-one being called Ubila'a, who contains in one entity such opposites as wife-givers and wife-takers, the sun and the moon, and the heavens and the earth. A sign of Ubila'a's great powers is the fact that he-she lives in a distant heavenly world "resplendent with gold." Ubila'a is associated not only with gold and nobility but also with height, foreignness, and abstractness. The god is the greatest of aristocrats, but it is important to note that he-she is also portrayed as a thief – Ubila'a holds all possibilities (McKinnon 1983:43-48).

Metal is important in several other ways in Tanimbarese myth. Miraculous spears figure prominently. Atuf, the single culture hero recognized throughout the Tanimbarese archipelago, created the present-day sky and its contents by wielding a magic lance he obtained by force from (in some versions) Ubila'a. The deity was forced to give up the weapon as a fine for making palm wine against *adat* law (Ubila'a first offered gold coins in payment of the fine but was informed that these were insufficient; see McKinnon 1983: 40-41, 45). With the lance Atuf speared the sun and thus created the moon and stars. In one version of the myth the sky was so near to the ground that the sun could not come up very far above the horizon. Atuf set sail for the east to remedy the situation, aided by his wondrous spear. After a number of adventures involving bizarre distortions of persons and the natural order (old women without body orifices, fruit that falls from the ground to the sky from upside-down trees), Atuf and his companions find the air growing hotter and hotter. They dunk themselves in coconut oil as protection from the heat. Then, McKinnon writes,

As they approached the horizon, they continually had to trim the top of the mast, as it kept scraping against the sky, which became increasingly lower as they moved east. Finally, when they were close enough to the sun, Atuf took up his shield – a wooden plank with a hole cut in the middle for his lance. He thrust his lance into the sun and the great hot disk shattered to pieces. The largest piece remained the sun. A smaller piece dropped into the sea and became the moon, while a thousand fragments splintered off in all directions to become the stars in the sky. (McKinnon 1983: 40-41.)

The Atuf narratives also involve gold jewelry worn by the mythical first brothers and sisters. For instance, in one version that relates how Atuf and his three sisters left their home in the Babar Islands and came to Tanimbar, Atuf placates his sister Inkelu with gifts of jewelry after a major argument (McKinnon 1983: 37-38).

Metal acts also as an important symbolic vehicle for talking about gender and marriage alliance. The contrast here, as in Sumba, Flores, the Batak regions, and the Dayak cultures, is with cloth. Hard metals and soft textiles are thought to balance each other as natural counterparts, like men and women. The Tanimbarese go beyond this, however, to conceptualize the *processes* of metal smelting and smithing and textile weaving in the same philosophical key (Figs. 148, 149, and 150). McKinnon's ethnographic research is particularly rewarding on this point (1983: 89-99). Before exploring these gender symbols, however, it would be useful to review the basic features of the Tanimbarese marriage system.

Kinship and Art in Tanimbar

Tanimbar has the sort of flexible asymmetrical marriage alliance system met so often in the Indo-

149. – Young man from the island of Selaru (South Tanimbar) with a head-dress made of bands of cotton in two colors and cock feathers. He wears silver or gold earrings (courtesy Kon. Inst. v/d Tropen, Amsterdam).

150. – Group of men in the island of Selaru (South Tanimbar) in the first quarter of this century (courtesy Kon. Inst. v/d Tropen, Amsterdam).

217

nesian cultures represented in this catalogue. In flat anthropological categories, Tanimbar has patrilineal clans and asymmetrical marriage alliance encouraging unions between men and their mother's brother's daughters – the female offspring of the houses that provided the man's father with a wife the generation before. Women ideally move in one direction only, from beneficent giver groups to indebted taker groups, and such ranked alliances (again ideally) remain in place over many generations. In actual village practice, it is mostly the aristocratic families that maintain the appearance of strict asymmetrical relationships over many generations. In their genealogies they hark back to founding ancestors who first established a fixed hierarchy of alliance relationships. They legitimate these in reference to the supreme deity and dramatize them through set "exchange pathways" (McKinnon's useful phrase) involving highly stereotyped gifts. Nobles live in houses that have names, as noted, and their house treasures include heirlooms with names and histories of their own (Fig. 152).

Commoner families, by contrast, live in unnamed houses, boast fewer prestige goods, and participate in marriage alliances with shorter pedigrees, which demonstrate less attention to strict asymmetrical relationships. McKinnon writes that the estates of commoners are inherently impermanent and that their exchange relationships with other houses are more provisional than set. Commoners suffer for this: through their genealogical ties to the supernatural, the noble families claim privileged access to the sources of life that wife-givers and women bring to wife-receiving houses. McKinnon suggests that Lévi-Strauss's concept of house societies (discussed briefly in the chapter on "Jewelry and Social Position," above) is a productive idea in investigating Tanimbarese village society, as houses are not only the salient folk category for talking about marriage and politics but dealing with houses allows anthropologists to avoid sterile debates about alternative forms of descent and marriage in the same culture. (McKinnon 1983:1-10.)

Jewelry is crucial in Tanimbarese kinship, for it gives the whole system a set of concrete symbols of surpassing beauty and local attractiveness. Jewelry is rather like the Tanimbar house: it objectifies the social order in tangible form. Tanimbarese noble houses contain things (house treasures) (Fig. 151)

and persons (living descendants of the lineage and their wives), and they symbolize both continuity to dead ancestors (Fig. 152) and alliance ties to other houses. Tanimbarese jewelry also "speaks" in two directions: house treasures descend down the patriline and in a sense serve as the "essence of the house," while marriage exchange goods, utilizing jewelry, give concrete form to alliance relationships between wife-givers and wife-takers.

Named houses are constructed about religiously powerful treasures which, as noted, sometimes carry names and have detailed histories. These named valuables include gold breast pendants or pairs of male or female earrings and are called the "master of the house." In Yamdena the core heirlooms that must not be alienated from the house through exchange are called the "riggings of the house" (McKinnon 1983:126, citing Drabbe 1940: 202). Great houses, like village altars and *adat* dance formations, are sometimes spoken of as boats. Some named heirlooms are thought to have been gifts from heavenly wife-takers, while others are said to have come from mythical creatures living in the Underworld. Treasure boxes for storing the heirlooms may also have exciting histories attached to them. (See McKinnon 1983:126-131 for specific histories of the gold pendants and metal earrings she investigated in her fieldwork.)

Aristocratic houses not only harbor permanent stores of heirlooms, they also trade precious goods among themselves at weddings and at the many other gift-giving occasions that presage or follow marriages. For any one marriage alliance the wife-giving house is designated "male" and the wife-receiving house is their "daughter" and deemed the "female" partner to the transaction. The bride-givers provide their bride-takers with female blood, or the "life source" for producing babies and keeping a steady flow of good luck coursing into the wife-receiving house and its agricultural fields. The wife-receivers for their part give back lavish bridewealth gifts. Jewelry, it happens, goes in both directions, although the pieces from the wife-givers take on a sense of femaleness and the jewelry from the bridegroom's side is seen as masculine. McKinnon's summary of the marriage gifts and countergifts describes the *adat* in detail and can be quoted in full:

"Male" wife-givers provide the following "female" gifts to their bridegroom and his side:

1. bakan: ikat-banded cotton sarongs woven indigenously and worn by women. Most valuable are those called "antique sarongs" (bakan mnanat), which are not only quite old, but in general originate from the Southwestern Islands, from which they have been imported.

2. kemene: pairs of imported gold filigree earrings worn by women. Among these filigreed earrings, the most highly prized are the ones which possess a string of beads (kmene ni lean) that link the two halves of the pair.

3. marumat: necklaces — made out of imported Venetian glass or sarodoine stone (a variety of chalcedon) beads and small bits of gold — that are worn by women. The most valuable necklaces are those called ungrela, which have an additional, long, single strand of beads which hangs down the back of the woman.

4. sislau: pairs of shell armbands; each of the pair consists of eight to ten shell rings that are cut by women from a variety of *Conus* shell and then lashed together. They are worn by women on the upper arms. The topmost ring of the most prized armshells is made from black shell.

5. af amtahan: all garden produce — especially rice (wanat) — which is grown and harvested by women; this may be given in either raw or cooked form.

From the side of the "female" wife-takers, the male objects given to the wife-givers include:

1. masa: large, important gold pendants which are worn by men (and in ceremonial dances, also by women); these most often represent a human face, alone or in conjunction with horn, boat, or half-moon motifs, but sometimes are simple, flat, round gold disks, golden kris handles, or are in the shape of some animal such as a turtle. The most valuable of these gold pendants boast a large gold link chain and clasp.

2. lela: imported elephant's tusks of varying lengths. The value of a tusk is determined by its size and length.

3. loran: pairs of imported or indigenously made silver, gold, or alloy earrings worn by men. They are solid, and pear-shaped in form, but with a split down the center in which a swatch of red cloth is usually lodged. There are many varieties of loran, but the most highly valued are those which are called Loran Luan (from the island Luang to the west), and those called "white loran" (loran nangiar), which are considered pure gold without any silver, or brass alloy.

4. suruk: antique swords. These are rarely to be seen nowadays, and the few that survive do not, in general, circulate in exchanges.

5. tuat: in all actuality, tuat refers to slightly fermented palmwine, which is, at least nowadays, rarely drunk and is never used in marriage exchanges. That which is, in fact, presented in exchanges would more properly be called palm brandy…

6. vavu and ian: pig and fish captured in the hunt by men: these may be given in either raw or cooked form. (McKinnon 1983:86-87.)

151. — Domestic altar in the form of a human figure. Skulls of ancestors and riches were kept on the plank above the altar (courtesy Kon. Inst. v/d Tropen, Amsterdam).

152. — Family altar from a nobleman's house in Tanimbar, in the shape of a stylized human figure. This panel was reportedly made to support a plank onto which was placed the skull of an ancestor, along with jewels and other prized possessions. This sculpture was on loan to the Tropenmuseum, Amsterdam, from 1915 before being sold. (Barbier-Müller Museum, No. 3568, height 130 cm. On permanent loan to the Dallas Museum of Art, plate 49 in the catalogue *Indonesian Primitive Art*).

Gender and Jewelry

Now we are finally in a position to see how gender concepts touch on jewelry and jewelry-making. McKinnon writes that feminine goods, such as the gold filigree earrings, bead necklaces, and of course the woven textiles are all lightweight, pliable open-work constructions (1983:88). Male goods, such as the oval-shaped silver earrings, tusks, and swords, are all dense heavy things formed of single pieces. Masculine valuables are also generally sharp and pointed. Noting that the erotic symbolism is obvious, McKinnon goes on to link these hard and soft gifts and countergifts to Tanimbarese concepts about the place of women and men in society: "like the valuables that speak of their qualities, males occupy single, permanent and fixed places in the world − in houses. The place of females is always shifting and composite; their role − like the lashing of armshells and the threads of a necklace − is to bind together a multiplicity of discrete houses through the encircling flow of the life-blood they bear" (1983:88).

The way in which the two types of valuables are manufactured also has strong connotations of masculinity or femininity, and with that, wife-giving or wife-taking (McKinnon 1983:90-99). This small corner of material culture also draws the Tanimbarese and any analyst of that culture into other parallel ranges of complementary ideas.

The manufacture of such female goods as cloth is designated a "cool" endeavor and sometimes involves ritual activities to cool the object produced. Alternatively, female goods are sometimes produced without the aid of any special "hot" plant roots (McKinnon 1983:89-90). Male valuables, such as certain metal treasures, by contrast are refined and shaped through heat and often require the use of "hot" roots, which demand the death of a living creature to provide heat. In fact, the linkage of death and metalworking goes one step further: smelting and working gold is said to "kill the gold" (McKinnon 1983:90-91). Heat was apparently thought to escape during the metalmaking activity and endanger the smith. McKinnon also notes that few Tanimbarese houses made their own metal earrings. Most of the ornaments were imported from outside the island, although some − thought locally to be of lower quality − were made in Tanimbar villages.

Citing Drabbe (1940) McKinnon reports that cutting elephant tusks (Fig. 142) into armband rings (a masculine endeavor for producing masculine goods) was also associated with heat and danger and was well regulated through ritual, while the feminine activity of lashing shells together into armbands posed no such threat and seems to have been a rather mundane activity (1983:91-92). An elephant tusk was likened to a human body, and cutting off one end to make rings for armbands was referred to as "severing the head" of the piece. Ivory cutting and carving were accompanied by gong and drum music and ritual dancing. McKinnon suggests that there may have been an implicit association between ivory-working and that other prime male pursuit, headtaking. Although the words of the songs accompanying tusk-cutting dances dwell on ivory-working, "One is nevertheless tempted to draw the comparison between this dance and the one which follows the taking of heads in warfare," McKinnon writes. "At the time of the final offering made to Ubila'a and the ancestor images, the man who has cut the tusk also makes an offering to the sawdust, in a way that is not dissimilar to the offering made to the heads captured in war." The cutter feeds ceremonial foods to the ivory dust left from the cutting work. "Like a head captured in warfare, the sawdust of the beheaded tusk is fed and then thrown outside the village wall, where it is asked to remain contentedly, and not seek vengeance for its death" (McKinnon 1983:92-93).

Male activity (Fig. 150) in the world is thus associated with threats, dangers, death, heat, and close ritual regulation of these things, but McKinnon notes that it is an oversimplification to say that "cool" female activity as a consequence produces life. Rather, in the philosophical pattern found in many Indonesian cultures, life flows from the union of opposites such as heat and coolness, masculinity and femininity, and, in Tanimbar, hunting and gardening.

Men enter the forest armed with inherited "hot" roots to ward off dangers. Pigs are sacrificed to aid in these protective efforts, and men consume the particularly hot parts of the animal such as the fat and internal organs (McKinnon 1983:94-95). The coolness of women can potentially sap some of the heat from men and their hunting implements, so the various rituals staged for the hunters of game (and the hunters of heads) are generally protected from feminine interference. Gardening success, by contrast, derives from the coolness of the land (making it ready to receive seeds) and the ministrations of *both* wives and husbands. Although hunting and hunting rituals are exclusively male activities, gardening and gardening ceremonies are performed by both sexes working in concert as married pairs. McKinnon makes an especially astute observation here:

[I suggest] that death involves the denial or absence of sexual complementarity, while growth and life explicitly requires the complementarity of male and female. The process which is productive of death always turns in on itself – it pits heat against heat, man against man (or pig, as the case may be). The process which is productive of life always turns towards an other, which is complementary in nature: it requires the union of male and female, and the union of objects which have been generated out of heat and death with objects which have been generated through coolness and growth. (1983:97.)

This idea that creativity comes from the union of complementary opposites colors Tanimbarese ideas about jewelry, for this theory about the life-giving process at work in humans and the world underlies marriage exchange. Women's sarongs are cool objects and can be used to cool such hot things as masculine metal objects. Thus, the rationale for Tanimbarese gifts and countergifts at marriage: female goods "cool" hot, danger-filled male goods. Female valuables given by the wife-givers are cool, like brides, while "male valuables given by the wife-takers may be more or less hot, depending upon their 'weight', history, and value" (McKinnon 1983:98). In this system of ideas, jewelry pieces can "marry" each other:

What is clear is that the process of exchange effects the symbolic union of male and female. That this is so can best be seen in the conceptualization of the exchange of the big, named valuables which travel along lolat rows between name houses. Such valuables "rest" for years in houses while they "search for their spouses"... They from house to house only when two pieces – which are perceived to be the "match" or "equal" (noka) of one another – can be directly exchanged. In the exchange, it is said that the two valuables "marry one another" (rsifa). (1983:98.)

Readers intrigued by these Tanimbarese ideas of "gendered jewelry" and ritual, familial, and agricultural fertility and creativity are encouraged to read McKinnon's rewarding thesis in its entirety.

SOUTH MOLUCCAS
Comb, wood & bone. Cat. No. 174. Description p. 334.

SOUTH MOLUCCAS
Comb, bone. Cat. No. 175. Description p. 334.

SOUTH MOLUCCAS
Earring, gold alloy. Cat. No. 177. Description p. 334.

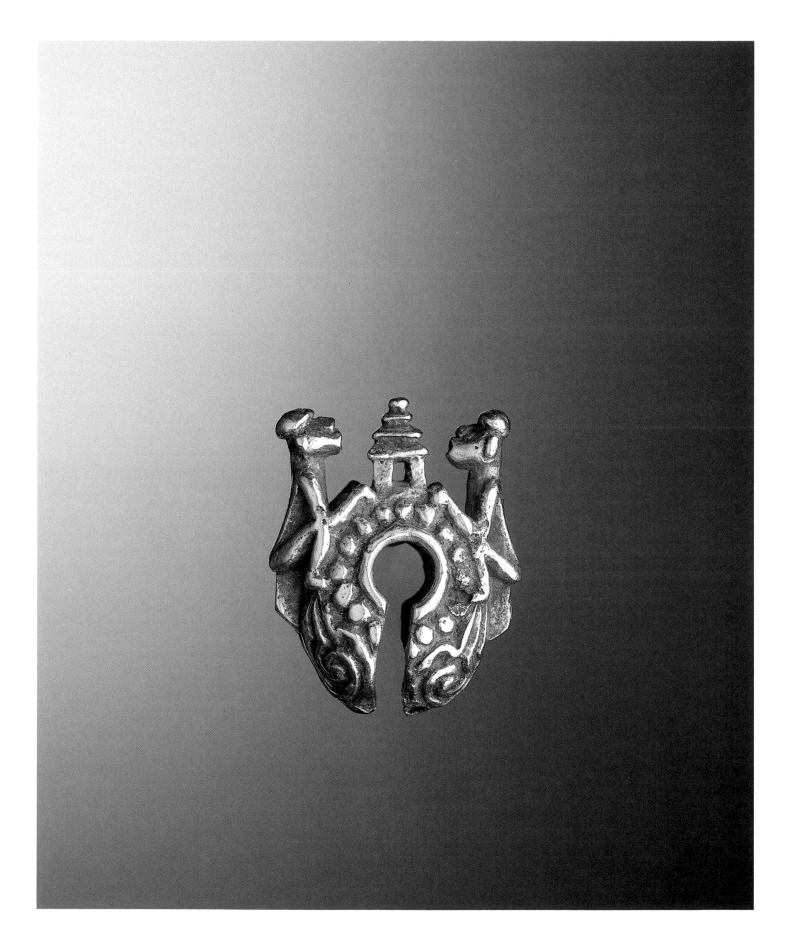

SOUTH MOLUCCAS
Earrings, gold. Cat. No. 180. Description p. 335.

229

SOUTH MOLUCCAS
Disk, gold. Cat. No. 185. Description p. 335.

SOUTH MOLUCCAS
Pendant, gold alloy, Cat. No. 186. Description p. 335.

SOUTH MOLUCCAS
Pendant, gold. Cat. No. 187. Description p. 335.

NORTHERN LUZON, PHILIPPINES

The seven thousand or so islands of the Philippine archipelago sweep northward from Indonesia, completing a huge crescent from Sumatra to Luzon that curls around the Southeast Asian mainland. Indonesia's intense historical interaction with Indic civilization, Middle Eastern Islam, and Dutch colonialism set it apart somewhat from the Chinese-influenced, largely Christianized Philippines, with its colonial contact with Spain (1521–1898) and the United States after the Spanish American War. The Philippines attained its independence in 1946. Indonesia and the Philippines are strikingly similar, however, on a number of fronts: both are composed of numerous ethnic societies (Indonesia with 250 to 300 societies, the Philippines with approximately 100); most of the many ethnic languages of each country belong to the Western Austronesian family; and a primary social and ecological distinction in both countries is that between lowland paddy rice farmers organized into relatively large and centralized societies and mountain slash-and-burn agriculturalists divided into small tribes and chiefdoms. Long-term contact between the peoples of partially Muslim Mindanao and seafarers from the northern rim of Indonesia (coastal peoples from North Kalimantan, Sulawesi, and Halmahera) has made the cultural unity of the two countries even firmer. In addition, in cultural anthropological terms, most of the peoples of the Philippines and Indonesia from North Sumatra through Luzon belong to a single, albeit rather roughly defined,

◀ Man's jacket. Cotton with embroidery. Bagobo. Mindanao, Philippines. Detail. (Barbier-Müller Museum (former Beyer collection, Manila), No. 3549-30, not exhibited).

11. NORTHERN LUZON

153. — These two mannequins, shown in the exhibition, are dressed with the clothes and regalia of a Bagobo nobleman (153) and his wife (154). Bagobo are highlanders of the Davao district in the southern part of Mindanao, a largely Muslim island today. The woman's sarong is made of the fiber of a wild banana tree (Musa textilis), rubbed with a piece of shell. This kind of textile is called *abaca* (Photograph Pierre-Alain Ferrazzini).

culture area separate on the one side from the lowland state peoples of mainland Southeast Asia and on the other side from Melanesia.

It is possible to make a finer cultural distinction within this area. Most of the Philippine jewelry in the Barbier-Müller collection comes from cultures in Northern Luzon (a few pieces are from the southern island of Mindanao; (Figs. 153 and 154). The mountain societies of Luzon show especially close cultural similarities to the societies of inland Sulawesi and Kalimantan. Recall that many of these Indonesian cultures did not participate in the sort of ranked marriage alliance relationships found among the Batak and many of the peoples of Sumba, Flores, Timor, and Tanimbar. Rather, ethnic societies in inland Sulawesi and Kalimantan traced their kinship relationship out through both parents instead of constructing great patrilineal clans. Northern Luzon kinship also is often focused on the bilateral family and overlapping personal kindreds. Recall as well the sort of jewelry found in that range of Indonesian societies: ornaments glorified men's prowess as warriors and hunters; provided amulet protection for those same masculine tasks; decorated marriageable girls in a sort of public advertisement of their family wealth; and announced the high social status of aristocrats and their ties to the supernatural world. Northern Luzon jewelry repeats all these themes. (Figs. 155 and 156) Further, it is interesting that one does not find any pronounced fascination with heritable house treasures that "glow with power," so common in the Indonesian societies with strong clans and asymmetrical marriage alliance. Northern Luzon peoples do have house heirlooms passed down through the family (treasures composed mostly of old Chinese jars, porcelain plates, gold earrings and necklaces, and metal weapons), but ideas of heirloom objects invested with supernatural powers do not seem to be as elaborate or well systematized as those found in Sumatra or Eastern Indonesia. Exchange involving Northern Luzon jewelry is also more similar to that found in Kalimantan and inland Sulawesi than to the kind of intricate exchange pathways linking ranked houses in the Batak areas, Sumba, Flores, Timor, and Tanimbar. Luzon jewelry is involved in exchange that tends to be between lowlanders and highlanders or between mountain ethnic groups. In addition, there are rather simple forms of exchange at marriage; these generally lack the complex ideologies of gifts and countergifts encountered, for instance, in Tanimbar.

The following brief introduction to Northern Luzon jewelry is taken from published sources, not field-work, and only sketches in the outlines of this part of Philippine culture. The Barbier-Müller collection includes pieces used by a number of societies: Ifugao, Tinggian, Gaddang, Kankanay, Kalinga, Ilongot, Bontoc and Isneg. As in Indonesia, it is usually inaccurate to assign set ethnic provenances to particular jewelry pieces, for many ornaments are worn in a variety of ethnic homelands and some-times acquire different names and different uses and interpretations as they are traded from group to group. Border areas between ethnic homelands are particularly problematic, for these are regions of enthusiastic borrowing. The ethnic identifications and the names assigned to the pieces in the collection are therefore suspect in this sense.

Northern Luzon has three broad ranges of cultures: Negrito societies (forest peoples who once de-pended on a nomadic hunting and gathering way of life but now sometimes practice slash-and-burn agriculture); coastal peoples such as the Ilocano (Christianized rural Filipinos participating to a large extent in the national culture; see Jocano 1982); and mountain societies like those represented in the Barbier-Müller jewelry exhibit. The highlanders, who are sometimes collectively called Igorots ("mountaineers"), have similar social structures and artistic systems. Far from being closed societies, they all interacted to some extent with lowland peoples and Spanish and American colonialists and missionaries. Northern Luzon represented consider-able wealth to the Europeans. The mountain region around the old Spanish *comandancias* of Ambu-rayan and Pepanto, in the Kankanay homeland, is a region of old gold and copper mines (Lebar 1975: 91). Spanish trails were carved into the mountains to take advantage of such mineral wealth and to convert the "pagans" to Christianity. Some Luzon groups retain portions of their indigenous religions and village cultures today, although assimilation into the Philippine national culture is proceeding as national development projects bring swift change.

Before national independence in 1946 — and in some cases before the twentieth century — Northern Luzon societies were based on small villages practic-ing a mixture of swidden (slash-and-burn) and wet-rice agriculture. In general, the societies with vast

154. – An elaborately dressed Bagobo woman from the island of Mindanao. The corresponding male costume is shown in Fig. 153. Like Northern Luzon peoples, the Bagobo cover the body at ritual occasions with hundreds of beads, pendants and cloth strips (Photograph Pierre-Alain Ferrazzini).

155. – Necklaces made of different kinds of earrings gave men an opportunity to show their wealth. Here, Mr. Makesset Marcellino Matbagan, ex Barrio-Captain, first councilman of Tep-Tepan Sul (West Bontoc), also wears an armlet with a small human figure, formerly related to headhunting practices (Photograph Roland Beday-Brandicourt, June 1984).

156. – Isneg woman at Kubidao, with an old chest ornament made of mother-of-pearl pendants and beads mounted on pineapple fiber, similar to Cat. No. 220 – 222 (Photograph Thierry David, 1983).

irrigated rice terraces (Ifugao, Kalinga, Tinggian, Kankanay, Bontoc, Gaddang) supported larger populations, larger and more socially complex villages, and somewhat more political centralization than those based on shifting cultivation. Stratified chiefdoms of the sort found among the Batak in Sumatra were not present, but a number of these irrigated rice cultures had a class of ritual aristocrats, who were often called *kadangyan*. This was a wealthy, ceremonial class who put on lavish feasts and commissioned village artwork (ritual altars, wood sculpture) to increase their prestige *vis-à-vis* their rivals. Much of Northern Luzon art, in fact, was produced by this class of status-conscious, small-scale nobles. (Figs. 155 and 156) The competition among aristocrats and the intensity of art production there, it should be noted, do not seem to have attained the superheated levels found in Nias or Sumba in Indonesia, but the basic thought systems were similar. Predominantly swidden societies, those that cultivated impermanent plots (Isneg, Ilongot, Ibaloi), tended to have less political stratification and a less prodigious production of material art. These peoples were, however, like the wet-rice cultivators, ritual orators of great sensitivity and technical accomplishment. Warrior status was stressed over class standing; settlements were not as permanent as in wet-rice societies; population density was also less. These people also tended to borrow their textiles from weaving peoples (Ellis 1981: 220).

Kinship, warfare, and economic relationships were similarly organized in all these societies in Northern Luzon. Kindred linked by marriage often harbored some hostility toward one other, a theme that showed up in lengthy marriage negotiations with an undercurrent of distrust. New husbands sometimes had to pay brideservice to their wives' family (that is, contribute their labor to that group for a set time). Gift exchange at marriage seems to have had relatively little defined gift-and-countergift organization of the sort found in Indonesia. Before modern times, headhunting raids were endemic. Taking a head was seen as the masculine pursuit par excellence and worked to free a man of the social and religious taints of immaturity (that is, taking a head made him a responsible adult). Headhunting, as in Kalimantan, was also thought to aid in the regeneration of human and agricultural life. Peace pacts, which developed as a companion institution to headtaking raids, were ritualized relationships that united distant regions into war-free partnerships. Pacts of this sort crosscut the highlands in many directions, sometimes connecting different ethnic groups. Practical and prestige goods were traded between pact-holding areas, most likely facilitating the energetic and long-term transmission of gold jewelry from one part of Northern Luzon to another.

Highland religions also had many similarities. They often posited a distant supreme deity (perhaps a mistranslation, as these figures were more like supernatural creative, aboriginal forces than anthropomorphic gods) and many layers of lesser deities, natural forces (thunder, lightning, volcanos), spirits, ghosts, and dead souls. Female spirit mediums were important human vehicles for contacting this spirit world, especially in times of illness. Male ritual specialists tended to focus on village-wide ceremonies and headtaking ventures. Many local religions divided the cosmos into five regions: the earth, the Skyworld, the Underworld, the Downstream region, and the Upstream region.

The different Northern Luzon cultures are related to each other in a theme-and-variations manner.

Isneg

Isneg (Fig. 157) is the modern ethnographic designation of a group sometimes referred to as Apayao (Wilson 1967), a term that may have come from the name that the Isneg gave to the major river in their region (Keesing 1962:154). Lebar lists eight synonyms for Apayo: Apayaw, Isneg, Isnag, Isned, Itneg, Mandaya, Kalina', and Payao (1975:97). Keesing clarifies matters by noting the great amount of migration in pre-colonial and Spanish times in this far northern section of Luzon (1962:154–159). Van Overbergh gives a useful lexicon of terms used by the Isneg to refer to themselves, as well as a list of ethnic designations their neighbors used for them (1932:15–25).

This was a fairly rich area of importance to the townspeople in the lowlands. Ilocos Norte was crosshatched with routes for trading rice, maize, sugarcane, fish, fine textiles, and gold, which was washed up from streambeds (Keesing 1962:162). Highland goods (tobacco, vegetables, mats, rattan, honey, and wax) were traded for coastal goods (livestock, cloth, ceramics, metal, and salt) (Lebar 1975:99).

Morice Vanoverbergh, a Catholic missionary, wrote

157. – Young Isneg boy, wearing a chest ornament made of mother-of-pearl pendants and beads, similar to No. 222 in this catalogue (from Vanoverbergh 1912).

241

158. – A Kalinga family at the beginning of this century. Note the earrings made of mother-of-pearl (Cat. No. 198) and the many bead necklaces (From Worcester 1912: No. 869).

159. – A Kalinga funeral, where the seated corpse of a girl is bedecked with ornaments. (From Worcester 1912: No. 876).

in his descriptive monograph on the Isneg that these people had permanent villages, at least in the sense that the houses stood from year to year, and smaller settlements in the hill swiddens (1932: 59–60). Permanent villages would sometimes stand virtually abandoned while everybody was off tending the hill plots. Kinship was bilateral, and traditional political leadership was closely associated with wealth and headhunting prowess. Heirloom treasures of powerful families consisted of the usual old jars, beads, and porcelain plates, which apparently also sometimes moved between houses as bridewealth (Lebar 1975: 99).

Kalinga

One of the most thoroughly decribed Northern Luzon societies, the Kalinga are wet-rice farmers situated in an unusually fertile mountain region (see Barton 1949; Dozier 1966; Magannon 1972; Lawless 1977; Lebar 1975: 92–95). Barton reports that in 1949 they were producing two rice crops a year and regularly exported the grain to other areas (1949: 9). They also grow dryfield rice, sugarcane, sweet potatoes, beans, taro, maize, betel, tobacco, and coffee. In northern Kalinga, like Ifugao, there are areas of spectacular steep green mountain slopes terraced with row upon row of rice fields. Kalinga villages in the north consist of six to thirty households, located between or along these mountain slopes. In the south, Kalinga towns support two hundred or so households (Lebar 1975: 92). Barton reports that there are two sorts of houses: square, for commoners, and octagonal, for aristocrats (1949: 9–10).

The social class system consists of four levels: the *kapus*, or poor people; the *baknang*, or wealthy class; the *kadangyan*, rich aristocrats who also head kinship groups; and the *pangat*, a small group of male political leaders drawn from the *kadangyan* (Barton 1949: 145–146). This last class is rather unusual in Luzon, according to Barton, and represents considerable political centralization and separation from simple kin-based leadership. The bilateral kindred (in which brothers and sisters trace relationships out through both their mother and father) forms the core of the kinship system (Lebar 1975: 93–94; Barton 1949: 32–83; Dozier 1966: 53–126). Another way of looking at the Kalinga kindred is to see it as the group of descendants of two pairs of great-grandparents (in the south, grandparents). Kindreds overlap and group

242

together into endogamous units (*bobolog*) living in set geographical regions (Lebar 1975: 93). Aristocratic families in the south may be developing something similar to bilateral descent groups with corporate title to land and other property (Lebar 1975: 93, citing Dozier 1966: 118).

Indigenous religions concentrated on the replenishment of creative forces to keep human society and agriculture going (Lebar 1975: 95; Barton 1949: 17–31). Barton cautions us, however, not to wax too eloquent on this point. He writes that central Kalinga has little faith in "miraculous increase" in farming and tends to expect the opposite, the diminishment of their crops (1949: 18). Their rituals guard against this unhappy circumstance. Ritual, in fact, is very much stressed over any formalized system of beliefs (Magannon 1972: 49). There are, however, rather vaguely defined deities, starting with Kabunian ("those to whom offerings are made"), the distant supreme deity or perhaps class of deities. Arranged below him are KiDul, the god of thunder, KiLat, the god of lightning, and several others associated with natural forces. The deities are associated with a Skyworld; the earthly world is filled with various spirits, demons, and souls of the dead; and in addition there are the Underworld, the Downstream region, and the Upstream region. This cosmology strongly recalls the pre-Christian religion of the Toba Batak in Sumatra (Barton 1949: 17–21).

The trade alliances common in many parts of Northern Luzon were particularly important in Kalinga society and may have been strengthened by the opening up of Spanish trails into the mountain provinces (Lebar 1975: 93). Barton suggests that *abuyog*, or ritualized trading partner relationships (rather similar to Kula relationships discussed in "Jewelry and Exchange"), may have long preceded the development of the Kalinga's ritualized peace pact, or *budong* (1949: 167–168). Pact holders included entire families, and dozens of Kalinga peace pacts snaked across the Luzon highlands and allowed for the carefully managed flow of food and prestige goods. Trading partners met periodically and regaled each other with oratory, dances, ceremonial foods, and gifts (Barton 1949: 167–208; Dozier 1966: 197–239; 269–291).

Kalinga art focuses on ceremonial gatherings, oratory, fancy dress, and ornamentation for the wealthy class. This is no surprise for a prosperous society based on irrigated rice cultivation. The *pangat* (the class of noblemen with political duties) solidified their positions through fine oratorical performances, by maintaining numerous peace pacts, and — at one time — though homicide (Barton 1949: 147–170). Barton reports that at the time of his research some *pangat* were unashamedly citing acquired rather than inherited wealth as part of the rationale for their high position (1949: 152), but headhunting was already on the wane.

Rice fields, house sites, and livestock constitute the bulk of heritable property, augmented in wealthy families by old Chinese jars, plates, gongs, and beads. Barton writes: "Like all Luzon mountaineers, the Kalinga is an antiquarian, and almost any old object, such as a bead, gong, jar, or plate, has, in addition to its use value and exchange value, an antiquarian value" (1949: 101). If an heirloom must be exchanged, because of dire economic straits, a Kalinga should ideally trade it to someone within the family. Heirlooms derive much of their value from their non-utilitarian nature, their patina of age (or rather, family history), and from their reputation in the neighborhood:

Gold earrings having an intrinsic value of 20 to 40 pesos are usually worth four to five times as much if old. Heirloom value might raise the price to ten times in the eyes of a particular family. It would be futile for anyone to cast a new earring or bead, however closely the color and form of the old one might be imitated in it, and try to get a high price for it, for every Kalinga knows all the old beads in his community or neighboring ones. He values ancient Chinese and Japanese jars (gusi) at considerably above their prices as antiques in the world market... I counted sixty-six [Chinese bowls] on the shelf for antiques (every house has one) in the house of Kanao.... The most valued heirloom gusi, together with some old plates or bowls, are kept on a shelf called pagud, and a guest is supposed to notice its position and not sit with his back toward it or spit toward it. Beads of carnelian or agate, even old glass beads, are valuable in proportion to their age, as also are Chinese imitations of ancient Greek beads. I look in vain for the genuine Greek beads. (Barton 1949: 102.)

Dozier writes that Kalinga have special terms for their treasures: heirloom beads are *onggoong*, jars are called *gossi*, and plates, *maokong*. Agate beads have three names, beginning with the most valuable: *masilap*, *abali*, and *kinawayan* (1966: 132). He also reports that heirlooms are rarely traded outside the boundaries of the subprovince today (1966: 149), although ancient trade in these goods must have been extensive. Some Kalinga heirlooms are probably over four hundred years old — and have been sitting on house shelves storing up

prestige all that time. In reviewing some theories about their historical origins, Dozier concludes that over many centuries the mountain peoples such as the Kalinga got a wide range of Chinese items from lowland peoples who traded more directly with mainland China. Trade in ceramics began as early as the tenth century and reached a peak in the fifteenth, during the Ming dynasty; it included ceramics from Sawankhalok (Thailand) and Annam (Indochina) (Dozier 1966: 27).

According to Barton, some Kalinga families also count spears and hand-adzes (made from broken cast-iron Chinese kettles) among their heirloom treasures. Textiles figure importantly in ceremonial gift exchange (Barton 1949: 102); they are woven and accumulated to exchange at births, weddings, funerals, (Fig. 159) and similar occasions. Kalinga art comes into its own, though, in costume. Barton refers to the "riotous adornment" of East Kalinga women, who wear many strings of bead necklaces as well as bead headbands and gold earrings (Fig. 158). Dozier cites a 1913 description of women's dress:

The women wear gaily colored upper garments and skirts. The wealthier ones have enormous necklaces of agate beads, while heavy and peculiarly shaped ear ornaments of brass and of mother-of-pearl are almost invariably in evidence. Their heads are adorned not only with abundant natural locks, but with switches made from the tresses of departed female ancestors or of relatives having long hair. Into the masses of hair thus built up are thrust gay scarlet and yellow feather plumes. (Dozier 1966: 17, citing Worcester 1913: 1213.)

Tinggian

This culturally heterogeneous group had ties to the Bontoc, Kalinga, and Isneg (Apayao), as well as historical contact with coastal societies in the time of ancient Chinese trade. Ilocano influence is also extremely strong, fostered by the construction of trails into the highlands (Lebar 1975: 95–96). Tinggian have maintained trading ties with other mountain groups for centuries. Irrigated rice as well as such garden crops as dryfield rice, vegetables, fruit, tobacco, and betel are grown. Some authors make a distinction between valley Tinggian, who practice wet-rice agriculture, and mountain Tinggian, who are dependent on swidden (see Keesing 1962: 149, 121). Tinggian have the usual assortment of Luzon livestock: water buffalo (important as prestige symbols), pigs, chickens, and dogs.

Villages have councils of elders and are joined together into defensive alliances of two or three settlements. In former times headhunting between villages more than 10 or 15 miles distant was customary, for such raids were necessary for the successful completion of funerals for important persons (Lebar 1975: 96–97).

Wealthy "headmen," who own many rice terraces, dominate village politics and have large stores of ceremonial wealth consisting of Chinese porcelain jars, copper gongs, and old beads (Keesing 1962: 121). A culture hero called Kaboniyan is said to be the original giver of rice, jars, gongs, and beads (Lebar 1975: 97). Valley Tinggian partake in elaborate rituals, while the upland swidden agriculturalists have a simpler ceremonial life and a less complex class structure. Female spirit mediums and male ritual specialists who lead village-wide ceremonies are important in indigenous religion. Aristocrats vie with each other for prestige by holding large ceremonies. Kinship is bilateral, with the same sort of emphasis on the personal kindred found in Kalinga (Lebar 1975: 96, 97). Ceremonial dress includes masses of beads. Keesing reports that a French surgeon travelling in Tinggian territory in about 1820 noted that women wore "sleeve-like bracelets of beads, and head ornaments of 'pearls, coral beads, and pieces of gold'" (Keesing 1962: 135–136, citing Gironière 1854).

Gaddang

This society is generally divided into the pagan and the Christian Gaddang. The converted group is much like any lowland Filipino population, while the Gaddang still practicing its own religion maintains a relatively distinct highland culture (see in general, Wallace 1970: 5–7, 31–32, 50–94; Lebar 1975: 100–102). Pagan Gaddang society (the subject here and henceforth simply called the Gaddang) relies on swidden agriculture, hunting, fishing, and trade in forest products. The kinship system includes bilateral personal kindreds with institutionalized spouse exchange (*solyad*) found in some areas, a practice serving to establish ties between different regions. Marriage is generally with people outside the local settlement, which can consist of as many as ten to fifteen houses. Gaddang settlements are distant from one another and in former times were easy prey for attack by neighboring Gaddang, a situation that fostered a climate of distrust and wariness.

Wallace writes that headtaking had apparently stopped by the time of his research (1965–1966), but raids were common up until World War II. Headtaking was apparently once thought necessary to assure good harvests, to secure blood revenge, and to increase a man's social status. Some of the prizes, or trophies, of raids were converted into jewelry:

In procuring a head, a party would usually ambush a lone person or an occupied house during the night. The head and fingertips of the deceased were severed from the body with a head-axe or knife. The men would then immediately return to the home settlement where the head was placed on a bamboo pole and a dance held in celebration of a successful hunting party. A considerable amount of frenzy and trance is reported to have been associated with the dance. Only the teeth, fingertips, and jawbone of a slain enemy were saved, the teeth and fingertips for necklaces and the jawbone as a gong holder. (Wallace 1970: 32.)

To some extent peace pacts between different areas controlled hostility and also had an economic effect: the distinct products of each region (say, spears) were exchanged for the other's products (say, forest products) during the periodic meeting of the pact-holders (Wallace 1970: 34).

Gaddang dress and decoration styles reflected the culture's trade ties to other highland peoples and their fairly extensive ritual system. Ceremonial dress for women consisted of beaded textiles, sarongs, decorated jackets, and masses of heavy beads (used as necklaces and head ornaments). Male ritual costume (Fig. 160) included a spear, decorated breechcloth and belt, and bead necklaces. Teeth were sometimes pegged with gold (Ellis 1981: 242).

Beads are important exchange items and markers of family wealth as well as being simply decorative. Wallace reports, for instance, that marriages are negotiated by a go-between, who carries a valuable "marriage bead" (*kiring*) from the boy's family to the girl's family. If the bead is accepted, the girl's parents agree to the wedding. Reckoned in value to equal one, two, and sometimes even three water buffalo, these beads are considered to be the first part of the young man's brideservice to his wife's family (again, the labor he contributes to them). If the engagement is broken by the man's side, they forfeit the marriage bead, but if the young woman's parents want to get out of the arrangement, they simply return the bead. Marriage negotiations also include some inheritance goods which in wealthy

161. – Ritual platform in front of a Bontoc men's house. This megalithic structure, called *fawi*, was the meeting place of old men, as well as a shelter for human skulls (from Jenks 1905, plate XXXII).

162. – Beheaded human body on its way to burial, in the Bontoc area, at the beginning of this century (from Jenks 1905, plate CXXXV).

families can include land, food, pigs, water buffalo, beads, and clothing (Wallace 1970:47–49). For about a year after the wedding the couple ideally should live in the bride's parent's settlement.

Jewelry is also associated with the institution of spouse exchange (*solyad*). Wallace found that forty percent of the forty-five married or widowed adults in the two communities he studied had participated in *solyad*. The basic system involves two married couples: the husbands agree to switch wives and ask their parents to negotiate the trade. The parents of husband A will bring a *kiring* marriage bead to the parents of the husband B. Wallace writes that both parties see this bead as a sort of collateral payment that assures that the reconstituted couple will conduct themselves properly. Sometimes the parents of the man B will offer to pay the other set of parents a *kiring* of their own, but more commonly B's parents will simply ask for a larger payment. Much negotiation ensues; side A repairs to their house and some days later returns, bearing a *lufay* (an expensive earring) along with the original bead. This earring is the customary second sort of collateral and must be forfeited along with the marriage bead if someting goes wrong with the temporary marriage. *Solyad* varies considerably according to where the houses of the original couples are located. If the two pairs live in distant villages, the wives each move to their new partner's houses for up to a year, rarely seeing their husbands during this time. If the two original couples live in the same community, the pairs will stay put in their own houses with the men making periodic night-time visits to the other house. Wallace notes that any functions *solyad* may serve beyond the two obvious ones – relieving childlessness and expanding the range of kin obligations – are obscure (1970: 50–53).

Jewelry is also connected to Gaddang religion. Women mediums go into trances to contact the spirit world and weigh themselves down with many strings of beads. Sometimes they ask for a bead along with a pig and maybe some clothing from a patient when they perform a curing ceremony (Wallace 1970: 101, 104). Gaddang houses, finally, envelop religiously charged ancestral treasures, called *unting*:

When a Gaddang family builds a house, before they live in it, six supernaturally endowed objects are placed inside, and a [ceremony] is held. Each time a new house is constructed these objects are moved to the new residence. The house objects hang from the rafters, protect the house and its occupants from illness and misfortune, and impose the taboo of not eating mudfish or corn inside the house. The most revered and powerful of the house religious objects is the kubang, on which the other five seem to depend. It consists of a bundle of clothing, generally a G-string, a skirt, and some beads, which belonged to the parents or grandparents of the male head of the household. Informants say that having the kubang in the house is a way of honoring their ancestors.... The second most important piece, according to informants, is the antolay. This is a piece of wood about two feet long and two inches square. One end of the piece is crudely carved into the shape of the head of a man.

Geometrical designs are cut just below the head. The quality of the realism in the head depends upon the skills of the carver, the male head of the household. The other four pieces, the alat, buririraw, lutong, and kuliwang are considered companion pieces to the kubang and antolay. The alat is a small woven rattan ball with a chicken feather attached to it. The buririraw is a small woven bamboo fan. The luton is a small piece of wood with rattan strings attached to it, and the kuliwang is the core of a piece of bamboo attached to a single string of rattan. (Wallace 1970: 112.)

In other areas, lowland influence has largely eliminated such house treasures.

Bontoc

Bontoc villages, centered on stone ritual platforms, are relatively large (300 to 2,000 residents, a size which makes them appproach towns; see Lebar 1975: 83). Villages are divided into *ato*, or wards, and generally have girls' dormitories and a men's house for council meetings. This stone council house and the ritual platform in the center of the ward were associated with headhunting in the past (Figs. 161 and 162). Dryfield vegetable and tuber crops supplement wet rice grown in terraces. The wealthy class in prosperous areas supported a fairly vigorous art tradition including gold jewelry, basketry, and stone structures for displaying heads. Bontoc also weave cloth, which they combine with gold, shell, and bead jewelry into elaborate dance costumes. War dances are particularly important (Fig. 164) (Alejandro 1978: 115).

Ato residence strongly affects the local conceptualization of kin relationship, which is bilateral with "some skewing toward patrilineality" with respect to men's ward affiliations (Lebar 1975: 84). A group of elders or *intugtukan* govern the ward and serve as a court. *Kandangyan,* the class of ritually defined aristocrats, dominate the ward councils, although they are not actual chiefs (Lebar 1975: 84–85;

163. – Kalinga girl with tattooed arms, bead necklaces and typical silver or gold earrings (Photograph Eduardo Masferré).

164. – Bontoc warrior wearing necklaces similar to those in Cat. No. 224 (Photograph Eduardo Masferré).

165. – Ifugao headhunter with his trophies (Barton, 1930 plate XLVIII).

166. – Ifugao man and his wife, at their elevation to Kadangyang rank. The man's headdress is similar to Cat. No. 193 in this catalogue (From Barton 1930, plate XXIII).

Cawed 1972: 11–15, 35–37). As is the case among the Ifugao, the Bontoc *kadangyan* class are basically a group of titleholders who endeavor to rise through the prestige ranks by hosting more and more elaborate feasts. As ceremonial nobles compete, many animals are sacrificed and their meat distributed to ward residents. At the same time, the *kadangyan* acquire more precious goods with which to outdo their competitors. Pre-modern Bontoc society practiced headhunting, another means of increasing prestige, and maintained peace pacts with other mountain societies (Cawed 1972: 20–25).

Family property of the wealthy includes rice land, dryfields, the house, and the granary. House heirlooms consist of gold earrings and necklaces, beads for head decoration, and old wine jars, which the Bontoc lovingly divide into six varieties, named according to the jar's color, design, and size (Cawed 1972: 40–41). Head beads receive similarly painstaking attention:

For a long time the women did not wear anything from the waist up; instead of clothing, the breast, neck, and arms had tattooes. Their hairs are held in place by colorful beads, some of which are rare and valuable like the apon-ngey made of red agate stone cut in different shapes; the fukas of white ivory having tapering oblong shape; of lesser value, like the moting, tiny red, white, and yellow porcelain beads; ing-ngit, which are bones of snake and teeth of the monkey. These two have other purposes than the one they were intended for. The snake bones are boiled now and then to cure stomach aliments; the monkey teeth are for protection against lightning.

The last is the koshao made of black stone, worn by a widow in mourning. Besides these, both sexes wear an earring of crudely fashioned gold material called the chinomog. This is inserted into the big holes of the ears, its weight pulling them down to shoulder length. Around their neck they wear a similar type of earring, tied singly or in a row by a black thread. This necklace is called uway. (Cawed 1972: 11–12.)

Men wore distinctive little basket-type hats on the back of their heads:

The colorful small rounded hat, beautifully adorned with beads, boar's teeth, and red feathers, called the fal-lake, is worn by bachelors; while a slightly larger one, brown and unadorned, is worn by married men. These hats, besides their decorative purpose serve as pockets for keeping pipes, tobacco leaves, matches, and other little things. (Cawed 1972: 10–11.)

Kankanay

This is another society that reckons descent bilaterally, relies on both wet rice and dryfield crops, and identifies high social status with the ability to mount lavish feasts. However, the Kankanay and their neighbors the Ibaloi have been subject to particularly heavy cultural influences from outside societies, because their homelands are located in the gold and copper mining areas of the highlands.

Bello reports that women today decorate their bodies chiefly through the use of hair ornaments, earrings, and bead necklaces, although other jewels and extensive tattooing were once common. Women wear upper blouses and woven, wrapped sarongs. Jewelry consists of copper or shell earrings, bead leglets, and copper coins worn around the neck. Men once wore black headbands for mourning, and aristocratic men wore red headbands as marks of high status. (Bello 1972: 35–36.)

Ifugao

Famous in art history circles for their wood sculpture, and well publicized these days in travel posters for their lush green terrace-covered mountains, the Ifugao have attracted considerable social science scholarship (Barton 1919, 1930, 1938; Dumia 1979; Hutterer 1973; see Conklin 1968 for a bibliography). They are similar in a number of ways to other Northern Luzon mountain societies. Ifugao live in hamlets of eight to twelve houses set on hills or along slopes, where they cultivate rice, taro, and sweet potato with rice wealth having great prestige value. Ritual organization helps control access to land and regulate farm labor tasks, kinship centers on an ideally exogamous bilateral kindred, and their religious cosmology posits the usual five realms (Lebar 1975: 78–82). However, Ifugao are distinctive in several ways. Their sculptural arts are extraordinary, and their aristocratic class, the *kadangyan*, (Fig. 166) maintained their status via an unusually rich array of prestige goods connected to lavish status-validating ceremonies. These goods included hornbill headdresses, gold beads, Chinese jars, gongs, and swords. The head ornament (difficult to see on fig. 165), worn by *kadangyan* women (Cat. No. 191) at rituals and possibly at their funerals (Ellis 1981: 241, citing Barton 1946: 172), is a good example of the Ifugao aristocracy's tradition of ostentatious display. This class also staged lavish rituals to increase their prestige. This was made possible by the fact that they were the only ones with enough rice land to produce a regular surplus. Traditional Ifugao society notably had no chiefs

167. – An Ifugao headhunter with some of his trophies: human or animal skulls (from Worcester 1912: 894).

168. — Ilongot man wearing on his forehead the extraordinary ornament made from the beak of a hornbill (see another example of this kind of head-dress, called *panglao*, in this catalogue No. 195) (Worcester 1912: 854).

in a practical, political sense, nor any well-institutionalized governmental forms such as a chiefly councils. *Kadangyan* status was largely one of ritual power and religious influence (Lebar 1975: 81).

The material arts in this culture were largely systems of objects designed to validate the special status of the *kadangyan* aristocrats. Wealthy families commissioned wooden deities (*bulul*) to insure full harvests and coincidentally to dramatize their own high social status (only rich families could afford the many animal sacrifices associated with *bulul* carving; see Ellis 1981: 196–197). Large hardwood benches called *hagabi* were constructed when a family attained *kadangyan* status (Lebar 1975: 81). Ifugao art resembles that of Nias in such practices, for Nias aristocrats also had to pass through several stages of feast-giving and art-commissioning before they could finally arrive at the apogee of status (marked by the construction of a great house in Nias, comparable to the *hagabi* bench in Ifugao). The prestige of warriors (again, in both societies) was demonstrated through the display of captured heads on a special skull shelf (Figs. 165 and 167).

In Ifugao, marriage unites "enemy groups" (Hutterer 1973: 37). In this, marriage is tied both to warfare and to prestige. Weddings usually entail an exchange of pigs and other gifts, but in the Kiangan area more extensive and elaborately defined bride-wealth gifts (*hakba*) are given to the bride's family. These gifts consist in part of death blankets, women's skirts, breechcloths, war knives, old jars, iron pots, spears, knives, and axes (Barton 1919: 16). Fines are also payable in rice-wine jars, knives, spears, pigs, chickens, baskets, and dishes (Barton 1919: 54–58, Plate 24). Barton writes that the Ifugao recognize two sorts of property, family property whose sale is ritually regulated, and personal property. *Ma-ibuy*, or family property, consists of rice lands, forest lands, and heirlooms, including gongs, rice-wine jars, gold neck ornaments, strings of amber-colored glass beads, and *bungol*, strings of agates and bloodstones. The current owner (rather, the family steward) of these treasures will outfit his family with the jewelry at ceremonies, at the same time that he displays the heirloom jars and gongs (Barton 1919: 32–34).

Ilongot

An uncommonly insular and unassimilated society with a reputation among lowlanders for fierceness, the Ilongot number about 3,500 and practice shifting cultivation. (See R. and M. Rosaldo 1975; M. Rosaldo 1980; R. Rosaldo 1980; Rosaldo and Atkinson 1976.) They live in scattered hill settlements made up of four to nine compound households, which are themselves dispersed somewhat within calling distance from each other. Dryfield rice is the staple, supplemented by root crops and hunting; pigs and chickens, rarely eaten, are raised for sale. Kinship is bilateral, dominated by a concept called the *bertan*. The definition of this shifts according to context, from one meaning that identifies *bertan* with the local group (a relatively endogamous group sharing a dialect and acting as the maximal unit for revenge raids in headhunting) to another that associates *bertan* with an ambilaterally claimed social category. People inherit their *bertan* from either their father or their mother and individuals claim no more than four *bertan*. Genealogical knowledge is shallow. In the northwest bridewealth is paid in a marriage which unites members of distant *bertan*, while in the northeast all marriages are accompanied by considerable gift-giving (including guns, bullets, cloth, and jewelry).

Dispute settlement is ritualized, and again headhunting was once the primary means of settling feuds and regulating relationships between distant groups. A man took a head to "relieve his heart" (R. and M. Rosaldo 1975:105) when unsettled by a festering feud or an unavenged death in the household. Renato Rosaldo (1980) writes that contemporary Ilongot remember their history as an ebb and flow of feuding times and peaceful times. Headtaking was associated with masculinity and male adult status (Fig. 168); a man first took a head not so much for the clichéd right to get married (a popular stereotype of Northern Luzon headtaking)

but rather to rid himself of the burdens and taints of immaturity (1980: 139–144). Once a young man had taken a head he had the right to wear the Ilongot's primary piece of male jewelry – the curved red hornbill earring called *batling* – in his upper earlobe (see Cat. No. 200). Headtaking reinvigorates the headhunter, but in a special sense:

Regarded as a ritual, headhunting resembles a piacular sacrifice: it involves the taking of a human life with a view toward cleansing the participants of the contaminating burdens of their own lives. Taking a head is a symbolic process designed less to acquire anything (whether so-called soul stuff or fertility) than to remove something. What is ritually removed, Ilongots say, is the weight that grows on one's life like vines on a tree. Once cleansed through participation in a successful raid, the men are said to become "light" in weight, "quick" of step, and "red" in complexion. Thus youths accentuate and older men recover – if only for a relatively short and gradually fading span of time – their characteristic youthful vigor as "quick ones." (Rosaldo 1980: 140.)

Rosaldo also notes that the red hornbill earrings move about when the wearer walks, and "Ilongots liken the motion of earrings to a light walk with quick steps, to gleeful laughter, to health and happiness." Further, the headhunter is praised in oratory and song in reference to his splendid ear ornaments (M. Rosaldo 1980: 149, quoted in Ellis 1981: 248):

Hear, here they are these men who have taken heads,
Wearing earrings, they have taken heads,
Hear, here they are, all lined up, the girls,
Wearing new red blouses, all the girls,
Ah, like a twisting vine, the thighs of the killers and the girls.

Symbols of this type and beauty surely exist for many Northern Luzon ornaments. Like the culture of jewelry in Indonesia, the symbolism of decoration in the Philippines awaits further study.

NORTHERN LUZON
Head ornament, brass. Cat. No. 191. Description p. 335.

NORTHERN LUZON
Headdress, hornbill skull, etc. Cat. No. 193. Description p. 335.

NORTHERN LUZON
Headdress, hornbill skull, etc. Cat. No. 195. Description p. 335.

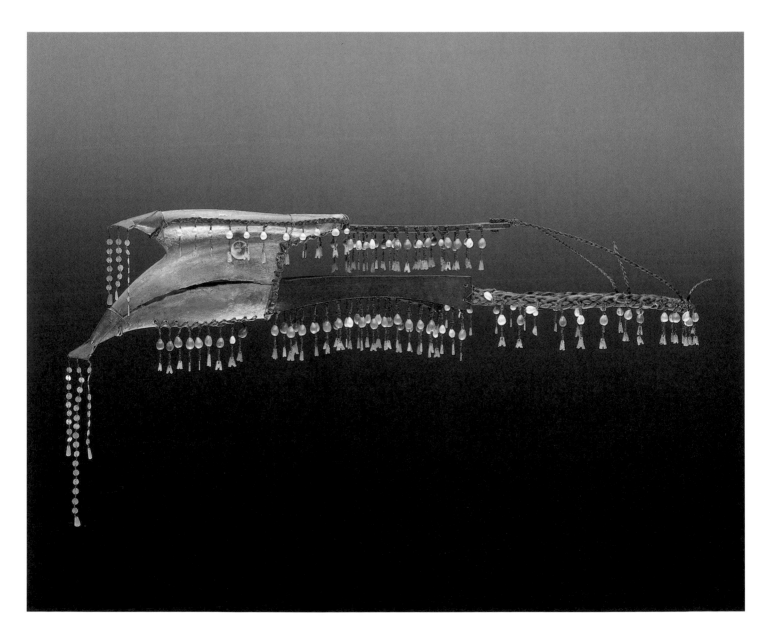

NORTHERN LUZON
Earrings, gold & brass. Cat. Nos. 205–208. Descriptions p. 336.

NORTHERN LUZON
Earring, brass. Cat. No. 215. Description p. 336.

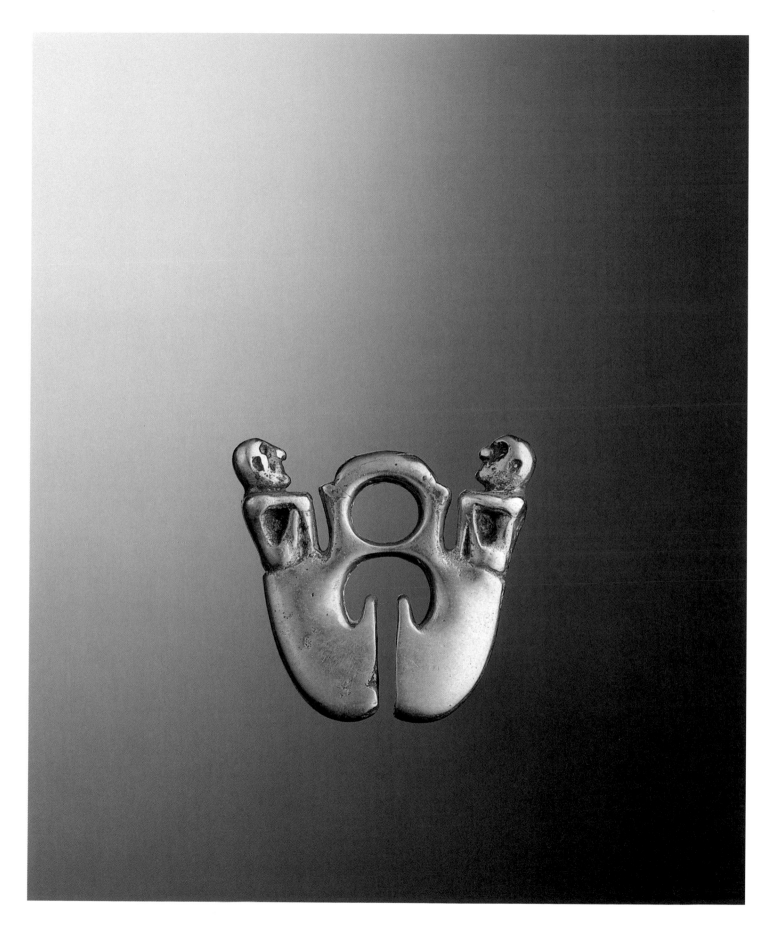

NORTHERN LUZON
Chest ornament, mother-of-pearl, etc. Cat. No. 220. Description p. 336.

NORTHERN LUZON
Belt, shell, etc. Cat. No. 234. Description p. 337.

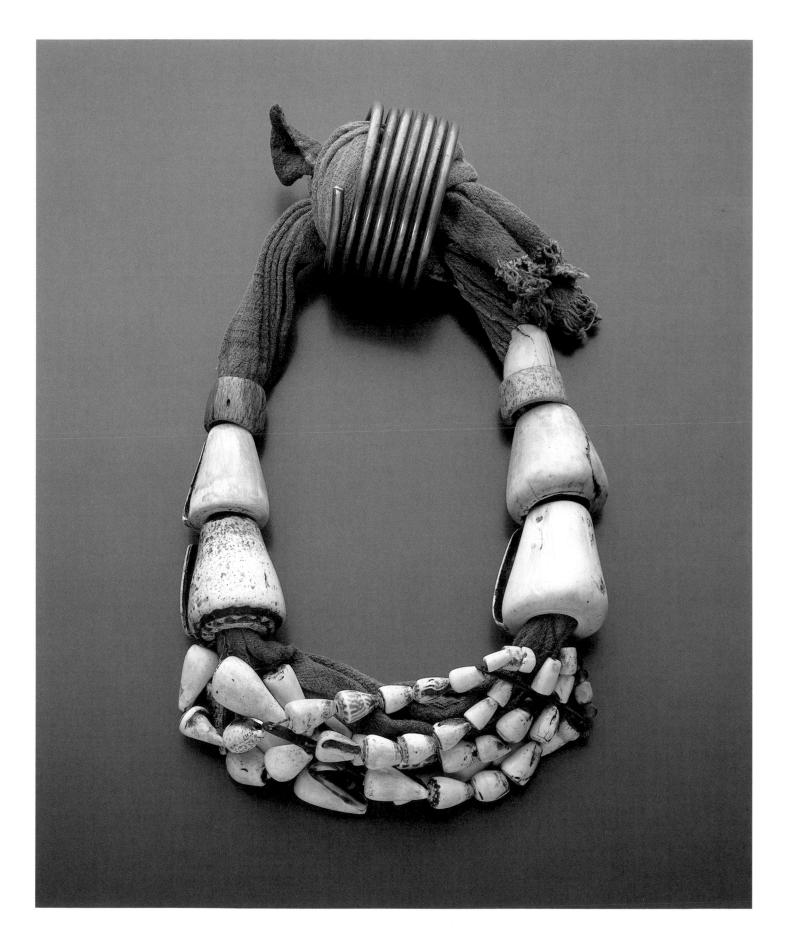

265

NORTHERN LUZON
Armlet, wood & tusks. Cat. No. 231. Description p. 337.

MINDANAO
Belt, brass. Cat. No. 250. Description p. 338.

13. NORTH SUMATRA, Batak (Karo), earrings, silver. H. 17.5 cm.

Description p. 320

13

14. NORTH SUMATRA, Batak (Karo), earring, silver. H. 16.3 cm.

15. NORTH SUMATRA, Batak (Karo), earrings, gilded silver. H. 12 cm.

Description pp. 320-321

Colour plate (14) p. 105

14

15

16. NORTH SUMATRA, Batak (Karo), earrings, gilded silver. H. 9 cm.

17. NORTH SUMATRA, Batak (Karo), earrings, gilded silver. H. 8 cm.

Description p. 321

16

17

18. NORTH SUMATRA, Batak (Karo), earrings, gilded silver. H. 5 cm.

19. NORTH SUMATRA, Batak (Toba), earrings, brass. H. 3 cm.

20. NORTH SUMATRA, Batak (Toba), earrings, brass. H. 4.5 cm.

Description p. 321

21. NORTH SUMATRA, Batak (Karo), necklace, gilded silver. H. 35 cm, W. 17.6 cm.

22. NORTH SUMATRA, Batak (Karo), necklace, gilded silver. H. 51 cm.

Description pp. 321-322

Color plate (22) p. 107

23. NORTH SUMATRA, Batak (Karo), necklace, gilded silver. H. 24 cm.

24. NORTH SUMATRA, Batak (Karo), pendant, silver. W. 16.5 cm.

Description p. 322

25. NORTH SUMATRA, Batak (Karo), jacket clasp, gilded silver. H. 25 cm.

26. NORTH SUMATRA, Batak (Karo), bracelet, gold & gilded silver. W. 17 cm.

Description p. 322

Color plate (26) p. 109

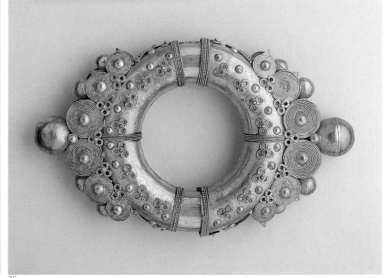

27. NORTH SUMATRA, Batak (Karo), bracelet, gilded silver. D. 7.3 cm.

28. NORTH SUMATRA, Batak (Toba), bracelet, brass. W. 10 cm.

Description p. 322

29. NORTH SUMATRA, Batak (Toba), bracelet, silver. D. 8 cm.

30. NORTH SUMATRA, Batak (Toba), bracelet, brass. D. 8 cm.

Description pp. 322-323

Color plate (29) p. 111

29

30

31. NORTH SUMATRA, Batak (Toba), bracelet, brass. D. 8.5 cm.

32. NORTH SUMATRA, Batak (Toba), bracelet, brass. D. 7.3 cm.

Description p. 323

31

32

33. NORTH SUMATRA, Batak (Toba), bracelet, silver. D. 7.3 cm.

34. NORTH SUMATRA, Batak (Karo), ring, silver & copper. H. 5.8 cm.

35. NORTH SUMATRA, Batak (Karo), ring, brass. H. 3.5 cm.

36. NORTH SUMATRA, Batak (Karo?), ring, gilded silver. H. 3.5 cm.

Description p. 323

33

34

35

36

37. NORTH SUMATRA, Batak (Karo), ring, gold. H. 2.2 cm.

38. NORTH SUMATRA, Batak (Toba), ring, brass. H. 4.3 cm.

39. NORTH SUMATRA, Batak (Toba), ring, brass. H. 2.5 cm.

40. NORTH SUMATRA, Batak (Toba), ring, brass. H. 2.5 cm.

Description pp. 323-324

Color plate (38) p. 113

37   38   39   40

41. KALIMANTAN, Dayak, headdress ornament (?), brass. H. 11.3 cm.

42. KALIMANTAN, Dayak, headdress ornament (?), brass. H. 14.2 cm. (Back view).

Description p. 324

41   42

43. & 43a. KALIMANTAN, Dayak (Kenyah-Kayan?), earrings, brass. L. 7 cm.

44. KALIMANTAN, Dayak (Kenyah-Kayan?), earring, brass. L. 11 cm.

Description p. 324

43   43a   44

45. KALIMANTAN, Dayak (Kenyah-Kayan?), earrings, brass. H. 8.8 cm.

46. KALIMANTAN, Dayak (Kenyah-Kayan?), earrings, brass. H. 8 cm.

47. KALIMANTAN or SARAWAK, Dayak, earring, silver. H. 8.3 cm. (Upside down).

Description p. 324

45

46

47

48. KALIMANTAN or SARAWAK, Dayak, earrings, brass. H. 6 cm. (Upside down).

49. KALIMANTAN or SARAWAK, Dayak, earrings, brass. H. 5.3 cm. (Upside down).

50. KALIMANTAN or SARAWAK, Dayak, earrings, hornbill beak. H. 3.2 cm. (Upside down).

Description p. 324

Color plate (49) p. 123

48

49

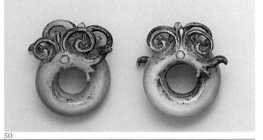

50

51. KALIMANTAN, Dayak (Kenyah-Kayan), earrings, brass. H. 13.5 cm.

52. KALIMANTAN or SARAWAK, Dayak, earrings, brass. H. 6.8 cm.

Description p. 324

Color plate (51) p. 125

51

52

53. KALIMANTAN or SARAWAK, Dayak, earring, hornbill beak. L. 12.8 cm.

54. KALIMANTAN or SARAWAK, Dayak, earring, hornbill beak. L. 9 cm.

55. SARAWAK, Dayak (Bidayuh), necklace, wickerwork, etc. D. 30 cm.

Description p. 324

Color plate (55) p. 127

53

54

55

56. SARAWAK, Dayak (Iban), armlet, clamshell. H. 4.2 cm.

57. SARAWAK, Dayak (Iban), armlet, clamshell. H. 3 cm.

Description p. 324

56

57

58. SARAWAK, Dayak (Iban), armlet, wood. D. 9.5 cm.

59. SARAWAK, Dayak (Iban), armlet, wood. D. 10 cm.

60. KALIMANTAN, Dayak, pendant, bone. H. 11 cm.

Description p. 325

58

59

60

61. KALIMANTAN, Dayak (Bahau?), pendant, wood. H. 15.5 cm.

62. KALIMANTAN, Dayak, pendant, wood. H. 12 cm.

63. KALIMANTAN, Dayak, pendant, wood. H. 12 cm.

Description p. 325

61 62 63

64. KALIMANTAN, Dayak, pendant, wood. H. 12.8 cm.

65. KALIMANTAN, Dayak, pendant, wood. H. 9.1 cm.

66. KALIMANTAN, Dayak, pendant, wood. H. 8.5 cm.

Description p. 325

64 65 66

67. CENTRAL SULAWESI, head ornament, brass. W. 22.2 cm.

68. CENTRAL SULAWESI, head ornament, brass. W. 21.5 cm.

Description p. 325

67 68

69. CENTRAL SULAWESI, head ornament, brass. W. 23 cm.

70. CENTRAL SULAWESI, head ornament, brass. W. 23 cm.

Description p. 325

Color plate (70) p. 139

71. SULAWESI, SELAYAR ISLAND, earring, gold. H. 2.6 cm.

72. CENTRAL SULAWESI, Toraja, necklace, wood, etc.
H. (element) 15 cm.

Description p. 325

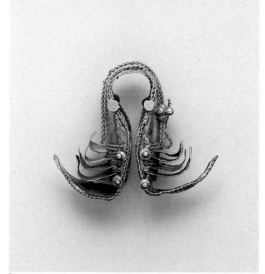

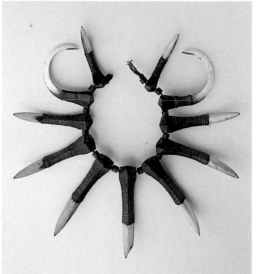

73. CENTRAL SULAWESI, pendant, brass. H. 6.8 cm.

74. CENTRAL SULAWESI, pendant, brass. H. 5.7 cm.

Description pp. 325-326

Color plate (74) p. 141

75. CENTRAL SULAWESI, pendant, brass. H. 5.2 cm.

76. CENTRAL SULAWESI, pendant, brass. H. 5.1 cm.

Description pp. 325-326

77. CENTRAL SULAWESI, pendant, brass. H. 5.6 cm.

78. SULAWESI, pendant, brass. H. 6.7 cm.

Description pp. 325-326

79. CENTRAL SULAWESI, Toraja, bracelet, silver & glass. D. 10 cm.

80. CENTRAL SULAWESI, figurines, brass. H. 7 & 7.9 cm.

Description p. 326

Color plate (80) p. 143

81. CENTRAL FLORES, Nage, frontal, gold. H. 47, W. 26 cm.

Description p. 326
Color plate (81) p. 155

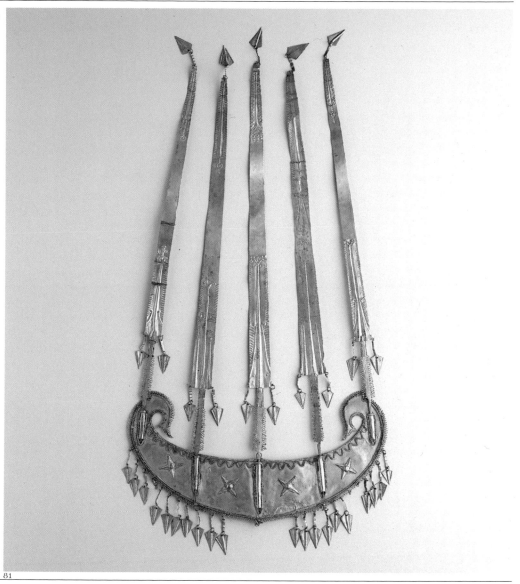

81

82. CENTRAL FLORES, Nage, frontal, gold. W. 28 cm.

Description p. 326

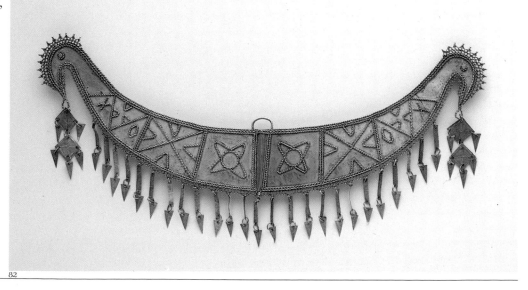

82

83. CENTRAL FLORES, Ngada, earrings, gold. H. 3.4 cm.

84. CENTRAL FLORES, Ngada, earrings, gold alloy. H. 4.7 cm.

85. CENTRAL FLORES, Nage, earrings, gold. H. 10.3 cm.

Description pp. 326-327

Color plate (85) p. 157

83

85

84

86. CENTRAL FLORES, Nage, Lio, earrings, gold. L. 5.6 cm.

87. CENTRAL FLORES, Nage, Lio, earrings, gold. L. 5.9 cm.

88. CENTRAL FLORES, Lio, earrings, gold alloy. H. 6.4 cm.

89. CENTRAL FLORES, Lio, earrings, gold. H. 4.5 cm.

Description p. 327

Color plate (86) p. 159

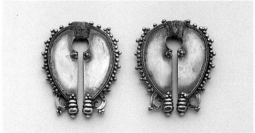

86

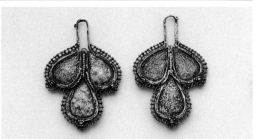

88

87

89

90. CENTRAL FLORES, Lio, earrings, gold. H. 3.5 cm.

91. CENTRAL FLORES, Lio, earrings, gold. H. 4.2 cm.

92. CENTRAL FLORES, Lio, earring, gold. H. 5.4 cm.

Description pp. 327-328

90

91

92

93. CENTRAL FLORES, Lio, earrings, gold. H. 5.4 cm.

94. CENTRAL FLORES, Lio, earrings, gold. H. 4.8 cm.

95. CENTRAL FLORES, Lio, earrings, gold. H. 5.3 cm.

Description p. 328

Color plate (93, 94 & 95) p. 161

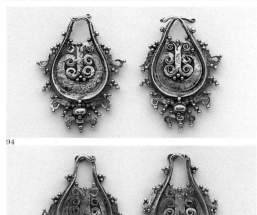

96. CENTRAL FLORES, Ende (?), earrings, gold. H. 13 cm.

97. CENTRAL FLORES, Lio (?), earrings, gold. H. 8.7 cm.

Description p. 328

98. LEMBATA, earring, silver. H. 4.5 cm.

99. LEMBATA, earrings, silver. H. 6 cm.

Description p. 328

100. Found in WEST FLORES, Manggarai, pendant, gold. W. 6.8 cm.

101. Found in WEST FLORES, Manggarai, disk, gold. D. 5 cm.

Description p. 328

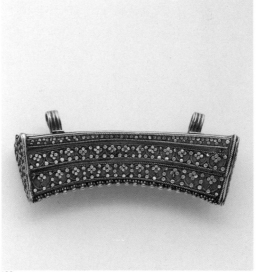

100

101

102. CENTRAL FLORES, Ngada, pendant/bag, gold. H. 10.4 cm.

103. CENTRAL FLORES, Ende (?), pendant, gold. H. 7.3 cm.

Description p. 328

102

103

104. CENTRAL FLORES, Ngada, pendant, gold alloy. W. 6 cm.

105. CENTRAL FLORES, Ngada, pendant, gold alloy. W. 7.7 cm.

Description pp. 328-329

104

105

126. EAST SUMBA, *mamuli*, gold.
H. 6.5 cm.

127. EAST SUMBA, *mamuli*, gold.
H. 7.9 cm.

Description pp. 330-331

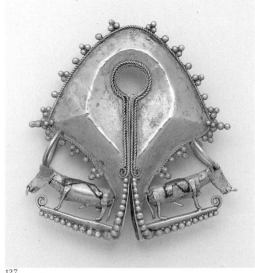

126

127

128. EAST SUMBA, *mamuli*, gold.
H. 7.2 cm.

129. EAST SUMBA, *mamuli*, gold.
H. 8 cm.

Description p. 331

Color plate (129) p. 183

128

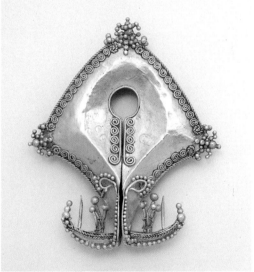

129

130. EAST SUMBA, *mamuli*, gold.
H. 7.2 cm.

130a. Detail.

Description p. 331

130

130a

131. EAST SUMBA, *mamuli*, gold.
H. 7.5 cm.

132. EAST SUMBA, *mamuli*, gold.
H. 6.6 cm.

Description p. 331

Color plate (132) p. 183

131

132

133. EAST SUMBA, *mamuli*, gold.
H. 7.2 cm.

134. EAST SUMBA, *mamuli*, gold.
H. 10.2 cm.

Description p. 331

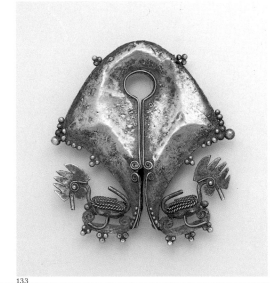

133

134

135. EAST SUMBA, *mamuli*, gold.
H. 10.2 cm.

136. EAST SUMBA, *mamuli*, gold.
H. 12.7 cm.

Description p. 331

Color plate (136) p. 185

135

136

137. EAST SUMBA, element of *mamuli*, gold. H. 3.7 cm.

138. SUMBA (?), statuette, silver. H. 4.5 cm.

Description p. 331

137

138

139. WEST SUMBA, pectoral, gold. W. 30 cm.

140. WEST SUMBA, pectoral, gold alloy. H. 20 cm.

Description pp. 331-332

Color plate (139) p. 189

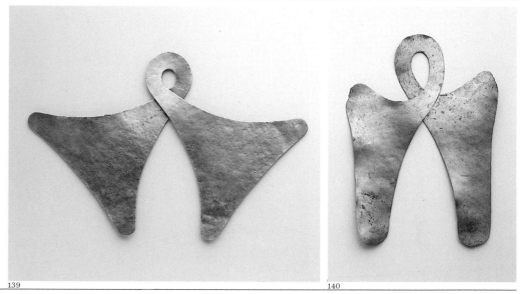

139

140

141. EAST SUMBA, disk, gold. D. 15 cm.

142. SUMBA, disk, gold. D. 8.8 cm.

Description p. 332

Color plate (141) p. 191

141

142

143. EAST SUMBA, chain, gold.
H. 74 cm.

144. EAST SUMBA, chain, gold.
L. 148 cm.

Description p. 332

Color plates (143 & 144) pp. 193 & 195

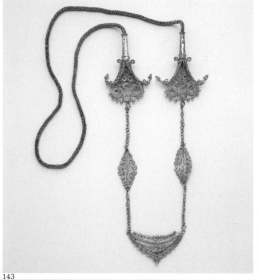
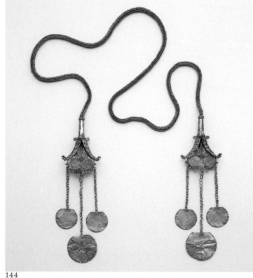

145. EAST SUMBA, bracelets, ivory.
D. 10.5 cm.

Description p. 332

146. TIMOR or SAVU, comb. wood
& silver. L. 14.2 cm.

147. CENTRAL TIMOR, comb,
turtleshell. H. 17 cm.

148. WEST TIMOR, hairpin, silver.
H. 11.5 cm.

Description pp. 332-333

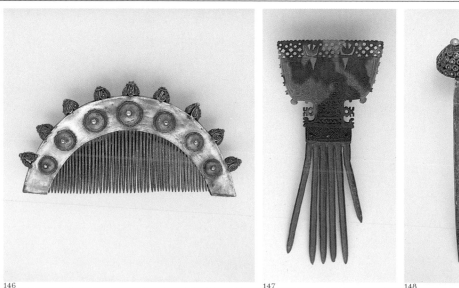

149. WEST TIMOR, Atoni, comb, horn, etc. L. 13 cm.

150. WEST TIMOR, Atoni, head cloth with silver elements. H. (element) 23 cm.

Description p. 333

Color plate (150) p. 205

See costume (150) p. 198

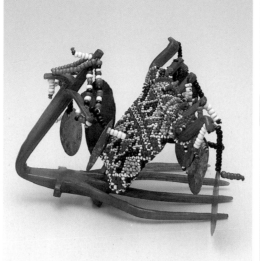

149

150

151. WEST TIMOR, Atoni, head cloth with silver elements. H. 28 cm.

152. WEST or CENTRAL TIMOR, frontal, silver. L. 32 cm.

153. CENTRAL TIMOR, frontal, gilded silver. L. 34.5 cm.

Description p. 333

See costume (151) p. 198

151

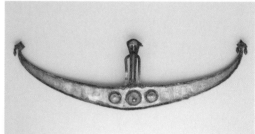

152

153

154. WEST TIMOR, Atoni, head ornament, silver. D. 6.5-7.5 cm.

155. WEST TIMOR, Atoni, head ornament, silver. D. 6.5-7.5 cm.

Description p. 333

See costume (154 & 155) p. 198

154

155

156. CENTRAL TIMOR, Tetum, earrings, silver. H. 7 cm.

157. CENTRAL TIMOR, Tetum, earrings, silver. H. 6.7 cm.

158. CENTRAL TIMOR, Tetum, earring, silver. H. 4.2 cm.

Description p. 333

Color plate (156) p. 207

157

156

158

159. WEST or CENTRAL TIMOR, disk, brass. D. 21 cm.

160. WEST or CENTRAL TIMOR, disk, gilded silver. D. 18.6 cm.

Description p. 333

159

160

161. WEST or CENTRAL TIMOR, disk, silver. D. 9.8 cm.

162. WEST or CENTRAL TIMOR, disk, silver. D. 13.7 cm.

Description p. 333

161

162

163. WEST or CENTRAL TIMOR, disk, gold. D. 11 cm.

164. CENTRAL TIMOR, bracelet, silver. W. 7.5 cm.

Description p. 333

163

164

165. WEST or CENTRAL TIMOR, bracelet, silver. W. 7.5 cm.

166. WEST or CENTRAL TIMOR, anklet, silver. W. 8.4 cm.

Description pp. 333-334
Color plate (166) p. 209

165

166

167. WEST TIMOR, Atoni, bracelet, silver. W. 8.5 cm.

168. WEST TIMOR, Atoni, bracelet, silver. W. 7.5 cm.

169. WEST TIMOR, Atoni, bracelet, silver. W. 8.4 cm.

Description p. 334

167

168

169

170. WEST or CENTRAL TIMOR, bracelet, silver. W. 7.7 cm.

171. WEST TIMOR, Atoni, bracelet, copper. W. 8 cm.

Description p. 334

170

171

172. TIMOR or SAVU, bracelets, silver. D. 6 cm.

173. WEST or CENTRAL TIMOR, anklets, silver. D. 7.8 cm.

Description p. 334

172

173

174. SOUTH MOLUCCAS, Tanimbar, comb, wood & bone. H. 24 cm.

174a. Detail.

Description p. 334

Color plate (174) p. 223

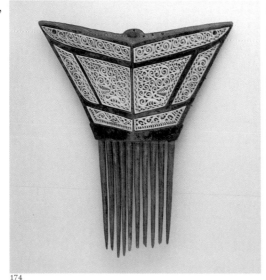
174

174a

175. SOUTH MOLUCCAS, Tanimbar, comb, bone. H. 8.8 cm.

Description p. 334
Color plate (175) p. 225

175

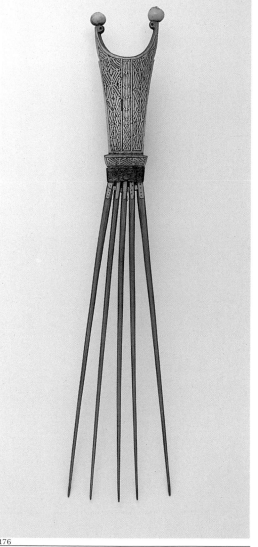

176

176. CENTRAL MOLUCCAS, Seram, comb, bamboo. H. 28.5 cm.

177. SOUTH MOLUCCAS, Tanimbar, earring, gold alloy. H. 3.3 cm.

Description p. 334
Color plate (177) p. 227

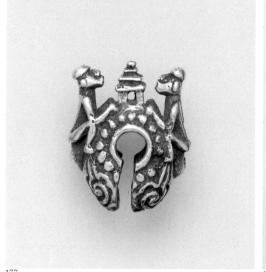

177

178. SOUTH MOLUCCAS, Tanimbar, earring, gold alloy. H. 3.4 cm.

179. SOUTH MOLUCCAS, Tanimbar, earrings, silver. H. 7.2 cm.

Description p. 334

178

179

180. SOUTH MOLUCCAS, Tanimbar, earrings, gold. H. 5.1 cm.

181. SOUTH MOLUCCAS, Tanimbar, earrings, silver. H. 4 cm.

182. SOUTH MOLUCCAS, Tanimbar, earrings, silver. H. 3.8 cm.

Description p. 335

Color plate (180) p. 229

181

180

182

183. SOUTH MOLUCCAS, Tanimbar, earring, gilded silver. H. 4 cm.

184. SOUTH MOLUCCAS, Tanimbar, earrings, gold. H. 4.1 cm.

185. SOUTH MOLUCCAS, Leti, disk, gold. D. 13.2 cm.

Description p. 335

Color plate (185) p. 231

183

184

185

186. SOUTH MOLUCCAS, Tanimbar, pendant, gold alloy. H. 4.4 cm.

187. SOUTH MOLUCCAS, Tanimbar, pendant, gold. H. 8 cm.

Description p. 335

Color plates (186 & 187) pp. 233 & 235

186

187

188. NORTHERN LUZON, Gaddang, hat, wooden & brass, etc. D. 7.2 cm.

Description p. 335

188

189. NORTHERN LUZON, Bontoc, headband, shell & beads. H. 78 cm.

190. NORTHERN LUZON, Bontoc, headband, snake vertebrae. D. 22 cm.

Description p. 335

189

190

191. NORTHERN LUZON, Ifugao, head ornament, brass. H. 10.5 cm.

192. NORTHERN LUZON, Ifugao, head ornament, brass. H. 7.5 cm.

Description p. 335

Color plate (191) p. 253

191

192

193. NORTHERN LUZON, Ifugao, headdress, hornbill skull, etc. W. 55 cm.

194. NORTHERN LUZON, Ilongot, head ornament, feathers, etc. H. 54 cm.

Description p. 335

Color plate (193) p. 255

See costume (193) p. 24

193

194

195. NORTHERN LUZON, Ilongot, headdress, hornbill skull, etc. L. 50 cm.

Description p. 335

Color plate (195) p. 257

195

196. NORTHERN LUZON, Ilongot, headdress, monkey skull, etc.
L. 28.6 cm.

Description p. 335

196

197. NORTHERN LUZON, Kalinga, earrings, mother-of-pearl, gold, etc.
H. 7.8 cm.

Description p. 335

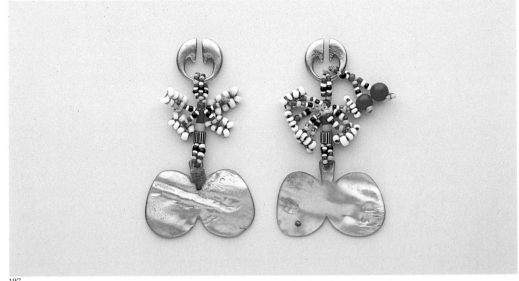

197

198. NORTHERN LUZON, Kalinga, earrings, mother-of-pearl, etc.
W. 13.6 cm.

Description p. 336

198

199. NORTHERN LUZON, Ifugao, earrings, mother-of-pearl, etc. H. 11 cm.

200. NORTHERN LUZON, Ilongot, earrings, hornbill beak, etc. H. 17.2 cm.

Description p. 336

199

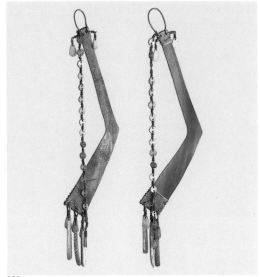

200

201. NORTHERN LUZON, Ilongot, earrings, mother-of-pearl, etc. H. 4.5 cm.

202. NORTHERN LUZON, Ilongot, earrings, mother-of-pearl, etc. H. 3.5 cm.

203. NORTHERN LUZON, Kalinga, earring, brass. H. 4.1 cm.

204. NORTHERN LUZON, Bontoc, earring, gold. H. 2.1 cm.

205. NORTHERN LUZON, Bontoc, earring, gold. H. 2.8 cm.

206. NORTHERN LUZON, Bontoc, earring, gold. H. 4 cm.

Description p. 336

Color plate (205 & 206) p. 259

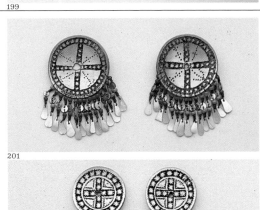

201

203

204

202

205

206

207. NORTHERN LUZON, Bontoc, earring, gold. H. 3.9 cm.

208. NORTHERN LUZON, Bontoc, earring, brass. H. 3 cm.

209. NORTHERN LUZON, Bontoc, earring, brass. H. 4.1 cm.

210. NORTHERN LUZON, Bontoc, earring, brass. H. 4.3 cm.

211. NORTHERN LUZON, Bontoc, earring, silver. H. 3.5 cm.

212. NORTHERN LUZON, Bontoc, earring, gold. H. 3.2 cm.

213. NORTHERN LUZON, Kankanay, earring, bronze. H. 4 cm.

214. NORTHERN LUZON, Kankanay, earring, brass. H. 4.9 cm.

Description p. 336
Color plate (207 & 208) p. 259

207

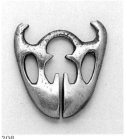

208

209

210

211

212

213

214

215. NORTHERN LUZON, Kankanay, earring, brass. H. 3 cm.

216. NORTHERN LUZON, Ifugao, earring, brass. H. 3.2 cm.

217. NORTHERN LUZON, Ifugao, earring, silver. H. 2 cm.

218. NORTHERN LUZON, Ifugao, pendant, brass. H. 2.8 cm.

219. NORTHERN LUZON, Ifugao, pendant, brass, H. 3.4 cm.

Description p. 336

Color plate (215) p. 261

216

217

215

218

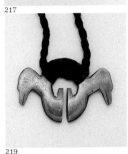
219

220. NORTHERN LUZON, Isneg, chest ornament, mother-of-pearl, etc. L. 109 cm.

Description p. 336

Color plate (220) p. 263

220

221. NORTHERN LUZON, Isneg,
chest ornament, mother-of-pearl, etc.
L. 92 cm.

Description p. 336

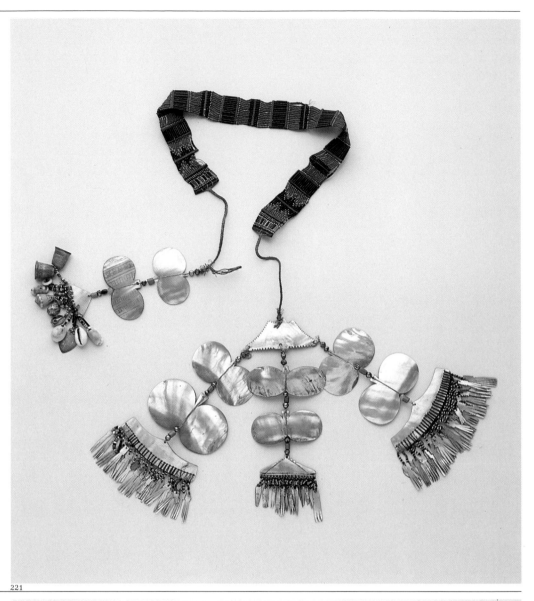

221

222. NORTHERN LUZON, Isneg,
chest ornament, mother-of-pearl, etc.
L. 80 cm.

Description p. 336

222

223. NORTHERN LUZON, Bontoc, necklace, brass & seeds. H. 29 cm.

224. NORTHERN LUZON, Bontoc, necklace, mother-of-pearl, tusks, etc. H. (element) 6 cm.

Description pp. 336-337

223

224

225. NORTHERN LUZON, Ifugao, necklace, mother-of-pearl. H. (element) 8 cm.

226. NORTHERN LUZON, Ifugao, necklace, brass. H. (element) 1.5 cm.

Description p. 337

225

226

227. NORTHERN LUZON, Ifugao, necklace, silver. H. (element) 2.2 cm.

228. NORTHERN.LUZON, Kalinga, pendant, brass. L. 5.2 cm.

229. NORTHERN LUZON, Ilongot, pendant, copper. H. (figure) 4.8 cm.

Description p. 337

See costume (227) p. 24

227

228

229

230. NORTHERN LUZON, Tinggian (Abra), armlet, wood & tusks. H. (figure) 15 cm.

231. NORTHERN LUZON, Bontoc, armlet, wood & tusks. H. (figure) 10 cm.

Description p. 337

Color plate (231) p. 267

230

231

232. NORTHERN LUZON, Bontoc, armlet, wood & tusks. H. (figure) 5 cm.

233. NORTHERN LUZON, Bontoc, bracelet, brass. D. 7.5 cm.

Description p. 337

232

233

234. NORTHERN LUZON, Bontoc, belt, shell, etc. D. 33 cm.

235. NORTHERN LUZON, Bontoc, belt ornament, shell. D. 19.8 cm.

Description p. 337

Color plate (234) p. 265

234

235

236. NORTHERN LUZON, Bontoc, belt, shell, etc.
D. (ornament) 15.7 cm.

237. NORTHERN LUZON, Ifugao, belt ornament, shell & turtleshell.
D. 14 cm.

238. NORTHERN LUZON, Ifugao, belt ornament, shell & turtleshell.
D. 9.5 cm.

Description p. 337

237

238

236

239. NORTHERN LUZON, Ifugao, belt & knife, wood, shell, etc.
L. (knife) 61 cm.

Description p. 337

239

311

240. NORTHERN LUZON, Ilongot, belt, brass & copper. H. 11.5 cm.

Description p. 337

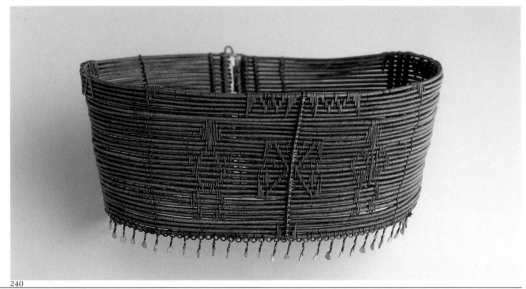

240

241. PALAWAN, comb, wood. L. 11.6 cm.

Description p. 337

241

242. MINDANAO, Bagobo, earplugs, ivory. D. 12 cm.

243. MINDANAO, Bagobo, earplugs, ivory, D. 7.9 cm.

Description p. 337

See costume (242) p. 238

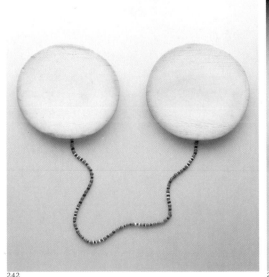

242

243

244. MINDANAO, Bagobo, ear-plugs, brass, bone, etc.
L. 22 cm.

Description pp. 337-338

See costume (244) p. 239

244

245. MINDANAO, T'boli, ear-plugs, wood, etc. D. 2.3 cm.

246. MINDANAO, Bagobo, necklace, snake vertebrae, etc.
H. 32 cm.

Description p. 338

See costume (246) p. 239

245

246

247. MINDANAO, Bagobo, necklace, brass. H. 33 cm.

248. MINDANAO, Mandaya, pendant, silver. D. 10.6 cm.

249. MINDANAO, Bagobo, belt ornaments, brass. H. 25 cm.

Description p. 338

See costume (247 & 249) p. 239

248

247

249

250. MINDANAO, Bagobo or T'boli, belt, brass. L. 73 cm.

Description p. 338

Color plate (250) p. 269

See costume (250) p. 239

250

251. MINDANAO, Bagobo or T'boli, belt, brass. L. 72 cm.

Description p. 338
See costume (251) p. 238

251

252. MINDANAO, Bagobo, belt, copper, brass & iron. H. (buckle) 9.7 cm.

Description p. 338

252

DESCRIPTIONS

Reproductions pp. 273–315

1. Nias H: 16.5 cm

Gold crown from South Nias, decorated with five Cosmic Trees(?), a symbol of continuity and tension between the Upperworld and the Lowerworld. Worn by women as part of the ritual display of gold house wealth. Gold ornaments like these were products of the intense rivalry between Nias high chiefs. To subdue a competitor and emerge as the paramount chief of several villages, a nobleman would attempt to build a greater *adat* house (called an *omo sebua* in Nias) and distribute more prestige goods than his rivals. Redistribution of valuables to the community was an indispensable part of constructing a fine *omo sebua*, and gold was an important symbol of nobility. Aristocracy itself was associated with height, magnificence, generosity, fertility, headtaking, and central spaces. A chief had to progress through several levels of festive activity to gain permission to dedicate a new house. Feldman (1979: 148-149) identifies four preliminary levels: the chief would have to (1) sacrifice at least twenty-four pigs, feed the community, and erect a *batu wa'ulu* (vertical megalith) to his ancestors; (2) distribute twelve more pigs at a feast; (3) commission and distribute great quantities of gold ornaments; and (4) bring back a human head from another district to "empower" the house. The fifth ceremonial level was the construction of the house itself, a structure whose form replicated the Nias conceptualization of the cosmos (the Upperworld, mundane world, and Lowerworld were represented by the attics, the living space, and the area under the floorboards). The new house was strongly associated with the persons of the chief and his wife. For instance, a representation of their full regalia was carved into the wooden panel in the house, so that in a sense the house itself wore jewelry. These carvings were called *laso sohagu*, and are shown in Fig. 80 in the ethnographic chapter on Nias. [3265]

2. Nias W: 12 cm

Gold earrings, made of thin ridged crescents, joined at the center. These can be worn by either men or women (see Holt 1971 for numerous photographs of old women wearing these as part of their dance costumes; the curved edges of the earrings point toward the top). Modigliani calls these earrings *gaule* (1890: 483-484, Fig. 92) and notes that chiefs wear them, aligned along the side of the head (with the rounded parts of the ornament pointed forward). Modigliani also writes that the sons of chief wear smaller earrings of the same type, called *wale-wale* (1890: 484, Fig. 94). He reports that the feminine version is called *saru dalinga* and shows how these earrings are attached to the ear (1890: 514, Figs. 121, 122).

It is possible that the shape of these earrings is a version of the double spiral, familiar throughout Southeast Asian art. In the section on Nias above there is a discussion of the political basis for the production of such gold ornaments in pre-modern times. For descriptions of Nias' several other types of ceremonial earrings, see Modigliani 1890 and Barbier 1978. There is some indication that men ideally wore just one earring while women were supposed to wear two. This would mean that the carved house panels combining feminine palm-frond motifs with portrayals of single earrings were possibly masculine-and-feminine-in-one objects. [3265–B A+B]

3. South Nias H: 8 cm

Woman's brass earrings, in the shape of a tropical laurel leaf. [3271–1 A+B]

4. South Nias H: 7.9 cm

Woman's brass earrings, in the shape of a tropical laurel leaf, smaller than No. 3. [3271–2 A+B]

5. Nias D: 22 cm

Pure gold necklace, with folded ridges. This is similar to the one that Modigliani discusses (1890: 483, Fig. 91), called *nifato-fato*, which

belonged to a chief from the north or the central part of the island. (In this region of Nias, according to Modigliani, women apparently did not have the type of earrings shown in No. 2.)

Golden breastplate-like necklaces of this sort were reproduced on South Nias house panels depicting the gold house treasure. Feldman says the necklaces were called *kalambagi* and were worn by both women and men (1979: 168). South Nias had three basic types of necklaces: (1) ones made of flat sheets of gold, like this one, either folded into little ridges or engraved with several motifs; (2) *kalabubu* headhunter necklaces (No. 6), of coconut shell disks, wood, or metal alloys; and (3) necklaces made of twisted lengths of bronze, silver, or gold. [3265–A]

6. Nias D: 20 cm

Headhunter's necklace, in some areas called *kalabubu*,[1] made of rings of coconut shells joined by a bronze clasp. A masculine ornament, symbolizing high prestige and war success. In pre-national Nias, headtaking was associated with royalty, creative power, and masculinity. This *kalabubu* necklace proclaimed that the wearer had taken a human head from an outsider group (sometimes in another region of the island) and had brought it back to the village, at the same time bringing creativity and protective forces to his community. Such an act also signified that the man was now an adult.

Heads (called *binu*) were placed in the men's ceremonial house (*bale* – see Fig. 22) as offerings to the god of the Upperworld and the god of the Lowerworld. Heads were also prominently displayed in the chief's house: planted under the house posts, attached to the ridgepoles, and inserted under the entrance planks of the floor (Feldman 1979). Nias wooden sculptures of men often show them wearing these *kalabubu* necklaces along with other religiously important jewelry (see the ethnographic text for a fuller discussion.) [3269]

7. South Nias W: 20 cm

Gold necklace with repoussé decoration. The central flowerlike motif is typical of the region. It is often seen on megaliths and wooden house panels. It may derive from the Indian *patola* motif (see No. 5 for a fuller discussion). [3272]

8. South Nias H: 7 cm

Bracelet made out of a giant clamshell (*Tridacna gigas*), with a raised central ridge, from South Nias (see Schröder 1917: 201; Modigliani 1890: 515). Modigliani notes that the bracelet for men is called *töla gasa* (1890: Fig. 125). These bracelets are also apparently called *töladsaga* in South Nias, and *tölagasa* in North Nias (Schröder 1917: Plate XXIV, Fig. 53). Schröder writes that they were made by rubbing the shell with a stone. The giant clamshell (*gima*) was found along the beaches and also inland, as a fossil (Modigliani 1890: 122). The bracelet comes in two sizes, which apparently have the same general name. [3257–B]

8a. South Nias H: 6.6 cm

Giant clamshell bracelet similar to No. 7. Not illustrated. [3257–C]

9. Nias D: 9 cm

Another giant clamshell bracelet smoothly finished. [3257–D]

---

1. It should be noted that the names of individual pieces of jewelry and information about them are based mainly on a small number of informants in the field in Indonesia. The descriptions of the Philippine pieces are due almost entirely to consultations with Roland Beday-Brandicourt.

10. Nias   D: 9.2 cm

A smooth giant clamshell bracelet, like No. 9 but with a more pronounced central ridge.   [3257–A]

11. North Sumatra, Karo Batak   H: 53 cm

Gilded silver *sertali* made of many separate pieces mounted on red cloth. These large gold and red ornaments were placed on top of a woman's cloth headdress as part of Karo bridal finery for wealthy aristocrats. The bride piled on her head *uis* textiles edged in rows of *pio-pio* or *pilo-pilo* (little metallic spangles which wave in the wind, showing hospitality – see Fig. 90). She placed a *sertali* over the whole assembly. The designs inside the oval-shaped pieces show clear borrowings from the Muslimized, Malay influenced sultanates such as those in Aceh. They also recall Minangkabau decoration styles. If the bride wears the *sertali*, her bridegroom should wear the heavy *bura layang-layang* (No. 22) around his neck (this piece is sometimes called a *sertali layang-layang*, according to Sitepu 1980: 59). The bride often wears the fancy *karabu kudung-kudung* earrings (No. 16) as well. The number three is used repeatedly in these bridal ornaments and symbolizes the three-part alliance between home lineage, wife-givers, and wife-takers.

Karo *guru* (sorcerer-diviners) sometimes fashion special jewelry pieces for their healing rituals by combining the feminine *sertali* with the masculine *bura layang-layang*. The *guru* use these two-in-one new ornaments to *panggil roh*, call back the escaped souls of sick people. This healing technique plays on a common religious idea found in many parts of Indonesia – the notion that creative and protective power comes from the temporary union of contrasting but complementary opposites such as male and female, village and forest, human and supernatural, and metal and cloth (the constituents of many Karo bridal ornaments). The *guru* grabs the combined *sertali/bura layang-layang* and swings it downward through the air, calling back the lost soul into the head of the patient. This ritual use of the Karo jewelry is somewhat similar to the way Sumba's larger *mamuli* are used to contact supernatural beings.

Karo goldsmithing also had religious overtones. Drawing on the work of W. Marschall (1968) Harrisson and O'Connor describe the special status of the Karo goldsmith in former times:

Before the goldsmith of the Karo Batak starts working, he must offer his blood, heart, liver, and lungs to the spirits in prayer. He is afraid of his tools which are seen as animate objects capable of changing their names. The result is an intricate "secret language" which the goldsmiths use. Anybody may become a smith but it is usual for the son of a smith to follow his father or he may fall ill. If he does not follow he will be ridiculed by the tools. If the son follows his father he will inherit the tools. They may not be sold or they will cause ill luck. (1970: 70-71.)

The detail photograph (No. 11b) shows one of the *sertali's* constituent elements, whose shape recalls both buffalo horns and motifs on the Karo *adat* house. Despite this strongly Batak interpretation, however, the piece's style suggests considerable influence from Muslimized sultanates such as Aceh, important contributors to Karo village art.   [3170–3]

12. North Sumatra, Karo Batak   H: 38 cm

Gilded silver ornament made of separate pieces mounted on red cloth, called *bura-bura* or *sertali ruma-ruma*. It serves as an ornament on the bridegroom's cloth headdress and is worn together with the *layang-layang* (No. 22). Here again the same elements used in No. 11 reappear; the *ruma-ruma* representing the *adat* house is particularly noticeable (see detail No. 12b). Karo families from non-aristocratic backgrounds are beginning to use these elaborate bridal ornaments today, especially in migrant communities in cities, since the jewelry is often available for rent from wealthy families.   [3150–14]

13. North Sumatra, Karo Batak   H: 17.5 cm

These huge and heavy silver earrings, used also as headdress ornaments, are called *padung* or *padung-padung* and are still worn today in ceremonies by women. Through the 1930s they were quite widely used by village women and appear in a number of old photographs. *Padung-padung* are perhaps the Karo culture's most ethnically distinct type of jewelry. The ornaments take the form of double spirals (a common and possibly ancient Southeast Asian shape), joined at the center with a long double extension that ends in a small loop for attaching the piece to the top of the earlobe or to the ceremonial headdress made of woven *uis* textiles. A common way to wear the *padung-padung* is to suspend one from the top of one ear and to attach a second one to the cloth headdress near the top of the other ear. This second ornament's double spiral points back away from the face.

Often the first earring is not really suspended from a hole in the ear, but is also hung from the headdress. In the past, even the old women who did insert the *padung-padung* in a hole in the ear also attached it to the head cloths, because the ornament's great weight needed extra support so as not to harm the ear. Some *padung-padung* are made of hollow tubes of silver, whereas others may have been made of solid metal. In former times metalsmiths reportedly sometimes attached the ornaments to women's ears as part of the manufacturing process. Some *padung-padung* are decorated with five-point stars (*bintang silima*) set into the center of the coil. One old *guru* from Lingga village said in a 1983 interview that the use of stars came from Aceh, Karo's northern neighbor which has greatly influenced Karo art. Before national times, when the Karo highlands had relatively little contact with Islam or Christianity, village life revolved around farming and the *adat* rituals that regulated planting, harvesting, and the various life stages from birth to death. At large *adat* festivities women of any age, married or unmarried, would wear *padung-padung* jewelry. Married women often combined it with ritual *uis* textiles. In fact, the mode of wearing *padung-padung* in pairs, with one hanging down and one pointing back toward the back of the head is sometimes linked to marriage. In a 1983 interview one Karo *adat* expert volunteered the idea that this style of using the ornaments symbolized the sometimes-up, sometimes-down relationship that holds between couples over the course of their marriage. In his handbook on Karo design motifs, Sitepu (1980) notes that the shape of the *padung-padung* is like that of a little scorpion. No such explanation was volunteered by the ten or so Karo Batak I interviewed in 1983.   [3150–15 A+B]

14. North Sumatra, Karo Batak   H: 16.3 cm

A single *padung* ear ornament or headdress decoration, similar to the preceding pair in No. 13.   [3150–1]

15. North Sumatra, Karo Batak   H: 12 cm

Pair of earrings called *karabu kudung-kudung* in gilded silver; very ornamental, possibly due to Indian influence via Sumatra's coastal states. The same type of earring is often found in a less ornate version, such as No. 16. *Karabu kudung-kudung* earrings were once signs of great wealth and aristocratic social standing. Today anyone with the cash to buy them from Brastagi pawnshops can use them. Another modern way to get the earrings is to borrow them from an upper-class family that has them in their house treasure. In the *adat* this type of earrings should come from *kalimbubu*, the wife-giving lineage. Before national times, aristocratic women wore these at major *adat* rituals. According to a female *guru* (sorcerer-diviner) and several other villagers from Lingga, women wore them at their wedding, with the *sertali* headdress ornament, and at the funeral of their husband's father or mother. In the last case, the younger woman served as a central ritual figure in the funeral, acting in a sense as a bridge between wife-givers and wife-takers. As an intermediary figure between these two factions the young woman was the subject of unusually elaborate ornamentation. Only the death of a very old and respected person called for this degree of finery on the part of the mourning family. The same Lingga *guru* mentioned above also asserted that *karabu kudung-kudung* earrings came to Karo from the Simelungun Batak homeland, during the time of Tuan Purba, an important *raja*. Another Lingga woman said wryly that "according to theory" these earrings are to be worn suspended from a big hole at the top of the ear but in actuality women often suspended them from their *uis* textile headdress.

Note that these earrings are closed at the bottom while the four leaves or petals of No. 16 stand open. An *adat* expert from Tanjung near Brastagi noted in a 1983 interview that a girl who wore the open type was announcing that she already had a *jodoh* (Indonesian for a boyfriend or a good match), while the girl with the closed earrings was saying that she was still searching.   [3150–5]

16. North Sumatra, Karo Batak   H: 9 cm.

Another pair of gilded silver *karabu kudung-kudung* earrings, in a less ornamented style than No. 15. There is some dispute about this type of earring: Sitepu has no listing for *karabu kudung-kudung* but labels a very similar sort of earring as *padung Raja mehulu* (1980: 55, 61). It is possible that these were produced by Chinese in Sumatra. The National Museum in Jakarta identifies this style of earring as Minangkabau, from West Sumatra. In 1983 all Karo informants in Medan, Brastagi, and Lingga identified these pieces as typically Karo. Their shape may represent a partially open fruit or flower, but no informant offered either explanation. Whatever the case, the earring is one of many examples in Karo of a style that probably originated outside the Karo highlands but has long been considered part of Karo "ancient *adat*."   [3150–7 A+B]

17. North Sumatra, Karo Batak   H: 8 cm

Gilded-silver filigree earrings called *padung curu-curu* for women, shaped like small cones with many tiny spangles (*pilo-pilo*) at the bottom. These dance in the air as the wearer walks, "waving in good luck." Filigree work decorates the sides of the cones, and the earring is attached to the ear with a post joined to a round disk, to which more spangles are attached.

These are basically baubles of rich Karo aristocrats, who wore them at grand *adat* festivals, although in 1983 a number of my Karo informants had never seen this style. A male *adat* chief and *guru* from Tanjung offered one explanation. The *padung curu-curu* were once worn by noble women to show how much house treasure they have. The shape of the earring is like that of the globular nest of a certain type of bird which keeps busy all day flitting around finding little twigs and berries to stuff into his nest. Similarly, the aristocratic woman occupies herself with gathering in more and more treasure to stash away in her *adat* house. Sitepu (1980: 55, 62) also identifies these earrings as *padung curu-curu* but writes that *raga-raga* is an alternative name. Two modes of acquiring these ornaments were suggested by 1983 informants: a father can give them to his daughter, or a girl can get them from her father's sister, who is ideally the mother of the girl's future husband according to the Karo system of asymmetrical marriage alliance.

                    [3150–12 A+B]

18. North Sumatra, Karo Batak   H: 5 cm

Small delicate gilded silver earrings for women, of the same type as No. 17 and also called *padung curu-curu*. The tiny gold spangles hanging from the conical body of the earring are called *pilo-pilo*. At Karo *adat* rituals many objects are decorated with rows of *pilo-pilo*: bamboo frames over the village entrance, horns of water buffalo, the front of women's long, flat-shaped headdresses made of *uis* textiles. The spangles signify that visitors are welcome to the ceremony, and they shower blessings on all participants.

                    [3150–19 A+B]

19. North Sumatra, Toba Batak   H: 3 cm

Highly ornamental brass earrings sometimes called *simanjomak* in the Simanindo region of North Samosir Island in Lake Toba. The earrings portray a curled insectlike creature, with its head pointing downward and sharp protrusions along its back. Some Toba Batak apparently call these earrings simply *ating-ating*; the related Indonesian word *anting-anting* means earring, or charm in a secondary meaning. The National Museum in Jakarta identifies a very similarly shaped earring as coming from the old court culture of Palembang, in South Sumatra, so the Toba usage may be an example of the Batak adoption of a more general Sumatran and perhaps even Malay style. The Simanindo Museum staff says that these are worn by brides or old women at *adat* rituals. The earrings are sometimes given to a young woman by her *amangboru* (father's sister's husband), as an encouragement to marry his son, her father's sister's son, the ideal marriage partner according to *adat*. It is not necessary to be an aristocrat to wear these, but owners are generally wealthy. The insect motif may represent protective forces.   [3170–15 A+B]

20. North Sumatra, Toba Batak   H: 4.5 cm

Earrings in brass of the same type and style as No. 19. Used on Samosir Island; probably in other Toba regions as well. It is possible that the mythic animal depicted in both pairs is the *sibaganding* snake, important in Toba myths in pre-Christian times. This particular pair of earrings was found attached to a *sigale-gale* funeral puppet. These puppets represented people who had died without heirs, a major Batak disaster, which was "corrected" by special funerals in which puppets served as spirit mediums.

                    [3170–16 A+B]

21. North Sumatra, Karo Batak   H: 35 cm, W: 17.6 cm

A gilded silver wedding ornament for women, normally called a *bura* or *bura-bura*. It is composed of one main pendant, which simultaneously represents the Karo *adat* house (the central piece) and water buffalo horns (the crescent shape), a sign of high social rank and prestige. A *rante* (chain) is joined to the pendant by red cloth. *Lepah-lepah* (rectangular pieces) in two sets of three are arranged along the chain, representing the wearer's husband's lineage and his wife-givers and wife-takers. This ornament is part of the bride's full set of jewels for her wedding rituals; she wears this piece plus a *sertali* headdress ornament (No. 11) and *karabu kudung-kudung* earrings (No. 15 – see Fig. 90). The shape of this pendant links Karo jewelry styles to the large number of other Indonesian cultures that employ the horizontal half-moon shape (an extremely common style, for instance, in Eastern Indonesia). See the ethnographic chapter on the Batak for more discussion of Karo wedding ornaments.   [3150–16]

22. North Sumatra, Karo Batak   H: 51 cm

Gilded silver *layang-layang*, a large necklace for men, made of three principal elements and pendants. Each piece is edged with "luck-bringing" *pilo-pilo* and has finely worked filigree covering its entire surface. This ornament, also called *bura layang-layang*, is worn by Karo bridegrooms when their brides wear the *sertali* (No. 11). Older men also wear this for the *adat* funeral of their parents. The ornament combines several elements: *ruma-ruma* (the two large elements right and left representing, in part, *adat* houses); *lepah-lepah* (the rectangles on the chain); *pilo-pilo* tassles or spangles; and the *bura layang-layang* center element, representing according to some informants a type of bird. Note the frequent use of the number three. Many wedding ornaments use this: it symbolizes the Karo marriage system involving bride-givers (*kalimbubu*), their ritually subservient bride-receivers (*anakberu*), and the groom's own patrilineal lineage mates (*sanina*). The three elements together form

Karo's *sengkep sitelu* (the three complete), the society's master symbol of social order. When combined with the feminine *sertali*, this piece becomes an extremely powerful "soul-calling" ritual object for male or female *guru* (see discussion of No. 11). [3170–4]

23. North Sumatra, Karo Batak   H: 24 cm

Rante, or necklace, made of small, oblong gilded silver pieces strung together on a rather wornout piece of cloth, making this a somewhat modest example of Karo's many metal and cloth, two-elements-in-one ornaments. This *rante* (the word is a generic term for chain or necklace, related to the Indonesian word *rantai*) is a common Karo piece often given to a little girl as an initial bridewealth gift to insure that she will eventually marry her father's sister's son, the perfect marriage choice in the *adat*. Two filigree work clasps are used to hook the necklace together and symbolize the following situation. The *rante* is given as a *tanda perjanjian* to a girl when she is still a small child. This Indonesian term means a promise-sign, and the necklace is used in this way: a woman with a young son will come to visit her brother's wife who has a small daughter. The children will grow up to be the ideal couple in Karo *adat*: the mother's brother's daughter and father's sister's son. The mother of the little boy gives the *rante* to the little girl as a sort of down payment on later bridewealth gifts. The boy's mother caters to the little girl in this way, hoping to later secure her agreement to go through with the ideal marriage (this sort of cajoling supplication is the typical stance wife-receivers take toward their wife-providers. Recall that the boy's mother here is from the same clan as the little girl – they both are supposed to marry into the same wife-receiving group). The necklace's two-part clasp can be screwed open or shut. This symbolizes the rather ambiguous relationship between the two children: their marriage may actually come about but it is equally possible that their early promise to marry may "come apart." Many ritual sayings in the various Batak cultures also show this sharp awareness of the difference between the ideal world of *adat* and the actual world of real social relationships and individual biographies. [3150–10]

24. North Sumatra, Karo Batak   W: 16.5 cm

A darkened silver pendant with filigree work, employing the double buffalo horn motif frequently seen on necklaces for wedding ceremonies. Note also the representation of a roof topped with the head of a highly stylized *singa* (a creature important in the myths of several Batak cultures). The piece could not be positively identified in 1983 field interviews with residents and *adat* experts in Lingga village and Brastagi. Several people did comment that the piece had the same shape as the centerpiece pendant of the man's *layang-layang* necklace (No. 22) worn as part of the wedding costume. This unusual piece may be an idiosyncratic version of one of the more usual wedding ornaments, developed for use by a particular family. [3183]

25. North Sumatra, Karo Batak   H: 25 cm

Gilded silver jacket clasp for women; all Karo informants contacted as well as Sitepu simply use the Indonesian term *kancing baju* for this piece (Sitepu 1980: 61). The top disk has a motif also employed in the bride's *sertali* headdress ornament. According to one old woman living in Lingga, these jacket clasps were used only by young unmarried girls during "happy" festive *adat* rituals such as rice planting celebrations. The girls would wear these decorative pins on the front of their jackets during *adat* dances, to make themselves more attractive to boys. This woman and a Lingga *guru* said that the star decorations were used so that the girls would be sure to get married soon or at least be sure to get boyfriends with no difficulty. The buffalo horn motifs are generally taken to signify chieftainship. The piece like many Karo ornaments uses many motifs found in the

arts of Sumatra's Muslimized trade states such as Aceh and Minangkabau. [3169]

26. North Sumatra, Karo Batak   W: 17 cm

Man's gilded silver and gold bracelet called *gelang sarung*. It is formed of three sliding tubes of metal, decorated with appliquéd gold-thread spiral designs and gold balls. According to a Tanjung *guru*, it is used by aristocratic bridegrooms, by men of the upper class during the funerals of their fathers, and as a sort of protective amulet by men when their "dreams are not good." Other informants corroborated the second use, noting that the deceased's son wears this bracelet during a special *adat* funeral dance called the *landek*. All also agreed that the piece is used by bridegrooms; indeed in today's renaissance of interest in *adat* ceremonialism, a number of city Karo wear these bracelets at their weddings. Its style resembles the regalia of nobles in Minangkabau, Aceh, and the Deli sultanates along the east coast of Sumatra. According to Jasper, the *gelang sarung* bracelet is used by the Toba Batak too, and the filigree work is called *tali pioe* (1927: 173). A number of Karo jewelry styles are used in the northern part of Samosir Island, which is quite nearby. See also Sitepu (1980: 52–53, 58) for further discussion. [3150–2]

27. North Sumatra, Karo Batak   D: 7.3 cm

Gilded silver bracelet or armband, made of three interlocking pieces. Like No. 26, it is decorated with appliquéd filigree work, ball designs, and narrow bands. This may have been a woman's bracelet. Jasper describes a somewhat similar bracelet (1927: 172, Fig. 231). [3150–17]

28. North Sumatra, Toba Batak   W: 10 cm

Brass bracelet decorated with geometric designs and rows of triangular, sharp, teeth-shaped motifs. The outside of the piece is ornamented with raised balls, recalling the sort of bracelet found in Timor in Eastern Indonesia. Its use is unknown, but it may have been a man's bracelet for dancing and other rituals. Clearly it was a possession of the wealthy class. Note the lack of mythic creatures on this bracelet, in contrast to other Toba bracelets such as Nos. 29 and 30. [3170–2]

29. North Sumatra, Toba Batak   D: 8 cm

Heavy silver bracelet cast in two parts which form a partial spiral around the lower arm; similar to No. 30. A large representation of a *singa* (mythical beast combining elements of dragons, serpents, and elephants) decorates the outside of the bracelet, accompanied by a lizard. *Singa* are associated with high chiefly status; the motif also decorated the carved wooden *adat* houses of wealthy Toba before national times. The lizard, called *boraspati ni tano* in Toba myths, is a crucial house-protection spirit. Vergouwen writes that "he lives under the earth and to him is due the fruitfulness of the land" (1964: 68). He was invoked in many ceremonies bringing people into contact with the earth (house building, village founding, driving an offering pole into the ground). This bracelet was owned by wealthy aristocrats and was normally worn on the right wrist. [3170–1]

30. North Sumatra, Toba Batak   D: 8 cm

Heavy brass bracelet for men made in two parts by the lost wax process, similar to No. 29. In this piece, a *singa* head is supporting a lizard on its back, while the lizard winds back to approach a *parsanggiran* bowl. This is a receptacle for holding sacred lemon juice that the village *datu* or traditional priest sprinkled around an altar or central village plaza to purify it during a healing ceremony or village purification ritual. *Singa* were symbols of royalty and supernatural power in traditional Toba thought, while lizards served as protective spirits for houses, warding off evil influences. In this they are said to resemble the friendly little *cikcak* lizards which chirp when intruders are near. This bracelet was normally worn by men and could form part of the inherited house treasure of wealthy families. Sometimes *hula-hula* (the Toba word for wife-givers) would bestow valuable metal bracelets on their supplicant *boru*, or wife-receivers. These ornaments would act as protective blessings (see No. 34, a similar Karo Batak ring). [3150–3]

31. North Sumatra, Toba Batak   D: 8.5 cm

Chiselled brass bracelet, decorated with a *singa* head which seems to have a snake body. This may be a reference to *singanaga*, a Toba mythological concept combining elements of the *singa* dragon-elephant and the *naga* dragon-serpent. If so, the piece may also be identified with Naga Padoha, a Toba mythological creature similar to the Indian serpent Sesha which supports the world. In Toba houses the side beams are in fact the body of the *singa* and are therefore connected to the *naga*, as here (Barbier 1983 : 79, Figs. 68 and 68-bis). Like many traditional *adat* houses in Indonesia, those in Toba represent not just homes but the world itself in all its constituent parts. [3170–12]

32. North Sumatra, Toba Batak   D: 7.3 cm

Brass bracelet in two parts, decorated with a *singa* motif; see the discussion of Nos. 29 and 30. [3170–11]

33. North Sumatra, Toba Batak   D: 7.3 cm

Silver bracelet with geometrical decoration, made in two parts. [3150–6]

34. North Sumatra, Karo Batak   H: 5.8 cm

Old silver and copper ring called *cincin kerunggun*. A high, raised cone is set onto a rounded ring base, which is itself decorated with filigree work. Several small ball-shaped pieces decorate the top. This large and heavy ring, a Karo kinship ring par excellence, is an *upah tendi* object, a magic piece that conveys luck, security, and "firmness" to the wearer's *tendi*, or soul. These *upah tendi* rings, quite important in Karo *adat* and healing ceremonies, are also marriage alliance goods, although they are not part of bridewealth. Rather, they are metal goods that go in the opposite direction, from wife-giver to wife-receiver, conveying blessings to the *anakberu*, the wife-taking lineage. The ring works this way. A complete *cincin kerunggun* includes two smaller plain rings inserted into the larger one. The set of three represents the wife-giving *kalimbubu*, the man's own *sanina* lineage, and his wife-receiving *anakberu*. When an *anakberu* has a run of bad luck (a child, say, who has been sick for a long while) he may petition his *kalimbubu* to give him some emergency aid in the form of spiritual blessings. The wife-givers may choose to convey such blessings via a ring like this one. In bestowing the *cincin kerunggun* on their hapless *anakberu* the wife-givers also transfer some of their "prosperity-force" to him. A *guru* from Tanjung said that the three-part *kerunggun* ring should be made of three metals – copper, iron, and brass – to insure its potency. The *cincin silima-lima*, also made of three metals (despite the reference to the number five in its name) is based on the same idea (Sitepu 1980 : 51). This last ring specifically symbolizes the fertility that *kalimbubu* bestow on their wife-receivers. It is because of the *kalimbubu*, in fact, that the dutiful *anakberu* can have children. The reference to five may be associated with the many *adat* meanings of that number in Karo thought. [3150–11]

35. North Sumatra, Karo Batak   H: 3.5 cm

This brass ring, called a *cincin tapak gaja*, employs a very common decorative motif also used on women's walking sticks (*ciken diberu*). The motif was probably adopted from a Malay-type trading sultanate (such as Aceh or Minangkabau); indeed a very similar ring in the collection of the National Museum of Malaysia in Kuala Lumpur is identified as coming from the old Malay state of Kelantan. Karo rings serve many purposes: they can be decorative pieces, amulets, conjurer's tools for *guru* sorcerers, or ornaments used to change a run of bad luck. Some Karo rings with large tops were apparently used as containers to hold magic potions. Several Karo informants said that this particular ring, which must be worn on the first finger of the right hand, was simply a decorative piece. Another informant, a *guru* himself, said that the *cincin tapak gaja* could be used to hold special potions or medicines under its broad top and thus was a type of sorcerer's ring. Sitepu (1980) includes drawings of many Karo ornaments that use the same cross-hatched design found on the top of this ring. [3150–8]

36. North Sumatra, Batak, Karo (?)   H: 3.5 cm

Gilded silver ring, delicately worked, with an open design decorated with little balls. The ring was unfamiliar to several people I talked to in Lingga, Tanjung, and Brastagi in 1983. No name for it was offered, and it is not identified in Sitepu's *Mengenal Seni Kerajinan Tradisional Karo*, although it looks someting like the *cincin puting* discussed there (1980 : 56). The *cincin puting* is used for *upah tendi* (soul-protecting) purposes. One old woman in Lingga did say that another grand-mother in that village owned such a ring, and she averred that it had to be worn on the third finger of the left hand. Like almost all Karo jewelry, this piece shows strong stylistic influence from Karo's Muslimized, Malay-influenced neighbors. [3170–7]

37. North Sumatra, Karo Batak   H: 2.2 cm

Gold ring with a double spiral decoration in filigree on each side. This decoration is very similar to the *padung-padung* ear ornament in Karo (Nos. 13 and 14). [3150–18]

38. North Sumatra, Toba Batak   H: 4.3 cm

Brass ring representing a cock, perched on a base decorated with a portrayal (according to one Toba informant) of *jolma sojolma begu so begu*, a mysterious and frightening "not-yet-human, not-yet-spirit" figure who exerts a powerful influence over the health and prosperity of villages. The piece reportedly came originally from the small market town of Siborong-borong and was last used in its distinctive *parmanukan* ceremony (involving a cock sacrifice) in the early 1920s. According to one informant in Prapat, the ring was just one part of a great *datu's* (traditional priest) armamentarium of ritual objects used to ask the village spirits why disaster or epidemic illness had befallen the community. These objects reportedly included a red cock, a *guri-guri* (a small ceramic jar for special potions), the *tunggal panaluan* or *datu's* magic staff, the *taha-taha ni manuk* (the breast flesh from a chicken, ripped from the living bird's breast to read for augury), and a sort of bark book, also called the *taha-taha ni manuk* in this case. The *datu* would read this for spiritual direction. He would also use a special knife. After consulting his auguries the *datu* would ritually cleanse the village plaza by sprinkling sacred lemon juice and water in a circle, then sacrifice the red cock and sprinkle its blood all around. The *datu* in Siborong-borong purportedly used this cock ring whenever performing this rare ceremony. No one else interviewed in the Toba area confirmed this story. [3170–5]

39. North Sumatra, Toba Batak   H: 2.5 cm

Heavy brass ring for men, incorporating a *singa* motif with a ringed serpent's body and an elephant's head. This is also referred to as the *naga-gaja* (mythical serpent-elephant). Apparently the *singa ni ruma* (*singa* used to decorate the *adat* house) were called *singa-naga* or *gaja ni ruma*. The elephant as well as the buffalo is identified with Naga Padoha, the great serpent who carries the earth. [3150–4]

40. North Sumatra, Toba Batak   N: 2.5 cm

Another type of brass ring, for men, again based on the *singa* motif. This one is curled around several times, making a wide, impressive ring. [3170–13]

41 and 42. Kalimantan, Dayak   41: H: 11.3 cm; 42: H: 14.2 cm

Brass ornaments with stylized human figures. These pieces are said to have been worn on the shoulder or on the head, tied to some kind of turban. No field information.   41: [3478]
42: [3480–1]

43. Kalimantan, Dayak (Kenyah-Kayan?)   L: 7 cm

Pair of brass earrings in the shape of snakelike creatures with wide-open mouths and fangs. These dragons or stylized serpents do not really resemble the usual representation of the *aso*, the mythical creature decorating many Kenyah-Kayan earrings and other arts (see Nos. 44 and 45). These earrings were probably attached to the ear with a thread. [3455 A+B]

44. Kalimantan, Dayak (Kenyah-Kayan?)   L: 11 cm

Single large brass earring in the shape of an *aso*, or mythical open-mouthed half-dragon, half-snake (even though the word means dog). This one has an unusually large number of curliques. The *aso* is the main decorative motif found on Kenyah-Kayan earrings, so these may belong to that culture. *Aso* motifs are very common throughout Dayak arts (including Iban) and are used in wooden relief and bamboo carving, beadwork, tattoos, house and coffin ornamentation, and weaponry. [3459]

45. Kalimantan, Dayak (Kenayh-Kayan?)   H: 8.8 cm

Pair of brass earrings, representing an *aso* (discussed in No. 44). [3457 A+B]

46. Kalimantan, Dayak (Kenyah-Kayan?)   H: 8 cm

Pair of heavy earrings in an abstract design based on a circle. Brass or lead earrings were signs of prestige and beauty in Dayak jewelry traditions, which also employed shell, bead, hornbill, and feather finery. The Kayan Dayak are expert metalworkers (Hose and McDougall 1966, I: 193–199). The curvilinear design of these pieces may be linked to the very common curlique *aso* motifs on wooden sculpture in parts of Kalimantan and Sarawak. [3458 A+B]

47. Kalimantan or Sarawak, Dayak   H: 8.3 cm

Heavy earring with *aso* motifs, similar to Nos. 48, 49 and 50, but made of silver. Some Iban peoples were extraordinarily fond of silver and covered women's sarongs with row upon row of silver coins and disks, topping off the ensemble with a silver spangle headdress and masses of silver bracelets (Chin 1980: 65). The Maloh people are the most well-known silversmiths in Sarawak. [3424 A]

48. Kalimantan or Sarawak, Dayak   H: 6 cm

Pair of heavy brass earrings, in the form of large circles closing with *aso* mouths. Such earrings were found among the Penan, Kenyah-Kayan, Apo-Kayan, Bahau, and possibly other Dayak groups. When worn by men, these large earrings were often accompanied by bone earplugs inserted into the top of the ear, pointed forward (Chin 1980: 66). [3424 B+C]

49. Kalimantan or Sarawak, Dayak   H: 5.3 cm

Pair of heavy brass earrings similar to No. 48, associated with the same Dayak cultures. [3460 A+B]

50. Kalimantan or Sarawak, Dayak   H: 3.2 cm

Pair of *aso*-motif earrings similar in shape to Nos. 48 and 49, but cut out of hornbill beak. [3476 A+B]

51. Kalimantan, Dayak (Kenyah-Kayan)   H: 13.5 cm

Very heavy brass earrings used by a wide variety of Dayak peoples, worn by either women or men. The ornaments are inserted in enlarged earlobes, which are eventually extended by several inches. There are large wooden earrings as well as iron ones in much the same globular shape tapering to a point at the bottom. Together with old beads and heirloom Chinese jars, brass earrings are kept as part of the house treasure in these cultures. Along with tattoos, wearing heavy earrings is taken as a mark of social maturity. Brasswork in general is highly prized by inland Dayak, but the only brass objects made locally are earrings. The Maloh (a Kalimantan Dayak society from the upper Kapuas river region) are renowned as brassworkers. They once produced much of the local brasswork, making it from Malay and Chinese brassware (Hose and McDougall 1966, I: 197).

Here, the spiral headdress of the little humanlike figure was passed through the hole in the earlobe. Name and exact meaning unknown. Anthropomorphic figures (often representing ancestral spirits) frequently appear in Dayak textile and sculptural arts as dangerous but potentially protective spirits that must be placated by humans (see Hose and McDougall 1966, I: 237). [3456 A+B]

52. Kalimantan or Sarawak, Dayak (including Kelabit, Kenyah-Kayan, Murut, Penan, Apo-Kayan)   H: 6.8 cm

Pair of heavy brass earrings. The National Museum in Jakarta has an old wooden earring from Wetar Island in Eastern Indonesia (No. 27178A) that has a similar shape, although it is not pointed at the bottom. [3466 A+B]

53. Kalimantan or Sarawak, Dayak (Kenyah-Kayan, Apo-Kayan, Kelabit (?), other Dayak societies)   L: 12.8 cm

Man's earring, cut out of hornbill beak, with *aso* motifs on the openwork part. A hook holds the earring to the wearer's extended earlobe, and the rounded, uncarved part of the earring points forward. The hornbill figures importantly in Dayak creation myths and is frequently represented in artwork, especially that associated with masculine tasks such as hunting and headtaking raids. [3461–2]

54. Kalimantan or Sarawak, Dayak (Kenyah-Kayan, Apo-Kayan, Kelabit (?), other Dayak societies)   L: 9 cm

Another earring for men like No. 53, cut out of hornbill beak. [3461–1]

55. Sarawak, Bidayah Dayak   D: 30 cm

Man's necklace made of honey-bear teeth, beads, and cowry shells mounted on wickerwork. [3480–2]

56. Sarawak, Iban Dayak   H: 4.2 cm

Man's bracelet or armlet cut out of a giant clamshell. Decoratively ribbed on the sides with the natural ridges of the shell (see the giant clamshell bracelets from Nias, Nos. 8–10). An Iban man in full ritual regalia would wear metal belts, necklaces, feather headdresses, brass and silver bracelets, and pairs of shell armlets (see Chin 1980: 65). [3435–B]

57. Sarawak, Dayak (Iban)   H: 3 cm

Clamshell armlet of the same type as No. 56. [3435–A]

58. Sarawak, Dayak (Iban)   D: 9,5 cm

Armlet in black wood, decorated with geometric motifs with a
central ridge. It was worn one at a time above the elbow, by
hunters.   [3463–A]

59. Sarawak, Dayak (Iban)   D: 10 cm

Another man's armlet in black wood.   [3463–B]

60. Kalimantan, Dayak   H: 11 cm

A little pendant made of bone, worked in an especially fine way. The
two horns on the humanlike figure end in the shape of two animals:
a fish and some sort of small animal like a weasel. This pendant is
probably very old. Little figurines of a similar type were strung
together in groups upside down, across the back of decorated
wooden baby carriers to confer protective blessings on the child and
keep him safe from illness (Museum Negeri Tenggarong, East
Kalimantan). The baby carrier, sometimes elaborately carved and
decorated with beadwork, was called a *bening aban* (Figs. 96 and
97). The Tenggarong Museum staff noted that groups of similar
pendants were hung together on a string stretched diagonally across
the chest of a *dukun*, a folk healer-diviner, for his curing rituals called
belian. Benuaq Dayak reportedly use the pendants this way. See
Vredenbregt 1981 for a discussion of other Dayak miniature
sculptures and their relationship to the full range of *hampatong*
sculptures.   [3407]

61. Kalimantan, Dayak (Bahau ?)   H: 15.5 cm

A wooden pendant from the Mahakam River area. This piece has
a suspension hole and is done in a particularly striking style: the
figure has his left arm outstretched and the whole body curves
backwards (see Hose and McDougall 1966, I and Vredenbregt 1981
for information on Dayak sculpture).   [3408]

62 and 63. Kalimantan, Dayak (Kenyah, Bahau, Benuaq?)
H: 12 cm.

Two little wooden figurines in the shape of a man. A suspension
hole at their base indicates that they may have served as protective
amulets for decorated baby carriers or were strung together on a
string pulled across the *dukun*'s (healer) chest when he performed
curing rituals (see discussion of No. 60).   [3405 A+C]

64, 65, and 66. Kalimantan, Dayak
64: H: 12.8 cm; 65: H: 9.1 cm; 66: H: 8.5 cm

Small wooden statuettes. Dayak peoples made a profusion of
hampatong, or protective charmlike figurines, ranging in height
from several inches to several feet. These fierce-looking *hampatong*
were used to frighten away evil spirits.   [3405 I, F, D]

67. Central Sulawesi, Lake Poso region   W: 22.2 cm

This curved, snake-shaped brass head ornament is often called a
sanggori. This example has a four-leaf decoration near the tail. The
sanggori conferred magical protective powers on its wearer. When
polished, the metal gleamed so brightly that it supposedly would
reflect back the weapons and evil influences of attacking warriors.
It continues to have other uses in the several ethnic groups near Lake
Poso: in Kulawi, women wear it for *adat* ceremonies; in Central
Sulawesi, *sanggori* are inserted into the tops of the heads of funeral
puppets. The West Central Sulawesi region was a copper-working
center for the island. See the ethnographic chapter on Sulawesi for
more discussion and catalogue information from the museum in
Palu.   [3629]

68. Central Sulawesi, Lake Poso region   W: 21.5 cm

A brass *sanggori* similar to No. 67, but here the snake's head is
replaced by what seems to be a delicately modelled human face. The
significance of this is unknown.   [3628–2]

69. Central Sulawesi, Lake Poso region   W: 23 cm

Another snake-shaped brass *sanggori*, with a ridged body and eyes
set onto the sides of the serpent's face.   [3635–1]

70. Central Sulawesi, Lake Poso region   W: 23 cm

A brass snake-shaped *sanggori* similar to No. 69, also with a ridged
body.   [3635–2]

71. Sulawesi, Selayar Island off Southwest Sulawesi
H: 2.6 cm

Small, rather fragile gold earring from the island of Selayar. No
information is available about the name or social uses of this piece,
but one can note the similarity of its shape to the *taiganja* pendants
(Nos. 73–77) from the Palu and Kulawi area of West Central
Sulawesi, north of the Toraja regions. The shape of the *taiganja* itself
is a variation on the very common open oval design found in earrings
and pendants throughout Eastern Indonesia, the Moluccas, and the
northern Philippines (see Fig. 44).   [3621 I]

72. Central Sulawesi, Toraja   H (element): 15 cm

This *tora-tora* necklace, made of wild boar teeth and tusks attached
to a piece of wood with wickerwork, was used by the Sa'dan Toraja
in ritual dances as part of a highly stylized war costume (Nooy-Palm
1979: 195). Male dancers outfitted themselves in brass versions of
water buffalo horns (signs of prestige and of success in warfare—see
Fig. 105) and wore *tora-tora* around their necks to symbolize
masculinity, fierceness, and invulnerability to attack. This war
dance, called *ma'randing*, was once performed by members of the
slave class. The necklace may also have decorated funerary puppets
(see Grubauer 1913: 261, Fig. 151).   [3605]

73–77. Central Sulawesi, Palu, Kaili, Pamona, Kulawi, Lake
Poso societies
73: H: 6.8 cm; 74: H: 5.7 cm;
75: H: 5.2 cm; 76: H: 5.1 cm;
77: H: 5.6 cm

Heavy brass *taiganja* pendants in the basic open oval shape with
curvilinear decorations at the top and two sides. The interior of the
open oval is decorated with small balls and designs representing
shafts of ripe rice; the upward-curving designs on the piece are
buffalo horns, according to some sources (interpretations of *taiganja*
motifs vary a good deal from region to region in this part of
Sulawesi). *Taiganja* design motifs are said to celebrate fertility,
prosperity, and invulnerability to misfortune. According to the
national museum in Palu, *taiganja* had a variety of functions:
decorative, ritual pendants worn by girls on headbands (see Fig. 106)
for their adolescent rite-of-passage ceremony; ornaments for
aristocratic women in the old Islamized coastal *raja*ships near Palu;
gifts to initiate negotiations for bridewealth payments. These uses
and interpretations seem to vary by social class in the West Central
part of Sulawesi where the pendants are found in abundance. Noble
houses in the coastal *raja*ships often have superb *taiganja* as part of
their inalienable, inherited house treasures. Since *taiganja* have
considerable holy powers, they must be securely housed in special
treasure chests deep inside the home between the ritual occasions
when they are used. At major *adat* rituals such as weddings the
taiganja are worn in groups as pendants, on heavy gold chains or
gold coin necklaces. According to several 1983 informants, *taiganja*

are no longer made. They seem to have been part of an old copper- and brass-working industry centered in West Central Sulawesi that produced *taiganja*, *sanggori*, and the *tau-tau* human figurines. Note how similar the basic *taiganja* shape is to Eastern Indonesian open oval earrings and pendants such as Sumba's *mamuli* (Nos. 119–136), Tanimbar's silver earrings (Nos. 181–184), and Central Flores earrings, such as Nos. 90–92 (see Fig. 44). See the chapter on Sulawesi for more detail on *taiganja* motifs and uses.

[3621 G, H, F, 3630, 3621 D]

78. Sulawesi   H: 6.7 cm

Very heavy brass object (probably a pendant) with one end twisted over the other. Name, use, and ethnic origin unknown. This piece may come from one of Sulawesi's Islamized coastal states such as Bugis. These old mercantile societies controlled large trade networks throughout the Sulawesi-Kalimantan area and Eastern Indonesia. The shape recalls similar designs of the Sumba *marangga* and the Flores *taka*, but they are flat pendants. [3621 J]

79. Central Sulawesi, Toraja   D: 10 cm

This intriguing composite magic bracelet for male hunters is made of two parts: silver sections and blue glass fragments from an old bracelet (said to be Chinese, possibly from the Sung Dynasty). Mamasa Toraja reportedly thought that wearing the bracelet would render the wearer invisible. Many Indonesian cultures greatly value old relics, and this piece may have derived some of its supposed powers from such concepts. The bracelet came with a carved wooden box and string. [3632]

80. Central Sulawesi, Kaili, Pamona, Kulawi, Lake Poso regions   H: 7 and 7.9 cm

Little brass statuettes, called *tau-tau* in some areas, that always come in male and female pairs (*tau-tau* is a generic term for a variety of art objects in human form). Both figures have exaggerated eyes, pronounced sexual characteristics, and digited hands and feet that extend forward. They stand upright, staring forward, and the male wears a head ornament in the shape of buffalo horns. The figurines are variously identified as marriage negotiation gifts, lucky amulets for warding off misfortune, and fertility objects a new couple carries into their marriage (sometimes accompanied by a brass statuette of a water buffalo). See the ethnographic chapter on Sulawesi for more discussion. [3631 A+B]

81. Central Flores, Nage   H: 47 cm, W: 26 cm

Gold frontal, a type of crown called a *lado* or *lado wea* (*wea* = gold), with small spangles and five gold feathers, which represents a gold version of an older feather headdress, thanks to the influx of gold coins into Flores with late Dutch colonial trade and Dutch attempts at political control of this part of Eastern Indonesia. The base of the frontal is a crescent-moon-shaped piece with four-pointed-star decorations. One could almost relate the general shape to a complete boat with masts, though this interpretation was not offered in field interviews in 1983.

This crown for Nage noblemen (see Fig. 116) was an indispensable part of a large range of protective objects used to insure continued prosperity in the village of Boawai (similar crowns may have been used throughout the Nage area). According to several elderly villagers interviewed in 1983, there were three types of *lado*: ones similar to this made of gold, *lado* made from the feathers of a cock, and *lado* made from the lontar palm. Gold *lado* were passed on to sons through the inherited heirloom treasure; alternatively a man could commission a goldsmith to make one. Fashioning a new *lado* called for special sacrificial rituals to ensure the success of the endeavor. *Lado* crowns were once buried with their owners and

figure importantly in a number of large-scale village rituals involving animal sacrifices (*pa sese* ceremonies). One important ritual of this sort demonstrates the link between the *lado* and the *peo*, the forked stake in the middle of Nage villages. According to several Boawai men, seven aristocratic men of the village would go into the forest to select a tree to make a new *peo* stake. Each man would wear a *lado* crown, made out of gold if possible. The forked stake would be carried back to the village with one man in full regalia sitting on the trunk and another similarly attired sitting on a plank stretched between the two branches. In 1983 interviews it was clear that Boawai people have an elaborate ideology about how each of their ritual objects relate to the others.

Similar crescent-shaped forehead pieces, called *rajo*, are found in the Lio region, and indeed the design is a common one throughout Eastern Indonesia. The small spangles hanging down from the Nage crown are also used on some local earrings and are again a very common decorative style throughout Indonesia (see the *pilo-pilo* spangles on Karo Batak jewelry such as Nos. 11, 12, 18, and 25).

[3525–5]

82. Central Flores, Nage   W: 28 cm

Lower part of a gold *lado* crown. The two ends of the crescent are decorated with birds' heads. The bird is frequently used as a decorative motif, in interior architecture as well as jewelry. At the back of the piece are five holes for the gold feathers which originally completed the crown. [3525–37]

83. Central Flores, Ngada and occasionally Nage   H: 3.4 cm

Circular flat gold earrings called *bela*, in a modified open oval form, decorated with bunches of tiny balls at three points on each side. These ornaments demonstrate the extensive trade networks in prestige goods that linked different parts of West and Central Flores. The *bela* are typical Ngada pieces, according to an *adat* expert in Bajawa and the son of the last Bajawa *raja*. Ngada kinship traces descendants through both the father's and the mother's lines, and the children are claimed by their mother's descent group if the full bridewealth has not been paid (a common circumstance). If the marriage transactions have been completed, children are claimed by their father's descent group. Two shrines in the village commemorate the two sorts of ancestors a person has (see Figs. 112 and 113). In Ngada these *bela* earrings are not normally used as part of the bridewealth payments, nor as engagement rings as the Nage *wea wunu wona* earrings (No. 85) are. Rather, girls generally get them from their parents to wear as simple decorations for *adat* festivities. In Bajawa, informants note that the *bela* shown here are simply a newer style than those in No. 84.

Bela figure importantly in Ngada house architecture. In the *raja's* house in Kampung Bajawa, for instance, this style of earring is carved in relief on long wooden panels in the innermost room of the dwelling (see Fig. 117), and representations of *taka* pendants (Nos. 104 and 105) are carved into the panels next to them. Perhaps this indicates that these jewels were part of noble house treasures as well as simply decorative ornaments for use in ceremonies, although no one confirmed this. Both Nos. 83 and 84 are also found in Nage and even to some extent in Manggarai. In the village of Boawai in Nage, elderly residents called these *bela* and said that women wore them as earrings at *adat* rituals. Young men can give them to their fiancées as preliminary bridewealth objects, to publically announce their engagement (that is, *bela* are alternatives to Nage's *wea wunu wona* earrings). In Olaewa, another Nage village, the headman and his wife gave another interpretation, saying these were called *sengo* and were used as bridewealth and as ornaments by both men and women at *adat* rituals involving water buffalo sacrifices. A ceremony to enter a new house, for instance, is one ritual that would call for this high degree of body ornamentation. In Lio, descendants of the last aristocratic family in Walotopo called the same pieces *riti fai* but said that although there were in fact a few of this type ornament in other parts of Lio, there were none now in Walotopo.

[3525–22 A+B]

84. Central Flores, Ngada and occasionally Nage   H: 4.7 cm

Gold earrings called *bela*, an older version of No. 83: see the discussion there, as the more oval-shaped *bela* are used in the same way as the smaller rounded ones. This pair are finely worked around the exterior, and old cloth is wrapped around the top of the earring. Manggarai informants in Kampung Ruteng identified these earrings as *wua lolong*, which refers in its literal sense to a certain type of fruit. These earrings are occasionally included in Manggarai house treasures.

[3525–25 A+B]

85. Central Flores, Nage   H: 10.3 cm

Pair of ornately worked gold earrings, in the shape of an oblong oval, decorated with filigree wire curlicues all around the sides and ornamented with spangles at the bottom. They are hooked onto the earlobe with a movable clasp. This is one of the most common types of Nage earrings, called *wea wunu wona* in Boawai and the nearby village of Olaewa. *Wea* simply means gold, *wula* means leaves, and *wona* is the name of a plant, so the name translates approximately as "swinging leaves gold earrings." The thin dangling strips of gold are of course the leaves. In Nage these are considered jewelry "in the middle range" of cost and social importance. They are used as a special sort of advance bridewealth payment: a young man presents them to the young woman he wishes to marry as a sign that they are engaged. In fact, the woman's family will often insist on such a gift, to make sure that the young man's intentions are serious. The earring on the right, it happens, is missing one of its swinging leaves. In a 1983 interview in Olaewa the village headman commented with a laugh that the parents of a girl receiving such an earring would be sure to point out its deficiency and demand that the man's family make up for it with the additional gift of a horse. Nage once had asymmetrical marriage alliance and fairly large bridewealth payments. Today the Roman Catholic Church is discouraging first-cousin marriage, and as the marriage system changes jewelry exchange too may become less strict.

Nage women commonly wear these earrings at *adat* ceremonies. some also wear *iti bholo* earrings, which are just like these but lack the dangling leaves. In interviews in other parts of West and Central Flores, Manggarai informants said that they had a few of the complete earrings in their house treasures, although the style was fairly rare there. They were "imported things," as indeed so much of Manggarai jewelry is. The small museum run by the Ministry of Education and Culture in Ende notes that the earring is also found in Ende and Ngada. Walotopo villagers, in Lio, called the earrings *riti eko* (*eko* means "tail") and said that none of the type was currently used in the village, although they had seen them.   [3525–19 A+B]

86. Central Flores, Nage, Lio   L: 5.6 cm

Pair of gold earrings in the shape of birds, decorated on their necks and legs with a tight spiral design also found in Timor jewelry. Probably decorative pieces, although they may have been part of a ritual ensemble. See discussion of No. 87.   [3525–27 A+B]

87. Central Flores, Nage, Lio   L: 5.9 cm

Pair of gold earrings portraying fish in a realistic style. Each fish, marked with scales, has two small spangles hanging from its underside. The earrings are probably decorative ornaments, although they may have been part of a house treasure. Central Flores aristocrats were enamored of little gold animal figurines, as the Lio

necklace picture in Fig. 109 in the Flores ethnographic chapter indicates. Earrings in the shape of fish and birds may fit into that tradition, although a series of *adat* experts contacted in Manggarai, Ngada, Nage, Ende, and Lio could not shed much light on the exact names and uses of these pieces. Most informants, if they had seen earrings like these at all, simply called them *ika*, which means fish (similar to the Indonesian word *ikan*). The *ika*, if that is what we must call them, are said to have come from Lio. Supposedly they were used in a ritual called *lawo*, as part of a set of ornaments including a crown and bracelets. In 1983 interviews in the Lio village of Walotopo, elderly men and women did say that the pieces were Lio but noted that only a few families own them. The museum run by the Museum of Education and Culture in Ende has photographs of the house treasures in Walotopo with several gold fish earrings very similar to these. Ndona villagers, again in Lio, confirmed that the pieces were used as earrings there and sometimes kept as part of house treasures. Nage villagers identified the Barbier-Müller photographs of these earrings as *wea ika* (gold fish) and said that there used to be a few pieces like this in Nage, always worn as pendants on a necklace.   [3525–15 A+B]

88. Central Flores, Lio   H: 6.4 cm

Pair of earrings in low-carat gold, in a trilobed shape. Some elements having this shape appear on the necklace worn by the Lio woman shown in Fig. 115.   [3525–35 A+B]

89. Central Flores, Lio   H: 4.5 cm

A pair of gold earrings called *wea* (= gold) from Lio similar to Nos. 90–92. Their shape resembles an open four-sided diamond, with little knobs at the sides. The earrings were slipped through an enlarged hole in the earlobe, or may have been suspended from strings. The *wea* are most closely associated with the Lio people around Ende. In Lio, earrings of this sort are indispensable parts of a bride's *teo kinga*, the collection of jewelry and other valuables that she brings with her to her marriage. Some of her bridewealth payments are used to supply her with a suitably impressive *teo kinga*. The approximate Indonesian term for this is *pembawaan*, "things brought along." The Lio bridewealth is called *toko liwa* or *weli tebo*, and a special name for these *wea* earrings used as part of the *teo kinga* goods is *ome mbulu ina*. The various *wea* are given specific names according to their weight. For instance, an earring weighing about 10 grams is called an *ome mbulu* and one weighing about 20 grams is termed an *ome mbulu rua*. *Wea* are also used as part of the house treasure of Lio noble families. The ancestral founder of the aristocratic lineage in Walotopo, a man called Da Seko, started his family's *pusaka* treasure with seven *wuli* (gold conch shell pendants) and two *wea*. Later descendants acquired a harlequin mix of gold chains, earrings, disks, and even a Sumbanese-style *mamuli* (locally called a *wea bara*, with no mention of any connection to Sumba).   [3525–4 A+B]

90. Central Flores, Lio   H: 3.5 cm

A pair of gold *wea* earrings, a variation on the more ornate style seen in Nos. 91 and 92. One earring has black thread wrapped around the top, presumably for suspending the piece on the ear with a string. *Wea* are sometimes also worn by male aristocrats on heavy necklaces, from which large gold disks are suspended. They form part of the heirloom treasure of noble houses.   [3525–7 A+B]

91. Central Flores, Lio   H: 4.2 cm

Another pair of *wea* gold earrings. See discussion of No. 89.

[3525–2 A+B]

92. Central Flores, Lio
H: 5.4 cm

Single gold earring, an unusually ornate version of the Lio *wea* style with appliquéd decoration. [3525-20]

93. Central Flores, Nage, Lio
H: 5.4 cm

Ornate gold earrings for women in an oblong oval shape with openwork curvilinear design, called *tebe*, or more properly, *ate saga* (terms from the Nage villages of Boawai and Olaewa). The top of the earring is a thin movable clasp for affixing the piece to the ear. Similar little ball decorations are used on many other Flores earrings. These are somewhat unusual in that they do not employ the open oval shape found so often in Eastern Indonesia. The earring is a much-admired style in both the Nage area and the Lio region. Its provenance may well extend beyond these two cultures, although 1983 informants in Manggarai and Ngada said that this piece was not a local ornament. In the name *ate saga* the word *ate* translates into the Indonesian word *hati*, a very complex concept that combines some of the ideas of "heart" and "mind." (*Hati* literally means liver, the supposed seat of the emotions).

Like the Nage *wea wunu wona* earrings (No. 85) these ornaments are presented to a young woman by her fiancé as a sort of engagement ring: the gift is a public announcement that they intend to marry, and the earrings also serve as a type of down payment on the larger bridewealth to be paid later. Boawai residents stressed that only the richest families used these *ate saga* in their marriage negotiations, and they noted that if a young woman received a pair of these as an engagement gift everyone in the village would know that "she was not just anyone." The village headman of Olaewa further stated that *ate saga* were *barang keramat*, or holy objects full of powers. He said that the earrings were important parts of the heirlooms treasures passed down through the exogamous patrilineal clans. It should be noted that these valuable jewels are considered part of an indivisible triad of highly valued, sacred property: the *peo* forked stake in the village plaza (see Fig. 19), the inherited farmland, and the *ate saga*. Selling any of these endangers the good fortune, health, and prosperity of the clan. The appearance of these pieces on the Bali art market, though, argues that this belief is changing.

In the Lio village of Walotopo on the coast near Ende, the same ornaments are called *riti* (apparently a generic term). Used as earrings or massed together on chains and worn as necklaces, the *riti* are part of the noble house treasures and have a sacred air about them. Walotopo residents said that when the gold ornaments in the treasure are stored in their special cabinet in the *adat* house, they sometimes begin to move about and emit little noises. This is taken as a sign that the ancestor spirits who own the treasure wish to communicate something to their living descendants. In Walotopo, the *wea* (such as Nos. 89–92) are considered to be more valuable than *riti*. [3525-3 A+B]

94. Central Flores, Nage, Lio
H: 4.8 cm

Ate saga gold earrings similar to No. 93. [3525-6 A+B]

95. Central Flores, Nage, Lio
H: 5.3 cm

A pair of ornate gold Lio earrings similar in use and interpretation to Nos. 93 and 94; the same general style is also found in Nage villages. [3525-38 A+B]

96. Central Flores, Ende (?)
H: 13 cm

Pair of earrings in low-carat gold and filigree decoration of an unusual upside-down-V shape, with spangles at the bottom. These earrings show a clear Muslim influence, found on several other types of jewelry used in coastal Flores, a region in long-term contact with the great trade empires that extended into Eastern Indonesia. [3525-34 A+B]

97. Central Flores, Lio (?)
H: 8.7 cm

Pair of rather delicate openwork gold earrings tentatively identified as Lio pieces by informants there. They are called either *ata wolo* or *mboko leba* (two versions given by informants). They are used as decorative pieces and sometimes form part of Lio bridewealth. The earrings are hollow cagelike constructions made of bent wire affixed to the ear by a small hook. Since they are said to be rare in Lio, perhaps they are found in more abundance in another ethnic area. [3525-18 A+B]

98. Lembata, Lamalohot Archipelago
H: 4.5 cm

A silver earring important in marriage exchange gift-giving (Barnes 1974). This ornament shows yet an other distortion of the open oval shape common in much Eastern Indonesian and Sulawesi jewelry but is more narrow and elongated than usual (compare, for instance, the Sulawesi *taiganja*, Nos. 73–77, or the Sumba *mamuli*, Nos. 119–136). Like the *taiganja*, however, this piece is decorated near the base by what seem to be ripe-rice-stalk motifs. Very occasionally this typical sort of Lembata (Lomblen) earring is seen also in Nage, where they are called *tibu*, and in Lio, where they are called *pusu manu* (which literally means "chicken heart.") [3525-28]

99. Lembata, Lamalohot Archipelago
H: 6 cm

Pair of silver earrings with a copper twisted ornamentation along the internal edges. The type is similar to No. 98 but is even more elongated. See Barnes 1974 for detailed descriptions and anthropological analysis of marriage exchange involving such objects on Lembata. [3525-29 A+B]

100. Found in West Flores, Manggarai
W: 6.8

Gold pendant with applied filigree work, which can also be used as a cheek ornament (in pairs, suspended from a band around the head). This piece was probably brought to Flores from the Islamized Indonesian trade states, as the Manggarai seem to be without an indigenous jewelry tradition for the most part. [3525-16]

101. Found in West Flores, Manggarai
D: 5 cm

Gold disk with applied filigree geometric decoration, apparently worn either as a pendant or as a cheek ornament, like No. 100. The disks are probably of Bugis (South Sulawesi) origin, but they are also found in Flores and Sumba, sometimes in bad imitations in poor-quality metal. [3525-30]

102. Central Flores, Ngada
H: 10.4 cm

Small bag formed by two gold plaques sewn together by a gold thread and suspended on a gold chain. This bag may be a luxury replica of small bags used for carrying betel, but nothing can be put in this one as it is completely flat. [3525-36]

103. Central Flores, possibly Ende
H: 7.3 cm

Small gold pendant in the shape of a cross, to which is added a small pouch decorated with double spirals. The cross recalls the early conversion of the Endenese to Christianity, and the pouch could represent the *pusaka* (heirlooms) container, thus creating a mixture of the old and the new religious sacred symbols. This is only speculation, however. [3525-39]

104 and 105. Central Flores, Ngada
104: W: 6 cm; 105: W: 7.7 cm

Gilded silver (or low-carat gold) pendant called *taka*, in a double-ax-head shape. The form is amazingly similar to the Sumba *marangga* (see, e.g., No. 139), but there does not seem to be an awareness in

Flores (from evidence of my 1983 interviews) that there is similar jewelry on the other island. From an outsider's perspective, however, the ornaments of the two islands are closely related. These *taka* pendants are typical Ngada pieces, used throughout the Bajawa area. *Adat* experts there asserted that the shape represents an ax.

Taka are worn by men or women around the neck on a chain or suspended singly from a headband worn above the eyebrows. They are used as part of the bridewealth payments and can also be inherited from one's parents. The *taka* apparently have a certain sacred quality, for they may only be taken out of their special strongboxes into the daylight after a small animal such as a piglet has been sacrificed. The animal's blood is then sprinkled on all the powerful gold objects, to ask permission of the ancestral spirits to use "their" jewelry in an *adat* ritual. *Taka* as well as *bela* earrings (No. 83) are represented in relief carvings on wood panels in the inner-sanctum room of Ngada *adat* houses (see Fig. 117).

[3525-26, 25]

106. Central Flores   W: 13.6 cm

Crescent-shaped gold pendant with a chain, decorated with a repoussé floral motif. Crescent-shaped ornaments can be used as pendants or as frontals like the *rajo* found in the Lio area.

[3525-32]

107. Flores   D: 11.8 cm

Pair of ivory bracelets with a dark patina. A bride often wore a pair of bracelets when she entered her new husband's family home. In the Lamalohot cultures east of Flores, bridewealth was paid in ivory tusks, which were considered countergifts to "feminine" woven textiles (Maxwell 1981). Trade in ivory in the Flores–Sumba area must once have been extensive, for etched bracelets are also found in East Sumba house treasures. [3525-33 A+B]

108. Found in West Flores, Manggarai   H: 3.8 cm

Small gold pyramidal ring with applied filigree work, in the coastal Islamic state style. A trade object, like many pieces in Manggarai.

[3525-31]

109. Central Flores, Ngada (?)   D: 10 cm

Little gold cup which was apparently never worn but kept stored away. No one in any of the other ethnic areas visited in 1983 recognized this piece. [3525-13]

110. East Sumba   H: 16.5 cm

Ceremonial turtleshell comb for girls and women, called *hai kara jangga*. Worn like a crown, right on top of the head, with the decorated part pointed forward (see Fig. 52). The top portion is carved into a profusion of animal figures on each side of a skull tree (*andung* tree), which was a sort of altar for displaying captured heads after war raids on other regions. Bringing heads back to the village was associated with bringing back prosperity and luck. East Sumba turtleshell combs generally employ motifs such as this, which are also used in local textile design. In some areas fathers gave these combs to their daughters while they were teenagers. Unmarried adolescents wear the comb perched above their short bangs — the sign that they have entered puberty. Adult women of the noble class also wear the combs. In the detail photograph cocks and horses appear, with a human figure off to the side, facing the skull tree. [3650 B]

111. East Sumba   H: 16 cm

Another *hai kara jangga* turtleshell comb for girls and women, similar to No. 110. The top portion has a multitude of animal figures

on each side of a crayfish. Lobsters, fish, and crocodiles are associated with the Underworld, while birds evoke the Upperworld (see Adams 1979 for a discussion of animal symbolism in East Sumbanese myth). This design of animals facing each other is found in other Indonesian areas and is particularly frequent in the ritual textiles from Kroë (Lampong district, in South Sumatra). The motifs are also found in East Sumba's ceremonial textiles, woven by noble women (Adams 1969), and in stone pole sculpture in the village plazas. All these works of art teem with animals and mythical figures, as do the fully attired Sumbanese women when they are dressed in their textiles and combs. [3650 A]

112. Sumba   H: 7.6 cm

Turtleshell comb, the upper part covered with repoussé silver, with a decoration of clover leaves perhaps inspired by Indian *patola* designs. Compare this to the more usual *hai kara jangga* (Nos. 110 and 111), which are made completely of turtleshell. This one resembles the small crownlike combs from Savu. [3681]

113 and 113a. East Sumba   W: 30 cm

Large gold frontal called *lamba* (similar pieces are called *tabelu* in West Sumba societies), with repoussé decoration of horses and riders. The edge of this *lamba* is supported all along the inside by a piece of wicker. The ornament is kept in a wooden box of the same shape (No. 113a), tied with plaited wicker links (many especially valuable and sacred gold treasures in East Sumba are kept securely housed in special compartments). This *lamba* is said to come from the Kapunduk treasure of East Sumba.

In that region *lamba* are forehead decorations for men. Once reportedly made by itinerant Savunese goldsmiths, these *lamba* are core parts of the royal house treasures of the traditional ruling families. Today in the national period these families are more ceremonial leaders than political powers, but in late Dutch colonial times they did rule villages and *raja*ship domains and were able to amass considerable wealth in gold (Forth 1981; Adams 1969). The heirloom treasures of such rulers were kept carefully boxed in the dark recesses of the *adat* house attic, where other sacred relics were stored. These heirlooms would "glow with power" and were considered to be the "possessions of the *marapu*," the lineage ancestor spirits who were thought to maintain an active interest in the fortunes of their living descendants. *Lamba* were normally considered part of the inalienable heirloom treasure of the household, not to be sold or even taken down from their storage compartment without careful ritual precautions. Very occasionally *lamba* and other parts of the treasure could be removed from storage, cleansed (sometimes with the blood of a sacrificed animal), and used as a sort of altar for contacting *marapu* spirits. In some villages the ornaments are still so used today.

A more usual use, during major *adat* rituals, is for men to wear the *lamba* tied onto their foreheads as part of the royal regalia, including pictured woven textiles (see Fig. 127), gold chain necklaces (such as No. 144), orange bead necklaces called *anchida langgelu* (see Fig. 126), and *mamuli* pendants. The last would be worn in pairs suspended from the *lamba* on either side of the forehead (see Fig. 120). Notably, in East Sumba it was not the *raja* himself who wore such finery (although his family owned it) but his favorite slave (see Fig. 127). The full array of gold ornaments was especially important in East Sumbanese religious thought during the funeral of the *raja*, when the slave bedecked with gold would go into a trance during ritual dancing and serve as an intermediary between humans and the souls of departed ancestors, toward which the *raja*'s soul was moving. Slavery has long been abolished in East Sumba. (See the chapter on Sumba for more discussion of such trance rituals and their connection to gold jewelry such as the *lamba*.) [3682]

114. East or West Sumba W: 31 cm

A gold-alloy frontal called *lamba*, decorated with a central motif resembling a sun. In one East Sumba *raja*ship I visited, the village priest said that only men of middle age and upward can wear these powerful objects. Another informant, a descendant of a royal family, said that the shape of the *lamba* represented water buffalo horns, which are placed under the doorframe in royal houses. In West Sumba (in Lauli), these pieces are not used in combination with *mamuli* suspended from them but are either simply kept in the recesses of the *adat* house as "*marapu*'s things" (possessions of the lineage spirits) or worn by the *raja*'s sons as regalia for dancing. The ornaments are not called *lamba*, but *tabelu* (often pronounced *tabela*). In West Sumba there is apparently relatively little knowledge about how similar ornaments are used in East Sumba. Ethnic parochialism is a characteristic of Sumba societies in general (Needham 1980). [3666]

115. East or West Sumba W: 26 cm

Another gold *lamba*, called *tabelu* or *tabela* in West Sumba societies. These ornaments are made of thin, beaten sheets of gold and sometimes are rather fragile. This one has a raised globular design in the center. The crescent shape is one of the primary design motifs of Eastern Indonesian art and is often worn like *lamba* as a forehead decoration or as a pendant piece on a chain around the neck. Compare the Nage gold crown (No. 81) from Central Flores. As noted in the chapter on Sumba, many gold treasures were made for local royal families by travelling goldsmiths from the small islands off the west coast of Timor. [3665]

116. East or West Sumba W: 21.9 cm

Another gold *lamba*, with repoussé circles and little raised bumps pressed into the borders. Note also that two upside-down *mamuli* shapes are used as decorations near the bottom edge of the piece. Sumba stone sculpture and textiles also use jewelry motifs as decoration. [3679]

117. Sumba L (element): 12.5 cm

Chin ornament, composed of two beaten-gold plaques placed near the ears, connected by a beaded string that hangs down under the chin. The whole assembly is tied onto the head with a string. Exact use unknown. Chin ornaments of this general type are found in the house treasure of the *rajas* of Kampung Ruteng in Manggarai (West Flores) and in Mindanao in the southern Philippines (see Casal et al. 1981: 151). Note the motif of the *mamuli* on the gold plaques, as on No. 116. [3680]

118. Sumba L: 19.5 cm

Two gold plaques which were part of an ear and chin ornament of the same type as No. 117. [3678 A+B]

119. East Sumba H: 5 cm

Pair of gold *woridi*, which are ornaments similar to *mamuli* (Nos. 124–136). Possibly made by Flores metalsmiths living in Sumba. Perhaps employed as marriage-alliance exchange gift. [3660-17 A+ B]

120. East Sumba H: 4.7 cm

Gold *woridi*, a variation of No. 121 and very similar to the pair in No. 119. Decorated with tight spirals around the edges. Largely unrecognized in 1983 interviews in East and West Sumba. [3660-10]

121. East Sumba H: 8.1 cm

Another, larger and more diamond-shaped *woridi*, decorated with tight spirals and virtually closed at the bottom. Compare this shape to that of *taiganja* from Sulawesi (Nos. 73–77). [3660-7]

122. Sumba (?) H: 4.7 cm

Gold ornament in a modified *mamuli* shape, seemingly halfway between the East Sumba *mamuli* shape and the Central Flores *wea* earrings (Nos. 89–92). Possibly a *woridi*. [3660-16]

123. West Sumba H: 5.2 cm

A gold pendant, earring, or jacket pin. Apparently an uncommon and perhaps idiosyncratic ornament, for it was unrecognized in most parts of Sumba visited in 1983. One *raja* in Lamboya (West Sumba) had a similar piece, called a *madaka*, which had been given to him before his marriage by his wife's father as an incentive to go through with the marriage. Upon his accepting the ornament, which he wore as a jacket pin, his family gave the older man's side a good *marangga* pendant (of the same type as No. 139). [3660-8]

124. West Sumba H: 8 cm

Mamuli earring or pendant, in silver. This particular type was called *pewisie* ("that which has feet"), and Jasper (1927: Fig. 168) gives its provenance as northwestern Sumba. The motifs at the bottom are stylized horse heads, a typical design in West Sumbanese art. Horses are crucial symbols of wealth and prestige throughout the island. West Sumba societies also had *mamuli* in their royal treasuries, but they tended to be less grand than those in East Sumba, just as West Sumba village *raja*ships were not as powerful or as profitably linked to the Dutch horse trade as their East Sumba counterparts. In Lauli in West Sumba plain masculine and feminine pairs of *mamuli* were given by wife-takers to wife-givers as bridewealth gifts, and more decorated *mamuli* (but generally without figurines) were kept as sacred house altar objects. Others were used in the ritual costumes of *rajas*' sons and daughters, for in West Sumba women as well as men could wear *mamuli* at *adat* ceremonies. Today *mamuli* are used in abundance by girl dancers in Lauli and Anakalang, sometimes worn in one earlobe and sometimes suspended around the neck by chains. [3660-11]

125. East or West Sumba H: 7.1 cm

Relatively plain *mamuli* of very pure, heavy gold. Pairs of *polos* (plain) *mamuli* were used (in matched male and female pairs) as initial bridewealth payments to the woman's father's lineage group, to get the negotiations off to a good start.

Different types of *mamuli* were variously marriage exchange goods given by wife-takers to wife-givers as bridewealth; lineage prestige items that could be used for dancing and other rituals; sacred altar objects employed by priests for contacting *marapu* spirits; or extremely holy lineage relics almost never taken down from their special storage cabinets. [3660-15]

126. East Sumba H: 6.5 cm

Gold *mamuli*, part of a *raja*'s house treasure. Very well worked at the bottom, with what looks like flowering bushes (a departure from the usual East Sumbanese mythic motifs — skull trees, horses, water buffalo, warriors). *Mamuli* like this one (and Nos. 127–136), with human or animal figures along the base, were part of the sacred house heirlooms of very wealthy royal families and were used as altar objects for summoning lineage spirits for advice and mystical aid. See the chapter on Sumba for a discussion of the several categories of *mamuli* in East Sumba. [3660-19]

127. East Sumba H: 7.9 cm

Very finely worked gold *mamuli* with figurines of two water buffalo at the base. The animals face outward and have silver crosses on their backs. Buffalo are a principal sign of wealth for Sumbanese families, and their horns are still kept to decorate the outside walls of *adat* houses, on the porch. This type of large *mamuli* was part of the royal house treasure and could be suspended from *lamba* forehead crescents (see Fig. 120) during the rare and extravagant *papangka* funerals of renowned *raja*. The even larger *mamuli*, such as No. 136, should never be taken out of the secret storage compartment of the house. This is said to come from the House of Pau's treasury.
[3660-18]

128. East Sumba H: 7.2 cm

Gold *mamuli* decorated with two *andung* trees (see No. 129 for an explanation of these skull trees, important in village religious life in pre-modern times). At the base of the trees repose pairs of water buffalo horns, making this *mamuli* particularly laden with symbols of high political prestige and power. A *mamuli* for ritual display, not for marriage exchange.
[3660-4]

129. East Sumba H: 8 cm

An ornately decorated gold *mamuli*, part of a *raja's* treasure (not for use as a necklace ornament and probably not directly involved in marriage exhange). This piece, like No. 128, has tiny *andung* trees (skull trees) at its base, which in past times were used like altars to display skulls of heads captured in raids, in order to ritually replenish the forces of life in the victorious village. The skull trees seem to be standing on the prows of boats. Just beyond are forked stakes, important in ancestor placation and linked to buffalo sacrifices and megalithic monument building in many parts of island and mainland Southeast Asia. From the House of Pau's treasury.
[3660-9]

130. East Sumba H: 7.2 cm

Gold *mamuli* with two *andung* trees, with forked stakes and pairs of water buffalo horns under each tree (shown in detail). *Andung* trees are also a common motif on the woven textiles of aristocratic families in East Sumba.
[3660-5]

131. East Sumba H: 7.5 cm

Gold *mamuli* decorated with birds (cocks or cockatoos?) standing in boats. Like Nos. 126–130 and 132–133, this one was an object of house treasure used to mediate between humans and spirits.
[3660-1]

132. East Sumba H: 6.6 cm

Gold *mamuli* with bird (a cockatoo?), branches, and a little cup. Highly ornamented *mamuli* like this one often played on mythic narrative themes. The choice of animal or skull tree representation may have been associated with the lineage history of the particular royal household that commissioned the piece.
[3660-3]

133. East Sumba H: 7.2 cm

Gold *mamuli*, with figurines of cocks, similar to No. 131. [3660-6]

134. East Sumba H 10.2 cm

Large gold *mamuli* with articulated monkeys holding fruit or little gold bowls (ritual offering cups?) in their paws. This extraordinarily large and luxuriant piece was part of the sacred treasure of a noble house, testament to the wealth and prestige of the *raja* whose family commissioned it. These huge *mamuli* ideally should never be taken

out of their "holy of holies" storage place in the depths of the *adat* house without extreme ritual precautions. Some pieces of this size, in fact, were never supposed to be taken out into the light, or misfortune would befall the family. Some *mamuli* (probably less grand than this type) may have been involved in practices resembling the classic potlatch rituals of the Northwest Coast Indian societies of North America: stacks of fine textiles and some *mamuli* were once buried with important *rajas*, and the jewelry was sometimes broken beforehand. Such destruction of wealth plus the fact that the *raja* bestowed *mamuli* on their lesser followers to secure their allegiance suggests that some form of the potlatch may once have operated in dry, ecologically variable East Sumba.
[3660-2]

135. East Sumba H: 10.2 cm

Another exceptionally large and splendid *mamuli*, with two horsemen and their female companions. Of the same general type as No. 134, a holy heirloom object that ideally passed down through the family line, under the ritual control of the *raja* and his priest.

The shape of *mamuli* in general may represent female genitals (an interpretation not offered by Sumbanese interviewed in 1983). If so, the ornament is a powerfully ambiguous one, for some *mamuli* are heirloom treasures often identified with *rajas* and their patrilineal lineages and other *mamuli* are masculine marriage exchange objects. Combining these sorts of "masculine" objects with a shape associated with femininity would make the *mamuli* one of Indonesia's male-and-female-in-one art objects, where the two-in-one pattern unleashes sacred powers and creative forces. See the chapter on Sumba for a discussion of the several categories of *mamuli*. This type was commissioned by the most prosperous *rajas* and kept hidden in the house treasure as a possession of the *marapu* who were themselves associated with the upper reaches of the house.
[3660-13]

136. East Sumba H: 12.7 cm

A large gold *mamuli* of extravagant concept: four fighting men with movable limbs, armed with lances and shields, decorate the base in realistic warlike poses. Like No. 135, this piece is a sacred treasure object, not a simple ornament or marriage exchange gift. At a social functional level such *mamuli* are lavish prestige objects of a privileged class able to amass a huge surplus of wealth, thanks in part to well-timed political alliances in the era of trade in horses with the Dutch. Said to be from the House of Pau's treasury. [3660-12]

137. East Sumba H: 3.7 cm

Little gold horse complete with tackle and male rider; the rider's female companion sits behind him (head redone). Once part of the decoration for the base of a big *mamuli*, the most sacred type that was ideally never removed from the house storage compartment. Many details are worked into this little figure, including the horse's short tail which sticks straight up, typical of Sumba's feisty mounts.
[3664]

138. East Sumba (?) H: 4.5 cm

Little silver horseman with detachable shield. The quality of sculpture is far superior to the horsemen found on *mamuli* such as the figure in No. 137; therefore it is unlikely that this was a *mamuli* piece. Unidentified and unrecognized by all interviewed in 1983 in Sumba and Flores.
[3667]

139. West Sumba, including Lauli, Lamboya, and others
W: 30 cm

Gold pectoral *marangga* (often pronounced *maragga*) made of beaten 18-carat gold leaf. It has the shape of two joined triangles, a form which seems to appear in the arts of various islands outside Sumba (see the Flores *taka* pendants, Nos. 104 and 105). Part of the heirloom treasure, the *marangga* is kept in the attic of nobles' *adat* houses and taken out into the light only for special ritual occasions, under the careful control of the village priests. With the *mamuli*, the *marangga* is often represented on West Sumbanese megaliths: on stone slab monuments at grave sites, and altars in the village plaza (see Fig. 132). In the Lauli region the *marangga* forms a triad with the *tabelu* (the gold crescent-shaped frontal called *lamba* in East Sumba) and special *mamuli*. These are all "marapu's things," holy objects that embody the essence of the lineage and the great house that shelters the family line. Large, important *marangga* like this one, then, are holy objects. This piece reportedly came from the Pau treasure in East Sumba, which would imply that the style is not confined to West Sumba societies and may have spread throughout the island through trade and perhaps marriage alliances.   [3676]

140. West Sumba   H: 20 cm

Gold alloy pectoral called *marangga* made of a very thin plaque of metal, of a more elongated shape than usual (compare whith No. 139, the usual shape). On stone ritual altars in the village plaza in Tarung near Waikabubak, there are relief designs that look like an abstract human figure composed of a circular head and two "wings", forming a sort of *marangga* shape. The *rato*, or priest, said that this shape was a *marangga* of a very ancient variety. This may indicate that the shape of this unusual *marangga* here is older than the shape of No. 139.   [3673]

141. East Sumba   D: 15 cm

Gold disk called *tabilu* (sometimes *tabili*) worn by men suspended from a gold chain around the neck. Decorated in repoussé geometric designs. Part of the inherited house treasure of aristocrats. In former times *tabilu* were worn by the *raja's* slaves as part of their full funeral regalia in trance dances at their *raja's* funeral. Recall that the word *tabelu* is used in West Sumba for the piece called *lamba* in East Sumba (the crescent-shaped forehead ornament). These gold *tabilu* disks have obvious ties to other disks used as male prestige objects in Timor and other parts of Eastern Indonesia. This piece is said to come from the House of Pau's treasury.   [3683]

142. East Sumba   D: 8.8 cm

Tabilu disk with intricate repoussé geometric motifs. Similar in use and interpretation to No. 141.   [3677]

143. East Sumba   L: 74 cm

Gold *kanatar* chain terminating in two stylized open-mouthed *nagas* (mythical snake-dragons). Sometimes called *kanatar ningu nganjang*. Attached to the *naga* heads is another chain that includes three decorative plaques with gold filigree designs. Without the plaques this East Sumba chain is very similar to the royal chains of office used by aristocrats on Savu (see Fig. 134) (see Fox 1977: 121). Goldsmiths from the small islands of Ndao, Savu, and Roti may well have carried this style throughout Eastern Indonesia (Central Flores *rajas* in Ngada also use similar chains). Kanatar chains of less elegant types than this one serve as marriage alliance gifts, and are presented to wife-givers by the groom's lineage. These fine, heavy chains, however, are regalia of high *rajaships*. In pre-national times, though, the old *rajas* themselves rarely wore the chains — their slaves did (see the discussion in the Sumba chapter, above). Some East Sumba noble families are reported to have *kanatar* chains so long that they can be wrapped around the waist eight times; this is an apt illustration of the prestige value they carry. Like other house treasure they are kept in special compartments in the dark upper reaches of the *adat* house. These chains are often worn with necklaces called

anchida langgelu (long ropes of orange *mutisala* beads which culminate in a group of old gold coins (see Fig. 126). Said to come from the treasure of Pau.   [3675]

144. East Sumba   L: 148 cm

A heavy gold *kanatar* chain, a royal badge of office for East Sumbanese aristocrats. This chain ends in stylized *naga* (snake-dragon) motifs, out of whose mouths spill three chains with disks attached. The disks are decorated around their edges with small puncture holes, a convention used on headhunters' disks in Timor. (There is also a possible *patola* cloth influence for these disk designs.) The *nagas'* mouths are filled with tight spirals made of gold wire, another Timor area jewelry technique — or, more accurately, a Savunese, Rotinese, and Ndao technique, for those islands supplied much of Eastern Indonesia from Sumba to Timor with goldsmiths and silversmiths. Somewhat simpler chains called *lulu amahu* were part of the masculine metal goods that the wife-takers presented to their wife-givers as bridewealth goods to counterbalance their wife-givers' feminine gifts of women, woven textiles, ivory bracelets, porcelain, and beadwork (Adams 1969: 47). Various combinations of gold chains and *mamuli* were paid to the wife-givers at different stages of contracting a marriage, from the time of a girl's birth through the course of the protracted wedding rituals. Said to come from the treasure of Pau.   [3672]

145. East Sumba   D: 10.5 cm

Pair of woman's ivory bracelets, decorated with connecting triangle designs composed of small circles. Ivory bracelets were part of the feminine goods that wife-giver lineages bestowed on their ritually inferior wife-takers. Accompanying the ivory bracelets are woven cloths, porcelain, beadwork, pigs, and, in former times, personal attendants (Adams, 1969: 47). These gifts are balanced with masculine metal goods (swords, gold chains, *mamuli*, heavy brass bracelets, and horses — and slaves, in pre-modern times). Ivory is an important marriage exchange good in many parts of Eastern Indonesia (Sumba, East Flores, Lembata), but its exact use and meaning varies from marriage system to marriage system (Maxwell 1981; Barnes 1974).   [3661 A+B]

146. Timor or Savu   L: 14.2 cm

A woman's decorated silver and wood comb, mainly associated with wealthy Savunese but also worn to some extent by Atoni women, who got much of their silverwork from Savu and Ndao. Savunese noblewomen who do not own the more expensive, elaborate, and prestigious gold "crown comb" (with little extensions coming out the top) sometimes substitute this simpler silver one. These silver combs come in gold versions; a West Sumba aristocrat, for instance, has a gold one in her bridewealth treasury, and reported in 1983 that it had come from Timor. The comb is in the shape of a semicircle, with seven raised knobs on the silver part, with wooden teeth extending below. Nine delicate filigree-work knobs adorn the comb along the top edge. One informant in Timor said the comb was called *kilinoni*. They are sometimes worn in pairs, one at the front of the head and another at the crown.   [3711–V]

147. Central Timor   H: 17 cm

Turtleshell or buffalo horn comb. Exact use (whether male or female) is unknown. At its top the comb has an openwork piece patterned with tattoo-like designs; below, a smaller section is decorated with busy geometric motifs. Vroklage shows a comb made of horn (called *sasuit reda*) very similar to this (1953, I: 165).   [3721]

148. West Timor, Atoni   H: 11.5 cm

A fancy silver hairpin of a style that is made in various metals besides silver. Probably a decorative hairpin, used by the wealthy class. May be found in Central Timor societies as well as in Atoni. Possible Javanese or Balinese stylistic influence, as is the case with much Timor jewelry. The decoration of flowers (rosettes) is typically Timorese. Vroklage reports that these are called *sasukun* in Central Timor (1953, I: 181).   [3711–D]

149. West Timor, Atoni   L: 13 cm

A warrior's decorated comb in horn, outfitted with brightly colored beadwork and small silver disks (once associated with headtaking). Part of the Atoni war costume. For more discussion (with details of the *meo* or warrior-headtaker's costume) see the chapter on Timor.   [3731]

150. West Timor, Atoni   H (element): 23 cm

Head cloth with silver elements, disks, and frontal in a tree shape, part of the headhunter's costume (see Fig. 133).   [3725]

151. West Timor, Atoni   H: 28 cm

Head cloth in embroidered cotton, to which are attached beaded decorations and silver disks, worn by headhunters. See descriptions of the headhunter's attire in the chapter on Timor and Fig. 133.   [3720–D]

152. West or Central Timor   L: 32 cm

Silver frontal shaped like a crescent moon or possibly a boat, with a human figure in the center. This motif, combining a horizontal crescent with a center figure, is an extremely common one throughout the arts of Eastern Indonesia and the Moluccas: it is found in chest pendants, forehead ornaments, sculpture designs, and ritual altars (see Figs. 20, 21). A structurally similar shape is the motif of a *Garuda* head with upraised wings, so important in Hindu-Buddhist art in Java. These frontals are reportedly called *kai bauk* in some Timor areas. Besides crescent moons and boats, their shape also recalls the horns of sacrificed water buffalo, a prestige symbol, so they may be a symbol of rank, perhaps linked to headhunting prowess.   [3711–U]

153. Central Timor   L: 34.5 cm

Gilded silver frontal with applied filigree decoration. The curve of this frontal definitely recalls water buffalo horns rather than a crescent moon.   [3711–Z]

154 and 155. West Timor, Atoni   D: 6.5 – 7.5 cm

Two pairs of silver disks linked by a beaded string, part of a head ornament (see Fig. 133).   [3720 A+B]

156. Central Timor, Tetum   H: 7 cm

Cast silver earrings with four sides, ending in a tiny bell. A flat earring, with the central space filled with tight spiral designs (found in Atoni bracelet work, which may also come from the same source). Vroklage reproduces such earrings in Sec. III, plates, in *Ethnographie der Belu in Zentral-Timor* (1953) and says they are called *kavata* (I: 179). The Tetum marriage alliance system involves the exchange of considerable amounts of metal goods. See the chapter on Timor.   [3711–W A+B]

157. Central Timor, Tetum   H: 6.7 cm

Cast silver earrings in the style of No. 156. In this pair one earring has an intricate four-pronged (broken?) design, ornamented with

tiny knobs. The same decoration in the other earring may have broken off.   [3711–S A+B]

158. Central Timor, Tetum   H: 4.2 cm

A cast silver earring employing basically the same style as No. 156 but in a sturdier, heavier version. The design has become more abstract, without an enclosing cage. The earring forms a triangle made of five tight spirals. Interior Timor peoples and islanders from Roti and Ndao are the silversmiths for Timor's coastal people such as the Atoni.   [3711–Q C]

159. West or Central Timor   D: 21 cm

Large brass disk with a crescent-shaped design in repoussé recalling the Timor frontals.   [3711–X]

160. West or Central Timor   D: 18.6 cm

Gilded silver disk with an extra central plaque with a hole in the center. See discussion, No. 161.   [3711–T]

161. West or Central Timor   D: 9.8 cm

Silver disk, probably once a headhunting emblem presented to returning warriors by the local aristocrats. Eight-pointed star motif in the center worked in repoussé. Possible influence of Dongson styles (see the introductory chapter on "Peoples and Arts of Island Southeast Asia"), although this is simply not documented. Men wore headtaking disks as badges of prestige and bravery. In addition, in Atoni when new mothers emerged from their post-childbirth seclusion, they were outfitted in the male warrior's costume, complete with headhunter disks. See the chapter on Timor for discussion of some of the symbolic dynamics of this. Vroklage writes that in the Belu region silver plaques are called *bellak mutiu* ("white") and the very rare gold ones, *bellak mean* ("red"). These disks have stars or less often *kae bauk*, moon-crescent motifs (1953, I: 178–179).   [3711–A]

162. West or Central Timor   D: 13.7 cm

Silver disk with a star design in repoussé. Identified in 1983 interviews as an Atoni piece.   [3711–R]

163. West or Central Timor   D: 11 cm

Gold disk worn on a man's headdress or around the neck as a pendant, signifying in former times that he had taken a head. This piece is edged by a row of small puncture holes, with an outside row of tiny raised dots. Probably an Atoni piece but similar ones may have been used in Central Timor as well. Headtaking regulated relationships between local groups and added to warriors' prestige (Schulte Nordholt 1971). Disks were common warrior ornaments throughout Eastern Indonesia, possibly deriving from contact with the old Indianized kingdoms of Java and Bali.   [3727]

164. Central Timor   W: 7.5 cm

Silver "bracelet" meant to be worn around the clutched fingers of a female dancer who shook the bells in rhythm to her dance. There is a bell inside the head and two tiny birds are perched on either side. Possible influence from the old court styles of jewelry from Java or Bali, whose Indianized kingdoms periodically extended their trade influence into Eastern Indonesia. Similar bracelets are found in Bali today.   [3711–F]

165. West or Central Timor   W: 7.5 cm

Silver hand "bracelet" similar to No. 164. This one has two tiny silver human heads on either side of the central bell. The Atoni used bells in abundance in their dance costumes. Ropes of bells were draped

around the body, and bells hung from anklets. Several Flores cultures also use bells in this way (e.g., Manggarai war costumes).
[3711–G]

166. West or Central Timor W: 8.4 cm

Silver bell anklet to be worn by men in ritual dances in a costume which includes *niti maskuna* (knobbed silver or copper bracelets such as Nos. 167 and 169). Called *nitbano* in Atoni, where this type of anklet is common. Savunese also have a version of this, called *wonali*, which men wear on horseback, creating an impressive sound as they gallop by.
[3729–B]

167. West Timor, Atoni W: 8.5 cm

A heavy silver bracelet for men, called *niti maskuna* (*kuna* = teeth). In the shape of an open circle, the bracelet has a simple base studded with big silver balls, the better to hurt an enemy in battle. Like No. 168 this one is more than an ornament; it was once used as a weapon in inter-village raids in hand-to-hand combat. Now it is worn as part of a war-dance costume, although this very common style can also be used for other *adat* ceremonies or everyday wear. In *adat* rituals, men wear *niti maskuna* with anklets outfitted with bells like No. 166.
[3711–L]

168. West Timor, Atoni W: 7.5 cm

Silver bracelet for men, called *niti maskuna*, similar to No. 167.
[3711–K]

169. West Timor, Atoni W: 8.4 cm

A silver *niti maskuna* bracelet for men. Now worn for *adat* dances but once employed as a brass-knuckles sort of weapon for punching opponents. Similar to Nos. 167 and 168 but this one has tight spiral designs on the sides as well as the usual raised balls. [3729–A]

170. West or Central Timor W: 7.7 cm

Silver bracelet used by either men or women, probably part of a dance costume. In an open circle form, decorated with five rows of tight spirals at the two open edges. Like No. 171, this bracelet curves inward at its center portion. The top and bottom edges are flat. Schulte Nordholt writes that Atoni get their silver jewelry from the Belu in Timor's central highlands and from the island of Roti (1971: 41).
[3711–M]

171. West Timor, Atoni W: 8 cm

An Atoni man's copper anklet or bracelet, in the shape of an open circle with a depressed, decorated center and two raised sides. Spirals decorate the center space, while abstract geometric designs mark the edges. Often used on metal betel containers, the same type of designs are common throughout much Timor art and influenced that of Flores as well. The anklet is reportedly at times called a *nit leof* (possibly misspelled). Most of Atoni's metal ornaments are made by smiths from Roti, Ndao, or Central Timor. This piece can be used either as an anklet or a bracelet, depending on where it fits.
[3711–N]

172. Timor or Savu D: 6 cm

Woman's silver bracelets, called *niti sao*. These are common Savunese pieces, but Atoni women are beginning to use them here of late. *Niti* means bracelet and *sao* means head, the head here being that of a snake (not a *naga*, according to informants in Kupang). Feminine bracelets do not have the knobs found on the masculine warriors' bracelets shown in No. 167. [3729–C+D]

173. West or Central Timor D: 7.8 cm

Silver anklets called *buku*, worn by Atoni warriors in full battle dress. Atoni got much of their silverwork through trade with the Belu and the peoples of the small islands off Timor's southwest coast. See the ethnographic chapter on Timor for a discussion of the extraordinary Atoni *meo* (headhunter-warrior) costume. [3730]

174. South Moluccas, Tanimbar H: 24 cm

Hunter's comb in hardwood with eight plaques of bone, which are carved into intricate curvilinear patterns. Tanimbarese were expert carvers in a number of mediums; see the magnificent carved wooden altar, in *Art of the Archaic Indonesians* (1982: 147). Tanimbarese considered hunting a masculine, "hot" activity, linked to death. This sphere was combined with "cooling" feminine activities such as weaving to unleash the creative forces of existence (McKinnon 1983). At the top of the comb there is a hole into which was introduced a very long ornament probably made of wicker-work and feathers. The detail photograph (No. 174 a) shows a *naga* serpent-dragon with a gaping mouth; use of such motifs, common throughout Southeast Asia, indicates the extent to which Moluccan arts were open to stylistic influences from other regions. [3557]

Ex coll. Berlin-Dahlem Museum.

175. South Moluccas, Tanimbar H: 8.8 cm

Small comb in bone, worn by women. The top portion seems to contain an anthropomorphic figure, with its arms bent inward at its sides. The style of the curvilinear motifs definitively recalls the large wooden altars (see Fig. 152) found in Tanimbar villages (see *Art of the Archaic Indonesians* 1982: 147 and the description of another altar, Barbier 1984: 150). [3561]

Ex coll. Berlin-Dahlem Museum.

176. Central Moluccas, Seram H: 28.5 cm

Bamboo comb with geometric motifs and two imported blue beads.
[3550-2]

Ex coll. Oldenbarnevelt, collected around 1900.

177. South Moluccas, Tanimbar H: 3.3 cm

Small gold alloy earring (or pendant or house treasure object) decorated with spirals and two crouching figures, facing some sort of houselike structure. The position of the figures is similar to that found on wooden sculpture of the same area, but the backs of the little men recall sculpture from the Solomon Islands. Whether worn as an earring or not, this piece was probably part of the inherited house treasure, a group of heirlooms with a storied past, names, and a central role in symbolizing the power of the house and its position in the village and in a network of marriage relationships (see McKinnon 1983 and the chapter on the Moluccas in this catalogue).
[3562]

178. South Moluccas, Tanimbar H: 3.4 cm

Gold alloy earring or pendant like No. 177. Note the general similarity of the open oval shape to the Sumbanese *mamuli* and the Sulawesi *taiganja*.
[3559]

179. South Moluccas, Tanimbar H: 7.2 cm

Silver openwork earrings, made from two main curved pieces joined together. The front is different from the back in that it has two little balls just below the suspension hooks. Possibly a feminine earring; see McKinnon 1983: 88 ff and this catalogue's ethnographic section on the Moluccas, based largely on McKinnon's work.
[3567 A+B]

180. South Moluccas, Tanimbar   H: 5.1 cm

Pair of delicate openwork gold earrings, probably *kemene*, constructed of little double spirals of thin wire (see Fig. 143). The two earrings are joined by a string of green glass beads, a configuration which would made this the most valuable category of this sort of earring.   [3571 A+B]

181. South Moluccas, Tanimbar   H: 4 cm

Solid, pear-shaped silver earrings, probably of the type called *loran*. The bottom parts are flat, instead of being round as is usual. Used in gift exchange between marriage alliance partners; wife-takers give these to the family of the bride. See McKinnon 1983 and the discussion in this catalogue's chapter on the Moluccas. There are several variants of this basic type of earring.   [3566 A+B]

182. South Moluccas, Tanimbar   H: 3.8 cm

Pair of silver earrings, a variant of No. 181. They still have the original black thread used to attach them.   [3564 A+B]

183. South Moluccas, Tanimbar   H: 4 cm

Gilded silver single earring, of the type of No. 181.   [3569]

184. South Moluccas, Tanimbar   H: 4.1 cm

Pair of gold earrings of fine quality, in the same basic shape shown in No. 181. They have kept the piece of red cloth which protects the ear when the earrings are worn and which has ritual significance. Tanimbar jewelry has been strongly influenced by trade with Java and Bali and other parts of Eastern Indonesia. These earrings may show such influence.   [3570 A+B]

185. South Moluccas, Leti   D: 13.2 cm

Gold disk with two dancing figures wearing some sort of ritual costume including headgear. Timor has many similar disks (see Nos. 159–163) denoting headhunter-warrior status in former times. Leti, northeast of Timor, is in the Eastern Indonesian cultural complex.   [3560]

186. South Moluccas, Tanimbar   H: 4.4 cm

Small pendant in silver or very-low carat gold, representing a human figure. Note the fine engraved decoration on the chest and the back. It is hung with a string of old Chinese beads (*mutisala*). This pendant may have been the sort Tanimbar upper-class families kept in their house treasures as relics of lineage founders (see McKinnon 1983). Such pendants often had special names and detailed, exciting histories.   [3563]

187. South Moluccas, Tanimbar (Selaru Island)   H: 8 cm

Rectangular gold pendant, with a figure seated cross-legged on a mat. The floral motifs in the background and the figure's position may indicate Chinese influence, although this particular seated position is common in artwork in much of Eastern Indonesia and the Moluccas. Men's pendants are important parts of Tanimbar bridewealth gifts, given by the wife-takers to the bride's father's family (McKinnon 1983: 86–87).   [3572]

188. Northern Luzon, Gaddang   D: 7.2 cm

Man's hat in wood covered with a sheet of brass, decorated with beads and two mother-of-pearl ornaments similar to the type of earrings worn in the area. This hat is worn strapped to the back of the head, and can be used for carrying personal items such as tobacco. See Fig. 16.   [3524 A]

189. Northern Luzon, Bontoc   L: 78 cm

Woman's headband called *bukas* made of glass and clamshell beads, worn only by married women. This one is quite long, and so was worn wrapped around the head three times.   [3547]

190. Northern Luzon, Bontoc   D: 22 cm

Snake vertebrae headband, reportedly called *duli*. It was worn by women as a protective charm against lightning. It was also used as an amulet for a safe childbirth (often placed on the belly).   [3538]

191. Northern Luzon, Ifugao   H: 10.5 cm

Brass female statuette called *dungdung* nailed on a wooden base. It was worn on the head by noblewomen at their marriage (the corresponding male headdress was the *yang-ngoh*, No. 193) and also at funeral ceremonies. This very realistic statuette is of a rare style.   [3512]

192. Northern Luzon, Ifugao   H: 7.5 cm

Brass female figurine, called *dungdung*, worn by upper-class women on the head during important ceremonies.   [3545]

193. Northern Luzon, Ifugao   W: 55 cm

Man's headdress called *yang-ngoh*, made of a hornbill skull with two side plaque of horn, attached to a "crown" covered with a ceremonial sash. Only the noblest and richest families had the right to own a *yang-ngoh*. They first had to reach the status that allowed them to have a *hagabi* (large wooden bench) and a *kanagbigat* (a large *bulul* statue which was part of the structure of the house itself, supporting the beams). The *yang-ngoh* was inherited by the first son and was worn on only two occasions: at his marriage (the female counterpart being the *dungdung*, No. 191) and at a *uhya-uhy* ceremony, a rare and expensive feast given between three and ten years after the marriage, to testify to the prosperity of the family. See Fig. 166.   [3541-1]

Ex coll. H.O. Beyer (1902-1912).

194. Northern Luzon, Ilongot (Tinglayan)   H: 54 cm

Headdress called *pinangpanga* made of feathers, colored cotton, brass and mother-of-pearl spangles, and horsehair. Attached to the back of the head, it could only be worn by the head shaman in Gaddang and Ilongot villages.   [3528-6]

195. Northern Luzon, Ilongot   L: 50 cm

Headhunter's headdress called *panglao*, made of a hornbill skull attached to a headband of wickerwork, with seeds and mother-of-pearl spangles. This headdress could only be worn by a hunter who had already taken two heads.   [3546]

196. Northern Luzon, Ilongot   L: 28.6 cm

Headhunter's headdress called *toc-bed* (?), made of a monkey skull attached to a wickerwork headband decorated with seeds and mother-of-pearl spangles.   [3534]

197. Northern Luzon, Kalinga   H: 7.8 cm

Pair of woman's earrings including a pendant in the shape of joined circles of shell, and a beaded decoration, attached to a gold *dinumug* (open oval ornament, found in a number of varieties under different names in Northern Luzon cultures. Note how the shape of this piece is similar in schematic form to such Indonesian ornaments as the Sumba *mamuli*, the Flores *wea*, and the Central Sulawesi *taiganja* – see Fig. 44). *Dinumug* are often combined with beads and shells to make striking composite jewelry.   [3530 A+B]

198. Northern Luzon, Kalinga W: 13.6 cm

Pair of woman's earrings in mother-of-pearl called *bawisak*, complete with their beaded loop for attaching the ornament to the ear. [3543–J A+B]

199. Northern Luzon, Ifugao H: 11 cm

Man's earrings in mother-of-pearl, with brass thread and clamshell disks. [3543–L A+B]

200. Northern Luzon, Ilongot H: 17.2 cm

Man's earrings called *batling*, made of a red hornbill beak and a metal chain with mother-of-pearl disks. See R. Rosaldo 1980; M. Rosaldo 1980; Ellis 1981: 248, and the short discussion of this earring in the ethnographic text. The *batling* was a proud sign of masculine prestige and headhunting prowess, and announced that the wearer was a full adult member of village society, since he had taken a head and thus shed the burdens of immaturity. Associated with praise poems about headhunter status and masculine virtues. [3535 A+B]

201 and 202. Northern Luzon, Ilongot 201: H: 4.5 cm
202: H: 3.5 cm

Earrings made of engraved mother-of-pearl disks with small spangles. [3536 A+B and C+D]

203. Northern Luzon, Kalinga H: 4.1 cm

Bronze *dinumug* in the basic open oval shape. This type of ornament is quite common in many Northern Luzon cultures, and comes in a variety of somewhat modified forms all built around the fundamental open oval. Such ornaments were used as earrings, singly or in pairs, or as pendants, on chains. Several different types of *dinumug* were sometimes grouped together on necklaces. Similar to the open oval *ling-ling-o* (Nos. 216–219) and related stylistically to the *pinangpanga*, Nos. 206–215. [3543–F]

204. Northern Luzon, Bontoc H: 2.1 cm

Gold *dinumug*, like No. 203. [3516–G]

205. Northern Luzon, West Bontoc H: 2.8 cm

Gold *iniming*, similar to the Bontoc and Kalinga *dinumug* ornaments. [3516–G]

206. Northern Luzon, West Bontoc H: 4 cm

Gold *pinangpanga* with figures of deer facing each other across the top. The shape of this piece is an elaboration of the simpler open oval seen in No. 205. From the village of Kilong (Mrs. P. Gungommo). [3543–A]

207. Northern Luzon, Bontoc H: 3.9 cm

Gold *pinangpanga* with stylized bird's or deer's heads. [3516–J]

208. Northern Luzon, Bontoc H: 3 cm

Bronze *pinangpanga*, in a rather abstract design. [3543–G]
Ex coll. H.O. Beyer (1905-1912).

209. Northern Luzon, Bontoc H: 4.1 cm

Bronze *pinangpanga* with animal head and snake motifs. [3543–E]
Ex coll. H.O. Beyer (1905-1912).

210. Northern Luzon, Bontoc H: 4.3 cm

Brass *pinangpanga* with stylized deer's heads. [3528–4]

211. Northern Luzon, Bontoc H: 3.5 cm

Silver *pinangpanga*, with stylized bird's (?) heads. [3516–F]

212. Northern Luzon, West Bontoc H: 3.2 cm

Gold *pinangpanga* with two human figures (*bulul*, in the generic term) crouched back-to-back. From the village of Guina-ang. [3516–K]

213. Northern Luzon, Kankanay H: 4 cm

Bronze *pinangpanga* with two stylized figures with raised arms. Bauko Valley. [3516–L]

214. Northern Luzon, Kankanay H: 4.9 cm

Bronze *pinangpanga*. [3543–H]
Ex coll. H. O. Beyer (1905–1912).

215. Northern Luzon, Kankanay H: 3 cm

Brass *pinangpanga*, with two crouched human figures (*bulul*) facing each other. [3516–N]

216. Northern Luzon, Ifugao H: 3.2 cm

Bronze *ling-ling-o* of an archaic type. [3543–D]
Ex coll. H. O. Beyer (1905–1912).

217. Northern Luzon, Ifugao H: 2 cm

Silver *ling-ling-o* with side "wings" (called *kawitor*). See Ellis 1981 for discussions of *ling-ling-o*. [3516–C]

218. Northern Luzon, Ifugao (Mayoyao) H: 2.8 cm

Brass *ling-ling-o* with two stylized human figures. [3516–M]

219. Northern Luzon, Ifugao H: 3.4 cm

Bronze *ling-ling-o* with side "wings", or *kawitor*. [3543–B]
Ex coll. H. O. Beyer (1905–1912).

220. Northern Luzon, Isneg L: 109 cm

Man's chest ornament called *sipatal*, composed of six butterfly-shaped mother-of-pearl ornaments (called *bissin*, possibly misspelled) joined by glass, agate, and Indian silver beads, mounted on pineapple fiber. The ribbon is made of tiny glass beads and ends in an element similar to the main ones. Given as a marriage gift in 1917 to the last owner. Village of Dataï. [3528–8]

221. Northern Luzon, Isneg L: 92 cm

Woman's chest ornament, similar in construction to No. 220. The end element here includes two silver thimbles, a small shell, and a small silver heart. From the village of Baduat. [3528–10]

222. Northern Luzon, Isneg L: 80 cm

Child's chest ornament, similar in construction to the preceding one, with smaller elements (the end element is missing). From the village of Baduat. [3528–9]

223. Northern Luzon, West Bontoc H: 29 cm

Necklace called *sengseng*, worn by widows and old women. Made of brass elements and seeds from a wild banana tree. [3549–36]

224. Northern Luzon, Bontoc   H (element): 6 cm

Headhunter's necklace called *boaya*, made of pieces of shell carved in the shape of animal's teeth, mounted on a wickerwork support. At each end are two wild pig's tusks (see Fig. 42). *Buaya* means crocodile in Indonesian.   [3528–2]

225. Northern Luzon, Ifugao   H (element): 8 cm

Necklace called *palangapang* made of six mother-of-pearl plaques on a wicker string. (See Ellis 1981: 246–247).   [3505]

226. Northern Luzon, Ifugao (Klanguya)   H (element): 1.5 cm

Necklace made of sixteen brass pointed *ling-ling-o*, mounted on a thread.   [3543–C]

Ex coll. H. O. Beyer (1905–1912).

227. Northern Luzon, Ifugao   H (element): 2.2 cm

Necklace made of five silver *ling-ling-o* mounted on a thread. See Fig. 155.   [3516–A]

228. Northern Luzon, Kalinga   L: 5.2 cm

Brass pendant in the shape of a small four-legged animal. This piece is probably very old. See a similar pendant in Ellis 1981: 243, tentatively identified there as Kankanay.   [3543–N]

229. Northern Luzon, Ilongot (Gingian)   H: 4.8 cm

Pendant in the shape of an anthropomorphic figure cut out of copper, called *simasin*. It is decorated with spangles which imitate coins. A religious medal is included among the spangles.   [3527]

230. Northern Luzon, Tinggian   H (figure): 15 cm

Tankil headhunter's armlet of wood and tusks with a stylized human figure (see Ellis 1981: 246–247). No. 231 is a similar *tankil* from the Bontoc area. This Tinggian one is reportedly from the Abra region.   [3543–K]

231. Northern Luzon, Bontoc   H (figure): 10 cm

Headhunter's armlet, called *tankil*, made of two tusks and a wooden figure, originally used as a gong handle. According to Beday-Brandicourt, when a young man has reached the age of initiation, he must go alone into the mountains to hunt for a wild pig, whose tusks will be used to make the armlet. If he is very brave and kills two pigs, he will have an armlet with four tusks (such armlets are also the prerogative of nobles, who are allowed simply to buy the second pair of tusks). Only after that can the young man participate in a headtaking expedition (see Fig. 162). If his first victim is female, he will carve a wooden female image to tie on his *tankil*, and if the victim is a man, it will be a male figure. The figures are carved in *nara* (red teak) wood and tied on with fibers. Often the victim's hair is added. Before he has killed anyone, the young man can only be tattooed up to the level where he wears the *tankil*; afterward he can enlarge the tattoos to cover his whole chest and face. The *tankil* are worn mostly during the *kañao* (a general name sometimes used for all ritual ceremonies throughout Northern Luzon, according to Beday-Brandicourt).   [3508]

232. Northern Luzon, Bontoc   H (figure): 5 cm

Headhunter's armlet or *tankil*, made of two tusks and a wooden couple, who sit facing each other. See Ellis 1981: 246–247.   [3526]

233. Northern Luzon, Bontoc   D: 7.5 cm

Bracelet made of a brass spiral, worn by older women with the *seng-seng* necklace, No. 223.   [3549–33]

234. Northern Luzon, Northeast Bontoc   D: 33 cm

Woman's belt called *sangilot*, made out of shells sewn on cloth. The brass spiral counterweight is worn at the back, and the pouch formed by the smaller shells is at the front.   [3528–5]

235. Northern Luzon, Bontoc   D: 19.8 cm

Large engraved shell (*tikam*) which, according to Beday-Brandicourt is called *cabibi* (spelling?) when mounted on a belt. The center is ornamented with a small disk of coconut shell. Ellis (1981: 244–245) writes that these shell disks were apparently purely ornamental. But Beday-Brandicourt asserts that they were signs of high noble status, or headhunter prowess, and were ideally confined to men who had taken at least one head. The ornaments were supposedly quite expensive. One explanation for this is that only a good hunter or a noble could afford to mount the necessary expedition to and from the coast — where the shells are found — without losing his head on the way. It is more likely that trade pact-holders controlled access to these.   [3515]

236. Northern Luzon, Bontoc   D (ornament): 15.7 cm

Complete Bontoc belt with shell ornament (see No. 235). The belt is made of wickerwork decorated with cowry shells. The shell ornament (called *tikam* by the Bontoc) can also be found hooked on a brass chain. Possibly a headhunter's belt.   [3543–I]

237 and 238. Northern Luzon, Ifugao   237: D: 14 cm
          238: D: 9.5 cm

Belt ornaments called *upud*, worn on a *ginutu* belt. They are carved out of a shell, with a central horn openwork decoration.

          [3540, 3511]

239. Northern Luzon, Ifugao   L (knife): 61 cm

Hunter's belt called *ginutu*, made of clamshell disks, rubbed in the riverbed until round and then mounted on wickerwork. The bigger disks go around the waist and the smaller ones hang at the front between the legs. The minimum number of disks must be thirty-two when the exchange value of the belt is one gold pendant (*balituk* in Ifugao), or two adult female pigs. The belt is complete with knife (*bolo*) and its sheath.   [3539]

240. Northern Luzon, Ilongot   H: 11.5 cm

Woman's belt made of rows of wicker covered with brass thread, resulting in a rigid structure like a corset. Decorated with two human figures whose outlines are worked into the wicker. Mother-of-pearl spangles at the bottom.   [3549–34]

Ex coll. Beyer.

241. Palawan   L: 11.6 cm

Wooden comb surmounted with a pig.   [3528–11]

242. Mindanao, Bagobo   D: 12 cm

Pair of man's ivory earplugs called *pamarang*, linked by a beaded string.   [3549–6]

243. Mindanao, Bagobo   D: 7.9 cm

Ivory earplugs called *pamarang* worn directly in the ear or attached to a wicker ring which goes around the ear.   [3528–3 A+B]

244. Mindanao, Bagobo   L: 22 cm

Women's earplugs in bone, with mother-of-pearl spangles and beaded and brass chains passing under the chin. See the Bagobo costume,

Fig. 154. Compare the similar earring-pendant in Casino 1981: 151.
[3549–17]

245. Mindanao, T'boli   D: 2.3 cm

Metal earplugs linked with a beaded string passing under the chin. See the somewhat similar Bagobo piece, No. 244. The Manggarai of West Flores, far to the south of Mindanao in Indonesia, have a similar sort of beaded chin ornament attached to the head near the ears (see Fig. 114).   [3516–H]

246. Mindanao, Bagobo   H: 32 cm

Hunter's necklace made of tusks, snake vertebrae, and plastic beads, mounted on abaca fiber. See Bagobo costume, Fig. 153.
[3549-7]

247. Mindanao, Bagobo   H: 33 cm

Woman's necklace called *solai* made of a brass chain, to which are attached smaller chains and bells. See Bagobo costume, Fig. 154.
[3549–18]

248. Mindanao, Mandaya   D: 10.6 cm

Chest pendant for women in hammered silver.   [3528–1]

249. Mindanao, Bagobo   H: 25 cm

Pair of brass ornaments made of a series of bells on slender chains, which were attached to the belt. See the Bagobo costume, Fig. 154.
[3549–9 A+B]

250. Mindanao, Bagobo or T'boli   L: 73 cm

Brass belt called *sabitan* with openwork buckle for men and women, decorated with many small bells on chains. These bells, popular in Bagobo costumes, were also attached to the belt. See the Bagobo costume, Fig. 154   [3549–11]

251. Mindanao, Bagobo or T'boli   L: 72 cm

Sabitan belt made of many brass chains and an ornate buckle, of the same type as No. 250 but without the bells. See the Bagobo costume, Fig. 153.   [3549–26]

252. Mindanao, Bagobo   H (buckle): 9.7 cm

Woman's belt made of copper and brass chains, with a copper buckle inlaid with iron, to which are attached little bells.

[3543 M]

GLOSSARY I

INDONESIAN AND ETHNIC-LANGUAGE TERMS
USED IN THE TEXT

The spelling used for transcribing Indonesian terms is the one now officially used in the country. The following letters represent:

c = **ch** as in **ch**air (*cabibi*)
g = hard **g** as in **g**o (*garuda*)
h = strong aspirate (*hampatong*)
u = **oo** as in y**ou** (*ulos*)
r = **r-r-r** (*rato*)
j = **dj** (Jata)

---

abali (Kalinga language, Northern Luzon, Philippines): Kalinga agate bead of middle-range value.

adat (Indonesian, and various Indonesian ethnic languages): village "ways of life" or custom, often taken to include rules, ritual customs, traditional political order, and styles of house architecture, social etiquette, dress, and adornment. An elastic, eminently adjustable concept, *adat* is often defined locally as "the ancient customs of our ancestors" but in reality is frequently a very contemporary idea shaped by a society's understanding of Islam or Christianity and its political interaction with other ethnic groups and with the Indonesian nation.

adu (South Nias language, Indonesia): wooden images important in preventing and avoiding illness and misfortune, in South Nias.

adu bihara (South Nias language, Indonesia): rows of little human figures attached to a stick, used in South Nias; usually roughly carved.

adu horö (South Nias language, Indonesia): wooden statues that combine male and female sexual characteristics. As two-in-one images, useful in invoking and controlling power.

adu siraha salawa (South Nias language, Indonesia): realistic statues of nobles, often wearing jewelry. These statues protected the village chiefs and celebrated their dead forebears.

adu zatua (South Nias language, Indonesia): ancestor effigies in South Nias.

agama (Indonesian): world religion (e.g., Islam, Christianity, Buddhism).

anakberu (Karo Batak, North Sumatra, Indonesia): wife-receivers.

anakboru (Angkola Batak language, North Sumatra, Indonesia): wife-receivers.

anak patalo (Sa'dan Toraja language, Sulawesi, Indonesia): aristocrats.

anchida langgelu (Kambera language, East Sumba, Indonesia): a very long chain of office made of orange beads, with gold coins at the end. Used by nobles in East Sumba.

andung (Angkola Batak language, North Sumatra; also used in other Indonesian languages): a special ritual language for mourning and leave-taking, composed of indirect references and complex metaphorical phrases (e.g., the Flickerer, for flames). In East Sumba *andung* trees were altars for displaying captured heads, in pre-modern times.

anting-anting (Indonesian): earring; charm.

aso (various Dayak languages, Kalimantan, Indonesia, and Sarawak, Malaysia): a highly stylized dragonlike mythical creature, with gaping jaws; omnipresent in Dayak art. Literally, "dog."

ata (Kambera language, East Sumba, Indonesia): slaves, in pre-modern East Sumba.

ata koo (Lio language, Central Flores, Indonesia): slaves, in pre-modern Lio.

ata ngandi (Kambera language, East Sumba, Indonesia): personal attendants for East Sumbanese aristocrats, in former times.

ate sage (Nage language, Central Flores, Indonesia): a type of Nage earring.

baju pa'barani (Sa'dan Toraja, Sulawesi, Indonesia): war suit for Sa'dan Toraja soldiers or male dancers.

balalungki (Kulawi dialect, Central Sulawesi): name for the coiled copper snake ornament, called *sanggori* in other regions of Central Sulawesi.

bale (various Indonesian languages, including Nias and Batak): village meeting houses of various sorts. In Nias, the men's council house.

balian (various Dayak languages, in Kalimantan, Indonesia, and Sarawak, Malaysia): shaman, healer, exorcist.

banda uma (Kambera language, East Sumba, Indonesia): *adat* house heirloom wealth.

banyan (Hindi, from Sanskrit): a magnificent tropical tree with an intricately folded trunk and canopylike branches. Numerous aerial roots grow down from the branches to the forest floor where they form auxiliary trunks. Used by many Indonesian societies as an important image for human society and the structure of the cosmos.

barang keramat (Indonesian): miraculous objects, possessions.

batik (Indonesian): cotton cloth with intricate patterns made by resist dyeing techniques using small dippers filled with heated wax. The ritual textiles of Javanese courts, now sold in markets all over Indonesia.

batling (Ilongot language, Northern Luzon, Philippines): red hornbill earring, worn by Ilongot warriors who have taken heads.

batu wa'ulu (South Nias language, Indonesia): vertical stone slabs erected in Nias villages to help raise the social and ritual status of living aristocrats.

begu (various Batak languages, North Sumatra, Indonesia): spirits, in Toba Batak.

bela (Ngada and Nage languages, Central Flores, Indonesia): term for gold earrings in Ngada, Nage.

belis (some Flores languages): bridewealth.

bellak mutiu (Belu language, Timor, Indonesia): silver plaques, Belu.

bening aban (some Dayak languages): baby-carrier, strapped on the back.

bintang silima (Karo Batak usage, or Indonesian): five-pointed star used in Karo jewelry.

binu (Nias language, Indonesia): head, and headhunting in Nias.

boru (Toba and Southern Batak societies, North Sumatra, Indonesia): a word with many meanings relating to daughterhood, wife-receiving, and femininity. In Toba, wife-receivers.

bukas (Bontoc language (?), Northern Luzon, Philippines): woman's headband, in Bontoc.

buku (Atoni language, Timor, Indonesia): silver anklets for Atoni warriors. (Also the Indonesian word for book.)

bulul (Northern Luzon languages, Philippines): wooden deities carved in various Northern Luzon cultures.

bupati (Indonesian): top administrator of a *kabupaten* (subprovince); a position in the Indonesian national government.

bura-bura (Karo Batak, North Sumatra, Indonesia): Karo bridal ornament.

bura layang-layang (Karo Batak language, North Sumatra, Indonesia): necklace with pendant, for bridegrooms.

cabibi (Bontoc language, Northern Luzon, Philippines): Bontoc headhunter's belt made of an engraved shell.

ciken diberu (Karo Batak language, North Sumatra, Indonesia): Karo woman's walking stick.

cincin (Indonesian): ring.

cincin kehrunggun; cincin puting; cincin silima-lima; cincin tapak gaja (Karo Batak language, North Sumatra, Indonesia): various terms for Karo Batak rings.

dalihan na tolu (Angkola Batak and Toba Batak languages, North Sumatra): literally, the arrangement of three stones on the hearth for balancing a cookpot. In ceremonial speech, the partnership of a man's own clanmates, his wife-givers, and his wife-takers.

datu (Toba Batak and Angkola languages, North Sumatra, Indonesia): village sorcerer-diviner, some of whom can cause and/or cure illnesses and soul maladies through spells and charms. Similar to the *guru* in the Karo Batak region.

dii sao (Nage language, Central Flores, Indonesia): a type of marriage in Bajawa, Nage, where it takes the husband's side years to pay the bridewealth. Children are claimed by their mother's clan.

dinumug (Bontoc and various other Northern Luzon languages, Philippines): open oval earring, similar to *ling-ling-o*.

dukun (Indonesian): folk healer, augury expert, charm-caster.

dulang (Indonesian): copper serving tray, important in *adat*.

duli (Bontoc language (?), Northern Luzon, Philippines): snake vertebrae headband.

dungdung (Ifugao language, Northern Luzon, Philippines): brass female figurine worn on the head by Ifugao noblewomen.

ere (South Nias language, Indonesia): priestesses in South Nias.

gana-ganaan (Toba and Angkola Batak languages, North Sumatra, Indonesia): potent substances and carved images for working charms in Toba or Angkola.

Garuda (Indonesian, from Sanskrit): mythical bird, of Indian origin.

gaule (Nias language, Indonesia): type of earring.

gelang (Indonesian): bracelet.

gelang kaki (Indonesian): ankle bracelet.

gelang sarung (Karo Batak usage, North Sumatra, Indonesia): gilded silver and gold Karo bracelet.

gima (Nias language, Indonesia): giant clamshell, in Nias.

gosi (Kalinga language, Northern Luzon, Philippines): Kalinga word for old heirloom jars.

guri-guri (Toba Batak language, North Sumatra, Indonesia): small ceramic jar for potions, in Toba sorcery.

guru (Karo Batak language, North Sumatra, Indonesia): shaman, sorcerer, priest.

hagabi (Northern Luzon, Philippines): ceremonial bench, for wealthy aristocrats.

hai kara jangga (Kambera language, East Sumba, Indonesia): East Sumbanese turtleshell comb for girls and women.

halus (Indonesian): smooth, refined in speech, manner, character, and dress.

hampatong (various Kalimantan languages): wooden sculptures carved by Dayak peoples to ward off evil and other dangers. These figures come in various sizes and often have fearsome facial expressions.

horja (Angkola and Toba Batak languages, North Sumatra): "a work," a ritual endeavor, any major *adat* ceremony involving the ritual sacrifice of a water buffalo, allowing the celebrants to play the gong and drum ensemble known as the *gondang*.

hula-hula (Toba Batak, North Sumatra, Indonesia): wife-givers.

huta: see *kuta*.

ika (various Flores languages): "fish"; term for fish-shaped earrings in Flores.

ikat (Indonesian): a technique used in processing cloth in which threads are tied off, in patterns, to produce a design when dye is applied.

iniming (Bontoc language, Northern Luzon, Philippines): Bontoc earring.

iti bholo (Nage language, Central Flores, Indonesia): Nage term for earrings.

ja heda (Nage language, Central Flores, Indonesia): large Nage wood equestrian statue.

Jata (Dayak languages): female supernatural figure or force, often associated with the moon.

jodoh (Indonesian): a person's "perfect match" for love.

kabihu (Kambera language, East Sumba, Indonesia): free commoners, in pre-modern East Sumba. Also refers to lineages.

kabisu (various West Sumbanese languages, Indonesia): clans, in some West Sumbanese cultures.

Kaboniyan (Tinggian language, Northern Luzon, Philippines): a Tinggian culture hero, originator of rice, jars, gongs, and beads.

kabupaten (Indonesian): subprovince.

kadangyan (various Northern Luzon cultures, Philippines): ritual class of aristocrats.

kae bauk (Belu language, Timor, Indonesia): moon-crescent motifs on Timor disks.

kai bauk (Timor languages, Indonesia): term for metal frontals in some areas of Timor.

kalabubu (Nias language, Indonesia): headhunter's necklace.

kalambagi (Nias language, Indonesia): necklace.

kalimbubu (Karo Batak language, North Sumatra, Indonesia): wife-givers.

kanatar (various Sumbanese languages, Indonesia): a general term for chain or chain of office.

kancing baju (Indonesian): jacket pin.

karabu kudung-kudung (Karo Batak language, North Sumatra, Indonesia): earrings for women.

kasar (Indonesian): rough, rough-mannered, rough-spoken; the counterpart to *halus*.

kawadaku (Kambera language, East Sumba, Indonesia): pieces of beaten metal, used as altar objects.

kemene (Yamdenan language, Tanimbar, Indonesia): women's gold filigree earrings used in Tanimbar marriage exchange.

keris (Javanese, also used in Indonesian): curved dagger worn with the ceremonial costume of male aristocrats; it is a repository of sacred powers.

kerunggun (Karo Batak language, North Sumatra, Indonesia): a special sort of luck-bringing ring. Given by wife-giver to a wife-receiver in need of spiritual aid.

kinawayan (Kalinga language, Northern Luzon, Philippines): heirloom agate bead of lowest value.

kiring (Gaddang language, Northern Luzon, Philippines): Gaddang marriage bead.

kuta (Karo Batak, North Sumatra, Indonesia): village. (Toba and Angkola Batak word is *huta*.)

lado (Nage language, Central Flores, Indonesia): Nage crown for nobles and warriors (*lado wea* = gold crown).

laiya (Kambera language, East Sumba, Indonesia): wife-receiving lineages.

lamba (Kambera language, East Sumba, Indonesia): gold crescent-shaped ornaments, called *tabelu* in West Sumba.

laso sohagu (Nias language, Indonesia): carved wood house panels, depicting gold ornaments. There are both masculine and feminine versions.

lela (Yamdenan language, Tanimbar, Indonesia): elephant tusks used in Tanimbar marriage exchange.

lepah-lepah (Karo Batak language, North Sumatra, Indonesia): rectangular plaques on Karo jewelry.

ling-ling-o (Ifugao and other Northern Luzon languages, Philippines): generic term for open oval earring, pendant.

loda (Ngada language, Central Flores, Indonesia): in Ngada, a gold chain of office.

loran (Yamdenan language, Tanimbar, Indonesia): solid, pear-shaped earrings of silver, gold, or alloy, used in Tanimbar marriage exchange.

lulu amahu (Kambera language, East Sumba, Indonesia): a type of gold chain.

madaka (West Sumbanese languages, Indonesia): term for gold ornament (pin? pendant? earring?) in West Sumba.

mambu ana's (South Nias language, Indonesia): the third type of ritual needed in South Nias to construct a new *adat* house. This one involves the production and distribution of gold ornaments.

mamuli (East and West Sumbanese languages, Indonesia): four-sided, somewhat diamond-shaped earrings or pendants, of gold or silver sheeting, used as marriage alliance gifts and house heirloom treasure by wealthy aristocrats on Sumba.

maradika (Kulawi dialect, Sulawesi, Indonesia): aristocrats in Kulawi.

maramba (Kambera language, East Sumba, Indonesia): noble families in East Sumba.

marangga (various West Sumbanese languages, Indonesia): beaten gold chest ornament, in the form of two crossed triangular plates, joined at the center.

marapu (Kambera and other Sumbanese languages, Indonesia): ancestral spirits, Sumbanese societies.

maru (Lio language, Central Flores, Indonesia): a Lio ritual involving groups of old women outfitted in full *adat* regalia and a male trancer, used during the dangerous period of constructing a new house.

marumak (Yamdenan language, Tanimbar, Indonesia): women's necklaces, Tanimbar.

masa (Yamdenan language, Tanimbar, Indonesia): large gold pendants worn by Tanimbar men.

masilap (Kalinga language, Northern Luzon, Philippines): most valuable sort of agate bead used in Kalinga.

maskong (Kalinga language, Northern Luzon, Philippines): Kalinga word for heirloom plates.

mbesa (various Sulawesi languages, Indonesia): valuable trade cloths kept as family heirlooms by aristocrats of various Sulawesi societies.

membuka kata (Indonesian): in *adat*, to open negotiations for a marriage.

meo (Atoni language, Timor language, Indonesian): Atoni heroic warrior.

mesjid (Indonesian): mosque.

modok (Tetum language, Timor, Indonesia): "the green vegetables"; symbolic prestation in Tetum marriage exchange.

mokesa (Kaili-Pamona languages, Sulawesi, Indonesia): rite of passage for girls passing into adulthood, marked by wearing three *taiganja* suspended from a headband.

moko (Alor language, Lamalohot archipelago, Indonesia): metal drums used as marriage exchange gifts in Alor.

mora (Angkola and Mandailing Batak, North Sumatra, Indonesia): wife-givers, in the Southern Batak homelands. Literally, "wealthy."

mosa laki (Lio language, Central Flores, Indonesia): Lio aristocrats.

mutisala (Indonesian): colored beads.

na'an (Tetum language, Timor, Indonesia): "the meat"; symbolic gift in Tetum marriage exchange.

naga (various Southeast Asian languages, from Sanskrit): a mythic serpent-dragon, often portrayed with a highly stylized open-jawed mouth. The design is found in the arts of many mainland and island Southeast Asian peoples.

Naga Padoha (Toba Batak language, North Sumatra, Indonesia): Toba mythical creature who supports the earth (and *adat* houses).

nandrulo (South Nias language, Indonesia): gold crown in South Nias. Other terms for gold crowns include *tuwu, rai, saembu ana'a,* and *takula ana'a.*

nieto (North and Central Nias languages, Indonesia): in North and Central Nias, an alternate term for *kalabubu,* the man's necklace of honor made of coconut shell disks, wood, or metal alloys.

ni'o woliwoli (South Nias language, Indonesia): coiled fern motif, used in Nias house design.

nit leof (Atoni language, Timor, Indonesia): Atoni term for silver anklet.

niti maskuna (Atoni language, Timor, Indonesia): heavy silver bracelet for men, Atoni.

noin funan (Atoni language, Timor, Indonesia): silver crescent, part of Atoni warrior's costume.

noin sunan (Atoni language, Timor, Indonesia): silver horn, part of Atoni war costume.

obat (Indonesian): medicine; potent curative or charm substance.

omas sigumorsing (Angkola Batak language, North Sumatra): an *andung* word for bridewealth, literally, "gold yellow yellowest gold."

ome mbulu (Lio language, Central Flores, Indonesia): a special name for *wea* earrings.

omo sebua (South Nias language, Indonesia): the great wooden houses of South Nias.

onggong (Kalinga language, Northern Luzon, Philippines): special name for Kalinga heirloom beads.

owasa (South Nias language, Indonesia): feasts of merit in South Nias.

owo'owo (South Nias language, Indonesia): horizontal stone slabs representing ships, built to commemorate the sponsor's ancestors.

pa sese (Nage language, Central Flores, Indonesia): Nage ritual to carve a new *peo* (*q.v.*) forked stake.

padung or *padung-padung* (Karo Batak language, North Sumatra, Indonesia): Karo Batak double-spiral earring for women, usually in heavy silver.

padung curu-curu (Karo Batak language, North Sumatra, Indonesia): Karo earring for women.

padung Raja mehulu (Karo Batak language, North Sumatra, Indonesia): Karo earring for women.

palangapang (Ifugao language, Northern Luzon, Philippines): Ifugao necklace.

pamarang (Bagobo language (?), Mindanao, Philippines): Bagobo term for man's earplugs.

Pande Besi (Sa'dan Toraja language, Sulawesi, Indonesia): master ironforger.

panggil roh (Indonesian): to call back lost or struggling souls.

panlao (Ilongot language, Northern Luzon, Philippines): Ilongot headhunter's headdress.

pangulubalang (various Batak languages, North Sumatra, Indonesia): small human-shaped stone protective statue at village's rim, in Toba and Angkola.

Pano Bulaan (Sa'dan Toraja language, Sulawesi, Indonesia): a girl in a Toraja myth. *Bulaan* means gold, while *pano* in one of its meanings refers to a scaly skin disease.

papangga (Kambera language, East Sumba, Indonesia): funeral procession for dead aristocrats in East Sumba, where the *raja*'s slaves dress up as *rajas* and go into trances.

parmanukan (Toba Batak language, North Sumatra, Indonesia): Toba sacrificial ritual (*manuk* = chicken).

parsanggiran (Toba Batak language, North Sumatra, Indonesia): bowl for sacred "sprinkling juice" (lemon juice) in Toba.

pasa (Nage language, Central Flores, Indonesia): a type of marriage in Bajawa in Nage, where the husband's side succeeds in paying the full bridewealth. Children are claimed by their father's clan.

pasisir (Indonesian): coastal.

pataca (used in Timor languages, Indonesia): old Mexican coin introduced into Timor by the Portuguese.

pemia (various Central Sulawesi languages, Indonesia): funeral mask held on a stick; sometimes it wears a *sanggori*.

pengaroh (Indonesian): charm, influence-substance.

peo (Nage language, Central Flores, Indonesia): forked stake, which is set in village center; a sacrificial altar.

pewisie (West Sumbanese languages (?), Indonesia): special term for silver *mamuli*.

pilo-pilo or *pio-pio* (Karo Batak language, North Sumatra, Indonesia): fringe of little spangles, on Karo jewelry.

pinangpanga (Ilongot and Gaddang languages (?), Northern Luzon, Philippines): shaman's headdress.

pingi marapu (Kambera language, East Sumba, Indonesia): "trunk of the *marapu*," in East Sumba.

piso (Toba Batak language, North Sumatra, Indonesia): literally, "knife," similar to the Indonesian word *pisau*. In Toba *adat*, *piso* gifts are given by wife-receivers to their wife-givers.

podo (Nage language, Central Flores, Indonesia): special box for storing jewelry, in Nage.

porsimboraan (Toba Batak language, North Sumatra, Indonesia): amulets in Toba.

proa (various Indonesian languages): sea-going ship.

pua kumbu (Iban languages, Sarawak, Malaysia): woven textiles, with representations of mythic beings who have contacted the weaverwoman.

Puang Matua (Sa'dan Toraja language, Sulawesi, Indonesia): the Sa'dan Toraja creator god, also known as To menampa, "the forger."

pusaka (Indonesian): heirloom treasure.

raga-raga (Karo Batak language, North Sumatra, Indonesia): possible alternative word for the Karo Batak *padung curu-curu* earring. Also means altar.

rai (Nias languages, Indonesia): gold crown for female aristocrats, with tree motifs. Other Nias terms for gold crowns include *nandrulo*, *tuwu*, *saembu ana's*, and *takula ana'a*.

rai bowo zicho (Nias languages, Indonesia): a type of crown for women, perhaps evoking the image of the Cosmic Tree important in creation myths. *Zicho* or *sicho* could mean either shrub or moon, or both. The *rai bowo zicho* is also called *soma-soma*, a magical plant perhaps used as a border marker.

raja (Indonesian, and various Indonesian ethnic languages; from Hindi, from Sanskrit): chief, or ceremonial chief, or *adat* expert.

rajo (Nage language, Central Flores, Indonesia): Nage crescent-shaped forehead piece.

rambu (Kambera language, East Sumba, Indonesia): an honorific title for high-born women in East Sumba.

rantai (Indonesian; many variants in ethnic languages): chain or necklace.

Ranying Mahatala Langit (Ngaju Dayak language, Indonesia): mythical hornbill.

rara' (Sa'dan Toraja language, Sulawesi, Indonesia): gold jewelry worn by upper-class Toraja women.

rato (Sumbanese languages, Indonesia): priests and public spokesmen of the *rajas*, in East Sumba.

riti (Lio language, Central Flores, Indonesia): generic term for earring in Lio.

sabawo gafasi (South Nias language, Indonesia): cotton sepals; decorative motifs for Nias house relief sculpture.

saembu ana'a (South Nias language, Indonesia): term for gold crown in South Nias. Other terms for gold crowns: *nandrulo*, *tuwu*, *rai*, and *takula ana'a*.

sahala (Angkola Batak language, North Sumatra): the magical powers and "glow" of the highest *rajas* and their heirloom relics.

sanggori (various Central Sulawesi languages, Indonesia): curved snake-shaped head ornament, Central Sulawesi.

sanina (Karo Batak language, North Sumatra, Indonesia): of-a-single-mother; patrilineal descent category in Karo Batak kinship.

sarong (Indonesian and various Indonesian ethnic languages): a long length of cloth reaching from the waist to the ankles.

sasuit redu (Belu language (?), Timor, Indonesia): Timor comb.

sasukun (Central Timor languages (?), Indonesia): silver hairpin, Timor.

sengkap sitelu (Karo Batak, North Sumatra, Indonesia): three-stones-on-the-hearth; the Karo partnership of a man's lineagemates, his wife-givers, and his wife-takers. Counterpart of *dalihan na tolu* in Angkola and Toba languages.

sengseng (Bontoc language, Northern Luzon, Philippines): old woman's necklace, Bontoc.

sertali (Karo Batak language, North Sumatra): Karo Batak bridal ornament, made of metal pieces joined with a metal bead and red cloth band.

si alawa (South Nias language, Indonesia): "that which is high," a praise phrase for South Nias nobles.

sibaganding (Toba Batak language, North Sumatra, Indonesia): mythic Toba snake.

si-gale-gale (Toba Batak language, North Sumatra, Indonesia): funeral puppets in the form of dressed human figures (with real earrings) that are used at the funerals of people who die without heirs.

silua na godang (Angkola Batak language, North Sumatra): literally, "the greatest gift"; Angkola praise phrase for referring to new brides.

simanjomak (Toba Batak language, North Sumatra, Indonesia): an insect, also used to describe a type of curled, knobbed earring.

simpanan (Indonesian): in a jewelry context, "stored things."

singa (Batak languages, North Sumatra, Indonesia; also related Sanskrit): mythical creature in Batak architecture, sculpture, jewelry.

singa-naga (Toba Batak language, North Sumatra, Indonesia): mythical Toba creature.

sislau (Yamdenan language, Tanimbar, Indonesia): pairs of shell armbands worn by women in Tanimbar.

siulu (South Nias language, Indonesia): noble families in South Nias; the term more recently means chief. *Ulu* refers to the ideas of upstream and river's source.

sofutö dzihöno (South Nias language, Indonesia): "the oracle of the people," a eulogistic phrase for speaking of South Nias nobles.

solyad (Gaddang language, Northern Luzon, Philippines): spouse exchange institution, in Gaddang.

söma-söma (Nias languages, Indonesia): another term for the *rai bowo zicho* crown for women. *Söma-söma* may refer to a magical plant located outside the houses of priests or priestesses. The plant may also be used to ritually mark borders.

suku terasing (Indonesian): minority ethnic groups; "isolated" groups.

suruk (Yamdenan language, Tanimbar, Indonesia): old swords, used in Tanimbar marriage exchange.

tabelu (various West Sumba languages, Indonesia): gold crescents used as forehead decorations in West Sumba cultures; called *lamba* in East Sumba.

tabilu (tabili) (Kambera language, East Sumba, Indonesia): gold disk, East Sumba.

taiganja (Kaili-Pamona and related West and Central Sulawesi languages, Indonesia): heavy bronze or sometimes copper or gold pendants decorated with curlique-shaped protrusions, from West and Central Sulawesi.

ta'io sebu (South Nias language, Indonesia): arm-braces; decorative motifs in South Nias relief-style house sculpture.

tai walu ana kalo (Lio language, Central Flores, Indonesia): Lio commoner class.

tajahan (Ngaju Dayak language, Kalimantan, Indonesia): a type of *hampatong* sculpture placed atop poles or pedestals; an ancestor figure.

taka (Ngada language, Central Flores, Indonesia): silver or low-carat gold pendant in double-ax-head shape, in Ngada.

takula ana'a (South Nias language, Indonesia): in South Nias, a gold crown with golden "branches," or *lagene*. Other terms for gold crowns: *nandrulo, tuwu, saembu ana'a, rai*.

tali-piu (Karo Batak language, North Sumatra, Indonesia): filigree work on ornate Karo bracelets.

tanda perjanjian (Indonesian): sign that a promise of some sort has been made.

tangawahil (Kambera language, East Sumba, Indonesia): tray for holding sacred jewelry in East Sumbanese noble houses.

tanggu marapu (various Sumbanese languages, Indonesia): "possessions of the *marapu*," sacred heirloom treasures "owned" by spirits of lineage ancestors.

tankil (Bontoc language, Northern Luzon, Philippines): Bontoc headhunter's armlet.

tau-tau (various Toraja and Central Sulawesi languages, Sulawesi, Indonesia): Toraja funerary statues; also sometimes used for small metal statuettes. From the word for "human."

tebe (Nage language, Central Flores, Indonesia): gold earrings in Nage; also called *ate saga*.

telögu (South Nias language, Indonesia): royal sword, in South Nias.

tendi (Karo Batak language, North Sumatra, Indonesia): soul in Karo Batak. A related Toba and Angkola word is *tondi*.

teo kinga (Lio language, Central Flores, Indonesia): in Lio, a prescribed set of gold jewels a bride brings with her to her marriage. Includes a gold bracelet, *ome mbulu ina* and *ome mbulu* earrings.

tetua ngata (Kulawi dialect, Sulawesi, Indonesia): religious specialists in Kulawi.

toc-bed (Ilongot language, Northern Luzon, Philippines): Ilongot headhunter's headdress.

tölagasa (töladsaga) (Nias languages, Indonesia): Nias giant-clam-shell bracelets.

tolak bala (Angkola Batak language, North Sumatra): to cast back evil influences. Special garments, amulets, and sayings are used for this purpose.

tongkonan (Sa'dan Toraja language, Sulawesi, Indonesia): Toraja *adat* house.

tora-tora (Sa'dan Toraja language, Sulawesi, Indonesia): Sa'dan Toraja warrior's necklace, of wild boar fangs.

tuat (Yamdenan language, Tanimbar, Indonesia): palm spirits used in Tanimbar marriage exchange.

tugu (various Batak languages, North Sumatra, Indonesia): stone or cement funeral obelisk erected to commemorate ancestors.

tuha (South Nias language, Indonesia): lord of the village, in South Nias.

tumpal (Indonesian): a design motif, associated with the so-called ornamental style of Southeast Asian art, composed of inverted triangles, which may have small protuberances at the bottom.

tunggal panaluan (Toba Batak language, North Sumatra, Indonesia): *datu*'s magical staff or wand. Intricately carved with mythic beings, who are "fed" potent substances.

tuwu (South Nias language, Indonesia): term for gold crown in South Nias. Other terms for gold crowns: *rai, nandrulo, saembu ana'a, takula ana'a*.

Ubila'a (Yamdenan language, Tanimbar, Indonesia): a Tanimbar deity.

uis (Karo Batak, North Sumatra, Indonesia): woven textile used for rituals and gift exchange related to marriage. The Karo word for *ulos*.

ulos (various Batak languages, North Sumatra, Indonesia): ceremonial woven textile, used as a "luck-conferring" gift that wife-givers bestow on their daughters and wife-receivers.

ulu (South Nias language, Indonesia): upstream, river's source, a reference to South Nias aristocrats. In other Indonesian languages (for example, Angkola Batak), *ulu* means head.

upah tendi (Karo Batak language, North Sumatra, Indonesia): amulets and words for protecting the soul, in Karo Batak.

updu (Ifugao language, Northern Luzon, Philippines): Ifugao belt ornament.

vavu (Yamdenan language, Tanimbar, Indonesia): pigs, in Tanimbar marriage exchange.

wale-wale (Nias language language, Indonesia): type of Nias earrings, for chiefs' sons.

wea (Lio language, Central Flores, Indonesia): a type of gold earring. In a number of Eastern Indonesian languages, *wea* or similar words mean "gold."

wea wunu wona (Nage language, Central Flores, Indonesia): Nage gold earrings.

wonga uwi (Ngada language, Central Flores, Indonesia): in Ngada, chain-link chest ornaments, sometimes made of gold.

woridi (Kambera language, East Sumba, Indonesia): *mamuli*-like gold ornament.

wula poda (Lauli language, West Sumba, Indonesia): agricultural increase ritual in Tarung village near Waikabubak, West Sumba.

wuli (Ngada language, Central Flores, Indonesia): gold necklaces made in the shape of fat conch shells. Part of warriors' and noblemen's dress.

yang-ngoh (Ifugao language, Northern Luzon, Philippines): Ifugao man's headdress, with hornbill skull.

yera (Kambera language, East Sumba, Indonesia): wife-giving lineages.

GLOSSARY II

PEOPLES AND PLACES MENTIONED IN THE TEXT

Aceh: Former muslim Kingdom. Now province (Daerah Istimewa, or "Special District") at the northern tip of Sumatra.

Adonara: Island off the east coast of Flores.

Alor: Island in Lamalohot Archipelago east of Flores, directly north of Timor.

Ambon: Island in the Moluccas, near Seram and Buru.

Amfoan: Traditional domain in Atoni area of West Timor.

Anakalang: Ethnic group and area in West Sumba.

Angkola: Ethnic group and area in the Southern Batak region, North Sumatra.

Apayao: Another word for Isneg, an ethnic unit in Northern Luzon in the Philippines.

Apo-Kayan: Dayak ethnic group, in interior Kalimantan.

Arafura Sea: Body of water bordered by the South Moluccas, Irian, and northern Australia.

Aru: Small island northeast of Tanimbar, near West Irian.

Atoni: Ethnic group in West Timor near Kupang.

Babar Island: Small island in Indonesia's Southwestern Islands, west of Tanimbar.

Baduat: Isneg village in Northern Luzon.

Bagobo: Ethnic group in Mindanao, southern Philippines.

Bahau: Dayak ethnic group in interior Kalimantan.

Bajawa: Town in the Ngada region of Central Flores.

Bali: Small island off the eastern tip of Java.

Batak: Group of ethnic societies in North Sumatra, between the Gayo-Alas and the Minangkabau; near Lake Toba and to the south.

Batavia: Old name for Jakarta, under the Dutch.

Bauko Valley: Area in the Kankanay region of Northern Luzon.

Bawömatuluo: Aristocratic village in South Nias, full of *adat* houses and stone sculptures.

Belu: Central Timor ethnic group, overlapping in part with the Tetum ethnic unit.

Benuaq: Dayak ethnic group in interior Kalimantan

Bima: Historically, a powerful trade kingdom centered in Sumbawa.

Boawai: A Nage high village.

Bontoc: Philippine ethnic group in Northern Luzon.

Borneo: Former name for the island now including Kalimantan, Sarawak, Sabah, and Brunei.

Borobudur: Buddhist-inspired temple in Java.

Brastagi: Karo Batak market town.

Brunei: Newly independent nation on the island (once called Borneo) including Sarawak and Kalimantan.

Bugis: Ethnic group in South Sulawesi near Ujuong Pandang. An important mercantile state whose influencee extended to coastal Kalimantan and Eastern Indonesia.

Buru: Isolated island in the Moluccas, west of Seram.

Cebu: Island northwest of Mindanao in the Philippines.

Celebes: Former name for Sulawesi during the Dutch colonial period.

Cibal: Old name for a Manggarai town in West Flores.

Dairi-Pakpak: Batak ethnic group(s).

Dataï: Isneg village in Northern Luzon.

Dayak: General ethnic designation for interior Kalimantan societies, taken here to include Sarawak's Iban.

Deli: Islamic sultanate on Sumatra's East Coast, near Medan.

Donggala-Palu: Region around the coastal town of Palu in Central Sulawesi. Donggala is the Kabupaten district.

Dongson (from the name of an archaeological site in North Vietnam): Stylistic period in Southeast Asian art (approximately 200 to 0 B.C.), associated with magnificent large bronze religious objects, including "thunder drums."

Eastern Indonesia: Corresponds roughly to the group of islands in the province of Nusa Tenggara Timor (Sumba, Flores, eastward to Timor). Some scholars include the Moluccas.

Ende: Port town in central Flores; can also be used as an ethnic designation.

Flores: Long, narrow, mountainous island north of Sumba, east of Sumbawa, in Eastern Indonesia.

Gaddang: Ethnic group in Northern Luzon in the Philippines.

Gayo-Alas: Ethnic group in Sumatra located between the Karo Batak and the Acehnese.

Gorontalo: Ethnic group in the long northern "arm" of Sulawesi.

Guina-ang: Bontoc village in Northern Luzon in the Philippines.

Halmahera: Group of islands in the north Moluccas, north of Seram and northwest of West Irian.

Ibaloi: Ethnic group in Northern Luzon in the Philippines.

Iban: General term covering a series of related Dayak societies in interior Sarawak.

Ifugao: Ethnic group in Northern Luzon in the Philippines.

Igorot: General ethnic designation for mountain peoples in Northern Luzon; used by outsiders.

Ilocano: Lowland, Christianized ethnic group in Luzon, Philippines.

Ilocos Norte: Province in Northern Luzon, Philippines.

Ilongot: Ethnic group in Northern Luzon in the Philippines.

Isneg: Ethnic group in Northern Luzon in the Philippines.

Java: Densely populated island, mostly islamized, in Inner Indonesia; ethnic designation.

Kabanjahe: Karo Batak town.

Kai: Small island near West Irian, in the South Moluccas.

Kaili: Dialect and ethnic designation for the region near Palu, in Central Sulawesi.

Kalimantan: Indonesia's geographically central island, once called Borneo. Peopled by coastal, Muslim societies, and Dayak groups in the interior.

Kalinga: Ethnic group in Northern Luzon in the Philippines.

Kampung Bajawa: Small village near the town of Bajawa, in the Ngada region of Central Flores.

Kampung Ruteng: Small Manggarai village near the town of Ruteng, in West Flores.

Kampung Tarung: High village near Waikabubak, in West Sumba.

Kankanay: Ethnic group in Northern Luzon in the Philippines.

Kapuas River: In Central Kalimantan.

Kapunduk: Old chieftaincy in East Sumba.

Karo: Batak ethnic group in North Sumatra.

Kayan: Dayak ethnic group in interior Kalimantan.

Kedang: Old *adat* domain in Lembata (Lomblen), east of Flores.

Kelabit: Dayak society in interior Kalimantan.

Kelantan: Province and old sultanate in peninsular Malaysia.

Kenyah-Kayan: Dayak ethnic group in interior Kalimantan.

Keo: Ethnic designation for a people closely related to the Nage of Central Flores.

Kodi: Ethnic group in West Sumba, along the west coast.

Kroë: Old court society in Lampong District, South Sumatra.

Kuching: Capital of Sarawak (sometimes spelled Kucing).

Kulawi: Town and ethnic designation, in the interior mountains south of Palu in Central Sulawesi.

Kupang: Capital of West Timor.

Kuta Beach: Resort area near Den Pasar, Bali.

Lamalohot Archipelago: Group of islands off the east coast of Flores.

Lamboya: Ethnic group and area in West Sumba.

Lauli: Ethnic group and area in West Sumba.

Lembata: New name for the island of Lomblen, east of Flores.

Lesser Sunda Islands: Chain of islands that extends eastward in a line from Java and Bali toward Timor.

Leti: Group of islands off the northeast coast of Timor, including the Islands of Leti, Moa, Lakor.

Lingga: A village in the Karo Batak region.

Lio: Ethnic group and area in central Flores near Ende.

Lombok: Island east of Bali.

Luzon (and Northern Luzon): Large, mountainous island in the northern part of the Philippines. Northern Luzon (the "Mountain Provinces") includes many ethnic groups not as firmly in the national orbit as lowland Filipinos — such as those near Manila — are.

Madura: Densely populated island northeast of Java, near Surabaya.

Mahakam River: Major trade artery in Eastern Kalimantan.

Makassae: Ethnic group in Central Timor.

Makassar: Old *entrepôt* in South Sulawesi. Now: Ujung Pandang.

Maloh: Dayak ethnic group.

Malocca: Entrepôt in Malaysia, on the Straits of Malacca between Sumatra and peninsular Malaysia.

Maluku: Province in Indonesia; "the Moluccas."

Minangkabau: Ethnic group and area in West Sumatra around Bukittinggi and Padang.

Mindanao: The Philippines' large southernmost island.

Moluccas: Island group east of Sulawesi, northeast of Timor.

Morotai: Island at the northern tip of Halmahera, close to the southern Philippines.

Murut: Dayak ethnic group and area, Kalimantan.

Nage: Ethnic group and area in Central Flores, around Boawai.

Ndao: Small island off the West Coast of Timor, near Roti and Savu.

Ngada: Ethnic group and area in Central Flores, around Bajawa, west of the Nage.

Ngaju: Dayak ethnic group and area.

Nias: Island off the West Coast of North Sumatra, West of Sibolga. Ethnic designation.

Nusa Tenggara Timur: Indonesian province extending from Flores and Sumba to Timor; its capital is Kupang.

Olaewa: Nage village near Boawai in Central Flores.

Orang Kubu: Hunting and gathering peoples in isolated regions of Sumatra; nearly gone today.

Outer Islands of Indonesia: Islands and ethnic societies beyond densely populated, Indianized Inner Indonesia (Java, Madura, Bali). Includes Sumatra, Kalimantan, Sulawesi, Moluccas, Eastern Indonesia.

Padang: Coastal city in West Sumatra, in Minangkabau.

Pakpak: Batak ethnic group and area, west of Lake Toba in North Sumatra.

Palawan: Long, narrow island in the Philippines, north of Kalimantan.

Palembang: City in South Sumatra; center of old trade state.

Palu: Coastal town in Central Sulawesi.

Pamona: Ethnic and dialect designation for the area around Palu (often used in the term Kaili-Pamona).

Pantar: Small island north of Timor between Lembata and Alor.

Pau: Old *raja*ship in East Sumba.

Penan: Dayak ethnic group and area in Kalimantan.

Poso: Sometimes used to refer to area around Lake Poso in Central Sulawesi.

Prapat: Toba Batak resort town on Lake Toba.

Rante Pao: Sa'dan Toraja town in Sulawesi.

Rindi: Traditional domain in East Sumba.

Roti: Small island off the southwest coast of Timor.

Ruteng: Town in Manggarai region of West Flores.

Sa'dan Toraja: Ethnic group and area in Sulawesi, in the interior mountains north of Ujung Pandang.

Sabah: Province of Malaysia on the island once called Borneo.

Samosir Island: Toba Batak island in Lake Toba, in North Sumatra.

Sarawak: Province of Malaysia on the island once called Borneo. Includes many Iban Dayak societies.

Savu: Small island (including many goldsmiths) off the west coast of Timor.

Selayar Island: Small island off the south coast of Sulawesi.

Seram: Island in the central Moluccas.

Sesean, Mount: Mountain in Sa'dan Toraja region of Sulawesi.

Siberut Island: Off the west coast of Sumatra, in Mentawai group of islands.

Sibolga: Batak port town, on the west coast of North Sumatra.

Siborong-borong: Tioba Batak market between the Lake Toba and Sibolga in North Sumatra.

Sikka: Ethnic group and area in Central Flores.

Simanindo: Toba Batak village in northern part of Samosir Island in Lake Toba in North Sumatra.

Simalungun: Batak sub-society in North Sumatra, east of the Lake Toba.

Solor: Archipelago: Flores and the island chain to its east through Alor.

Southwestern Islands: Southern Moluccas islands group, including Roma, Damar, Nila, Teun, Serua, Wetar, Kisar, Leti, Luang-Sermata, Babar.

Spice Islands: Old name for the Moluccas.

Sulawesi: Large island east of Kalimantan (formerly: Celebes.)

Sumatra: Large island in the far western part of Indonesia.

Sumba: Island in eastern Indonesia, southwest of Flores.

Sumbawa: Island east of Lombok, with Islamic, mercantile history.

Tambora: Volcano on Sumbawa whose explosion in 1815 weakened the trade state of Bima.

Tana Toraja: "Torajaland."

Tanimbar: Island group in the South Moluccas.

Tanjung: Village in Karo Batak area in North Sumatra.

Tarung: High village near Waikabubak, West Sumba.

Tarutung: Market town in the southern part of Toba Batak region in North Sumatra.

T'boli: Ethnic group and area in Mindanao in the southern Philippines.

Ternate: Island in the Moluccas; center of an old trade kingdom.

Tetum: Ethnic group and area in Central Timor.

Tidore: Small island in Halmahera, near Ternate; part of an old trade state.

Timor: Island in Eastern Indonesia, near Irian.

Tinggian: Ethnic group in Northern Luzon in the Philippines.

Toba Batak: Batak sub-society in North Sumatra.

Toba, Lake: Large lake in the Batak areas, North Sumatra.

Trobriand: Island group off the southeastern coast of New Guinea.

Tomok: Toba Batak village on Samosir Island in North Sumatra.

Tomini, Gulf of: Located in Sulawesi, north of the town of Poso.

Toraja: Group of ethnic societies in the interior mountains north of Ujung Pandang in Sulawesi.

Ujung Pandang: City in South Sulawesi in the Bugis area.

Waikabubak: Capital of West Sumba.

Waingapu: Capital of East Sumba.

Walotopo: Lio village on the south coast of Flores, near Ende.

Wehali: Central Timor traditional state.

Weitabar: Town in West Sumba.

Wetar Island: Island located off the northeastern point of Timor, north of Dili.

Yamdena: Island in Tanimbar Archipelago in the South Moluccas.

GLOSSARY III

ANTHROPOLOGICAL TERMS USED IN THE TEXT

ambilateral: Descriptive term referring to both sides of a person's family (relatives through the mother and relatives through the father).

ambilineal: Descent is a rule of descent that affiliates an individual with groups of kin related to him via women or men.

asymmetrical marriage alliance: A type of economic and political relationship between two lineages of different clans forged through marriages between their sons and daughters. Lineage A provides its daughters as brides to Lineage B, who may not give their own daughters back as brides to A but must pass their women in another direction, to Lineage C. (If B could "repay" A's gifts of women with their own daughters the marriage system would be symmetrical.) Wife-providers are generally deemed the ritual superiors of their wife-receivers, who are in A's eternal debt. A range of material gifts and labor services are often associated with the basic marriage alliance, and village political organization and relationships between chiefly houses and commoners are sometimes symbolized in the same language of giving and receiving. The ideal marriage is with the matrilateral cross cousin in some of these systems. In Indonesia the type of descent found in this type of marriage system is often patrilineal, with variations.

bilateral kinship: A type of kinship system lacking descent groups in which individuals affiliate about equally with their mother's and father's relatives.

bride-giver, wife-giver: A lineage or part of a lineage that gives its daughters and sisters to another lineage as wives, in cultures that have asymmetrical marriage alliance.

bride-taker, wife-taker (or -receiver): The lineage or part of a lineage that receives women as brides from a marriage alliance partner, in kinship systems with asymmetrical marriage alliance.

bridewealth, brideprice: Valuables presented to the family of the bride by the family of the groom; such wealth is sometimes transferred over a long period of time.

brideservice: Labor service that a new husband does for his wife's family as an obligation of legitimate marriages.

clan: A set of kinspeople whose members believe themselves to be descended from a common ancestor (patrilineal clans) or ancestress (matrilineal clan).

Sometimes divided into smaller groups of people who trace descent to a more recent ancestor or ancestress (this yields lineages).

countergift: In Indonesian societies with asymmetrical marriage alliance, gifts that are presented to the alliance partner to "balance" or "complete" that group's prestations. Metal goods including certain types of jewelry are common countergifts to cloth.

culture area: In ecological terms a broad geographical area in which a number of cultures have made similar adaptations to a similar environment and have developed similar social forms; in more general terms, a closely relate group of cultures, such as Melanesia, Polynesia, or Island Southeast Asia.

descent group: A group of kin who are lineal descendants of a common ancestor or ancestress, extending beyond two generations. A *descent category*, not an actual group of people, is a concept relating to all the people who might ideally be included in a descent group. Descent is of several types, including *patrilineal* (traced from fathers to all their children and then, in the next generation, to the children of the sons) and *matrilineal* (traced from mothers to all their children and then, in the next generation, to children of the daughters.)

house wealth, house treasure: Heirloom relics of the family house and its previous occupants in the family line. Such treasures often symbolize the "essence" of the family and its forebears.

kindred: A group made up of all the people thought to be related to an individual, through both his mother and his father.

kula: Ritualized trade circuit in Trobriand region of Melanesia.

lineage: A group of kin whose members trace descent from a known, common ancestor; a unit within a clan, whose ancestor or ancestress supposedly existed in the more distant past than did the lineage ancestor. Lineagemates are one's fellow members of the lineage.

matrilateral cross-cousin marriage: One's cross cousin is the child of one's father's sister or mother's brother (that is, one figures relationship via one's parent's sibling of the sex opposite from the parent. A child of one's mother's sister or father's brother is a parallel cousin).

"Matrilateral" means on the mother's side, so a matrilateral cross cousin, for a man, is his mother's brother's daughter. In cultures with asymmetrical marriage alliance, matrilateral cross-cousin marriage is often idealized and encouraged: it means that a young man has gotten a bride from the same household that provided his father with his mother a generation ago. From a woman's perspective, young girls growing up are encouraged to follow their father's sisters footsteps to marry where those women did, and eventually marry their father's sister's sons.

matrilineal descent: Descent traced down through a number of generations via women. In a culture with matrilineal clan descent a woman's children will all belong to her clan, but only her daughters can pass on membership to the third generation. The children of sons belong to their mothers' group.

matrilocal residence: A convention of residence after marriage where the couple lives with or near the wife's family.

patrilineal descent: Descent traced down through a number of generations via men. In a culture with patrilineal clan descent a man's children will all belong to his clan, but only his sons can pass on membership to the third generation.

patrilocal residence: A convention of residence after marriage where the couple lives with or near the husband's family.

potlatch: A ritualized "party" in which rival chiefs try to outdo each other through profligate gift-giving and destruction of valuable prestige goods such as cloth or metal. Sometimes this is a mechanism for redistributing practical goods such as food in the absence of central political control. The classic potlatch was found among Northwest Coast Indian cultures in North America.

prestation: A gift whose form and mode of giving symbolizes the total social relationship between the giver and the recipient.

rite of passage: A ritual that takes a person from one social status (such as childhood) and transforms him into a different sort of social person (such as a marriageable adult).

Rites of passage have a predictable three-part structure, involving separation from the first social state, a ritual transition between states, and reincorporation into the new status.

swidden cultivation: Slash-and-burn agriculture, which involves replicating the structure of the tropical forest in miniature, well-controlled form. Farmers first cut down the tropical vegetation, then burn it, and utilize the nutrients from the ash as fertilizer for their mixed-crop plot. Once the strip of land is exhausted after several years, the plot is allowed to lie fallow, sometimes for decades. New swidden plots are opened and old ones are rotated, with the possibility of considerable population movement.

wet rice cultivation, paddy rice cultivation: A more intensive and productive form of agriculture than swidden, involving the painstaking construction and maintenance of flooded paddies, bordered with dikes. Nutrients are brought to the growing rice via the circulating water, and huge crops can be produced if more labor is used. Often supports a denser human population than swidden, and sometimes involves more social complexity and centralization, to regulate access to water.

SUGGESTED READING

There is a copious amount of published research on Indonesian, Malaysian, and Philippine cultures, but unfortunately there have been relatively few recent investigations focused directly on the arts of the peoples of Outer Island Indonesia, Sarawak, and Northern Luzon. The lack of simple documentation of local art traditions is especially regrettable in this era of rapid social change and national consolidation. Much of the art history research on island Southeast Asia is concerned with the court arts of the old Indianized kingdoms of Java and Bali. Thus, one finds innumerable studies of Borobudur but very few analyses of the wooden prowboards of Tanimbar, the earrings of Flores, or the bridal headgear of the Karo Batak. Happily, there is something of a renaissance of cultural anthropological field-work going on now in Indonesia, and much of that research touches on village ritual, oratory, dance, and gift exchange – all topics that help elucidate the meanings, styles, and social uses of the sort of jewelry in the Barbier-Müller collection. The following is a brief guide for the general reader to some of the most rewarding and most accessible books and articles on art, ritual, and ornamentation in the cultures included in the exhibit. English-language sources are highlighted, although there is considerable additional literature in Indonesian, Dutch, German, and French. This guide proceeds according to the sections of the catalogue.

1. Ornaments and Heirlooms Beyond the Old Court Societies

The People and Art of the Philippines (1981), by Gabriel Casal, et al., provides a wealth of information about jewelry in Northern Luzon and Mindanao societies, while Morice Vanoverbergh's "Dress and Adornment in the Mountain Province of Luzon, Philippine Islands" (1924) is a more specialized source. See also the many citations on ornaments in the bibliography to *The People and Art of the Philippines*.

For Indonesia, J.E. Jasper and Mas Pirngadie's fourth volume of their *De Inlandsche Kunstnijverheid in Nederlandsch Indie* (1927), is a classic source on metal jewelry traditions in both Outer and Inner Indonesia. This volume, entitled *De Goud- en Zilversmeedkunst*, includes many detailed line drawings of individual ornaments. H. Ling Roth's *Oriental Silverwork: Malay and Chinese* (1966) is a useful illustrated catalogue of pieces from those two traditions. Many descriptive monographs by colonial-era Dutch civil servants, linguists, and ethnographers pay a good deal of attention to dress and ornamentation. A number of these are cited in the ethnographic sections of this catalogue.

2. The Peoples and Arts of Outer Island Southeast Asia

Casal, et al., *The People and Art of the Philippines* (1981) is both an enjoyable and a scholarly introduction to the arts of that country.

For Indonesia there is no comprehensive, recent book dealing in any detail with art outside Java and Bali. Claire Holt's excellent *Art in Indonesia: Continuities and Change* (1967) remains the landmark survey, but because it is so comprehensive (treating everything from ancient temple art to modernist painting in the national period), the book devotes little attention to the arts of specific Outer Island cultures. Tibor Bodrogi's *Art of Indonesia* (1972) is a well-written survey with detailed sections on Kalimantan and Sulawesi, derived from Dutch sources. The essays in *Art of the Archaic Indonesians* (1982) all deal with Outer Island cultures and often discuss their arts in considerable detail against the backdrop of local ritual and myth. Some of the essays are drawn from rather dated sources, however. See also the much briefer catalogue *Indonesian Primitive Art*, by Jean Paul Barbier (1984), written and published for the Dallas Museum of Art. Introductory works emphasizing the Indic heritage in Indonesia include Philip Rawson's *The Art of Southeast Asia* (1967) and Frits Wagner's *Indonesia, The Art of an Island Group* (1959).

Indonesia's woven and batiked textiles have received a good deal of recent attention. In fact, thanks to a number of museum exhibitions, research into the symbolic meanings and social uses of cloth has dominated art studies in the Outer Islands of the archipelago. Since the woven textiles of these cultures are often marriage gifts and ritual objects, they have proved to be wonderful entry points for catalogue authors to explore local cultures. Mattiebelle Gittinger's *Splendid Symbols: Textiles and Tradition in Indonesia* (1979) is a consistently well-documented, well-illustrated catalogue dealing with all types of Indonesian cultures. Her sections on the Batak peoples and the culture of Eastern Indonesia are especially fine. Also valuable and understandable to the nonspecialist are the anthology *Indonesian Textiles*, edited by Mattiebelle Gittinger (1980), and Mary Hunt Kahlenberg's *Textile Traditions of Indonesia* (1977).

The folk aesthetic systems of the peoples of Sumatra, Kalimantan, Sulawesi, and Eastern Indonesia are attracting considerable attention from anthropologists. Much of this very new research concentrates on the way aesthetic feelings and ideas are coded into language. For a taste of this approach, see the essays in *The Imagination of Reality: Essays in Southeast Asian Coherence Systems* (edited by A.L. Becker and Aram A. Yengoyan, 1979). Many of the essays in *The Flow of Life: Essays on Eastern Indonesia* (edited by

James J. Fox, 1980) explore the same type of symbolic domains, although the book's overt aim is the study of comparative social structure. *Five Essays on the Indonesian Arts*, edited by the ethnomusicologist Margaret Kartomi (1981), addresses music, textiles, drama, and modern art of several Indonesian societies (see especially Robyn Maxwell's piece on Flores textiles). *Art, Ritual and Society in Indonesia*, edited by Judith Becker and Edward M. Bruner (1979), contains anthropological and art history articles on the Batak and Nias peoples. *Perceptions of the Past in Southeast Asia*, an anthology edited by Anthony Reid and David Marr (1979), deals at some length with folk aesthetics as those ideas relate to history-telling and myth-making.

For a general ethnographic introduction to Indonesia's many cultures, one might profitably start with Volume I of Frank M. Lebar's *Ethnic Groups of Insular Southeast Asia* (1972). Volume II of this series covers the Philippines and Taiwan. The entries, many based on anthropological fieldwork, include information on kinship, language, political organization, and religion. After some sessions with Lebar, the reader might want a closer look at the cultures of Java and Bali, and here the work of Clifford Geertz is consistently rewarding and challenging. See his books *The Religion of Java* (1960), *Agricultural Involution: The Process of Ecological Change in Indonesia* (1963), and *Negara: The Theatre State in Nineteenth-Century Bali* (1980). Geertz's celebrated article "Deep Play: Notes on the Balinese Cockfight" (1972) explores the aesthetics and politics of game-playing and ritual in Bali, with methodological implications for the study of art and ritual all over the archipelago. (See also Boon 1977.) The literature on the arts of Java and Bali is huge but does not directly concern us here.

Many monographs on the individual cultures represented in the Barbier-Müller collection are cited in the ethnographic sections of this catalogue. For a fascinating deep-immersion introduction to Outer Island cultures, try Hetty Nooy-Palm's *The Sa'dan Toraja* (1979), H.G. Schulte Nordholt's *The Political System of the Atoni of Timor* (1971), J.C. Vergouwen's *The Social Organisation and Customary Law of the Toba-Batak of Northern Sumatra* (1933; republished 1964), Marie Jeanne Adam's *System and Meaning in East Sumbanese Textile Design* (1969), and Gregory Forth's new *Rindi: An Ethnographic Study of a Traditional Domain in Eastern Sumba* (1981).

3. Looking at Jewelry

There are relatively few books on jewelry which have an anthropological focus or discuss the artistic tradition of jewelry from the viewpoint of comparative art history. Oppi Untracht's monumental and encyclopedic *Jewelry: Concepts and Technology* (1982) deals with all aspects of jewelry use and design and has some excellent introductory sections on jewelry exchange in different cultures. Paul and Elaine Lewis's *Peoples of the Golden Triangle: Six Tribes in Thailand* (1984) includes hundreds of color illustrations, many of them showing people in full ritual dress complete with silver ornaments; groups of jewelry pieces are also photographed according to type. The ethnographic film *Miao Year* also has many shots of Northern Thai ethnic jewelry styles.

For a valuable discussion of a jewelry tradition quite distant from Southeast Asia, see *Southwest Indian Silver from the Doneghy Collection*, edited by Louise Lincoln. The essays here put Navaho jewelry in its social and religious contexts, with particular emphasis on folk aesthetics.

4. Jewelry and Social Position

Two good 1983 articles that explore the concept of social location in Bugis society in Sulawesi are Shelly Errington's "Embodied

Sumange in Luwu" and Susan B. Millar's "On Interpreting Gender in Bugis Society." Clifford Geertz's "Deep Play: Notes on the Balinese Cockfight" (1972) shows some of the ways that social location in Bali is created and changed via rituals and games. For valuable essays on Indonesian political systems, see *Pre-Colonial State Systems in Southeast Asia*, edited by Anthony Reid and Lance Castles (1975).

5. Jewelry and Exchange

Bronislaw Malinowski's *Argonauts of the Western Pacific* (1922, reprinted 1961) is the classic anthropological analysis of jewelry and ritualized trade circuits. Wilhelm G. Solheim II has a good discussion of ancient exchange among small island groups in the Philippines in the essay "Philippine Prehistory," in Casal et al., *The People and Art of the Philippines* (1981). *Economic Exchange and Social Interaction in Southeast Asia: Perspectives from Prehistory, History, and Ethnography* (1977), edited by Karl Hutterer, is a provocative set of articles asking scholars to rethink the history of the region in terms of an exchange framework (see especially Hutterer's own article, "Prehistoric Trade and Evolution of Philippine Societies: A Reconsideration," pp. 177-196).

6. Jewelry and the Supernatural

A great deal of the Western scholarship on Indonesia touches on what Westerners call "religion," probably because mythic frame-works and ritual activities permeate virtually all sectors of pre-modern Indonesian thought. Investigations of Indonesia's stunning Outer Island ethnic religions include Hans Schärer's *Ngaju Religion: The Conception of God among a South Borneo People* (1963), Hetty Nooy-Palm's *The Sa'dan Toraja* (1979), the various monographs mentioned in the ethnic sections of this catalogue, the essays in Becker and Yengoyan's *The Imagination of Reality* (1979), and the articles in Fox's *The Flow of Life: Essays on Eastern Indonesia* (1980). For the Northern Philippines, Michelle Rosaldo's *Knowledge and Passion: Ilongot Notions of Self and Social Life* (1980), opens up much of Ilongot religion through careful symbolic analysis, and Renato Rosaldo's *Ilongot Headhunting* (1980) approaches questions of Ilongot concepts of society, history, and myth via a study of headtaking. For speculations on the connections between ideas of metalworking and the supernatural, one might start with Tom Harrisson and Stanley J. O'Connor's *Gold and Megalithic Activity in Prehistoric and Recent West Borneo* (1970). A source to follow this might be Charles Zerner's superb 1981 article "Signs of the Spirit, Signature of the Smith: Iron Forging in Tana Toraja." Wolfgang Marshall's "Metallurgie und frühe Besiedlungsgeschichte Indonesiens" (1958) provides much information and analysis of local metalsmithing traditions in their ritual and mythic contexts.

7. Jewelry in Contemporary Island Southeast Asia

This is an under-researched topic at the moment. Nelson Graburn's introduction to *Ethnic and Tourist Arts: Cultural Expressions from the Fourth World* (1979) is a provocative guide to the sort of work that *should* be done on island Southeast Asia's changing arts.

Nias

E.E.W.Gs. Schröder's *Nias: Ethnographische, geographische en historische Aanteekeningen en Studien* (1917) and E. Modigliani's *Un Viaggio a Nias* (1880) are standard descriptive works with much information, photographs, and drawings on Nias art. Peter Suzuki's *The Religious System and Culture of Nias* (1959) provides good summaries of much of the older work in European languages, while Wolfgang Marshall's *Der Berg des Herrn der Erde* (1976) is a valuable modern anthropological study. Three rewarding works in the field of Nias art are Jean Paul Barbier's *Symbolique et Motifs du Sud de Nias* (1978), Jerome Feldman's 1977 Columbia Ph.D. thesis,

"The Architecture of Nias, Indonesia, with Special Reference to Bawömataluo Village" and his essay "The House as World in Bawömataluo, South Nias" (1979).

North Sumatra: Toba and Karo Batak

There is a huge literature on the Batak peoples, a considerable amount of it in English; see Toenggoel P. Siagian's 1966 bibliography, which covers sources in Indonesian, English, Dutch, and German. A standard ethnography is J.C. Vergouwen's monumental *The Social Organisation and Customary Law of the Toba-Batak of Northern Sumatra*, first published in 1933. A more recent ethnographic study is Masri Singarimbun's *Kinship, Descent, and Alliance among the Karo Batak* (1975). Kipp and Kipp's 1983 *Beyond Samosir: Recent Studies of the Batak Peoples of Sumatra* is a collection of anthropological articles based on fieldwork in Toba, Karo, Pakpak, Simelungun, and Angkola. See the bibliographies of those articles for recent publications on these societies, as well as citations of Edward M. Bruner's work on social change in Toba. Jean Paul Barbier's *Tobaland: The Shreds of Tradition* (1983) documents the swiftly disappearing house architecture and sculpture of that area.

Kalimantan and Sarawak: Dayak

Lucas Chin's *Cultural Heritage of Sarawak* (1980) is a good introductory catalogue on the Sarawak Museum's collection of Iban art, with information on jewelry. Hans Schärer's *Ngaju Religion* (1963) is perhaps the best general text on a Dayak culture seen via its symbolic systems. Hose and McDougall's two-volume *The Pagan Tribes of Borneo* (1966) is an exhaustively detailed descriptive account done in old-fashioned style (a chapter on magic and spells, a chapter on soul concepts, and so on); the sections on ear ornaments are especially good.

Central Sulawesi

The Sa'dan Toraja are a popular subject for Western ethnographers, but the peoples around Palu and Lake Poso are less well studied. See Hetty Nooy-Palm's *The Sa'dan Toraja* (1979), which has a great deal of information on artistic motifs as well as a lengthy bibliography. Eric Crystal, Shinji Yamashita, Elizabeth Coville, Toby Volkman, and Charles Zerner have all done fieldwork in the last ten years on Sa'dan ritual and traditional belief systems. Tangdilintin's *Toraja dan Kebudayaannya* (1975) is a good introductory work in Indonesian. For the so-called West Toraja peoples, see Kruyt and Adriani's *De Bare'e Sprekende Toradjas van Midden-Celebes* (1912-1914) and also Albert Grubauer's *Unter Kopfjägern in Central Celebes* (1913), which has information on jewelry. The *Monografi Daerah Sulawesi Tengah* series (published in Jakarta by the Departemen Pendidikan dan Kebudayaan) is a rich source of historical, demographic, and anthropological information, with sections on bridewealth payments involving jewelry. See also the excellent museum catalogue of the new national museum in Palu, compiled by M. Masyhuda (1982-1983).

Flores

Flores cultures are notably under-researched, even in the current wave of new Eastern Indonesian anthropology studies. Art research is rare, the exception being Robyn Maxwell's fine essays "Textiles and Tusks: Some Observations on the Social Dimensions of Weaving in East Flores" (1981) and "Textile and Ethnic Configurations in Flores and the Solor Archipelago" (1980). Robert Barnes' book *Kedang: A Study of the Collective Thought of an Eastern Indonesian People* (1974) deals extensively with bridewealth exchange and prestige objects. Two articles in Fox's *The Flow of Life* relate Flores area ethnography to Eastern Indonesianist theoretical concerns: Barnes' "Concordance, Structure, and Variation: Considerations of Alliance in Kedang," and John Gordon's "The Marriage Nexus among the Manggarai of West Flores" (1980). Current research is being conducted in Manggarai by David Hicks and Maybeth Erbe, while Nancy Lutz has done recent research in East Flores.

Sumba

East Sumbanese art is wonderfully well described and analyzed in a long series of works by Marie Jeanne Adams: *System and Meaning in East Sumba Textile Design* (1969), "Structural Aspects of a Village Art, East Sumba," (1973), "The Crocodile Couple and the Snake Encounter in the Tellantry of East Sumba" (1979), and "Structural Aspects of East Sumbanese Art" (1980). See also Gregory Forth's book *Rindi* (1981), which has a good deal of information on gold jewelry. L. Onvlee's work in East Sumba provided the basis of much of this more recent research. The government-sponsored *Budaya Sumba* series, published by the Departemen Pendidikan dan Kebudayaan, is also a good source on sculpture and jewelry. The indefatigable East Sumbanese social historian Oe. H. Kapita has published an invaluable series of books on *adat* and oratory, much of it related to jewelry (see his 1976 *Masyarakat Sumba dan Adat Istiadatnya* as well as *Sumba di dalam Jangkauan Jaman*, *Ludu Humba Pakangutuna* (1977), and *Lu Ndai: Rukuda da Kabihu dangu la Pahunga Lodu* (1979). See also the articles on Sumba in Fox's *The Flow of Life* (1980).

Timor

For introductions to Timor cultures, see Vroklage's three-volume *Ethnographie der Belu in Zentral-Timor* (1952), Schulte Nordholt's *The Political System of the Atoni of Timor* (1971), and the articles by Shepard Forman, Claudine Friedberg, Elizabeth Traube, and Gerard Francillon in Fox's *The Flow of Life*. Clark Cunningham's "Order in the Atoni House" (1964) is also an excellent source on Atoni symbolic systems as they are presented in traditional house architecture.

Moluccas: Tanimbar

Drabbe's 1940 *Het Leven van den Tanembarese* is the classic description of Tanimbarese village society. Susan McKinnon's 1983 Ph.D. thesis, "Hierarchy, Alliance, and Exchange in the Tanimbar Islands," is the benchmark modern report.

Northern Luzon, Philippines

Shiro Saito's 512-page *Philippine Ethnography: A Critically Annotated and Selected Bibliography* (1972) lists both dress and adornment.

Good basic sources that touch on the social history and prehistory of the northern Philippines include Wilhelm Solheim's article "Philippine Prehistory" in Casal, et al., *The People and Art of the Philippines*; Karl Hutterer's *Economic Exchange and Social Interaction in Southeast Asia: Perspectives from Prehistory, History, and Ethnography* (1977); Felix M. Keesing's *The Ethnohistory of Northern Luzon* (1962); and William Henry Scott's *The Discovery of the Igorots: Spanish Contacts with the Pagans of Northern Luzon* (1974). There are a large number of anthropological monographs on Northern Luzon societies, many including information on dress and adornment. A good sense for these cultures can be gained by reading R.F. Barton's *Ifugao Law* (1969) and *The Kalingas: Their Institutions and Custom Law* (1949); Edward P. Dozier's *Mountain Arbiters* (1966); Michelle Rosaldo's *Knowledge and Passion: Ilongot Notions of Self and Social Life* (1980); and Renato Rosaldo's *Ilongot Headhunting: 1883-1974* (1980).

REFERENCES CITED

1969 ADAMS, Marie Jeanne
System and Meaning in East Sumba Textile Design: A Study in Traditional Indonesian Art. New Haven: Yale University, Southeast Asia Studies, Cultural Report No. 16.

1973 "Structural Aspects of a Village Art, East Sumba, Indonesia." *American Anthropologist* 75: 265–279.

1979 "The Crocodile Couple and the Snake Encounter in the Tellantry of East Sumba, Indonesia," in Becker and Yengoyan, 1979.

1980 "Structural Aspects of East Sumbanese Art," in Fox 1980: 208–220.

1912 ADRIANI, N. and KRUYT, A. C.
De Bare'e-sprekende Toradjas van Midden-Celebes. Amsterdam: North-Holland.

1923 ALDER, W. F.
Men of the Inner Jungle. New York and London: Century.

1978 ALEJANDRO, Reynaldo G.
Philippine Dance: Mainstream and Cross-currents. Quezon City: Vera-Reyes.

1972 ANDERSON, Benedict
"The Idea of Power in Japanese Culture," in Claire Holt, Benedict Anderson, James Siegel, eds., *Culture and Politics in Indonesia.* Ithaca: Cornell University Press.

1976 APPELL, G. N.
The Societies of Borneo: Explorations in the Theory of Cognatic Structure. American Anthropological Association Special Publication, No. 6. Washington, D.C.: American Anthropological Association.

1982 *ART OF THE ARCHAIC INDONESIANS.* Exhibition catalogue. Dallas: Museum of Fine arts.

1983 ATKINSON, Jane M.
"Religions in Dialogue: The Construction of an Indonesian Minority Religion." *American Ethnologist* 10, (No. 4): 684–696.

1982 AVÉ J. B.
"The Dayak of Borneo, Their View of Life and Death, and Their Art," in *Art of the Archaic Indonesians*, 1982: 95–100.

1977 BARBIER, Jean Paul
Indonésie et Mélanésie, Geneva: Collection Barbier-Müller.

1978 *Symbolique et Motifs du Sud de Nias.* Geneva: Collection Barbier-Müller, Etudes et Monographies.

1983 *Tobaland: The Shreds of Tradition.* Geneva: Musée Barbier-Müller.

1984a *Indonesian Primitive Art.* Dallas: Dallas Museum of Art.

1984b *Art of Nagaland.* Geneva: Musée Barbier-Müller.

1974 BARNES, R. H.
Kedang: A Study of the Collective Thought of an Eastern Indonesian People. Oxford: Clarendon Press.

1980 "Concordance, Structure, and Variation: Considerations of Alliance in Kedang," in Fox 1980b: 68–97.

1930 BARTON, R. F.
The Half-Way Sun. New York: Brewer and Warren.

1938 *Philippine Pagans.* London: George Routledge and Sons.

1949 *The Kalingas: Their Institutions and Custom Law.* Chicago: University of Chicago Press.

1969 *Ifugao Law.* Berkeley: University of California Press.

1979 BECKER, A. L.
"Communication Across Diversity," in Becker and Yengoyan 1979: 1–5.

1982 "Modern Philology." Unpublished manuscript.

1979 BECKER, A. L. and Aram A. Yengoyan, eds.
The Imagination of Reality: Essays in Southeast Asian Coherence Systems. Norwood, N. J.: Ablex.

1972 BELLO, Moises C.
Kankanay Social Organization and Culture Change. Community Development Research Council, University of the Philippines.

1982 BIRO PUSAT STATISTIK
Statistik Indonesia: Statistical Yearbook of Indonesia. Jakarta: Biro Pusat Statistik.

1882 BOCK, Carl
The Head-Hunters of Borneo. London: Sampson Low, Marston, Searle, & Rivington.

1972 BODROGI, Tibor
Art in Indonesia. Greenwich, Conn.: New York Graphic Society.

1977 BOON, James A.
The Anthropological Romance of Bali, 1597-1972. Cambridge: Cambridge University Press.

1973 BRUNER, Edward M.
"The Expression of Ethnicity in Indonesia," in Abe Abner Cohen, ed., *Urban Ethnicity.* ASA Monograph, London: Tavistock.

1979 BRUNER, Edward M. and BECKER Judith, eds.
Art, Ritual and Society in Indonesia. Athens: Ohio University Papers in International Studies, Southeast Asia Series No. 53.

1981 CASAL, Gabriel, REGALADO TROTA JOSE, Jr., CASINO, Eric S., ELLIS, George R., SOLHEIM II, Wilhelm G.
The People and Art of the Philippines. Los Angeles: Museum of Cultural History, University of California, Los Angeles.

1981 CASINO, Eric S.
"Arts and Peoples of the Southern Philippines," in Casal et al. 1981: 123–182.

1975 CASTLES, Lance
"Statelessness and Stateforming Tendencies among the Bataks before Colonial Rule," in Reid and Castles 1975.

1972 CAWED, Carmencita
The Culture of the Bontoc Igorot. Manila: MCS Enterprises.

1980 CHIN, Lucas
Cultural Heritage of Sarawak. Kuching: Sarawak Museum.

1968 CONKLIN, H.
Ifugao Bibliography. New Haven: Yale University, Southeast Asia Studies, Bibliography Series 11.

1966 COOLEY, Frank L.
"Altar and Throne in Central Moluccan Societies." *Indonesia* 11: 135–156.

1976 CORNELL UNIVERSITY LIBRARIES
Southeast Asia Catalogue. Compiled under the direction of Giok Po Oey. 7 vols. plus supplements. Boston: G.K. Hall.

1973 CORONESE, Stefano
Una civiltà primitiva. Cremona: ISME.

1982 CRYSTAL, Eric and SHINJI, Yamashita
"Power of Gods: Ma'Bugi Ritual of the Sa'dan Toraja." Unpublished paper, delivered at the 1982 Indonesian Studies Conference "Religion in Indonesia." Athens: Ohio University.

1922 CURLE, Richard
"The Netherlands: Mixed Races and varied

1966 DOZIER, Edward P.
Life in the Dutch Indies" in *Peoples of all Nations* vol. V: 3673–3740.

1979 DAVIS, Gloria, ed.
What Is Modern Indonesian Culture? Athens: Ohio University Papers in International Studies, Southeast Asia Series No. 52.

1982 DE HOOG, J.
"The Lesser Sunda Islands and the Moluccas," in *Art of the Archaic Indonesians* 1982: 121–127.

Mountain Arbiters. Tucson: University of Arizona Press.

1940 DRABBE, P.
"Het Leven van den Tanémbarees: Ethnografische Studie over het Tanénbareesche Volk." *Internationales Archiv für Ethnographie.* Supplement to Vol. 37.

1944 DUBOIS, Cora
The People of Alor: A Social Psychological Study of an Eastern Indian Island. Minneapolis: University of Minnesota Press.

1979 DUMIA, Mariano A.
The Ifugao World. Quezon City: New Day Publishers.

1978 DUNSMORE, S.
Beads. Kuching: Sarawak Museum, Occasional Paper No. 2.

1903 DURKHEIM, Emile and MAUSS Marcel
Primitive Classification. Translated with an introduction by Rodney Needham. London: Cohen and West, 1963.

1979 EBIN, Victoria
The Body Decorated. London: Thames and Hudson.

1963 ECHOLS, John M. and SHADILY Hassan
An Indonesian-English Dictionary. Ithaca: Cornell University Press.

1981 ELLIS, George P.
"Arts and Peoples of the Northern Philippines," in Casal et al. 1981: 183–263.

1983 ERRINGTON, Shelly
"Embodied Sumange' in Luwu." *Journal of Asian Studies* 40 (No. 3): 545–570.

1977 FELDMAN, Jerome A.
"The Architecture of Nias, Indonesia with Special Reference to Bawömataluo Village." Columbia University, Ph. D. thesis.

1979 "The House as World in Bawömataluo, South Nias," in Bruner and Becker 1979.

1909 FISCHER, H. W.
Catalogue van 'sRijks Ethnographisch Museum, Leiden.

1961 FISCHER, John L.
"Art Styles as Cultural Cognitive Maps." *American Anthropologist* 63: 79-93. Reprinted in Otten 1971.

1980 FORMAN, Shepard
"Descent, Alliance, and Exchange Ideology among the Makassae of East Timor" in Fox 1980b: 152–177.

1981 FORTH, Gregory L.
Rindi: An Ethnographic Study of a Traditional Domain in Eastern Sumba. The Hague: Martinus Nijhoff.

1972 FOX, James J.
"Sikanese," in Lebar 1972: 88–90.

1977 *Harvest of the Palm: Ecological Change in Eastern Indonesia.* Cambridge, Mass.: Harvard University Press.

1980a "Figure Shark and Pattern Crocodile: The Foundations of the Textile Traditions of Roti and Ndao," in Gittinger 1980: 39–55.

1980b Ed.
The Flow of Life: Essays on Eastern Indonesia. Cambridge, Mass.: Harvard University Press.

1980c "Models and Metaphors: Comparative Research in Eastern Indonesia," in Fox 1980b: 327–334.

1980 FRANCILLON, Girard
"Incursions upon Wehali: A Modern History of an Ancient Empire," in Fox 1980b: 248–265.

1966 FRASER, Douglas
The Many Faces of Primitive Art. Englewood Cliffs: Prentice-Hall.

1980 FRIEDBERG, Claudine
"Boiled Woman and Broiled Man: Myths and Agricultural Rituals of the Bunaq of Central Timor," in Fox 1980b: 266–289.

1946 FÜRER-HAIMENDORF, Christoph von
Die nackten Nagas: dreizehn Monate unter Kopfjägern Indiens. Wiesbaden: Brockhaus.

1957 GEDDES, W. R.
Nine Dayak Nights. London: Oxford University Press.

1960 GEERTZ, Clifford
The Religion of Java. Glencoe, Ill.: Free Press.

1963 *Agricultural Involution: The Processes of Ecological Change in Indonesia.* Berkeley: University of California Press.

1972 "Deep Play: Notes on the Balinese Cockfight." *Daedalus* 101:1–37. Reprinted in Geertz, *The Interpretation of Culture.* New York: Basic Books, 1973.

1973 "Thick Description: Toward an Interpretive Theory of Culture," introductory essay to *The Interpretation of Culture.* New York: Basic Books.

1980 *Negara: The Theatre State in Nineteenth-Century Bali.* Princeton: Princeton University Press.

1979 GITTINGER, Mattiebelle
Splendid Symbols: Textiles and Tradition in Indonesia. Washington, D.C.: Textile Museum.

1980 Ed.
Indonesian Textiles. Proceedings of the Irene Emery Roundtable on Museum Textiles, 1979. Washington, D.C.: Textile Museum.

1929 GOLOUBEW, Victor
«L'âge du bronze au Tonkin et dans le Nord-Annam». *Bulletin de l'Ecole française d'Extrême-Orient* XXIX: 1–46.

1980 GORDON, John L.
"The Marriage Nexus among the Manggarai of West Flores," in Fox 1980b: 48–67.

1979 GRABURN, Nelson H. H.
Ethnic and Tourist Arts: Cultural Expressions from the Fourth World. Berkeley: University of California Press.

1913 GRUBAUER, Albert
Unter Kopfjägern in Central Celebes. Leipzig: R. Voigtlanders.

1905 HADDON, Ernest B.
"The Dog-Motive in Bornean Art". *The Journal of the Anthropological Institute of Great Britain and Ireland* vol. XXXV: 113–125.

1976 HARDI, Lasmidjah et al.
Kain Adat: Traditional Textiles. Jakarta: Djambatan/Intermasa, for Himpunan Wastraprema.

1969 HARRISSON, Tom and O'CONNOR, Stanley J.
Excavation of the Prehistoric Iron Industry in West Borneo. Ithaca: Cornell University Southeast Asia Studies Program, Data Paper No. 72. 2 vols.

1970 *Gold and Megalithic Activity in Prehistoric and Recent West Borneo.* Ithaca: Cornell University Southeast Asia Studies Program, Data Paper No. 77.

1974 HART, Donn V.
An Annotated Bibliography of Philippine Bibliographies: 1965–1974. DeKalb: Northern Illinois University Center for Southeast Asian Studies.

1974 HARVEY, Barbara
"Tradition, Islam, and Rebellion: South Sulawesi 1950–1965." Ithaca: Cornell University Ph. D. thesis.

1846 HEIJMERING, G.
"Een Inlandsche Oorlog op het Eiland Timor." *Tijdschrift voor Nederlandsche-Indië* 8 (3): 204–222.

1966 HEINE-GELDERN, Robert
"Some Tribal Art Styles of Southeast Asia: An Experiment in Art History," in Fraser 1966.

1976 HICKS, David
Tetum Ghosts and Kin: Fieldwork in an Indonesian Community. Palo Alto, Calif.: Mayfield.

1984 *A Maternal Religion.* DeKalb: Northern Illinois University, Papers in International Studies.

1967 HOLT, Claire
Art in Indonesia: Continuities and Change. Ithaca: Cornell University Press.

1971 "Dances of Sumatra and Nias: Notes by Claire Holt." *Indonesia* 11: 1–21.

1926 HOSE, Charles
Natural Man: A Record from Borneo. London: Macmillan.

1966 HOSE, Charles and McDOUGALL, William
The Pagan Tribes of Borneo. 2 vols. London: Frank Cass.

1983 HOSKINS, Janet
Cambridge, Mass., Ph. D. thesis Harvard University.

1973 HUTTERER, Karl
"Reciprocity and Revenge Among the Ifugao." *Philippine Quarterly of Culture and Society* 1: 33–38.

1977 "Prehistoric Trade and Evolution of Philippine Societies: A Reconsideration," in Karl Hutterer, ed.
— *Economic Exchange and Social Interaction in Southeast Asia: Perspectives from Prehistory, History, and Ethnography*, pp. 177–190. Ann Arbor: University of Michigan Papers on South and Southeast Asia.

1974 INDONESIAN MONOGRAPHS
A Catalogue of Monograph Publications 1945–1968. (Monographs from Cornell, on microfiche.) Switzerland, Bibliotheca Asiatica 10.

1927 JASPER, J.E. and PIRNGADIE, Mas
De Inlandsche Kinstnijverheid in Nederlandsch Indie. Leiden: Mouton.

1905 JENKS, Albert Ernest
The Bontoc Igorot. Manila: Bureau of Public Printing.

1882 JOCANO, F. Landa
The Ilocanos: An Ethnography of Family and Community Life in the Ilocos Region. Diliman, Quezon City: University of the Philippines.

1980 JOSSELIN DE JONG, P.E.
"The Concept of the Field of Ethnological Study," in Fox 1980b: 317–326.

1977 KAHLENBERG, Mary Hunt
Textile Traditions of Indonesia. Los Angeles: Los Angeles County Museum of Art.

1973 *KALIMANTAN: MYTHE EN KUNST*
Delft: Tentoonstelling Indonesisch Ethnografisch Museum.

1976a KAPITA, Oe. K.
Masyarakat Sumba dan Adat Istiadatnya. Dewan Penata Layanan Gereja Kristen Sumba. Jakarta: Bpk. Gunung Mulia.

1976b *Sumba di dalam Jangkauan Jaman.* Dewan Penata Layanan Gereja Kristen Sumba. Jakarta: Bpk. Gunung Mulia.

1977 *Ludu Humba Pakangutuna.* Dewan Penata Layanan Gereja Kristen Sumba. Jakarta: Bpk. Gunung Mulia.

1979 KAPITA, U. H.
Lu Ndai: Rukuda da Kabihu dangu la Pahunga Lodu. Dewan Penata Layanan Gereja Kristen Sumba. Jakarta: Bpk. Gunung Mulia.

1981 KARTOMI, Margaret, ed.
Five Essays on the Indonesian Arts. Monash University.

n.d. KATALOG PERPUSTA KAAN-KONINKLIJK
Institut voor Taal- Land- en Volkenskunde, n.p.

1929 KAUDERN, Walter
Results of the Author's Expedition to Celebes 1917–20. Vol. IV "Games and Dances in Celebes." Göteborg: Elanders Boktrycheri.

1962 KEESING, Felix M.
The Ethnohistory of Northern Luzon. Stanford, California: Stanford University Press.

1934 KEESING, Felix M. and KEESING, Marie
Taming Philippine Headhunters. London: Allen & Unwin. Reprinted New York: AMS Press.

1975 KEESING, Roger M
Kin Groups and Social Structure. New York: Holt, Rinehart, and Winston.

1955 KENNEDY, Raymond
"Field Notes on Indonesia: Flores, 1949-50," in Harold C. Conklin, ed., Human Relations Area Files (Source No. 5 in OBI Indonesia File). New Haven: Yale University.

1982 KIPP, Rita S.
"Terms for Kith and Kin," paper delivered

at the annual American Anthropology Association meeting. Forthcoming, *American Anthropologist*.

1983 "A Political System of Highland Sumatra, or Rethinking Edmond Leach," in R. S. and R. Kipp 1983: 125–138.

1983 KIPP, Rita S. and KIPP, Richard, eds. *Beyond Samosir: Recent Studies of the Batak Peoples of Sumatra*. Athens: Ohio University Papers in International Studies, Southeast Asia Series No. 62.

1983 KIPP, Richard
"Fictive Kinship and Changing Ethnicity among Karo and Toba Migrants," in R. S. and R. Kipp 1983.

1913 KLEIWEG DE ZWAAN, J. P.
Die Insel Nias bei Sumatra. The Hague: Martinus Nijhoff.

1972 KOENTJARANINGRAT, M.
"Manggarai," in Lebar 1972: 81–83.

1982 KUIPERS, Joel
New Haven: Yale University, Ph. D. thesis.

1977 LAWLESS, Robert
Societal Ecology in Northern Luzon: Kalinga Agriculture, Organization, Population, and Change. Vol. 18, No. 1. Norman: University of Oklahoma.

1951 LEACH, E. R.
"The Structural Implications of Matrilateral Cross-Cousin Marriage," reprinted in Leach 1961: 54–104.

1954 *Political Systems of Highland Burma*. Boston: Beacon Press.

1961 *Rethinking Anthropology*. London: Athlone Press.

1976 *Culture and Communication*. Themes in the Social Sciences Series. Cambridge: Cambridge University Press.

1972 LEBAR, Frank
Ethnic Groups of Insular Southeast Asia. Vols. I and II. New Haven: Yale University, Human Relations Area Files.

1966 LEIGH, Michael B., comp.
Checklist of Holdings on Borneo in the Cornell University Libraries. Ithaca: Cornell University Southeast Asia Program, Data Paper No. 62.

1974 LEMBAGA PENELITIAN MALUKU
Bibliografi Maluku (1950–1973). Jakarta.

1979 LESSA, William and VOGT, Evon, eds.
Reader in Comparative Religion. 4th ed. New York: Harper & Row.

1944– LÉVI-STRAUSS, Claude
1945 "Split Representation in the Art of Asia and America," reprinted in Lévi-Strauss 1967.

1949 *The Elementary Structure of Kinship*. Boston: Beacon Press. Reprinted 1969.

1955 "The Structural Study of Myth." *Journal of American Folklore* 78 (270): 428–444. Reprinted with slight modifications in Lévi-Strauss 1967.

1967 *Structural Anthropology*. New York: Doubleday, Anchor Books.

1982 "The Social Organization of the Kwakiutl," in Lévi-Strauss, *The Way of the Masks*. 2nd ed. Seattle: University of Washington Press.

1984 LEWIS, Paul and LEWIS, Elaine
Peoples of the Golden Triangle: Six Tribes in Thailand. London: Thames & Hudson.

1982 LINCOLN, Louise, ed.
Southeast Indian Silver from the Doneghy Collection. Austin: University of Texas Press.

1968 LOEHR, Max
Ritual Vessels of Bronze Age China. New York: The Asia House Society Inc.

1956 MACDONALD, Malcolm
Borneo People. London: Jonathan Cape.

1972 MAGANNON, Esteban T.
Religion in a Kalinga Village. Quezon City: University of the Philippines, Community Development Research Council.

1922 MALINOWSKI, Bronislaw
Argonauts of the Western Pacific. New York: E. P. Dutton. Reprinted 1961.

1958 MARSCHALL, W.
"Metallurgie und frühe Besiedlungsgeschichte Indonesiens." *Ethnologica* 4: 29–263.

1976 *Der Berg des Herrn der Erde.* Munich: Deutsche Taschenbucher.

1982 "Enggano and Nias," in *Art of the Archaic Indonesians* 1982: 17–27.

1971 MASYHUDA, M.
Bahasa Kaili Pamona. Palu: Yayasan Kebudayaan Sulawesi Tengah.

1977 *Mongrafi Daerah Sulawesi Tengah.* Vol. I. Jakarta: Departemen Pendidikan dan Kebudayaan.

1982– *Katalogus Koleksi, Museum Negeri, Sulawesi*
1983 *Tengah.* Palu: Museum Negeri Sulawesi Tengah.

1959 MAUSS, Marcel
The Gift. New York: Free Press.

1980 MAXWELL, John
"Textiles of the Kapuas Basin–With Special Reference to Maloh Beadwork," in Gittinger 1980: 127–140.

1981 "Textiles and Tusks: Some Observations on the Social Dimensions of Weaving in East Flores," in Kartomi 1981: 43–62.

1983 "Ceremonial Textiles of the Ngada of Eastern Indonesia." Connaissance des Arts Tribaux, No. 18. Geneva: Musée Barbier-Müller.

1980 MAXWELL, Robyn J.
"Textile and Ethnic Configurations in Flores and the Solor Archipelago," in Gittinger 1980: 141–156.

1979 McKINLEY, Robert
"Zaman and Masa, Eras and Periods: Religious Evolution and the Permanence of Epistemological Ages in Malay Culture," in Becker and Yengoyan 1979: 303–324.

1983 McKINNON, Susan M.
"Hierarchy, Alliance and Exchange in the Tanimbar Islands." Chicago: University of Chicago, Ph. D. thesis.

1982 MILLAR, Susan B.
"Lahireng/Bateng: An Analysis of Religion and Social Action." Unpublished paper, delivered at 1982 Indonesian Studies Conference, "Religion in Indonesia." Ohio University, Athens, Ohio.

1983 "On Interpreting Gender in Bugis Society." *American Ethnologist* 10 (No. 3): 477–493.

1942 MILLER, C. C.
Black Borneo. New York: Modern Age Books.

1890 MODIGLIANI, Elio
Un Viaggio a Nias. Milan: Treves.

1932 MÖLLER, A.G.
"Religion des Niassens." *Inter. Archiv für Ethnographie* XXXII (I, II).

1983 MUDE, H. B.
"Perhiasan Kodi." Unpublished manuscript.

1962 NEEDHAM, Rodney
Structure and Sentiment: A Test Case in Social Anthropology. Chicago: University of Chicago Press.

1980 "Principles and Variations in the Structure of Sumbanese Society," in Fox 1980b: 21–47.

1979 NOOY-PALM, Hetty
The Sa'dan Toraja: A Study of Their Social Life and Religion. Vol. I: *Organization, Symbols, and Beliefs.* The Hague: Martinus Nijhoff.

1980 ONVLEE, L.
"The Significance of Livestock on Sumba," in Fox 1980b: 195–207.

1971 OTTEN, Charlotte M.
Anthropology and Art: Readings in Cross-Cultural Aesthetics. Austin: University of Texas Press.

1977 PAKAN, Priyanti
"Orang Toraja: Identifikasi, Klasifikasi, dan Lokasi." *Berita Anthropologi* (Nos. 32–33): 21–49.

1965 PIDDOCKE, Stuart
"The Potlatch System of the Southern Kwakiutl: A New Perspective." *Southwestern Journal of Anthropology* 21: 244–264.

1981 POLMAN, Katrien
The North Moluccas: An Annotated Bibliography. The Hague: Martinus Nijhoff.

1977 *PROYEK PENGEMBANGAN PERPUSTA-KAAN*
Katalog Anthropologi Indonesia. Koleksi Perpustakaan Museum Pusat. Jakarta: Departemen P dan K, Sulawesi Selatan.

1978 *PROYEK PENGEMBANGAN PERPUSTA-KAAN SULAWESI SELATAN*
Bibliografi Daerah: Sulawesi Selatan. Ujung Pandang: Perpustakaan Wilayah, Departemen P dan K, Sulawesi Selatan.

1980 *PROYEK PENGEMBANGAN PERPUSTA-KAAN SUMATERA UTARA*
Bibliografi Daerah: Sumatera Utara. Medan: Perpustakaan Wilayah, Departemen P dan K, Propinsi Sumatra Utara.

1967 RAWSON, Philip
The Art of Southeast Asia. New York: Praeger.

1975 REID, Anthony and CASTLES, Lance
Pre-Colonial State Systems in Southeast Asia. Kuala Lumpur: Monographs of the Malaysian Branch of the Royal Asiatic Society.

1979 REID, Anthony and MARR, David, eds.
Perceptions of the Past in Southeast Asia. ASAA Southeast Asia Publications Series. London: Heinemann.

1886 REIDEL
De Sluik − en Kroesharige Rassen tusschen Seiebes en Papua. The Hague: Martinus Nijhoff.

1980 ROSALDO, Michelle Z.
Knowleduge and Passion: Ilongot Nations of Self and Social Life. Cambridge: University Cambridge Press.

1975 ROSALDO, Michelle and ATKINSON Jane
"Man the Hunter and Woman," in Roy Ellis, ed., *The Interpretation of Symbolism*: 43–75. London: Malaby.

1975 ROSALDO, Renato and ROSALDO, Michelle
"Ilongot," in Lebar 1975: 103–106.

1979 ROSALDO, Renato
"Red Hornbill Earrings: Ilongot Ideas on Self, Beauty, and Health." Paper read at the annual meeting of the Association for Asian Studies, Los Angeles.

1980 *Ilongot Headhunting.* Stanford, Calif.: Stanford University Press.

1966 ROTH, H. Ling
Oriental Silverwork: Malay and Chinese. Kuala Lumpur: University of Malaysia Press.

1972 SAITO, Shiro
Philippine Ethnography: A Critically Annotated and Selected Bibliography. Honolulu: University of Hawaii Press.

1963 SCHÄRER, Hans
Ngaju Religion: The Conception of God Among a South Borneo People. Trans. Rodney Needham. The Hague: Martinus Nijhoff.

1917 SCHRÖDER, E. E. W. Gs.
Nias: Ethnographische, Geographische en Historische Aanteekeningen en Studien. 2 vols. Leiden: Brill.

1971 SCHULTE NORDHOLT, H. G.
The Political System of the Atoni of Timor. The Hague: Martinus Nijhoff.

1974 SCOTT, William Henry
The Discovery of the Igorots. Quezon City: New Day Publishers.

1966 SIAGIAN, Toenggoel P.
"Bibliography on the Batak Peoples." *Indonesia* 2 (Oct.): 161–84.

1975 SINGARIMBUN, Masri
Kinship, Descent, and Alliance among the Karo Batak. Berkeley: University of Californai Press.

n.d. SOELARTO, B.
Budaya Sumba. 3 vols. Jakarta: Departemen Pendidikan dan Kebudayaan.

n.d. SOELARTO, B. and ALBILADIYAH, S. Ilmi
Adat Istiadat dan Kesenian orang Kulawi. Jakarta: Departemen Pendidikan dan Kebudayaan.

1976 SOLHEIM, Wilhelm G., II
"Coastal Irian Jaya and the Origin of the Nasantao (Austronesian-Speaking People)," in Chosukey, Serizawa, ed., *Le peuplement de l'archipel Nippon et des îles du Pacifique: chronologie, paléogéographie, industries*: 32–42. Nice n.p..